THIRD EDITION

# THE
# CAMPER'S
# COMPANION

## The Pack-Along Guide
## for Better Outdoor Trips

Rick Greenspan and Hal Kahn

Foghorn Press
BOOKS BUILDING COMMUNITY™

ISBN 1-57354-000-5

51595

9 781573 540001

Publishing Manager
Foghorn Press
555 DeHaro Street, Suite 220
San Francisco, CA 94107

To order a book, please call Foghorn Press:
1-800-FOGHORN (364-4676) or (415) 241-9550.

Foghorn Press titles are distributed to the book trade by Publishers Group West, Emeryville, California. To contact your local sales representative, call 1-800-788-3123.

No liability is assumed with respect to the information or content of this book. No one should participate in any of the activities described in this book unless they recognize and personally assume the associated risks.

Library of Congress ISSN Data:
February 1996
*The Camper's Companion: The Pack-Along Guide for Better Outdoor Trips*
*Third Edition*
ISSN: 1086-7864

CREDITS

| | |
|---|---|
| Editing/Book Production | Ann-Marie Brown |
| Illustrations | Gordon Ohlinger, I. Magnus, Kirk McInroy |
| Cover Photo | Charlie Borland |

**The Color of Commitment**

Foghorn Press has always been committed to printing on recycled paper, but up to now, we hadn't taken the final plunge to use 100-percent recycled paper because we were unconvinced of its quality. And until now, those concerns were valid. But the good news is that quality recycled paper is now available. We are thrilled to announce that Foghorn Press books are printed with Soya-based inks on 100-percent recycled paper, which has a 50-percent post-consumer waste content. The only way you'd know we made this change is by looking at the hue of the paper—a small price to pay for environmental integrity. You may even like the color better. We do. And we know the earth does, too.

Printed in the United States of America

# THE
# CAMPER'S
# COMPANION

### The Pack-Along Guide
### for Better Outdoor Trips

Rick Greenspan and Hal Kahn

Foghorn
Press

BOOKS BUILDING COMMUNITY™

# Acknowledgments

The people who made this book possible are the ones who have traveled with us, sharing our pleasure in wilderness camping and helping us test the depths of our ability to improvise and have fun. They are all in the book, mostly under their own names, though sometimes shaded by a "moniker." To them our thanks have often been spoken privately; here it is made public, and we hope they enjoy reading the words as much as we enjoyed writing them.

A new edition of a book accumulates layers of obligation, and if you're a true archaeologist, you'll look up the earlier editions to see the names of the editors, critics, friends, relatives and ex-spouses who got us started. Now, standing at the head of the line, hardened to our nuttiness and excesses, tolerant of behavior only marginally acceptable in normal social circles, are the friends who got us on, in, and off the Internet with heroic good grace. Monica Wheeler and Randy Stross coddled us when others would have throttled us, wasting huge stretches of their own time to teach us to pedal our tricycles on the back roads of the information highway. Backing them up with technical advice were Russ Allbery, Jane Norris, Carol Oliver, Larry Schwimmer, and Greg Smith. They've got better things to do with their lives, but they never said so. Stephen Johns and Mike Thoma gave us permission to cite their Home Pages on the World Wide Web. They're the kind of folks who give the Net a good name.

Bonnie Lewkowicz, as always, updated us on the problems and prospects of camping with physical disabilities, and Dean Martineau did the same via the Internet. Tireless workers on the Web offered much advice, and though we don't know them personally, we thank them nonetheless. Shimon Schwarzschild helped us with Forest Service publications, Ann-Marie Brown wired her mouth into a smile and edited our stuff, and Maureen

McClain, who hates adjectives, surgically removed the worst offenders.

We arc grateful to the editors of *Sierra* for permission to cite a passage from Joan Hamilton's lovely article on children, and to the International Mountain Bicycling Association for permission to reproduce their "Rules of the Trail." The American Canoe Association, American Hiking Society, American Red Cross, National Forest Service, National Park Service, U.S. Geological Survey, and the Sierra Club kindly provided us with helpful information. Netscape and Yahoo have respectively permitted us to reproduce several of their Internet screens. GORP has granted similar permission, and the University of Washington has permitted us to cite its on-line publication, DO-IT. We thank them all.

Finally, all those anonymous trail crews, rangers and strangers we've met in the mountains deserve a nod and a note of thanks as well. There is a great store of friendship in the backcountry, and we seem to have drawn on it more than most. Our book is a little gesture of repayment, and we hope our friends take it as that.

*Rick Greenspan and Hal Kahn*

# Permissions

# Preface

It was Jimmy the Greek who first said, referring to Aristotle, "Ya don't tamper wit da Classics." Or was it Walt Hriniak watching Rod Carew? No matter. It's a self-evident truth. Look what happened to Coke when they tried to fix a formula that wasn't broke. Or those learned scribblers who set out to modernize the King James version of the Bible. Didn't work, did it?

Well, that's the way we feel about *The Camper's Companion*. We've heard it described by some critics (none of whom are related to us by blood or debt) as "the VW Repair Book of camping." To that we say, "Aw shucks." Modesty aside, however, we want to assure readers of this new and improved edition that the original hasn't been gutted and restuffed. Rather, it's been upgraded, updated and uplifted. The single all-new addition is a chapter on how to use the Internet to enrich your outdoor life. No other outdoor book can make that statement! Aside from that we still offer you the most complete and accessible single-volume introduction to the outdoors available. Still the wiliest and wisest how-to manual for the wilderness. Still filled with sage advice, and a lot of oregano, basil and thyme on top of that. And still the most burned book in America! For we continue to give you tear-out pages of recipes and lists as fuel for thought and the campfire. Our old motto, "Learn and Burn," has worked wonders for a legion of hikers, bikers, campers and canoeists. We hope it will work for you too.

All facts and figures have been checked and revised where necessary. All the informational resources in Chapter 2—park services, organizations, clubs, phone numbers, faxes, e-mail and snail-mail addresses—have been updated. Obsolete equipment has been replaced with information on the newest products now (or about to be) in the camping stores. We have discovered new quick-cooking foods in out-of-the-way places, and we tell you what they are and how to get them in Chapter 5. All the lists in

Chapter 6—have been revisited and repaired where necessary, and of course reproduced in cut-out form at the back of the book. New recipes have been added to Chapters 9 and 10, making this the most comprehensive cookbook-within-an-outdoor-book ever written. We have completely revised the Book List to give you easy access to the best information out there in the publishers' world, and where available, we've added throughout the book useful World Wide Web addresses to get you quickly to this new and powerful source of information.

As one or more of our late grandparents would no doubt have put it, "If that is all you have added, *Dayenu*." Which means, Enough!

We hope you'll agree. We insist that you let us know what you think. That way, the next edition will be an even better model than this one. If that's possible!

*RG and HK, San Francisco, 1996*

# Contents

---

# Introduction

## Brooklyn Boy Meets Wilderness

Steve looks like a surfer but sounds like a mobster. Behind the day-glo tan and obedient muscles is a bookish film critic from Flatbush who'd never been closer to the wilderness than summer camp at Bear Mountain. The Great Outdoors ("outta daws") meant Belmont Racetrack and Shea Stadium. The only trails he'd ever hiked were asphalt; the only lonesome roads he'd traveled under his own power were the sidestreets off Queens Boulevard on a three-speed bike he had lifted from his cousin Jimmy.

But like many young city slickers, he craved the country. We'd never taken anyone camping who was so eager to "tame" the wilderness. He couldn't wait to strap on the pack and get started. He was strong and fit. He was ready for bear! He lasted about three hours. Several miles from the trailhead, he began to mutter and grumble. How in hell could anyone enjoy schlepping a forty-pound pack uphill in 80-degree heat all afternoon toward some abstract promise of a cool mountain lake? The farther we got from the last beer, the darker his mood became. His boots were good-looking but a size too small; long before we reached our destination, they had rubbed his heels raw. His pack felt like some mythic burden of the damned. The route was incomprehensible. By the time we stopped for dinner, he was ready for a hotel. But a quarter-inch foam sleeping pad was not his idea of the Waldorf Astoria.

The second day brought no relief. Up too early, we climbed 1,500 feet in the first mile, then set off cross-country around a mountain bowl strewn with rock slides, boulders and steep pitches into space. The streets of Brooklyn seemed safe by comparison. Steve's every muscle ached from yesterday. We kept up a steady stream of encouragement, however, and by mid-afternoon, Steve made a monumental discovery. You can make the pack work *for* you, keeping the weight on the hips and off the shoulders. He began to notice that the view before him was improbably remote and beautiful, something he couldn't see elsewhere. And when we finally climbed down to a granite-girded lake, filled with trout and inaccessible enough to promise a week of solitude, Steve remembered why we came: five days of fishing, cooking, eating and relaxing.

His contentment lasted until we set out to catch our supper. Steve regarded the fishing rod with suspicion. We put a lure on the line and taught him how to cast. But that did nothing to dispel his skepticism. How could you catch fish with a spoon-shaped piece of metal at the end of a nylon string? He cast and cast—aspersions and oaths as well as lures and flies and bubbles. Around the lake he went. No luck. He announced his early retirement from the game.

His mood blackened as the clouds rolled in, necessitating another trauma—setting up his tent. He hesitated. We cajoled. He procrastinated. We insisted. He refused. We quickly erected it. It began to pour. It rained all night. In the morning, Steve's tent looked like a collapsed dream the day the circus leaves town. Somewhere under that heap of netting, nylon and wind-sundered rainfly lay a sodden camper converted to the virtues of foul-weather protection. While the sun dried his sleeping bag, Steve spent an hour erecting the tent in the ideal place with geometric fanaticism. It looked great, and he never spent another moment in it. But he was glad it was there, waiting.

The next day Steve caught his first fish, an eight-inch brown trout, with a grasshopper. Well, perhaps he'd consider coming out of retirement. Two days later, he returned with seven little rainbows after a tough solo hike to a lake beyond the razor-back ridge. And he began to *talk* fishing. He studied the "hatch" of flies on the water's surface, invented fishing knots, and experimented with salmon eggs as extra enticement on his lures. Trout with almonds, trout baked in soy sauce, ginger and garlic, fish grilled over red-hot coals at sunset—all helped make the talk better. Camping began to look—and feel—like fun.

On our fourth day, Steve set out to bake a cake. He'd never before baked anything, anywhere. He had, however, been impressed with the cinnamon nut bread and the chocolate cake with icing we'd pulled from the coals. He hauled out flour and baking powder, corn meal (which he mistook for milk powder), RyKrisps, raisins, apricots and sugar; mixed them all in a pot; added some margarine, sugar and an egg; then poured in just enough water to make the batter run off the spoon like a ribbon. We reminded him to grease the pot before surrounding it with hot coals, wished him luck and went fishing. When we returned, an apricot cornbread awaited us, and Steve carved another notch on the stock of his outdoor knowledge.

After that, we had a wilderness fanatic on our hands. He insisted on doing everything: fishing, sewing, cooking and gathering wood. We managed to keep busy swimming, sunning, eating and reading. Together we invented ways to cook fish, fry corn cakes and coin new names for constellations in the night sky because we weren't sure of their classic names and didn't care. By the time we walked out, Steve was a confirmed camper and we were convinced that anyone could become one, too.

## What This Book Is About

There are enough texts on hiking, cycling, canoeing, backpacking, car camping, mountaineering, survival and fishing to fill a four-year curriculum on the fine art of leaving your house. This book doesn't duplicate the other guides. Rather, it illustrates how imagination, improvisation and commitment can unfold the possibilities of the outdoors, whether you get there by car, foot, bike, canoe, llama, horse or wheelchair. It takes an agnostic view of what defines the outdoors. For some, it is a campground filled with RVs and barbecues, sort of a downtown with trees. For others, it is a remote off-trail lake two days away from the nearest human voice. For many, it is somewhere in between—a state park, a riverbank or a day hike away from the madding crowd.

This book recognizes that whatever the outdoors means to you, its pleasures can be enhanced by some common-sense planning, a willingness to slow down and hang out, and a disposition to indulge in minor adventures. The book is based on the Pleasure Principle: A camping holiday is neither boot camp nor a triumph of the will. It is not (necessarily) uplifting or ennobling. It is, or *should* be, more fun and less expensive than a motel tour of the world's Disneylands and watering holes. And this book shows you how.

This book is practical. It tells you four things—how to plan a trip; how to get where you're going; how to cook and eat as never before on a camping trip; and what to do in the long hours between sumptuous meals. If you're a novice, we'll show you how to get started and how to finish gracefully, even if you've gotten egg on your face along the way. If you are an old hand at camping, we'll give you new and useful information about fishing, cooking, trail-finding, stargazing, family entertainment and all-purpose, world-class hanging out. If you've ever come back from a camping trip bored or discontented, this is the book you need.

A book can't paddle a canoe, catch a fish or bake a cake. It *can*, however, provide your initial inspiration, point you in the right direction and above all, cut the time, cost and hard knocks of learning. We'll show you how to stay dry, stay full, stay busy and stay friends. We'll run you through the basics—how to get the information you need, including access to the Internet, and how to think about equipment, packing, maps and trails. We'll then give you hints on improvising: drying food, fishing in the rain, repairing boots and entertaining children. We are equal-opportunity enthusiasts and want you to get a feel for the limitless possibilities of a camping trip.

We do make several assumptions: that you like to camp and love to eat; that you want a vacation, not a forced march; that you like to get away from the grind. (Rick's grandmother used to complain, "If you've seen one tree you've seen 'em all." This book is not for her.) We also assume that you are not necessarily a mountain climber, spelunker, Yukon guide or even a member of the Sierra Club. You may never have set foot in a national park or on a wilderness trail, or you may have been haunting them for years. You are reasonably fit but not a triathlete. You may be too young to read this book or too old to believe all its claims; you may be "abled" or disabled. You believe that locomotion by foot or boat or bike or wheelchair is an honorable and even enjoyable way to travel. And that financing a camping trip does not require a seat on the New York Stock Exchange.

The style of camping espoused in this book requires no exceptional skills. Getting a canoe across a lake or down a slow-moving river is not the same as taking a raft or kayak through whitewater with the family's Waterford crystal on board. Our book is about the first, not the second. Riding a mountain bike on a dirt trail or a touring bike into a campground does not require experience in the *Giro d'Italia*. We know something about the former, nothing about the latter. Backpacking in the wilderness, on or off-trail, takes ordinary, not extraordinary, know-how.

One of us is afraid of heights, but gets along fine even on steep trails. We've been lost and even without radar have managed to figure out where we were and how to get to where we were going. We don't have the newest, most expensive equipment. But we've lived on fish we caught, baked breads and cakes, read some of the world's longest novels, kept our clothes dry and spirits up in 48 hours of steady rain, and come back to spin tales that made our friends' feet itch and our own thoughts turn to the next trip out. Everything that we write about, we (or our friends) have done ourselves, and most of it we learned by doing. All the stories are true. And if we haven't done something—for example, performed triple bypass surgery with a Swiss Army knife or coped with a serious injury—we don't write about it. We prefer to go easy on the detailed information you can get better elsewhere. But we make every effort to show you how to get that information (in Chapters 2 and 3 and in the Book List in the back of the book).

## How to Use This Book

We've never met anyone who has actually read a camping book from cover to cover. Unless you can't bear to skip a single page, you'll want to cut in at functional points and then cut out again. To that end, we divide the book into four parts: Planning a Trip, Outdoor Basics, Cooking and Eating, and the Pleasure Principle: Creative Loitering. Here's a brief summary of each.

## Planning a Trip

Planning a camping trip takes time and energy, though the amount of each depends on your mode of travel. Car and canoe camping are relatively easy. Think of your "vehicle" as an extra-large steamer trunk. Toss in anything you want and get out of town before the IRS comes calling. Biking and backpacking take more planning. You need to consider total weight, packing constraints, route difficulty, the number of people involved, and travel distances. In all cases—however you travel—planning requires making lists, deciding where to go, when to go, how to get there, whom to go with. Then you have to assemble gear, maps, permits, and then more gear.

In Chapter 1, we show you how to plan trips by car, bike,

canoe, horse and foot, for one person, two, four or more, for families and extended families—bringing babies, great-grandmothers and disabled friends takes only a little special forethought. We also discuss the great philosophical question, How far should one go? Not on the first date, but on the first day, and on subsequent days, too. We have a formula that operates here and you're going to like it. It has to do with resting as much as moving, and will prepare you for the great culture shock of PHO (Planned Hanging Out).

Chapter 2 puts at your fingertips the kind of information everybody always asks for: Where do we get maps and permits, find campgrounds, get in touch with experts and guides and like-minded enthusiasts? Where do we find the right fix-it manual, the local or regional outdoor club or clinic, the best advice on equipment, the meaning of life? Let your ham-handed fists do the walking through its pages.

Chapter 3 takes you by the hand down the yellow brick road of the Internet, the biggest information avenue in the world. We show you how to get and give advice about the outdoors on the Net, and how to answer the big questions: How do the on-line services work? How does the World Wide Web work? What's there for the camper, backpacker, paddler, cyclist? Is it worth the time and effort? How much effort does it take? Armed with this chapter, you can be your own compiler and multiply a thousand-fold the kind of information we give you in Chapter 2.

Chapter 4 is all about equipment—with a twist. We show you how to stay warm, dry and comfortable, *without spending a fortune.* Canoeists, we argue, don't need the latest second-skin raingear, bicyclists don't need the newest genetically engineered lightweight frames, and backpackers don't need freeze-dried tent stakes. What everybody needs is a make-do attitude and a sympathetic sales clerk.

Chapter 5 concerns food: what and how much to take, where to buy it, how to weigh and pack it, what kind of utensils and stoves and pots you will need, even how to cache food on a long trip. Once you've got this part of the planning done, the cooking and eating will be a piece of cake! In short, it will take you an hour to read these suggestions, two hours to absorb them, and a few more hours to put them into practice. But we guarantee it'll save you countless hours, dollars and hassles.

So will Chapter 6, which is devoted to the exquisite art of making lists. We show you basic lists and arcane, Gothic lists. We'll help you make equipment lists, tool kits and medicine chests. Even book lists! If after this chapter you forget something, don't call us, we'll call you.

## Outdoor Basics

You've planned and prepared for your camping adventure for a week. You've got everything. You're in the saddle, on the dock, or at the trailhead. Chapter 7 takes you from there to your destination. It shows you how to read maps, load and adjust a pack, pannier or canoe, and how to hike or bike a trail and negotiate off-trail terrain. It gets you through weather and around obstacles. It tells you how to get acclimated to altitude, heat and cold. Above all, it stresses the importance of remaining flexible. A blister, a storm or just a meadow full of wildflowers may slow you down and make you change your plans. This is a vacation. Look around, enjoy and take it easy.

Chapter 8 shows you how to choose a site and set up camp. If you don't know where to pitch your tent or stow your canoe, how to build a fire, protect your food from small and large creatures of the night (your partner excepted), stash your gear, enjoy or at least survive a storm, the information is there. Use it.

## Cooking and Eating

Eating is at the heart—well, gut—of the outdoor experience. Our attitude is this: If you enjoy eating in your own kitchen, why deprive yourself of the pleasure just because you're three days and 9,000 feet away from a home with a range? Stick with us and you'll be able to have your cake and eat it, too!

Chapter 9 tells you how to avoid the library-paste peril of freeze-dried foods by preparing your own dried meals at home, simply and inexpensively. It takes you through cooking basics with the expectation that even if you have never boiled an egg, you can still bake a trout or make the best Brazilian black bean soup this side of Rio.

Chapter 10 is the collection of recipes that have made us famous from Kneejerk Junction to Toehold Lake, from Chez Panisse in Berkeley to the Oyster Bar in Grand Central Station:

freshwater fish, homemade soups and sauces, stewed fruits, jams and chutneys, baked breads, cakes and pizzas. The recipes are keyed for time, ease, heat source (stove or fire) and perishability. Read 'em and drool. Chapter 10 is also full of useful how-to information for preparing food in the outback. Need to clean or bone a fish? Cook in the rain? Use a camp stove? Need to eat fast and travel light? Want to carry a 40-pound reflector oven and microwave blaster into a campground? We have answers to all these questions and more. We show you how to become an outdoor chef without burning yourself, the food or the forest.

## Pleasure Principle: Creative Loitering

Bikers and canoeists sometimes want to take a day off. Day hikers and car campers have loads of time on their hands. And backpackers—at least those dedicated to the Kahn & Greenspan school of sequential hiking and loafing—love long days wondering if it's worth getting up to bag a grasshopper as bait or read the world's second longest novel. Children need to be busy, amused, content, dirty, startled and entranced by the simple wonder of it all. This is the part of the book that caps the journey and makes it all worth while.

Chapter 11 pulls together all the good things to do on a lazy day (well, all the good things fit to print), whether you're in a paved campsite or stuck in an aerie below the summit of Mount Vertigo. This is a chapter dedicated, but not limited, to children. Whatever your age, if you don't know what to do with time on your hands 200 miles from the nearest game show, take heart. Help is at hand. Here. Now.

Chapter 12 is the amateur angler's guide to the briny deep. Some people fish for sport. Others fish to relax. We fish to eat. Here is the info on everything from gear to casting to landing the big cahoonga. You even get a fish-eye view of the whole thing: where they hang out and why, what they're looking for and at. We don't use the latest in laminated fly rods, and purists might cringe, but we've never gone hungry and never left a lake or stream dissatisfied, even when we didn't catch a thing.

Chapter 13 is an introduction to the heavens. Stars are just about the only nighttime-viewing entertainment in the backcountry, and viewing them is the second most popular sport conducted in a prone position after dark. We have tried in this chapter to give you a couple of working methods for making personal sense out of the slice of sky above you; it is legitimate to see constellations with your own mind's eye. Just as ancient Greeks and Chinese discovered different formations in the same stars, you may rearrange the classical sky for yourself with much pleasure and no damage to the astronomical establishment. On the other hand, if you're a traditionalist and want to know how to read a star map, the information is here. But either way, you'll never know how bright the night sky is until you see it unobscured by city lights and a pall of smog.

# CHAPTER 1

# Variables:
# Who's Going Where
# and How?

## Getting Ready

Anyone who has ever camped out in the backyard as a kid or whose children have waved goodbye after supper and gone off down the back steps and disappeared into a tent knows that there are things to do to get ready. Complex things: Which cookies to take? Which friend? And simple things: Knowing the fastest, safest escape route back to bed in the event that the yard is overrun by goblins. A grown-up camping trip farther afield isn't much different. While you don't have to gird for battle to get ready, you do need to answer some fairly basic questions: Where to go? When? How far? How long? With whom? And the answers depend in the first place on the great locomotion dilemma: To go or not to go by car, by bike, by canoe, by horse, by foot. Once you resolve that, proceed to the section which applies to you, and then browse the others. You may be persuaded to try another way another time.

## Car Camping

We know two people whose names are Ed and Edna. They are not related. They have never met. They have nothing to do with one another. But combined, their stories ought to prove once and for all that car camping comes in as many hues as a smoggy sunset in Passaic or L.A.

Edna is a biker. She rides a 750cc Harley, wears leathers and a tattoo, and is, we swear it, sixty years old. She looks *bad* and we've heard teenagers exclaim, "Awesome, dude!" when she pulls into the parking lot. The parking lot in question abuts REI (Recreational Equipment Incorporated), the great Western states' equivalent of EMS (Eastern Mountain Sports) and other outdoor provisioners. Twice a year without fail Edna shows up there to check out the latest in camping gear, everything from stoves to tents to orienteering compasses. She plunks down a bundle and leaves the staff agog from the tales she tells of her latest adventures on the camping trail. Edna and her women pals have been to every campground from the San Juan Islands in Puget Sound to Death Valley. She likes to keep moving, but she also knows how to hike, cook, fish and strip down her bike and rebuild it in a campground. She rides for the feel of the wind and the speed of her wheels, and camps for the companionship and the beauty of the places she finds off the road. She's one of our all-time favorite campers—daring, eccentric, funny and good at what she does.

Ed is a retired body shop owner whom we met in a campsite on the Oregon coast a couple of years ago. Every summer he takes off in his camper truck, fishing the coastal rivers and the ocean beaches for three months. But when we met him he was a shattered man. He hadn't slept for a week before he pulled into this particular campground. This was no insomniac. He told us he could sleep through a fender job on Al Capone's Packard. But he had made a mistake and tried the mountain campgrounds in the Cascade Range. They were clean, accessible, friendly and uncrowded. Still, he couldn't get to sleep. It was too quiet! He realized when he got back to the shore that what he had missed was the sound of the sea. It was part of his routine; it defined his environment, and he swore he would never leave the coast again. For him, being confined to the coast was a blessing, not a constraint. His vistas were bounded by tidewaters, but within them he found unlimited possibilities.

You'd be surprised at the number of people who settle into a favorite campground for a whole summer (or winter in the warmer climes). They're called "seasonals," and you'll recognize them by the little gardens and workshops they create in their campsites, the neighborly village atmosphere they create for all comers. And while most of us can't afford to take off three months to camp out of our cars, the number of people visiting parks and campgrounds for a few days *alfresco* is growing. And camping with your vehicle has a lot of advantages which other kinds of camping (such as backpacking) lack. You don't have to haul anything anywhere but out of the trunk of your car. (And if you have a motor-home, you don't have to haul anything out at all!) Your tent can be old or new, heavy or light, or you can sleep in the backseat of your car. You can bring a lightweight backpacking stove or a four-burner extravaganza with a cantilevered oven or a ten-pound bag of briquettes for the campground grill. Car camping is great for small kids, who can't carry a pack or walk for miles. It's also just the ticket for disabled people if the campground has the necessary access facilities and construction. For campers who like conveniences like showers, flush toilets, picnic tables, and possibly a nearby Foster's Freeze, it provides a happy alternative to urban life.

## Campground Reservations

Most campsites, whether in county, state or national parks, are available on a first-come, first-served basis, and it is possible and often necessary to reserve a site by mail or phone well before you leave on your trip. In the northern tier states and Canada, where the summer season is short, camping pressure is heavy and often campsites are sold out by January! The same is true in heavily populated or touristed parks (e.g. Yosemite, Yellowstone and Acadia). So:

- Reserve early.

- Call your local, county or state Parks and Recreation Department for reservation information and requirements.

- Call the National Park Service (see Chapter 2 for numbers) for reservation info at specified parks. Many parks will not accept reservations before a certain date.

- Cancel reservations as soon as you know you can't use them. That's a courtesy to others on the waiting list.

- If you don't have a reservation, you may still get a campsite on a first-come basis at the park itself.

- Try to avoid the big holiday weekends if you don't have a reservation.

Once you get to a campground, you may want to hike the local trails for a day. That means you may need a map (and may want to know how to read it), a day pack, and some food and water to bring along. You may want to take your all-terrain bicycle for a trail ride. You may want to fish in a nearby lake or stream, spend some time cooking, or just sit in the shade and read.

Whatever your preferences, you can enhance your experience by using the sections below which apply to you and your particular needs. If you want to hike off the trail, read the section on topographic maps; if you like to fiddle with the menu, go to the chapters on food and cooking; if you're bringing a bicycle, check your tool set against the list in Chapter 6. And if you're a first-timer, you'll want to know what equipment is necessary, what is optional, what can be rented, and what is useful to buy if you're on a limited budget. Check out Chapter 4 for hints and some unconventional wisdom.

## Crime in the Campground

Alas, the age of innocence is over. It's a fact of life that there's crime out there in the outback. Not surprising given some estimates that almost 35 million Americans camped in a tent in 1993! In 1994 there were 398 reported burglaries in the National Parks, 3,180 reports of theft (excluding motor vehicles), 201 reports of stolen vehicles, and 237 assaults (with firearms, knives, sticks and fists). The Park Service produces annual figures on all reported crimes, from aggravated assault to sex offenses, from fraud to drug violations, and if you're interested in this sort of thing, a call to the Park Service's Division of Ranger Activities in Washington (202/208-4874) will get you a copy of the report. Unreported cases would swell these figures. Car camping grounds are a lot safer than the mean streets you left behind, but still you need to take some common-sense precautions to assure that your holiday remains a holiday.

- Ask the park rangers what the local safety protocols are. They know best.

- Don't assume that gear locked in your car or trunk is safe if you head off for a day on the trail. Leave as little behind as possible. Ditto with your tent.

- Hike or travel in groups.

- Party in moderation. Park rangers report more assaults among people who know each other than among strangers.

- If you don't need your diamond tiara, leave it at home.

# Bicycle Touring and Mountain Bikes

A bicycle is one of the best ways to reach choice and remote camping spots. You move faster than on foot, and you notice things that you would miss in a car. Bike touring is marked above all by self-sufficiency. You carry all your own gear in panniers, the cyclist's equivalent of saddlebags. You can cover a continent or your local neighborhood, cross Canada or mosey through the backroads of Denmark: As long as you are camping along the way, you'll find a great deal of useful information here.

## *Bike Touring for the First Time?*

- Take day trips before trying an extended tour. Build your stamina.

- Take short "shakedown" tours *with all your gear* before trying a long one. These will accustom you to the feel of a fully loaded bike, allow you to iron out glitches in equipment, and probably persuade you to lighten your load!

- Plan to travel with someone else or a group.

- Take advantage of "walk-in" campsites. They are almost always available for cyclists (and hikers) without reservations. They're cheap, convenient, friendly.

- Learn basic repair skills for your bike: tire changing or patching, chain and cable repair. Or tour with somebody who knows how to fix your bike.

- Carry a lock and use it.

- Protect against sun and heavy weather.

Mountain biking means using your bicycle to travel on hiking trails or rough logging roads. As these are often steep and rugged, it's nearly impossible to carry a lot of weight on the bike. Furthermore, mountain bikes are heavier than touring bikes, for they have to stand up to the constant jolting of rough terrain. You don't take the *Encyclopedia Britannica* along on such a vehicle. Mountain bikers are essentially day hikers on bicycles, and they need to have map-reading skills, adequate food and drink, and protection from sun and rain, just as day-hikers do. In addition, they have to deal with the possibility of breakdowns miles from the nearest shop. That often requires innovation and ingenuity, as well as having the proper equipment and parts in the toolbag.

Talk to touring cyclists or mountain bikers. You'll discover that most of them love and know the outdoors and take pride and pleasure in combining camping and cycling. Like canoeists and backpackers, some camp in order to travel and some travel in order to camp. Either way, it's the combination that counts, and you'll find a wealth of valuable camping and traveling hints in this book, in addition to the specific sections which deal with bicycles and the outdoors.

*VeloNet is a great starting point for all the cycling information you'll ever need.*

## Bikers and Hikers

A great trail-use controversy has surfaced in the past few years as more and more mountain bikers are beginning to show up on what once were exclusively hiking (or horse packing) trails. We know of one case in Northern California where mountain bikers secretly carved out a trail on county backwoods land and used it for several years before it was discovered. Feelings flared, sides were taken, politicians got into the act, and the trail was filled in at the cost of public monies and a lot of excess spleen.

Six years ago there were some 15 million all-terrain bikes in the U.S. Now that figure is close to 30 million, and some experts estimate that over seven million bikes are being used in forested and mountain areas, along some of the 77,000 miles of trails maintained by the National Forest Service outside of designated wilderness areas. Who has got the right of way? Do peace and solitude take precedence over equal access rights? Are the trails being ruined? The answers aren't in yet, and the partisans on each side still outnumber those who are trying to work out compromise solutions.

---

*Hikers vs. Bikers*—The hikers: "It's like weeds taking over grass. Pretty soon we'll have all weeds. Better they go to quarries with their rocky bases." The bikers: "...Mountain biking is a new sport, and people better get educated....We're the hikers of the '90s, and we're getting a bad rap." (*New York Times*, May 30, 1995.)

---

Researchers meanwhile are trying to come up with hard facts which may change the tone of the debate. Debbie Chavez of the U.S. Forest Service's Pacific Southwest Research Station (PSW), for example, completed a mid-1995 national study of "Mountain Bike Use in Our National Forests: A Management Perspective," in which she found the following: 6 in 10 managers of the forests found evidence of mountain bike damage to the natural resources; 5 in 10 reported mountain bike accidents; 7 in 10 reported conflicts between bikers and horse-riders and hikers. Just who was at fault varied from report to report. The good news is that conflicts are being mediated by the provision of information, use of signs and posters, and through active Forest Service cooperation with the various trail users. Addictive readers may also want to check out "Conflict and Issues Related to Mountain Biking in the National Forests: A Multimethodological Approach," in the USDA Forest Service's second *Symposium on Social Aspects and Recreation Research (February 23-25, 1994),* published in October, 1995. You can get copies of these and more from the PSW Research Station, USDA Forest Service, P.O. Box 245, Berkeley, CA 94701.

Meanwhile bikers are beginning to learn the art of "soft cycling," walking their bikes over fragile terrain, slowing down on heavily hiked trail sections, making way for hikers and horses, learning trail etiquette. Here are the six "Rules of the Trail" put out by the International Mountain Bicycling Association (for their address and phone, see Chapter 2):

- Ride on open trails only.
- Leave no trace.
- Control your bicycle.
- Always yield trail (to hikers and pack animals).
- Never spook animals.
- Plan ahead.

# Canoeing

Helen Kass is a self-professed klutz. She doesn't know a rocker from a gunwale, freeboard from waterline. She insists that the genes for grace and athletic skill were removed surgically from her body by aliens at an early age. Yet she proudly points to almost 40 years of New England canoeing experience and insists with a kind of triumphant resignation that if she can do it, you can too. Helen thinks that it's the only way to travel on Maine's rivers and on the inter-island itinerary along the coast. She and her family have been at it for a couple of generations, and the first time you find yourself waking up unexpectedly in a field of wild strawberries (having disembarked after dark), or the first time you take a wrong turn up the local sewer outlet with a dachshund who abandons ship, you will not be a pioneer. They beat you to it and lived to tell the tale.

Canoeing is the nautical equivalent of cross-country skiing, an invitation to random discovery. In many areas, you can combine hiking and canoeing, taking day trips on land and then heading out for another site down or up stream. In other areas, you can combine river and lake canoeing and literally go on for weeks, portaging between launching sites. Canoeing is also one of the easiest ways to transport yourself, your gear, and your entire family across a lake to your favorite campsite in the woods. A 70-pound, 16.5-foot canoe holds just about as much as a VW Bug, so you can toss in the lawn chairs and the old five-person canvas tent along with the spouse and close relatives. (An 18-footer will induce comparisons with the QE2, and you might as well bring along the dance band.) Made of everything from ye olde wood and canvas to hybrid miracle laminates, canoes are almost indestructable, and for Class 1 (lake) and Class 2 (slow-moving river) travel, no special repair kit is necessary (see Chapter 6, page 151). Because it's a shallow-draft craft, the canoe is ideal for exploring tidal waters. Other boats are at the mercy of the tides. Not the canoe.

Canoeing, like car camping, is a glorious way to travel with small children. You can stop as often as they like—to explore a tidal pool or mud hole, to examine a bird's nest, to romp and stretch, swim or pee. On a lazy river, you can always have a hand free to get food, comfort a crank, play a game, steady a fussbudget or pet the dachshund. Children even love the tipover drills you put them through before their first trip, and the drills themselves help demystify water-borne transport. You can even let small children help paddle. They'll grow up to take *you* canoeing.

Experienced canoeists agree that the "tippy" issue is much exaggerated. Of course, you can tip over a canoe. You can tip over a Volvo, too, if you're not careful, or fall off a bike or trip over your shoelaces while hiking. With a modicum of care and a sense of weight displacement that should come naturally, you'll board and exit the canoe, shift positions, pack, and paddle it safely and smoothly. If you've never paddled a canoe, take the Red Cross hands-on course, pass their test and be on your way. Read their big book, *Canoeing* (see Chapter 2), and you'll get all the hard information you need, from loading a canoe on your car to portaging, from handling a canoe in rough weather or water or fog to stashing gear and dealing with emergencies. After that, come back to us here, for all the news you need to make a canoeing trip a fabulous camping trip as well. What we say about backpacking below applies to you, too.

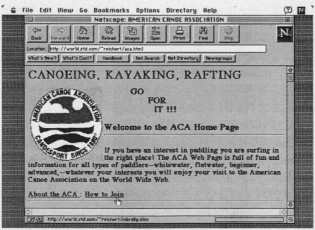

*The American Canoe Association is the best one-stop resource for reliable paddling information.*

## Whaddya Do With Your Car While Canoeing?

- Take a loop trip which brings you back to the car.

- Have friends or a canoe livery service (ask the park ranger station for information) drive your car to your destination point. Don't forget to take a set of keys for yourself!

- Hitch a ride back to the car while the rest of the party stays with the canoe. This only works on short trips and only where you feel safe hitchhiking.

- Sell the canoe to a passing farmer, walk into town, buy a new car, drive it back to your old car, sell it to a passing farmer, and drive off into the sunset.

# Backpacking

Some years ago, Rick discovered a gem of a lake in the high Sierras by just the method we want to get across to you here: a combination of memory, guile, imagination, curiosity, map reading and schmoozing. Here's the story.

Back in college when he was young and spry (he is now old and spry), Rick had a classmate whom we shall call Alice for national security reasons. Alice came from one of those unconscionably rich families that owned real estate—like half the South Pacific. As a little girl, she would be taken to the mountains by the family, its well-lardered pack train, a couple of spare aunts and uncles, and of course, its retainer, a grizzled wilderness guide right out of central casting named Big Buck. B.B. got them to this storied lake filled with giant golden trout and pure water, and Alice's fragmented memory of it provided Rick with the first shards of the information he needed.

The horses were left at a base camp, before the terrain got rough. The party had to hike, climbing ridges and walking through snowfields. "We hiked forever," Rick recalls Alice saying, "upwards, always upwards." (Alice, it must be noted, has never won a drama critics award.) The trail climbed a steep ridge over an 11,000-foot pass, and then at some predetermined point— there were no markers—Buck turned off the trail and began winding his way up a rocky streambed. The going was slow and steep. "I remember thinking that the top of the mountain was near, only to find that over each crest lay yet another rocky basin. And over the crest of that basin, there was still another."

Finally, of course, the party stopped at Big Buck's command and followed his gaze and ancient arm. There below, couched between snowfield and evergreen grove, lay Lake Nirvana, Buck's private Shangri-la, and the most beautiful place on Earth.

Years later, Rick was determined to find that place. He knew the lake's name and its general location. He gathered up maps and guidebooks, checked indexes and keys, and finally found it on a topo map. It was several miles off a main trail, nestled in a bowl surrounded by steep pinnacles and spires. Big Buck's route was easy to spot, over one crest, then another, then another, climbing upwards from the main trail toward the single passable entrance among the tall crags. Even the snowfields were on the map.

The map told him even more. The stream flowed into the lake year round, providing fresh water even in the late summer when the trip was planned. Just below the lake there were several flat, meadow-like areas in the forest. These could provide a sheltered campsite with running water nearby. So Rick set off by himself for the lake in mid-September.

The trip itself was too good to be true: wonderful fishing, secure campsite, superb weather, and above all, a breathtaking panorama of domes, spires and steep crags burnished by the late summer sun. Using maps, a compass, planning and common sense, Rick had decoded Big Buck's secret. To this day, he is touched by the memory of that experience. Before it, he had never left the trail with a pack. But his trip to Lake Nirvana gave him a new sort of confidence about backpacking. The wilderness beyond the trail was no longer a mystery. Shangri-la was open for business.

Backpacking doesn't always take you to a special place like Lake Nirvana. We have hiked "off trail" all day only to come to a lake that recently had a logging road cut into it. Four-wheel drives and boom boxes greeted us at a shoreline fouled with soap suds, garbage and dead fish. At that point, it was nice to know that we could keep on hiking—over another ridge, to another stream—to a campsite still untouched by civilization.

Like all the other forms of camping, backpacking requires planning, knowledge, practice and desire. But done well, it confers special rewards: a feeling of independence as you and your pack comprise a total environment for survival and pleasure, an exhilarating sense of distance from the nervous noise and speed of the city, a knowledge that the only way into this arena of high mountain grandeur was by foot, and a total conviction that it was worth every hard step.

### Horses, Mules and Llamas

Hal wouldn't get on a horse unless he lost an election bet; Rick's an old hand at packing into the wilderness on horseback. It doesn't matter—the point is that you don't need to be an expert equestrian to utilize pack animals and saddle horses to enhance the possibilities of a backpacking trip. Small children can be carried in the saddle with you. They love it. Disabled hikers, if secure in the saddle, can get farther into the wilderness than they would otherwise, and their special gear can be carried in on the pack animals.

Pack stations will help you arrange your trip (see page 43 for information). If you're an experienced rider and have the facilities for transporting a horse, you may be able to rent a mount and take it on your own. If not, a station hand will accompany you and lead the mules and your horse to your destination. You can contract to be left off and picked up a week later for the long trek out, or you can arrange to have the pack station "do" your whole trip for you.

All National Forest Service and National Park trails are required to be maintained for horse travel. That means clearance for a mounted rider and secure footing on the trail. Don't expect horses, mules or llamas (increasingly available as pack animals), to leave the trail when you want to go cross country. They can't and won't, so plan to have the animals tended during the time you are gone, be it hours or days.

# Special Considerations

### Camping with Children

Traveling with the very young—ages one to seven—has been a special and wonderful experience for us, and it can be for you. But it requires special forethought and follow-through. After all, *they* don't necessarily want to go camping; you do. They're following Mom, Dad or some other irrational parental figure who positively insists on getting back to nature. If they're too young to care, they're probably in a pack on your back, happy to be along for the ride. If they're old enough to think about it, they may have decided that they're doing you a favor. Hal's cousin Elizabeth remembers four things about her early days in a canoe: the black flies, the mosquitos, the dachshund, and the fanatical enthusiasm of parents who insisted that everyone was having a good time. Children are not necessarily born to the outback, littler versions of John Muir. They have to learn, too.

Car and canoe camping are naturals for the very young. Horse camping can be, too. In all of these cases, small legs don't have to go far, and big appetites and natural curiosities can be immediately satisfied. We don't know anyone who has ever tried long-distance bicycle touring with a young child, though it no doubt has been done, too. Backpacking takes a little more care in planning, but we've done it pleasurably with infants, toddlers and active five-year-olds. Special arrangements for sharing loads and responsibilities need to be worked out beforehand. *Really* worked out. Otherwise one or two people will end up harassed, over-worked and unhappy. Throughout this book you'll find ideas and suggestions to make kid camping so good that they'll want to come back for more. And that's the point, isn't it?

## Camping with Kids: A Starter Set

- Involve children in trip planning. Let 'em help shop and pack.

- Keep car travel brief. Break up the journey with frequent stops. A highway rest area may be the highlight of a young child's trip. Enjoy it.

- Car games. Keep a good supply in your head: license plate lotto, roadsign alphabet, stories, songs and riddles. (See the Book List on pages 381-386 for references.)

- Special equipment: favorite games, toys, teddy bears. (See Chapter 6 for packing for babies and the very young.)

- Food. Take what they *like* to eat, not what you think is good for them. Children, like adults, will not expire of malnutrition if they eat nothing but marshmallows (or carrots!) for three days. (See Chapter 5 on food planning for children.)

- Keep things simple and choose easy trails. The fewer ups and downs the better. Hal's first trip with his daughters covered two miles in two days. On the way back (downhill), it took only two hours! Rick spent each of four summers traveling all of three-quarters of a mile (the *same* three-quarters of a mile!) when his daughters were very young.

- Play while hiking. Walking can be fun or a bore. Make it fun. Play "ambush." Stop to check out a mud puddle or a bug. Catch a toad. Get to camp before your nerves and inspiration give out.

- Play while canoeing.

- Let kids participate. Let them help set up the tent, light the fire or stove, mix the batter, bake the cake, lick the pot, lead the way, paddle the canoe, hold the reins. Figure in extra time for all this, so you're not fuming when you put up the tent at midnight.

- Put on their rain suits at meals. Saves clothes; makes cleanup a snap.

- Wrap sock-clad feet in plastic bags before putting on tennies. Keeps feet dry when shoes get soaked by rain or puddles.

- Hang a whistle around their necks. They blow when lost. You find.

- Use a mix of diapers: disposables for inclement weather, cloth for sunny days.

- Pack along a cellular phone if you are worried about emergencies.

- Give adolescents and teenagers lots of leeway, but assume that they may need and want to learn how to do things, too (but may not know how to ask without seeming "dumb").

## *"Camping With Kids": A Sampler*

*"Around Katie's third birthday, we discovered pack goats. An eight-year-old nanny goat...carried 30 pounds with faithful devotion over the course of two summers...We formed an odd but able pack string in those days: mother, child, father, grandfather, dog and goat, united in common endeavor."*

*"The hike becomes a game. You walk for half an hour and get a lemon drop, some raisins, or a chocolate square. It takes us 45 minutes to fit in half an hour of pure walking, since we often stop for birds, bugs, and berries...But Katie never lags behind. In fact, she brags about her prowess....After those grim first steps, there is astonishingly little grumbling."*

*"'Horsey!...Horsey!' shrieks Pat [the two-year-old]. We peer into the*

*woods to find a small mule deer just 20 feet away....We watch quietly until the deer crosses the trail and heads downhill. The kids are quiet and big-eyed with their new knowledge: The woods are alive!"*

*[As they reach the trailhead and the car at the end of the journey:] "'There's the outhouse, Mom...There's the sign....There's the cars! We're home!'....'Aren't you glad, Mom?' Katie asks. 'Not really,' I say. 'It was a wonderful trip.' 'It was a stupid trip,' Katies says. 'No garbage cans, no picnic tables, no bathrooms. When I get home, I'm going to stay indoors for a long time.' I have no rejoinder. Preaching wilderness appreciation to Katie is futile....She's young...stubborn. [But] she's determinedly on the way to discovering hiking, camping and snooping around the woods for herself."*

Joan Hamilton, "Camping with Kids," *Sierra*, July/August 1986.

## Camping with the Disabled

Bonnie Lewkowicz, an experienced outdoor hand, took 30 Japanese disabled persons on their first camping trip. There were the usual language and first-timer problems but everyone muddled through. There were also the usual *unusual* problems which disabled people have to deal with all the time: inadequate transportation and assurances of campground accessibility by operators who don't understand what "accessible" means to disabled people. For example, a sandy campground, which on the surface looks comfy, may be so soft that a disabled person can't get enough purchase to turn over at night, or can't negotiate a wheelchair sunk to its hubs in the sand. One wheelchair-accessible restroom is better than none, but is so inadequate for large numbers as to render "accessible" meaningless. Some trails are in fact wheelchair accessible—for example some old fire roads; some are accessible to the blind and are known as "braille trails."

Things are getting better, if all too slowly, and for any disabled person who wants to participate in outdoor activities, including all the forms of camping we talk about here, there are a growing number of resources—organizations and publications—to turn to for assistance and advice. Need to know about adaptable equipment? About the kinds of questions you should ask about a campsite—are food-storage lockers reachable? Are picnic-table extensions available for wheelchair access? About rafting and canoe gear? About transportation? About clinics and clubs? About the "rails to trails" conversion program to make old railroad beds suitable for hiking by those with disabilities? See our resources list in Chapter 2, pages 48-51. Disability need not be a constraint on outdoor enthusiasms. Don't take our word for it. Take Bonnie's. Though she uses a wheelchair, she hasn't let the barriers overshadow the joy of being outdoors.

## Agenda for Improvements

- A new classification system of "accessibility."
- Federal legislation requiring wheelchair lifts on major transportation carriers.
- Adequate, as distinct from token, facilities in publicly maintained campgrounds.
- Less expensive specialized conversion equipment.
- A change of mind among the "abled." The outdoors belongs to all of us. Lend a hand.

# Where to Go

The absolutely best way to find a destination for a camping trip is by word of mouth. Ask your friends. Ask their friends. Check with salespeople at the outdoor outfitters, seek out local photographers, ask old-timers. Get in touch with the Sierra Club, local outdoor clinics and clubs, even the Boy and Girl Scouts. Check with resort owners, guides and camp counselors.

Another way to choose a camping destination is through a book or magazine. Check the library, bookstore, or camping store for trail, stream or route guides and commentaries. Local newspapers, newsletters and magazines often describe campsites and trails. (See Chapter 2 and the Book List on pages 381-386 for suggestions.) Be careful to notice the difference in difficulty between outings for beginners and those for experts. Don't start toward a scenic wonderland only to discover that you overlooked the section that mentioned the whitewater you have to negotiate, or the cliff face.

The precision of the answers you get from your research will be determined by the precision of the questions you ask. Figure out in advance how far you want to drive, and how far you want to hike, bike or paddle. Do you expect to hang out in a campsite or pile up the miles? Do you expect to catch fish? Need firewood?

Well-defined trails or routes? Then hit up the experts with, "We're looking for easy paddling downstream for a four-day trip with really good fishing and no portages." Don't worry if the answers are vague, and don't limit yourself to one or two suggestions. Any spot you might choose has its advantages and disadvantages. Keep checking out people, places and possibilities. If you're car camping, call the campground authorities for this kind of information: campsite availability, fire restrictions, entrance and overnight fees, opening and closing dates, fishing, swimming and boating info (are boat ramps open or closed?). Collect people's secret spots like a CIA agent collects microfilm.

Then locate the spots on a map. If you can't find them on paper, there's no sense setting out into the wilderness to look for them. Figure the distances and elevations; study the maps for possible difficulties: obstructions, streams to ford, logging trucks to avoid. (See Chapter 7 for a short course on how to read maps.) Once you've had a little practice, this will be easier than you think. Once you've figured out where to go, you can start thinking about how far to go and for how long.

## How Far Can You Go?

It's one thing to return from camping feeling exercised and healthy; it's quite another to limp home with blisters and sore muscles. A slow pace starts you off on the right foot.

A lot of people, especially beginners, take off after work on Friday, fight traffic on a long drive to a trailhead or campsite, and start out bright and early Saturday morning after five hours of sleep toward a destination that is just beyond their ability. By the time Saturday evening rolls around, they're exhausted, blistered and cranky. Whether you head for your campsite via bike, canoe, horse or foot, it's important that you don't overextend yourself, especially in the first day or two. The muscles you use on your daily job and those you use on a camping holiday are very different.

Long uphill grades can be disheartening if you're on foot or on a bike, and you should plan to stop often. If you're riding horses, remember that they need rest, too. If you're canoeing upstream or against the wind, you'll work harder and need more rest. Make time for it.

Backpacking is a little more complicated because pack weights vary according to the length of a trip. A half day of hiking is plenty on the first day, regardless of how much ground you cover. Most people can cover three to five miles uphill with a heavy pack in that time, usually at a rate of about 45 minutes per mile (about four hours of hiking). Reach your destination in early afternoon, have a swim, lunch, and then hang out for the rest of the day. You'll be able to hike farther as you acclimate to the altitude and as the pack gets lighter. If time permits, try a day or two of rest and relaxation after two days of hiking. And don't even think of the hike home. It's always easy. Most of the food is gone, the packs are light, and it's mostly downhill. That's the day you can expect to cover 10 to 12 miles, back to the trailhead and the ride home.

## A Guide to Moderation

- Almost every morning of travel, whether by bike, canoe or foot, deserves an afternoon of rest.

- A full day of travel deserves a full day of rest.

- The first day: by bicycle, no more than 30 miles in distance and 750 feet in elevation; by canoe, no more than four hours of paddling; by foot (backpacking), no more than five miles in distance and 1,500 feet in elevation.

- On succeeding days, no more than 50 miles/1,000 feet by bike; five hours by canoe; seven miles/2,000 feet by foot.

- The last day: Go for broke! Vacation's over, and you can sleep at work the next day.

- On horseback: Know your horse's limits and don't exceed them. Follow the advice of the pack station or your leader.

# How Many Are Going?

There are no rules about the number of people that can go on a trip, but you should have some idea of what the different numbers mean. Going alone is a lot different from going with one other person, or with two or twenty. We once met a party of 15 far off the trail in the Sierra wilderness who seemed content and happy. We never figured out how such a large group could hold together, and we shudder at the thought of having to organize such an expedition, but clearly it can be done. However, if the object is to recapture a bit of solitude and to relax, keep your forces down. We've traveled alone, as a pair, in a threesome, with four and with six.

## Soloing

Solo camping is a special and satisfying art, though going one-on-one with nature has its own requirements. Four or five days is a long time to spend by oneself. And while being alone is not the same thing as being lonely, it does call for a good set of inner resources in top working order. Keeping busy isn't hard, but since the kind of trip we're describing isn't a 20-mile-a-day grind, if you don't like tinkering with fishing lures or boat repairs, devising new ways to cook trout or just sitting, you may get antsy. That's okay, you've got plenty of room in which to be restless and plenty of space to pace. When solo camping, all your emotions become more intense: the questions, worries, phobias, as well as the rewards, highs and joys. Also, you alone get to make and unmake all the plans. And the only problem you'll have with "human dynamics" is figuring out how to get along with yourself.

If you go solo on foot, you'll have to sacrifice some weight that would otherwise be shared. The inflatable raft you might want for those lazy days on the lake will stay behind. The extra cooking pot, set of lures, roll of film, cinnamon container—may have to go as well. But for almost everything you leave behind, you can improvise with what you've got. You can make a raft, roast fish in the coals, sketch instead of taking pictures, fashion lures with your hooks, or substitute flaked chocolate for cinnamon.

The more experience you have camping with others, the better equipped you'll be to go it alone. The same is true of solo hiking off the trail: Experience *in a group* is a prerequisite. Any kind of hiking is safer, more fun and more confidence-building when done with others at first.

## With Others

But how many others? First, it's useful to understand that camping is not a personality-altering experience. For all the solace and rejuvenation that a trip in the backcountry provides, you're apt to take in and bring out the same likes, dislikes, habits and concerns that you carry around every day. The same is true of your friends. What pleases you or irks you about them will tag along, and may well be heightened by the unfamiliar environment.

The more people there are, the harder it is to achieve compatibility, and the more time and patience are necessary to make the trip work well for everybody. With larger groups, decision-making takes longer and is more emotionally draining. There are more ideas and opinions to deal with. Complications increase exponentially. A six-person trip is not three times as complex as a two-person trip: it's nine times as complex.

Try to straighten things out as much as possible beforehand. Talk over what you each like to do and eat, and what you can't stand. Discuss relative experience, physical fitness, allergies and ailments. Figure out who knows what. Share any information you can. The expert who makes you feel like a fool is dispensable; leave him or her at home. The one who makes *you* feel like an expert is, at 9,000 feet, the most wonderful human being on earth.

There are other advantages and disadvantages to numbers. The more people, the more you can bring—an extra book, additional chocolate bars, a tripod. Tasks can be shared and loads lightened. On the other hand, some lakes you want to camp at have only one small campsite, barely room for two. And the bigger the party, the harder it'll be to concentrate on the sounds of silence.

Count animals in your calculations, too. Dogs are wonderful companions in the wilderness and can carry their own food on the trail, but off-trail you must carry it for them: The probability of their tearing a pack on rough terrain and losing the food is high. And remember, unless you have a Siberian husky, malamute or some other pooch who is happiest in inclement weather, you'll share limited tent space with wet fur on those rainy nights. But as long as the trail is not too rocky for their footpads or off-limits to pets (as in National Parks), they're great to have along.

## Traveling with Dogs

- Prevent dehydration. Carry water in the car for them.

- Exercise dogs if confined to a campground or a long canoe ride.

- Keep 'em on a leash in cattle or sheep country. A dog that starts a stampede is fair game for ranchers.

- Keep 'em on a leash if they're carrying their own food. They can lose their packs if they go off-trail chasing local wildlife.

- Don't overload a dog's pack. They get tired, too.

- A name-and-address tag is essential. Dogs lost in the wilderness *have* been found and returned. Ask Rick: He lost Punkie in a thunderstorm. She was carried out by campers who found her, paws cut to shreds. Great campers!

- Protect a dog's feet above the tree line. Pads are easily cut on the granite high ground, and they are easily burned on extremely hot terrain. If you plan long hikes in those areas, consider fitting out your dog with dog booties, or apply commercially available treatments to toughen his or her pads. Ask your vet.

- Dogs are *not allowed* on trails in National Parks.

Regardless of the number of people and pets, there are several useful rules to go by:

- The slowest person sets the pace. Plan distances for the day or week with this in mind. If you have to stop short of those goals, well—it just doesn't matter. This is particularly important with children.

- Stay together. This is crucial if you're going off the trail ("cross country") or into new waters by canoe. If there are four of you, you can go in pairs, but even then all four should follow the same route. Stop at all trail forks and wait for the others. Most serious accidents occur when one person goes off alone.

- Cater to individual needs. If people hate to cook, don't make them feel they must. This isn't a test, it's a vacation. If others don't know how to cook but want to, help them out, but let them do it. This isn't a three-star French restaurant, and if the bread burns or the fish falls in the fire, so what? You'll still eat and you'll go home with a funny story.

- Share leadership and decision-making as much as possible. Let everyone take the lead on the trail. This is a matter of courtesy, and it's important. Many guidebooks suggest appointing a leader, someone who knows in advance he or she will have the final say in any difficult decision. This is good advice in emergency situations. The person with the most experience might be best to lead you up a mountainside or through rough water, but in most cases, there doesn't need to be much structure. Most decisions are better made by consulting everyone and finding a common denominator. Flexibility is the key: stay loose and happy.

# Resources and Guides: Getting the Information You Need

## Yellow Pages and Hot Lines: Working the Local Angle

The most frequent question we're asked is, "Where do I find out...?" Instead of leaving you in the dark till you get to the "end matter" of the book, we want to answer the question now, when you need it. Here and in the following chapter you'll find the addresses, telephone and fax numbers, e-mail addresses and World Wide Web sites (identified here as URLs) of the people or organizations that can help you plan a camping trip and find your way. If you learn to use a phone, fax or e-mail strategically, you can get information fast and reasonably cheap. Of course if you have more time, write and get the same.

Rather than try to be comprehensive and definitive, we give you here a finder's guide—sort of a Camper's Yellow Pages. One call or letter will lead to others until you have the information you need. Then in Chapter 3, we introduce you to that bottomless pit of information, the Internet. There you'll find literally hundreds— sometimes thousands—of parks, trails, routes, snippets of gear advice, organizations, recipes, and just about everything else you've ever imagined concerning the outdoors. Careful, though. You may never leave your monitor!

Look for local help first, then regional or national. Sometimes the fastest way to that end, however, is to start the other way around. Example: You want to find out local canoeing information: clubs, routes, trips and tips. Yet you don't know any local outlets and the phone book is no help. What to do? Call or write the American Canoe Association and ask for the names, addresses and phone numbers of their local affiliates. Sometimes it will be a club and sometimes an individual (the local "commodore"). Now you're back to square one, and in a few minutes you ought to have the information you seek.

You may need help on several fronts at the same time. The format in this chapter lets you package information. Example: You want maps, consumer guidelines for buying a mountain bike, park access and reservations info, and some literature to read on hiking and biking. Scan the categories and subcategories. No use writing away for a Forest Service map if what you need is a topo map. No use calling the bike shop in East Missoula if you live in Rattler Bend 2,500 miles away. Identify the park or parks you intend to visit then go to the information here on the national, state or county agency which administers those parks. Check our Book List on pages 381-386 if you don't find the book or magazines you need here. Assemble *all* the information first, then make your calls or write your letters. Do it early. You'll be surprised how helpful people are.

## Local Clinics, Clubs and Bulletin Boards

Experienced backcountry types tend to congregate at local outfitters and outdoor clinics or clubs. Local outdoor stores often serve as the hot-stove leagues for their immediate areas. They'll have bulletin boards (the old fashioned, pre-Internet kind) announcing all sorts of information—second-hand equipment for sale, offers to join a trip or expedition, learning clinics, rides to share to Mount This or River That. Store staffers are more often than not outdoor fanatics themselves and will give you enthusiastic and usually sound advice. And there will always be a couple of grizzled experts just hanging out swapping lies and tips on their own particular thing. They're human resources. Use 'em.

If you live near a college, community college or university, look up the name of the appropriate club—mountaineering, river/ water sports, hiking, environmental concerns—and give them a call. You may not be able to join such a group or get paid service—many are limited to staff and students—but almost certainly you'll get friendly advice as to where to turn for the information you need. Some of these services are run by professionals, some are co-ops, and some are student-operated. Most will let you run at the mouth with questions and let you look at their bulletin boards and brochures. It's a small community, after all, and they like interested people, whatever their connections.

If none of the above exist in your immediate neighborhood, get in touch with the local environmental organization. They usually have reliable and helpful advice on outdoor recreation: trips and activities for members (and non-members), local clubs or private groups, names of individuals or organizations you can call, pamphlets on the National Parks and trail systems, and the like.

# Where are the Forests, Where are the Parks?

Recreation follows politics, and thus parks, forests and wilderness areas are administered under different and sometimes competing jurisdictions. You don't need to be a Washington lobbyist to find out what you want to know, however; you just need an up-to-date phone book. Once you get someone on the line, you'll get friendly, informative service. We've dealt with federal and state agencies, departments, offices, field headquarters and ranger stations, and over the years they have been almost uniformly helpful. The fat cats are in Washington or the state capital; the outdoor experts are in the local and regional offices.

National Parks are administered by the National Park Service, a branch of the U.S. Department of the Interior. For travel information, brochures on all the national parks, and advice, call or write:

U.S. National Park Service
Public Enquiries Office
U.S. Department of the Interior
Washington, D.C. 20240
(202) 208-4747

The Park Service also has a dandy Home Page on the World Wide Web where you can "visit" each of the national parks by name, by state (located on a map of the U.S.), and by theme. Each of the parks then has its own page with 19 basic points of information including reservations and campground status, travel directions, main attractions, and other vital data. It's a great way

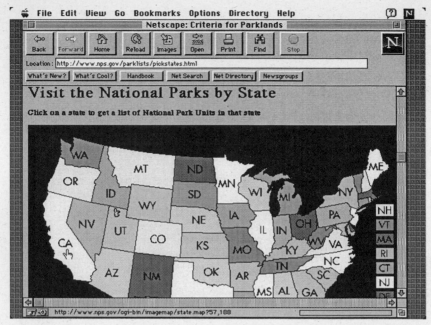

*Click on any state for a list of national parks on the National Park Service's Web Page.*

to find out what you need to know. The Web address (or URL) is: http://www.nps.gov

National Forests are administered by the National Forest Service, a branch of the U. S. Department of Agriculture. Wilderness areas are specially designated areas *within* National Forests. For information about trails, maps, permits, location, availability, rules and regulations in your state or local region, check the U. S. government pages in the phone book. First find "Department of Agriculture." Under that heading locate "National Forest Service." And under that heading locate the office of "Recreation." Then go to work with your questions. Otherwise write or call:

U.S. Forest Service
201 14th Street SW
Washington, D.C. 20240
(202) 205-1760

State and county parks are administered by their respective Parks and Recreation Departments. If you're not sure who oversees which park, call the state offices. They will tell you the park's status and refer you to the proper office and phone number.

# Printed Trip Guides

The National Parks and Forests are huge recreational areas, big management complexes. They don't look like Wall Street, but they're run by agencies that want the paying public to spend time and money in them. Hence they produce publicity and detailed information. Want descriptions of their facilities and camping possibilities? Write for their printed matter. Get the Sierra Club's booklet on the National Parks. Check your local library for literature. State parks also have printed brochures. Regional and state guidebooks are often complete, entertaining, and filled with the kinds of information you need: route information, number of campsites, recreational facilities (swimming, boating, fishing, trail hiking), amenities (showers, laundry facilities, cabins, shops), and maps. Don't buy a guidebook that doesn't have this kind of information. (See the Book List on pages 381-386 for a partial guidebook list.)

Trail guides are indispensable for trip planning. Most of the major forest, park and wilderness areas are now covered by convenient individual hiking guides. For example, Wilderness Press (2440 Bancroft Way, Berkeley, California 94704, 510/843-8080) produces detailed trail descriptions, itineraries, suggested number of days needed for round-trip hiking at various levels of expertise, altitude changes, flora and fauna to be seen, camping and fishing possibilities for almost all wilderness areas in the western United States. Similar guides exist to other wilderness areas. Mountaineering guides, which grade peaks by their climbing difficulty, make the high country accessible and safe. See our Book List on pages 381-386 for a selection of such Tote Books put out by the Sierra Club. Ask your local camping store to show you what they have or tell you what they know about.

# Maps and Permits

## Maps

There are four types of maps you may need to plan a camping trip: road maps, Forest or Park Service maps, topographical maps, and, if you're canoeing in coastal or large lake waters, nautical charts.

# Road Maps

Reliable road maps are updated every two years or so and will distinguish, by color, various road types: interstate highways, state highways, county roads, paved and unpaved local roads. Wherever you get your map, from the supermarket, the local auto club or map store, check the date of publication. A state road map may serve you best for long-distance driving; a sectional map (part of a state) may be drawn on a larger and hence more readable scale. If you are traveling through several states, try to collect similarly printed and scaled maps for the entire trip. Check the Yellow Pages for map sources. Call the state automobile association. Or ask Aunt Phionia, whose cross-country trip was planned by the swank travel agency you can't afford, if you can borrow the maps they gave her.

## Forest and Park Service Maps

The National Park Service, National Forest Service and some state park services put out maps of specific parks and forest lands, updated every ten years or so to show changes in access roads, jeep trails, campgrounds, parking areas and new hiking trails. If you're serious about getting access to the wilderness, you'll need such a map. Otherwise, you won't know how to navigate to the trailhead, which may be miles up a warren of logging roads and washboard tracks. These maps can be obtained from the appropriate agency office. Often this can be done with a phone call, and the maps will be sent to you free of charge, though sometimes you have to send a check or money order. You'll find that the more camping you do, the less you'll need to send away for maps. Not because you use them less, but because you'll keep returning to the same parks and forests year after year.

It is one thing to get to the trailhead, another to walk the trail or climb the mountain. Hiking requires topographical ("topo") maps, which bring you face to face with the lay of the land.

## Topographical Maps

Mountains and valleys normally don't change as fast as roads and other human structures. True, Mount Saint Helens can rearrange things dramatically. So can the San Andreas Fault. But by and large, the topo map drawn thirty years ago will still represent physiographic reality pretty accurately. Unfortunately, it won't show the latest trails and may show trails long since abandoned. That's why you should work with a combination of topo and Park/Forest Service maps. They'll allow you to chart a trip with reasonable accuracy.

Computer-generated mapping techniques promise to revolutionize the field, and already some topo maps are appearing color-coded for altitude and characteristic terrain features. Some are being produced on lightweight, foldable plastic, perfect for wilderness camping and hiking.

Topo maps are obtained from the U.S. Geological Survey, which is a sub-unit of the U.S. Department of the Interior. Victimized by big budget cuts in recent years, the U.S.G.S. has closed offices and cut staff. Still, it's worth a check in the phone book to see if there is a Geological Survey office in your area. If so, go down and get the maps you need from them. If not, try the local map vendors or camping stores. More and more of them sell the U.S.G.S. maps. The maps for any area in the United States are also available by mail, though you'll first need to send for a free "key" or index map if you don't know the name of the particular quadrant (of the entire area of a state) you want. The key divides the whole land area of the state into small squares. Each of these squares is numbered and titled, representing one topo map. After you pinpoint the area(s) you want, order the relevant maps by number and name. If there's not a U.S.G.S. office, map source or camping store in your area, write, e-mail, log on, or call:

U.S.G.S. - Map Distribution
Box 25286
Denver Federal Center
Denver, CO 80225
(303) 202-4700
(800) USA-MAPS *(From the menu tree you can get map and pricing information and place map orders.)*
URL: http://www.usgs.gov

## Nautical Charts

Most river canoeing can be done with Forest/Park Service maps and topo maps. Coastal canoeing, island hopping, and large lake travel may require nautical charts. These you obtain locally through map stores or independent dealers who specialize in nautical travel (salt-water fishing specialists, boat dealers, tour operators). Or write to:

Distribution Branch (N-CG 33)
National Ocean Service
Riverdale, MD 20737-1199
(301) 436-6990

## Permits

Permits are gatekeeping and safety devices, similar to campground reservations for car campers. They allow local forest or park rangers to keep track of the number of people entering each part of their jurisdictions each day, and to control the use of campfires in hazardous conditions. One permit that grants access and states fire conditions usually serves the two purposes. The idea is to maintain a balance between nature and human visitors to the maximum benefit of each. And while evidence shows that fewer people are backpacking in the wilderness, more people than ever are car camping, and hiking the most popular and accessible trails. It's not unusual for 200 people a day to pass some scenic spots on the John Muir Trail in Sequoia National Park, for example. Trails are fragile; numbers need to be controlled. Fire rangers also need to know where you are in case of a major emergency, such as a forest fire.

It's best to apply for a permit after you've had a chance to look at the maps and decide exactly where you want to go. Call or write the appropriate ranger station, which issues the permit. Addresses and phone numbers are available from the National Park or Forest Service office nearest you. Get the permit early. Along with it, you'll get any information that the rangers feel is important to pass on to hikers. This includes warnings about bears in the area, cautions involving drinking water and possible disease transmission, notices of areas closed to camping and rules regarding firewood, fires and fishing. These are all important to know about before you arrive on the scene with your backpack bulging, only to discover, for example, that you've mistakenly forsaken the campstove, expecting to cook with firewood. It's possible to get permits at the last minute, but rules differ depending on the area. Sometimes, you can arrive at a ranger station, get a permit immediately, drive on to the trailhead and begin hiking. Sometimes you can telephone ahead and have the permit waiting for you in the "night pick-up" box outside the ranger station door for late-night arrivals. Other times, you'll find that the trail is full for the day; permits will be issued for the following day only. It pays to have alternate routes and destinations in mind for just such eventualities.

One year, we drove to a National Forest area in the evening, planning to get a permit the following morning. A sign in front of the ranger station said that half the permits were issued in advance by mail (only until the end of April). The rest were issued that day, with the last few to be distributed the next morning at 6 a.m. We got to the door of the ranger station at 5:45, only to find ourselves behind nearly 40 other early risers. Our first choice was booked solid, and we had to settle for a second-choice route. Plan your trip well in advance. Make campground reservations early. Start ordering maps during rainy winter afternoons; send off for July and August permits in March. Especially if you're planning a week-long trip, the more time you give yourself to plan, the smoother it will go. It's possible to camp "spontaneously," but trips invariably work out better if they are thought out and arranged months in advance.

## Pack Stations

If you want animal transport into the mountains, call or write the pack stations closest to your destination. The National Forest Service requires all pack trains which enter National Forests to be licensed by them, so you can get a list of accredited pack stations from the appropriate regional National Forest office or its field station. The National Park Service runs its parks through concessionaires which either directly provide pack service or lease it out to local pack stations. Check with the National Park of your choice for information.

## Equipment

If there isn't a good camping, biking or boating store in your area, use the mail. The number of excellent illustrated catalogs of camping, biking and canoeing equipment is growing, and the information in them is reliable, often accompanied by expert technical advice, and the prices are usually fair and competitive. A growing number of companies are going on-line, complete with illustrated catalogs and order forms. Buy a canoe on the Net? It's been done!

## General Suppliers

REI Catalog
1700 45th Street East
Sumner, WA 98352
(800) 426-4840

REI stands for Recreational Equipment, Inc., one of the country's oldest outdoor suppliers. Meets all the outdoor needs covered in this book. Expert advice. Buying made easy through the mail. REI is a co-op, and holds regular clinics, talks and demonstrations for the public.

Eastern Mountain Sports (EMS)
1 Vose Farm Road
Peterborough, NH 03458
(603) 924-9571; FAX (603) 924-9138

The equivalent of REI in the eastern part of the U.S. Equally expert and reliable. They do not have a mail-order service, but they do have 43 stores. Call or write them for the one nearest to you.

L.L. Bean, Inc.
Freeport, ME 04032
(800) 221-4221

Old favorite, though it has gone awfully upscale in recent years. Even sells its own brand of bicycle and cycling accessories, as well as its old line of standard camping equipment. Threatens to become the Abercrombie and Fitch of the late 20th century. Still, they know their stuff and it's good.

Campmor
Box 700
Saddle River, NJ 07458
(800) 525-4784; Orders: (800) CAMPMOR
FAX (800) 230-2153
E-mail: catalog-request@campmor.com
URL: http://www.campmor.com/index.html

Lots of choices; good prices.

Early Winters
P.O. Box 4333
Portland, OR 97208-4333
(800) 821-1286
Stylish outdoor merchandise, but not cheap.

McHale & Co.
29 Draws Street
Seattle, WA 98109-1604
(206) 281-7861
Expensive and high quality packs.

The Rain Shed
707 N.W. 11th Street
Corvalis, OR 97330
(503) 753-8900
Kits to make your own gear; a good source for hard-to-find fabrics.

Stephensons
22 Hook Road
Gilford, NH 03246
(603) 293-8526
Expensive, high quality tents, sleeping bags, packs; specialists in "vapor barrier" systems.

Bibler Tents
5441 Western Avenue
Boulder, CO 80301
(303) 449-7351

## Canoes and Marine

Mad River Canoe Annual Catalog
P.O. Box 610
Waitsfield, VT 05673
(802) 496-3127
Catalog and Customer Service (800) 843-8985
FAX (802) 496-6247 or (802) 496-4724
A comprehensive, superbly illustrated catalog with enough technical information and non-technical advice to appease the appetites of beginners, experts and everybody in between. Mad River Canoe people also travel, giving demonstrations at outdoor stores all over the country. The catalog contains a calendar of appearances. The same people also issue a brochure on inn-to-inn canoeing vacations.

### Voyageur's Definitive Action Gear
P.O. Box 207
Waitsfield, VT 05673
(802) 496-3127

The Mad River folks under a different label. They hold a lock on waterproof storage bags and flotation systems for canoes and other water craft. You want dry sacks, sea sacks, fanny thwarts, portage harnessses, tandem end-bag flotation systems, or lash kits? These are the folks to write. Their catalog is, well, definitive. And easy to read.

### Old Town
58 Middle Street
Old Town, ME 04468
(800) 848-3673; (207) 827-5514

One of the great old names in canoeing. Fine catalog.

### Easy Rider Canoe and Kayak Company
15666 West Valley Highway
Seattle, WA 98188
(206) 228-3633; FAX (206) 277-8778

Has made Royalex, Fiberglass, and Kevlar canoes since 1970.

### We-no-nah
P.O. Box 247
Winona, MN 55987
(507) 454-5430; FAX (507) 454-5448

Making canoes since 1966. Catalog lists local dealers.

### West Marine
Box 50050
Watsonville, CA 95077-5050
(800) 538-0775; (408) 728-4430
FAX (408) 728-4360

General marine mail order, from inflatable kayaks to GPS devices to life jackets.

## Bicycles

### Rhode Gear
A Division of Bell Sports
160 Knowles Drive
Los Gatos, CA 95030
(800) 776-5677; (408) 370-1010
FAX (800) 888-9009; (408) 370-3146

High-quality cycling equipment including parts, clothing, and specialized gear.

Bikecology
1515 Wilshire Boulevard
Santa Monica, CA 90403
(310) 451-9977; FAX (310) 451-5651
Catalog of bicycles, frames, parts, components, clothes, exercisers and more.

Performance Bicycle Shop
P.O. Box 2741
Chapel Hill, NC 27514-2741
(800) 727-2453; (919) 933-9113
FAX (800) 727-3291
Prices for quality equipment—bicycles, accessories and clothing—are considerably cheaper than those offered by some of the glitzier places.

The Third Hand
12225 Highway 66
Ashland, OR 97520
(503) 455-4800; FAX (503) 482-0080
Every bicycle tool known to man, plus a wide assortment of spare parts not generally available elsewhere, such as derailleur bolts and nuts, seatpost binder quick-release and much more. If you do your own repairs and maintenance, you need this catalog.

Colorado Cyclist
3970 East Bijou Street
Colorado Springs, CO 80909-9946
(800) 688-8600; (719) 591-4040
FAX (719) 591-4041

Excel Sports
2045 32nd Street
Boulder, CO 80301
(800) 627-6664

The Womyn's Wheel, Inc.
P.O. Box 2820
Orleans, MA 02653
(800) 795-7433; (508) 240-2437
Specializes in clothing and equipment for women.

# Outdoor Services for the Disabled

The number of resources for disabled campers is growing exponentially, and we list here only those most readily available, or those which are resource guides themselves.

## *Contacts*

Breckenridge Outdoor Education Center
P.O. Box 697
Breckenridge, CO 80424
(303) 453-6422
Offers year-round outdoor adventures to people with special needs. Includes skiing, rock climbing, backpacking and canoeing.

Environmental Traveling Companions
Fort Mason Center
Building C
San Francisco, CA 94123
(415) 474-7662

Whole Access
517 Lincoln Avenue
Redwood City, CA 94061
(415) 363-2647

SOAR (Shared Outdoor Adventure Recreation)
P.O. Box 14583
Portland, OR 97214
(503) 238-1613

Wilderness Inquiry II
1313 Fifth Street SE
P.O. Box 84
Minneapolis, MN 55414
(800) 728-0719

Wilderness On Wheels Foundation
7125 West Jefferson Avenue, #155
Lakewood, CO 80235
(303) 988-2212
Dedicated, among other things, to building a trail in the Rockies.

P.O.I.N.T.
(Paraplegics on Independent Nature Trips)
c/o Shorty Powers, Director
403 Pacific Avenue
Terell, TX 75160
(214) 534-4231

C.W. HOG
(Cooperative Wilderness Handicapped Outdoor Group)
Idaho State University
P.O. Box 8118
Pocatello, ID 83209
(208) 236-3912

Jumping Mouse Camp
215 North Bonito
Flagstaff, AZ 86001
(602) 774-9608
Grand Canyon river trips for people with special needs.

Bay Area Outreach Recreation Program
830 Bancroft
University of California
Berkeley, CA 94710
(510) 849-4663

National Sports Center for the Disabled
P.O. Box 36
Winter Park, CO 80482
(303) 726-5514, Ext. 179

Outback Adventures
3104 Dartmouth Street
Bakersfield, CA 93305
(805) 871-4363
FAX (805) 872-7752
Provides travel camping for individuals with disabilities.

# Printed and Electronic Information for the Disabled

Spinal Network
P.O. Box 4162
Boulder, CO 80306
(303) 449-5412

Spinal network is a major publishing source for the physically disabled. It puts out books and a magazine. *New Mobility,* the "extra" issue of the magazine, under its earlier name Spinal Network, has a comprehensive annotated listing of resources and suggestions for outdoor activities, such as hiking and camping, fishing, kayaking and canoeing, biking and other summer sports. An indispensable guide. For an even fuller listing, see Spinal Network's big book of the same name.

*Access America, An Atlas and Guide to the National Parks for Visitors with Disabilities*
National Cartographic
P.O. Box 133
Burlington, VT 05402
(802) 860-2886

Also available through Spinal Network Bookstore. Separate volumes for the Eastern, Rocky Mountain, Western, and Southwestern national parks. They contain access information on travel, parking, restrooms, medical facilities, dining, campgrounds and everything else you can think of. Expensive ($45), but a valuable resource.

*California Parks Access: A Complete Guide to the State and National Parks for Visitors with Limited Mobility,* by Linda Mitchell and Allen Mitchell. Cougar Pass Press: Escondido, CA, 1992. 3225 North Broadway, Escondido, CA 92026; (800) 735-3805.

Contains excellent information about the access features of the many state and national parks in California. Worth using as a model for other states.

*Disabled Outdoor Magazine*
2052 West 23rd Street
Chicago, IL 60638
(708) 358-4160; (708) 366-8526

Specializes in outdoor recreation, with useful information on access, wilderness possibilities, fishing, etc.

*DO-IT and the Internet: Disability-Related Resources*
DO-IT stands for Disabilities, Opportunities, Internetworking, and Technology. It's an electronic publication which lists such resources as LISTSERV and LISTPROC mailing lists, electronic newsletters, newsgroup discussion groups, bulletin board systems accessible via telnet, World Wide Web home pages and gopher servers. It is constantly being updated. You get the list on the Gopher server by e-mailing hawking.u.washington.edu. You send comments and new information to another e-mail address: deamar@u.washington.edu

*Easy Access to National Parks*
Sierra Club National Headquarters
730 Polk Street
San Francisco, CA 94109
(415) 776-2211

A comprehensive guide to all 50 National Parks for people with mobility impairments. It includes information on trails, campgrounds and natural history. Ask for it as Item #6202. The Sierra Club also puts out a companion video: *Easy Access Video* (30 minutes), Sierra Club Item #V1995.

*Palestra*
Challenge Publications
P.O. Box 508
Macomb, IL 61455
(309) 833-1902

A research-oriented magazine covering sports and recreation for people with a wide range of disabilities.

*Sports & Spokes*
P.B.A. Publications
2111 East Highland #180
Phoenix, AZ 85016
(602) 224-0500

A magazine largely devoted to cycling sports.

## Adaptive Equipment

If you're looking for adaptive outdoor equipment or information on how to get it made, try:

Access to Recreation: Adaptive Equipment for the Physically Challenged
2509 East Thousand Oaks Boulevard #430
Thousand Oaks, CA 91362
(800) 634-4351; (805) 498-7535

This is a free mail-order catalog. Illustrated.

ABLEDATA
Adaptive Equipment Center
Newington Children's Hospital
181 East Cedar Street
Newington, CT 06111
(800) 346-2742; (203) 667-5405

This is a computer database which indexes products useful for people with disabilities. An electronic Yellow Pages for adaptive equipment.

# Bicycling

## *Touring Information and Organizations*

Adventure Cycling
P.O. Box 8308
Missoula, MT 59807
(406) 721-1776; Orders: (800) 721-8719
FAX (406) 721-8754
E-mail: acabike@aol.com
Excellent maps, clothing, camping gear and a great tour organizer.

British Cycling Federation
36 Rockingham Road
Kettering, North Hamptonshire NN168HG
England
(011) 44-412211
Maps, hostel info, advice on touring the British Isles and Europe.

Canadian Cycling Association
1600 James
Glouchester, Ontario K1L 8H9
Canada
(613) 748-5629

Cyclists' Touring Club
Cottereil House
69 Meadrow
Godalming, Surrey GU73HS
England
Touring info on the British Isles and Europe, including a handbook with cyclist-friendly lodging information.

International Mountain Bicycling Association
(IMBA)
P.O. Box 7578
Boulder, CO 80306
(303) 545-9011; FAX (303) 545-9026
E-mail: imba@aol.com
Fosters mountain biking as an environmentally sound and sustainable activity. See their "Rules of the Trail" in Chapter 1, page 20.

League of American Bicyclists
190 West Ostend Street, Suite 120
Baltimore, MD 21230-3755
(410) 539-3399; FAX (410) 539-3496
The oldest bicycle organization in the U.S.

U.S. Cycling Federation
(and National Off-Road Bicycling Association)
1 Olympic Plaza
Colorado Springs, CO 80909
(719) 578-4717; FAX (719) 578-4596
A major sponsor of competitions, races and other events.

If you really must have a longer list, proceed directly to the
Web. There, under the URL http://cycling.org/org you'll get a
list of all the cycling organizations in the world!

## Bicycling Publications

There are so many cycling publications now that any listing
will necessarily be incomplete. In the Book List on pages 381-386,
we note some of the more useful books. Here we list the major
magazines, many of which are the house organs of the groups
listed above. Thus the name in parentheses here means "Publication of (this group)." Note too that many of these magazines also
come in electronic format on the Internet.

*Bicycle Forum*
(Adventure Cycling)
P.O. Box 8308
Missoula, MT 59807
(406) 721-1776; FAX (406) 721-8754

*Bicycle USA*
(League of American Bicyclists)
190 West Ostend Street, Suite #12
Baltimore, MD 21230-3755
(410) 539-3399; FAX (410) 539-3496

*Bicycling*
(Rodale Press)
33 East Minor Street
Emmaus, PA 18098-0099
(610) 967-5171; FAX (610) 967-8960
Back issues: (800) 551-6634
Reader service: (610) 967-8093
E-mail: dwbicmag@aol.com
This is the oldest U.S. bicycling magazine.

*Cycling USA*
(U.S. Cycling Federation)
1 Olympic Plaza
Colorado Springs, CO 80909
(719) 578-4581; FAX (719) 578-4596

*Mountain Biking*
(Challenge Publications)
7950 Deering Road
Canoga Park, CA 91304
(818) 887-0550; FAX (818) 883-3019
E-mail: mtbikingmg@aol.com

*Recumbent Cyclist News*
Box 58755
Renton, WA 98058-1755
(206) 630-7200; FAX (206) 631-5728

*Outside*
1165 North Clark Street
Chicago, IL 60610
(312) 951-0990
One major cycling piece per issue.

## Hostels

Still called "youth" hostels, these organizations house cyclists and other travelers of practically any age. The two listings here will point you to hostel resources in the areas you expect to be cycling through.

Hosteling International - American Youth Hostels
National Office
P.O. Box 37613
Washington, DC 20013-7613
(800) 444-6111; (202) 783-6161

Hosteling International - Canada
400-205 Catherine Street
Ottawa, Ontario K2P1C3
Canada
(800) 663-5777; (613) 237-7884

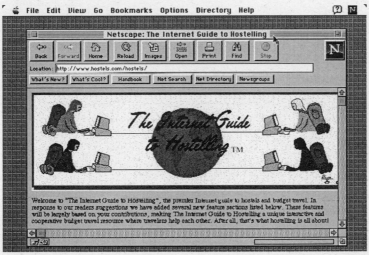

*You can get up-to-the-minute hostelling information on the Net.*

# Canoeing

## Organizations and Informal Groups

American Canoe Association
7432 Alban Station Boulevard
Springfield, VA 22150
(703) 451-0141; FAX (703) 451-2245
E-mail: acadirect@aol.com
URL: http://world.std.com/~reichert/aca.html
This is the godfather of canoeing organizations in the U.S.; it's over 100 years old.
It's the place to call or write for information on clubs and groups in your area. Its
club membership list is huge, so there will be something for you unless you live in

the desert. It has a book service with over 250 publications on canoeing, river guidebooks and maps, and instructional manuals. Also videotapes and films on canoeing. And, of course, it publishes its own magazine, *The American Canoeist.*

## American Red Cross

Contact your local chapter for training programs. See also the comprehensive illustrated book, *Canoeing* (Doubleday, 1977), which the Red Cross put out as the complete manual of canoeing. It's invaluable.

## American Whitewater Affiliation
c/o Phyllis Horowitz
P.O. Box 85
Phoenicia, NY 12464
(914) 688-5569

## Canadian Recreational Canoeing Association
c/o Joseph Agnew
1029 Hyde Park Road #5
Hyde Park, Ontario NOM 1Z0
Canada
(519) 473-2109

## Friends of the River
Fort Mason Center
Building C
San Francisco, CA 94123
(415) 771-0400; FAX (415) 442-3396
E-mail: ftr@igc.apc.org

## National Organization for River Sports
314 North 20th Street
P.O. Box 6847
Colorado Springs, CO 80934
(719) 579-8759; FAX (719) 576-6238

## United States Canoe Association
c/o Jim Mack
606 Ross Street
Middletown, OH 45044
(513) 422-3739; FAX is the same number

## Canoeing Magazines

There are not as many publications as the bikers have, but still more than you might expect. We list only two more here (see American Canoe Association and American Red Cross), and expect that will keep you afloat during the long dark winter nights.

*Paddler Magazine*
(The Paddling Group)
P.O. Box 1341
Eagle, ID 83616
(800) 752-7951; (208) 939-4500
E-mail: paddler@micron.net

*Canoe and Kayaking Magazine*
P.O. Box 3146
Kirkland, WA 98083
(800) MY-CANOE; (206) 827-6363
FAX (206) 827-1893
E-mail: canoekay@canoekayak.com
URL : http://www.canoekayak.com/canoekay

Videos and other canoeing publications can be found on the Net. The following URL will get you there:
http://www.gorp.com/gorp/activity/paddle.htm

# Camping, Hiking and Backpacking Resource and Advocacy Organizations

The following organizations focus on efforts to maintain and enhance the outdoor environment through national and local political efforts, trail development and maintenance programs, national park maintenance, hands-on environmental work, and information resources. These are the real "good hands" people.

Alpine Club of Canada
Box 2040
Canmore, Alberta T0L 0M0
Canada
(403) 678-3200

American Alpine Club
113 East 90th Street
New York, NY 10028
(212) 722-1628

American Hiking Society
1015 31st Street NW
Washington, D.C. 20007
(703) 255-9304; FAX (703) 255-9308
E-mail: ahsinform@aol.com

An advocacy group which seeks to protect, maintain and develop trails on federal land, organizes volunteer opportunities for trail development, campground posts and archaeology work on public lands. Has listings of trail clubs and organizations in almost any area. Want to learn how to build a horse trail, stop erosion or clear a trail? They'll tell you who to see.

Appalachian Mountain Club
5 Joy Street
Boston, MA 02108
(617) 523-0636; FAX (617) 523-0722

This is a big New England organization that helps to maintain the northeast portion of the Appalachian Trail.

Appalachian Trail Conference
P.O. Box 807
Harpers Ferry, WV 25425
(304) 535-6331; FAX (304) 535-6331
E-mail: appalachiantrail@charitiesusa.com
URL: http://www.fred.net/kathy/at.html

The umbrella organization that oversees maintenance of the Trail. Its members are the various Appalachian Trail clubs.

The Green Mountain Club, Inc.
RRI Box 650
Waterbury Center, VT 05677
(802) 244-7037; FAX (802) 244-5867

Like the Appalachian Trail Conference, this group helps maintain the Appalachian Trail, as well as the Long Trail which runs between Canada and Vermont.

Mazamas
909 West 19th Avenue
Portland, OR 97207
(503) 227-2345

Activities oriented. Mountaineering.

The Mountaineers
300 Third Avenue West
Seattle, WA 98119
(206) 284-6310; FAX (206) 284-4977
E-mail: mtneers@scn.org

National Campers and Hikers Association
7172 Transit Road
Buffalo, NY 14221
(716) 668-6242; FAX is the same number
Activities oriented.

New York-New Jersey Trail Conference
232 Madison Avenue Room 401
New York, NY 10016
(212) 685-9699; FAX (212) 779-8102
Maintains and develops trails. About 5,000 members.

The Prairie Club
940 Lee Street #204
Des Plains, IL 60016
(708) 299-8402; FAX is the same number
Instrumental in developing the Prairie Path, a long trail across the Great Plains.

Sierra Club National Headquarters
730 Polk Street
San Francisco, CA 94109
(415) 776-2211
The great environmental organization also provides outdoor recreational activities
for its members, including national and international outings. Local chapters—57
main chapters and 382 clubs in the U.S. and Canada—put on local activities,
often open to non-members, too. Also publishes books and pamphlets on all
aspects of the outdoors, including information on the National Parks and the
National Trail System, and a bimonthly magazine, *Sierra*. If you don't know where
the nearest chapter is, call or write the national headquarters.

# Gay and Lesbian Resources

### Adventuring/IGLOO
URL: http://access.digex.net/~erewhon/
     http://access.digex.net/~erewhon/igloo.html
A very useful Internet resource for gay and lesbian outdoor folk. IGLOO stands
for The International Gay and Lesbian Outdoor Organization. Includes address
lists, trip leaders guide, related information, and other IGLOO groups.

# Wilderness Training

Leadership and survival training is another way to "do" the outdoors. It's not quite the laid-back experience you'll get from our kind of camping, but it's compelling, challenging and an altogether legitimate alternative to the "one-step-at-a-time" camping which most of us do. People who have gone through these programs feel themselves special.

National Outdoor Leadership School
288 Main Street
Lander, WY 82520
(307) 332-6973; FAX (307) 332-1220
E-mail: admissions@nols.edu
URL: http://www.nols.edu

Outward Bound
Route 9D
R2 Box 280
Garrison, NY 10524-9757
(914) 424-4000; FAX (914) 424-4280

# CHAPTER 3

# Outdoors On-line

These days it's hard to remember that Isabella Bird made it through the Colorado high country (*and* the upper Yangzi Valley) without a laptop; that Ansel Adams captured Half Dome without a mouse or a modem. Paddlers and pedalers, trekkers and day-trippers don't need virtual space to navigate real terrain. The backcountry is rich in its own palpable information and it can be gathered like berries, handful by satisfying handful, just by being there. Antiques that we are, we still think the best advice comes from face-to-face contact, sometimes over a campfire, sometimes at a ranger station, an outdoor store, a bike shop, or a lake shore. Still, it'd be perverse to ignore what's new in the world, and what's new is that bottomless pit of information, the Internet. It's astonishing what's out there.

It's also overwhelming, unsystematized, chaotic, inscrutable, seductive, charming, magical, even useful. What we want to do here is show you how to look for and find information which may help you organize and enhance your outdoor ventures; how to communicate with others who have common interests; how to avoid the pests who clutter the lanes of the information highway. But this advice comes with a warning label: Beware—Amateurs at Work. We're not computer mavens. We can boogie board the Net but we sure as hell can't hang ten. But that's the point. If *we* can find our way along the electronic trail, so can you. And if you happen to be a techno-star, you can get on the e-mail (see our addresses on page 400, "About the Authors"), set us straight, point us in new directions, get acknowledged in the next edition, and tell tales out of school. Like the following:

## Chapter Three

# True Tales from Cyberspace

If you spot a weather-worn couple huddled around a phone booth diddling the wires, don't be alarmed. They're probably tour cyclists hooking up their pocket modem to log on to the Internet. Whadda they want? Well, in one attested case, backroad information from a small town in Connecticut to the same in Vermont. Sure, they could have bought a road map at the nearest gas station, but, hey, there are hackers all over the world begging to give away local information and lore to make things better on the road. And a lot of it is terrific. So Larry and Sue pack their powerbook along with their spare underwear, rain gear and socket wrenches, and cycle happily up the orchard circuit on the quietest of back country roads.

Then there's this from a self-styled comic discussing ways to die in the wilderness: "Can't speak for appendicitis, but I froze to death once. Quite a pleasant experience. Brrrr!"

Or Dale from Central Texas lamenting about bugs: "Does anyone know how long chiggers have been around? How did people that lived here 200 to 30,000 years ago avoid them? It is hard to imagine that they just learned to deal with having hundreds of chigger bites all the time. This is a really relevant subject to those of us in chigger country." No one seems to have responded to him.

Or the advice to parents from an expert on how to keep rock-climbing kids in shoes without going broke: glue a climbing-shoe replacement sole onto a pair of sneakers for around $15.

Heli-hiking (hiking with a helicopter transport to the trail-head) exercises folks pro and con; so does campground etiquette, gun totin' women, environmental politics. How to get rid of tent smells? Make seawater potable? Get trail advice for the Trinity Alps (or any other place on earth)? Marmot-proof your radiator hoses? Compare camp stoves and filtration systems? Order topo maps or canoes? Read the latest issue of an outdoor 'zine or an article from a back issue? Make campground reservations? Or make a date to go birding?

It's all there, the good and the bad, the serious and frivolous, the useful and irrelevant: Filenes meet Saks, Mad Hatter meet Einstein. If you're like us, you'll quickly fix on what you want or need and ignore the rest. After the first rush of success rappelling down the "hot spots" into the backcountry info-world, you'll figure out how many "forums" or "newsgroups" or "chat rooms" you really need in your life, how many wildlife graphics and mountain- and river-scapes you want on-screen. Remember when you got that first encyclopedia? How often you were going to use it? How much knowledge was at your fingertips? How it now sits on the shelf, rarely consulted but still valued for its occasional utility? That's what's going to happen with your on-line service or access to the World Wide Web. It'll become a tool rather than a sacra- ment. And once the mystery goes, routine settles in and you can roll up your sleeves and ignore the damn thing. In the meantime...

# What Do You Need?
# What Do You Need to Know?

We are *not* computer outfitters and we're not going to sell you anything. But to get on the Internet or onto one of the commercial on-line services, you need a computer—either a Mac or an IBM- compatible—and a modem, unless you're one of the few lucky ones "hot wired" to a large computer system. Got it? Computer, modem, money. The money buys you a subscription to an on-line service like America Online, Compuserve, Microsoft Network, or Prodigy, or it buys you the software and access directly to the World Wide Web and the whole Internet. (Crystal-ball gazers predict that eventually access to the Internet will be free, a give- away by your computer system, such as Windows or the Macintosh system.) We assume you have these things or want 'em and can get or borrow them. (Disabled users will need to check the on-line services to see which ones are access-friendly. Some are better prepared to offer command-based technologies in place of "graphic interfaces," those icon-filled screens accessible only with a mouse.) Once "logged on," the on-screen aids will take you by hand through the steps necessary to browse what's available and to get where you want to go.

What you don't need is a lot of hotshot computer jargon. You may want to know some of it, and that's what the definitions on pages 64-66 are for, but if you never know a server from a proto- col, a hypertext from a home page, you'll be fine. You're a camper, not a hacker, and we want to get you off-line and out-of-doors.

# What's in a Name?

*Caution:* The following definitions may cause irreversible damage to the computer-literate. Read at your own risk.

• **The Internet** (the Net). The Mother of all computer linkages. Think of ABC, NBC, CBS, Fox, BBC, and all the other TV networks in the world, with all their local affiliates and even you and me with our little ol' home broadcasting outlets (our Macs and PCs) tied together in an electronic embrace. No central headquarters churning out prime time schlock or power lunches. Zillions of images zooming along the wires in no particular direction ready to come into your living room if you've got a receiver and a wish list.

• **World Wide Web** (WWW; the Web). A system of communication which uses the Net to get the goods delivered. Slices and dices information into endless page-size chunks and sends 'em wafting hither—to you—and yon—to anybody else—as swiftly and smoothly as a Spiderman move on a good night. Techies will want to look under the hood to see how it works; the rest of us will settle for results by clicking on hot spots and icons.

• **Web site**. A "station" on the Web. A home page is a Web site. So are sub-sections of a home page.

• **HTTP** (Hyper-text transfer protocol). Sort of a semaphore flag that says, "Yo! Web page here!" In ways inscrutable, it lets you know you're in Paradise rather than Paducha.

• **HTML** (Hyper-text mark-up language). The language that converts ordinary homespun text into the gossamer worn at every Web site. You won't see it and don't have to know how to use it. But it makes the magic possible: all those hot spots and buttons, whistles and bells that let Net visitors read the message, see it in color, enjoy the pictures, and move on to related Web pages close at hand or miles away.

• **URL** (Uniform resource locator). A WWW address. Every Web page at every site has a URL; every component (or hot spot) of a home page has a URL. A URL looks like this:

http://www.foghorn.com

If you type a valid URL into a "search" box, electronic couriers will fan out across the Web (WWW) and retrieve that particular page for you.

• **Browser**. A tool that helps you determine what's out there and connect up to the Web. It's the super sleuth of the Net, knowing how to decode the language and addresses of Web pages and all their parts. *Examples:* Netscape, Mosaic, Internet Explorer.

• **Directory**. An index to the Web. Think of it as an encyclopedia with elephantiasis. Tells you where to go and takes you there if you click onto hot spots. But life and death on the Net are quick and fast, and even the best Directory pants and wheezes to keep up and keep current. *Example:* Yahoo.

• **Server**. A computer where the Web information is physically stored.

• **Home Page**. Closest thing to a homeboy in this town. A subject- or interest-specific site on the Web. Anyone with an account with a computerized organization can create a home page. *Examples:* U.S. Geological Survey Home Page; Mike Thoma Nature Hikes-1995. This latter is a personal home page. Its URL is http://www.thoma.com/thoma/hikes95.html

• **Hot spot**. A chrome-plated convenience with a silly name. It's a highlighted (or underlined) string of words, or an icon, which, when clicked on, sends you to the information promised. *Example:* Under Mike Thoma Nature Hikes-1995 is <u>Cataract Creek</u>. Click on that and you'll get three paragraphs of description. This is followed by a sub-category, Birds, under which are <u>Turkey Vulture</u>, <u>Raven</u>, <u>Acorn Woodpecker</u>, <u>Chestnut-backed Chickadee</u>. Click on any one of those hot spots and you'll get a picture and description of the bird in question.

• **On-line Service**. A commercial service which gives you access to a chunk of information on the Internet. *Examples:* America Online, Compuserve, Prodigy. These are powerful and popular services, cost a monthly fee plus hourly rates, and lead you to most of the information you might need. They also allow you access to the Web, or a sizeable portion of it.

• **FAQ** (Frequently Asked Questions). Just that. A way that servers organize answers to the most common questions asked by their clients, i.e., you and me.

• **Bookmark**. Also called **Favorite Places**. A convenient organizing tool for your personal use. You make the bookmarks, allowing you to bypass all the other junk in the way of the Web site you want to get to.

• **Newsgroup**. A gathering of like-minded individuals who exchange information and ideas on a specific subject. Essentially a continuous flow of e-mail messages that go to an electronic bulletin board. On occasion these may actually include news! *Example:* rec.backcountry.

• **Usenet**. The great democratic bazaar of newsgroups. Almost anyone can start up a newsgroup. Usenet introduces itself with two pages of what it is *not*. If you've got access to a Web browser, you can get at all of Usenet's FAQs as well. The URL is: http://www.cis.ohio-state.edu/hypertext/faq/usenet/FAQ-List.html. It lists FAQs both by topic and, glory be, by newsgroup. So, for example, if you want to know all about rec.backcountry, click on B, then on backcountry and all of the questions you've ever had or could imagine are asked and answered there.

• **Forum**. A site where people meet to share advice on a particular interest or subject. Forums can contain bulletin or message boards.

• **Bulletin Board/Message Board**. Sometimes shortened to "Boards." Terms used by the commercial services and others to function the way newsgroups do. Best for getting out a moderate amount of information to a broad audience. They also allow group discussions. Within Boards are "folders," more specific topic areas.

• **Library**. A bank of information made up of files which you can download. Best used to distribute large amounts of information, including text files, graphics, programs, etc.

• **Chat Room**. Where all the lonely people meet. Allows interactive communication, like a phone call or a conference call. Like the "Talk" function on e-mail.

---

## Getting Started

Outdoor information on the Net comes in two forms: interactively, where you participate in a "conversation," and statically, where you search for and find information that you want. We'll show you how to get at both, but first you need to know where to go. If you're a subscriber to one of the on-line services, you'll first encounter their Home Directory or Main Menu, a column of glitzy icons with such titles as "Entertainment," "Travel," "News," etc. It won't take you long to figure out that outdoor information is a subset of "Travel," and once you click on that icon, you'll get some obvious choices, with names like "Great Outdoors Forum," "Outdoor Activities Forum," "Outdoors Support Forum," "Outdoor Adventure Online," "Outdoor Products," "Outdoor Associations and Conservation Groups," etc. etc. ad infinitum. Some of these are stacked under others, so, for example you'll find an on-line magazine, say <u>Backpacker,</u> or <u>Outside Online</u>, and under *those* hot spots you'll get lots of other choices, including shopping marts where you can order gear, chat groups, opportunities to schmooze with the editors, even other magazines tucked in under a biggie, such as <u>Canoe and Kayak Magazine</u>, found via the Activities icon under <u>Outside Online</u>.

You may feel like you're getting lost, but remember that there's no *there* there. You can always back up the highway by clicking on the "Back" button, or you can check where you've been by clicking on the "Go" button which lists the places you've been in the order you went to 'em. Best of all, at any point you can create a "bookmark" or "favorite places" list and then never have to worry again about navigating the line to get where you want to be. Just as easily, you can tear up a bookmark when you no longer find it useful. Let's see how it all works.

## Show and Tell

It's the middle of winter, there's three feet of snow on the roads, the wind chill factor is off the charts, the space heater's on the blink, and the only thing up and running is your computer. Thoughts turn to the Boundary Waters, hot summer days in a canoe, mosquitos, 14-inch trout, the call of the wild and love in bloom. Thoughts also turn to the attic. You've got a broken down orienteering compass and a yen to find out if a GPS (global positioning system) will be a good substitute. What to do? Log on and tune in. You'll get answers alright. In spades.

One of the great things about the commercial on-line services (and the Usenet newsgroups which you'll meet below) is that you can give and get almost instant advice and opinions about camping, hiking, cycling, and everything else connected with the outdoors. Interactive communication is one of the super resources of the Internet, and even if you have nothing to say, you can check in on what others are thinking about. Experts and amateurs are out there at their keyboards just aching to show and tell.

Okay, you're on the trail of GPS advice and have moved down-country from a general category called, say, "Travel" to an information hot spot called <u>Outdoors 'R Us.</u> On some systems this is called a "forum," a gathering of like-minded people run by a moderator who knows the subject or can call on experts to deliver the goods. The moderator does the forum's housekeeping, bringing new stuff in and getting rid of dated or useless shards of information left over from a bygone era (say, ten minutes ago).

Whatever it's called, you'll find a number of icons to choose from. Check the <u>Gear Reviews</u> hot spot first. You may find everything you need to know about the GPS right there. Sure enough, there's a "GPS" line in the scroll box. Click on it and up comes a recent review of a couple of GPS's on the market. It compares prices, utility, ease of handling, weight. If it's thorough, it will also give you the 800 number of the manufacturer's customer service desk.

So far so good. You've got a start, but you really need more. Can a GPS stand in for a compass? Do you need both to fix your position off trail in the backcountry? How do the damn things work? You need a couple of paragraphs from the folks who know these things. You've got two options: Use the **Search** facility in the <u>Outdoors 'R Us</u> forum, or go to the **Library** within the forum. Let's try both.

At the **Search** facility, type in "GPS" or "GPS, uses" and see what you get. If you're lucky, you'll get a reference to that GPS review you've just read, as well as a reference and access to nine "articles" or mentions of "GPS" somewhere in the system. (Of course five of them may be to the "Government Printing Service," but four will be on the real thing.) Click on those articles and see what you can see.

Instead of making a **Search**, you can go another route, directly to the **Library**, which some of the services provide *within* any particular forum. There you call up its table of contents, and sure enough, there's an article on GPS. It's written by someone who's used them or sold them. It's too long to read on line, because you're paying by the hour, so you download it to your own system, log off, print it out, and mine it for nuggets. (You could also print it out directly from the screen on line.)

What'd you find? Well, *some* of the necessaries, especially on how the GPS works and how reliable it can be under certain travel conditions. You've got more comparison-shopping advice, and a few words quoted from an old bush pilot who used to fly by the seat of his pants till he invested in one. But you *haven't* got an answer to your question, "Will it do in place of a compass?" Don't give up. Proceed directly to the **Message Board** icon under Outdoors 'R Us, and prepare to post a message. Somebody out there's going to know the answer. Follow us here.

Click on the **Message Board** icon. What appears before your very eyes is a box, **Outdoors 'R Us Message Board**. In the box are three information lines and four icons. The three lines list Categories: 14; Messages: 16822; Latest: 03/15/96. The four icons give you some choices: **List Categories, Find New, Find Since, Help & Info**. At the bottom of the box is a line that says, "Date of last visit [03/15/96]", which tells you that the information on the message board is up-to-date.

Well, you're nowhere yet, but that's okay. Click on the **List Categories** icon. Remember there were 14 such categories promised? They're now going to show up on the screen in a scroll box. Up and down you browse till you spot Backcountry Sports. As you highlight it, you'll see that there are maybe 50 topics with over 5,000 postings all devoted to that topic! You'll also learn that the latest posting was, yep, today. Double click on the Backcountry Sports line (or go down to the **List Topics** icon and click on that) and presto! another box, this one called Backcountry Sports. Among the 50 topics in the scroll box are Backpacking Tips, Trail Reports, Canoeing and Backpacking Gear. That last one's it!

Double click on Backpacking Gear. A new box appears with that title at the top and a status line under it giving the following: Messages 29; Author; Responses; Latest. Let your mouse do the walking down the **Messages** column. It will encounter, among others, "Advice Needed," which garnered 3 responses, "Compasses" (1), "Tents" (14), "GPS" (9), "Replacing Pack Parts" (0), "Equipment" (6), "Stoves" (27). At the bottom of the box you're given five choices: Read Message, List Responses, Post Message, Find New, Find Since.

You want to check the "GPS" messages. Highlight "GPS." Nine messages isn't so many, so you decide to read 'em all. Click on the **Read Message** icon to get the original query, and then on

**List Responses** to read the replies. (If you didn't want to wade through all of them, click on the **Find Since** icon which will give you a choice of reading only the last [fill in the blank] number of days' responses.)

Read 'em and weep. The original query was, "Should I invest in a GPS?" and the responses, from friend and foe alike, debate the pros and cons. Some of it's interesting, some informative, some both. But no one's quite answered your question. So now you're ready to **Post Message.** Click on the blank form and fill it in with your question. The more precise and concise the better. Don't expect an immediate answer. This is not a "Chat Room," where folks natter back and forth at each other a line at a time.

Wait a few hours or a day or two and you may have several responses. You'll know you do as soon as you log on, because the postbox flag will be up telling you you've got mail. And sure enough, there's an answer from a guy named Rick: "GPS *ought* to incorporate a real compass but doesn't. Also, GPS may not register at all in a valley or a forest. Bottom line—you need both, the compass to guide you as you walk, the GPS (and map) to find out where the blazes you are when you get to an open meadow or ridge. My opinion: go for it. It's fun and useful, and the price is coming down."

Note that this is a long response. More common are short ones: "Nah. GPS ain't a compass. Use both." But Rick is long-winded and in this case you're grateful. You can even post a "thanks" to him.

Finally, if you're really anxious for an immediate reply, go to the "Chat Room" in the forum and try your luck. We've found most of the exchanges to be more noise than knowledge, but who knows, you might find the GPS sage of your dreams just waiting to chat up a storm.

Usenet, that wondrous world of freelancers, yentas, and electronic buccaneers, needs a nod here. It is to the Net what all those message boards are to the commercial services. It's Newsgroup Central, and it's a helluva place to chat up like-minded folks. Almost everybody's outdoor home page, commercial or amateur, is indebted to information gleaned from Usenet groups. It's hard to leave home without them!

You can get to the Usenet groups directly from your on-line service or from a Web browser like Netscape or a directory like

Yahoo. And you can subscribe to an unlimited number of news-groups for free. But be prepared to be overwhelmed. Volume is the Life Force of this sprawling system. And there is no moderator or manager to tidy things up. We're dealing with popular democracy here, although some would call it anarchy. There's no limit to the amount of correspondence on even the most recondite subjects, and woe is you if you don't keep up. Hal ignored the "rec.backcountry" newsgroup for a couple of weeks and got this message when he touched base: "Unread news in rec.backcountry ...1294 articles." (Yes, there are ways to delete the old and unwanted stuff, ways to browse only sub-topics of interest to you, say tent smells as opposed to the pros and cons of cotton clothing on the trail.)

When you start out at Usenet, subscribe to their new user group: news.announce.newusers. It's filled with useful guidelines. And to give you a sense of the riches in store, here's a sampling of some of the things available:

*Selected Usenet Newsgroups on the Outdoors*

| | |
|---|---|
| Camping: | rec.backcountry |
| | alt.rec.camping |
| Paddling: | rec.boats.paddle |
| Cycling: | rec.bicycles.misc |
| | rec.bicycles.off-road |
| | rec.bicycles.marketplace |
| Fishing: | rec.outdoors.fishing |
| | rec.outdoors.fishing.fly |
| | alt.fishing |

## Follow the Yellow Brick Road

Subscribers to the Web will have their own pathfinding tasks, and we'll take you through some of them below, but the principle is the same: Get out of the Entertainment warehouse and down into the outdoor stuff as quickly as possible. There you'll find more choices than you ever thought possible. There also you'll be able to use those URLs—Web site addresses—which we define on pages 80-81. If you know a Home Page's URL, you can type it in the box at the top of your screen and be taken directly to it without passing Go or collecting $200.

A couple of other things at the start may save you some grief: 1) All of the commercial on-line services allow you access to the Internet, so you can move back and forth between exclusive choices available only to subscribers and inclusive choices on the Net available to anybody who's got access. And for those who can't afford the commercial services, there are cheaper options. Look for "Internet Providers" in the Yellow Pages. 2) What's here today may be gone tomorrow. The Internet is a volatile medium and lots of Web sites come and go. For example, one of the world's great outdoor stores had a site on the Net for a while and then packed it in. Wasn't worth it yet, they told us: not enough response or sales. So be prepared for changes. When you get a "404 Not Found— The requested URL...was not found on this server," just sigh and move on. They'll be back one day or move to one of the commercial services. 3) Remember that the Net is alive with both commercial and non-commercial interests. A ".com" ending to a Usenet group or to a URL, for example, identifies a commercial player. That's not a value judgement, just an identification.

OK, you've got your toes wet and hands held as you've explored the cozy pastures of the commercial services. Now it's time to move on to the Big Time. Armed with a browser (like Netscape) you're off to see the Web.

First thing to do is get thee to a directory (like Yahoo). Easy. Click on "Exploring the Net" icon on your browser and you'll come up with a screen that offers four major choices: "What's New?," "What's Cool?," "Internet Directories," and "Internet Search." You want "Internet Directories."

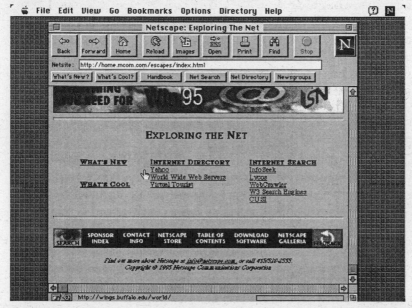

Click. Up comes <u>Yahoo Directory</u>, followed by a brief description and table of contents.

Click on that hot spot and you're at the Yahoo Home Page:

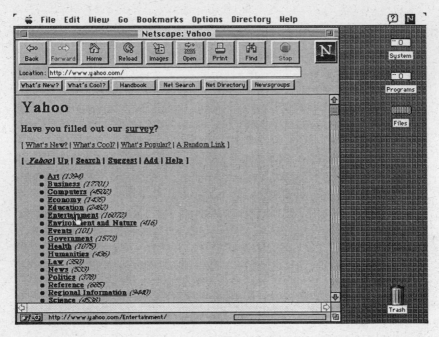

Check out the screen from top to bottom:

*1) Top status line.*

"Go" will show you *in the order you've traveled* where you've been during this current session on the Web. You can go back and forth to any of the sites by highlighting the one you want and double clicking on it. It's a cyberspace itinerary and beats keeping notes.

"Bookmarks" are your visas to immediate delivery to the site of your dreams. Make 'em and keep 'em whenever the mood strikes. Say you find yourself at the CHAOS (California Hiking and Outdoor Society) home page. Say you like what you find there. Say you forgot how the hell you got there and don't much care. Say you wanna come back. Up you go to "Bookmarks." CHAOS will be there waiting to be approved. Give the command to save it as a bookmark and you're set. Next time as soon as you log on to the Web, go directly to "Bookmarks," and CHAOS will be there along with the other favorite sites you've saved. Click "on" and fly away home.

*2) Button line.*

"Back" is a godsend. You've had it with CHAOS and want out. Hit the "Back" button and it'll take you back up the ladder, either all the way back to Yahoo or Netscape if you've just used your CHAOS bookmark and nothing else, or back to the Local Pages list if you've come to CHAOS via, say, The Backcountry Home Page. You can now go down to another site on the Local Pages list, say The Library or Recipes or Gear Review and Recommendations, click on and visit that site, after which the "Back" button will haul you back up the Local Pages list again. Hit the button one more time and you'll end up at The Backcountry Home Page and its introductory matter and list of options. "Back" again and you'll move up another level, maybe to the GORP (Great Outdoor Recreation Pages) if that's the site that sent you originally to The Backcountry Home Page. (We'll have more on both of these home pages below.)

The "Home" button will take you all the way back to your starting point—the first page you visit when you log onto the Net. In this case it would be the Home Page for the Netscape browser which we called up to get launched above, but it could be *any* page you define as your home base.

*3) Location line.*

Gives you the all-important URL or address. Sometimes you may want to write down a URL and later enter it in a "Search" bar to revisit a site. Note that *every* page and *every* hot spot has a URL. Watch how it grows as we move down the screens.

*4) "What's New?" line.*

More information about the directory.

*5) Yahoo / Up / Search line.*

If you don't see what you're after below, try the "Search" facility. And if you know something they don't—a new home page, a little-known site—hit the Suggest hot spot and let 'em know. They'll be grateful. They usually pay people to find these things, and they'll appreciate a freebie.

*6) The list.*

Here's where we start moving. Your cousin Lodestone may

want to check out "Science" stuff, but you want "Outdoors." So do we. It's under "Entertainment," and that's what we're going to click on. But hold on. Look at the bottom of the screen. As soon as we highlighted "Entertainment," the URL grew. It now includes / Entertainment/ at the end (see screen, page 74). The address is now more complete. OK, click away. What you get is:

The screen looks pretty much the same, but now we've got a long list of "Entertainment" choices. Second cousin Jerry G. wants "Drugs" but we want "Outdoors." Highlight it, check the bottom status line to see how the URL has grown again, click on it and away we go. Finally:

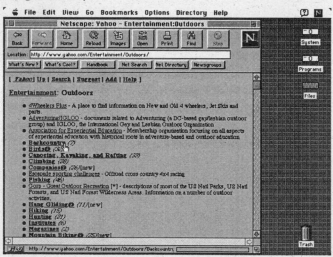

Now we've got some real choices, and they're worth checking
out. Just for the hell of it, and just because that's where we'd like to
be, we've gone to <u>Backcountry</u>, highlighted it, scoped out the
bottom status line, noted that /Backcountry/ has been added to
the string (lower screen, page 76), and clicked on that hot spot:

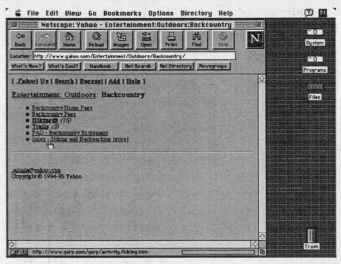

This could go on, but by now you've got the point. Hal would
go directly to <u>The Backcountry Home Page</u>, one of his favorites;
Rick would go to <u>Hiking</u>, one of his.

## Personal and Commercial

<u>The Backcountry Home Page</u> is the heroic effort of a fanatic.
He's got a name, Stephen Johns, and though we've never met him,
we like what he's put up there on the Web for all of us. His home
page says this: "This page is an attempt to organize and archive
the backcountry-related information that is available on the
Internet. Some of the information contained in these pages has
been taken from the rec.backcountry Usenet group. Much of the
information has been contributed by individuals...." That last is
important. This is both a personal and a collective effort, and
lovers of the backcountry are welcome to help out. He gives his e-
mail address: johns@swri.edu and advises potential contributors to
consult <u>A Beginner's Guide to HTML</u> to learn how to "mark up"
a document, that is, prepare it for Web acceptance.

The Backcountry Home Page then gives you several options, the most useful being the command, Click here to jump to Pages. Click away. You get a list of "Local Pages," "Links to Other Pages," (e.g., to Backcountry Home Pages, Individual Home Pages, Government Home Pages, Miscellaneous Home Pages, Commercial Home Pages), and something delightfully offbeat called "Odds and Ends." One of those local pages was the Hiking Clubs mentioned above under our discussion of the "Back" button. Another is The Library. Click on that and you get an enormous list of books, arranged alphabetically by author, all on some aspect or other of the backcountry. For example Edward Abbey's eco-warrior books are there. So are John Muir's. And sure enough, under G for Greenspan is the very book you're reading. Some of the entries have comments, appraisals, where-available advice. Another hero of the Net, John McCollum, put the list together and apparently maintains it. Nice work.

GORP, Great Outdoor Recreation Pages, by contrast is a commercial effort, and has to be one of the most comprehensive of all the outdoor sources on the Net. Its home page starts with a monster "Ingredients in the GORP Mixture" which is an annotated array of hot spots:

**Attractions** - National Parks, Forests, Wilderness Areas, Wildlife Refuges, National Monuments, National Wildlife Refuges and much more!

**Activities** - Hiking, Biking, Climbing, Fishing, Paddlesports, Skiing, Bird Watching, Wildlife Viewing, Caving, Windsurfing, Hang Gliding and Scuba Diving!

**Locations** - Travel & Outdoor Recreation information arranged geographically. Current listings include Africa, Antarctica, Asia, Australia, Canada, Central America, Europe, Mexico, New Zealand, South America, and USA.

**Books and Maps** - including: The Adventurous Traveler Bookstore - On-line database of over 1,700 books and maps for outdoor adventure in the USA and around the world. Centennial Publications produces specialty books related to classic tackle and fly fishing. Adams Angling Books lists an excellent selection of books for fly fishermen or collectors.

**Trips/Educational Opportunities** [which is a list of trekking destinations serviced by a commercial trek outfit].

**Himalayan Travel/World Adventure** [commercial adventure trips].

**Alaska Discovery** [a wilderness expedition company and its canoe, kayak and raft trips].

**Geostar Travel** [eco-tours].

**Gear** - including: The Classic Angler - extensive listings of products of interest to fly fishermen and classic tackle collectors. Northwest River Supplies offers the widest selections of quality paddlesport gear anywhere!

**The Newsstand** - Magazines, E-zines, newsletters and mailing listings.

**Food** - Stay healthy while you travel!

**General Travel Resources on the Internet**

**Clubs, Associations, Nonprofit Groups and Volunteers Opportunities**

Despite the hyperventilated prose and breathless hype for its clients, this home page puts a vast array of resources at our fingertips. For example this is what its "Hiking and Backpacking Resources on the Internet" page looks like:

Each one of those hot spots is loaded with tips, advice, directions—probably more than you'll ever need but which you'll be grateful for having nonetheless.

The journey on the Net will be as long or as short as you want to make it. Once the bloom is off the rose, you'll be able to resist the temptation to go on and on and on. And when the crocuses push through the snowmelt, you'll log *off* and head for the hills, more knowledgeable than ever if no wiser. It could be worse.

# The E-mail Connection

Suppose you've got a yearning to belong, to talk, to exchange, to hear the latest on that special outdoor subject of yours. But suppose you don't have access to the Net and can't afford the on-line services. All you've got is an e-mail account. You're in biz. There are computers out there, all over the world, that act as "list servers," that is, the home base or source of "mailing lists." There are literally hundreds of mailing lists. They're generated by individuals and groups, and they all come into your home via e-mail. Subscribe to a mailing list and before you can say "Shazaam!" you've probably got more mail on that subject than you can handle in three coffee breaks. Think of it. Every day you're guaranteed mail in your box on, say, D-Sports (Sports for those with disabilities), or wilderness preservation, or, for all we know, sex, drugs and rock 'n roll. And it's free.

Most of us find our mailing lists by word of mouth. Or from one of those message boards on the Net. Once you find the one you want, you e-mail a request for subscription, they send you the details, and you're signed up. They also tell you how to unsubscribe, a useful bit of information, because sooner or later you're going to have had enough, or you're going to want to move on to greener pastures.

## Some Useful URLs

• Adventurous Traveler Bookstore:
  http://www.gorp.com/atbook.htm

• American Canoe Association:
  http://world.std.com/~reichert/aca.html

• The Backcountry Home Page:
  http://io.datasys.swri.edu/Overview.html

• Foghorn Press:
  http://www.foghorn.com

- GORP - Great Outdoor Recreation Pages:
  http://www.gorp.com/

- GORP's Activities:
  Paddlesports:
  http://www.gorp.com/gorp/activity/paddle.htm

  Hiking and Backpacking:
  http://www.gorp.com/gorp/activity/hiking.htm

  Climbing:
  http://www.gorp.com/gorp/activity/climb.htm

  Biking:
  http://www.gorp.com/gorp/activity/biking.htm

  Nature & Wildlife:
  http://www.gorp.com/gorp/activity/wildlife.htm

- National Park Service:
  http://www.nps.gov

- Netscape: Internet Search:
  http://home.netscape.com/home/internet-search.html

- On-line Bicycle Sites:
  http://www.cs.wisc.edu/~condon/sd/links.html

- Outside Online *(Outside Magazine* on-line):
  http://web2.starwave.com:80/outside/online/sites/intsites.html

- USGS (United States Geological Survey):
  http://www.usgs.gov/

- USGS Map Sales (backcountry topo maps):
  http://info.er.usgs.gov

- World Wide Web Bicycle Lane:
  http://www.cs.purdue.edu/homes/dole/bike.html

- Yahoo:
  http://www.yahoo.com/

- Yahoo - Entertainment: Outdoors:
  http://www.yahoo.com/Entertainment/Outdoors/

# CHAPTER 4

# What to Bring

## Danger! Big Bucks

Those faded photographs of the early mountaineers like John Muir and his pals are probably banned in better camping stores. There's not enough equipment in them: no aluminum frame wraparound packs, self-standing dome tents, color-coordinated climber's shorts, not even sleeping bags. Just wood and wool. In those days, goose down was still the underside of Christmas dinner. Nylon and Gore-Tex® were not even a gleam in an inventor's eye. Nevertheless, those pioneer trekkers were well prepared and equipped. They just weren't fashionable.

We don't subscribe to the "old is beautiful" or "back to basics" nostalgia. The revolutionary lightweight equipment is breathtaking and extremely valuable—sleeping bags weighing as little as three-plus pounds and efficient at zero degrees Fahrenheit, five-pound tents with archery-shaft poles, featherweight self-inflating ground pads, Kevlar canoes. But that doesn't mean you have to go broke using it. Camping and cycling have become big business, and it's easy for ads and sales pressure to convince you that you'd better buy a lot of costly equipment in order to safely, comfortably or competently hit the trail.

The way out of this financial bind is through "functional shabbiness," with the emphasis on functional. Hal is a classic practitioner. He began hiking in a pair of work boots, which he repaired at every campsite. After they fell apart on the trail, he bought a pair of irregular hiking boots on sale at a factory outlet and has worn them ever since. He used a Taiwan-made sleeping bag for eight years until there was no loft left, then got a

PolarGuard® bag. He bought his used 12-speed bike for $76, and though it looks like it was built by committee, it's just fine for day touring and local camping trips. He's never owned a backpack, preferring to borrow a 19-year-old model with a re-welded frame, so disreputable that a shoe store, asked to replace a pouch zipper, refused to work on it. Hal isn't very pretty on the trail; but he does keep safe and solvent.

Like most people, you don't have a lot of money to spare, but you can manage by scavenging, improvising, borrowing and renting. An old shower curtain can become a tarp or tent (wash it first!); a padded book mailer can serve as a camera case. You'd be surprised at the number of ways to recycle plastic, wire or bits of material into functional camping necessities. Hal, for example, developed a list of 47 different functions for a bandana with a safety pin! And the more familiar you become with the routines and rhythms of camping, the more inventive you'll be.

If you plan to borrow, some rules should be followed carefully. Make an accurate list of everything you need to borrow. Then make duplicate lists of everything you *do* borrow. Keep one and leave the other with each lender. Make sure you both agree on its contents. Check the condition of the borrowed gear with the lender. Know what shape it's in before you use it. Return all items clean. Replace and repair (or have repaired) every piece of lost or damaged equipment, even if the damage is minute or superficial. Don't assume that the owner won't notice a missing strap, torn parka, clogged fuel vent or a half-empty Band-Aid box. Finally, make a voluntary cash contribution to the lender when you return the equipment. This is both a gesture of thanks and a way to let the lender add a little something to the equipment stash. Gear is expensive and anyone who lends it to you is a real friend. If you use care and consideration, you'll maintain the friendship and be able to borrow again.

Renting equipment is useful for testing items you're considering buying, or for things you use infrequently. Renting also makes sense if you aren't sure how much you'll like camping in the first place, or if seven avid first-timers show up on your doorstep ready to head into the Great Void with nary a kerchief to their names. Many camping and recreational stores have rental services from which it's now possible to get almost everything you need for a trip.

If you have some money to invest, it's worthwhile to buy

equipment that will last. Plan to assemble a set of decent equipment over several years. Shop slowly and carefully. Get advice from friends, experts and sales people. Also, study the semi-annual catalogs of the great outdoor stores. Their information is reliable, fastidious and based on expert experience and testing. Their prices are competitive and fair (see Chapter 2 for catalog addresses). You'll also want to visit the electronic malls on the Internet, complete with gear reviews, comparative testing, price quotes, graphic images of sales items, and even order forms.

# Sandwich of Warmth

## Clothing

Car campers and canoeists don't have clothing problems. They can take the entire summer wardrobe and a full-length mirror if they want. All they need to do is stay dry and, if elevation is a factor, warm. Cyclists and backpackers need to pack with an eye to weight and space. That wrinkled, drip-dry camper next to you at Ranger Ron's fireside chat is probably the world's bicycle touring champ just off the road for a night in the woods. She discovered years ago that Levis were too heavy and parkas too bulky to pack and went for thin cotton polyesters and a wool sweater. She's spent *her* extra cash on Gore-Tex® raingear and maybe a pair of cycling shorts to prevent chafing during all those hours in the saddle. Hikers don't need to make a fashion statement either. Tastes will vary. Some people are cool and comfortable in shorts; some hate having their bare legs covered with dust and sweat. Some women swear by halter tops, others by T-shirts to keep pack straps from rubbing the skin raw. Hats and underwear are as much articles of faith as clothing: "To wear or not to wear?" is thus a religious question. Follow your conscience. And check the clothing lists in Chapter 6 for variations and suggestions.

Our English friend Claire began her first backpacking trip in white shorts. Five minutes after we hit the trail, they were no longer white. And eight days later, they were nearly ready for the dumpster. Another friend discovered after four days that his three ragged woolen sweatshirts were too heavy to carry and unnecessary for summer weather. He burned them one afternoon while baking bread, along with his "spare" hiking boots, thus anticipating the latest innovation to hit the outdoor showrooms, lightweight throwaway backpacking clothes. Don't get too attached to your camping togs. They're going to go sooner or later.

The minimum hiking kit goes something like this: two T-shirts, a warm shirt, a sweater or sweatshirt, a pair of jeans, a pair of long johns or light pants (sleepwear on cold nights), a pair of shorts, as much or as little underwear as you like, three pairs of heavy socks, a warm jacket (down or fiber-filled are lightest), a wool hat, a sun visor or baseball cap, and a rain poncho that can double as a ground cloth. We'll discuss boots below. If you can get everything in a normal sleeping-bag-sized stuff sack and it weighs no more than 12 pounds, you're in business.

There are several extras that we always take along backpacking: a pair of gloves for warmth, wood gathering and pot holding; a bandana for the brow, nose and neck; a pair of lightweight moccasins, old sneakers or thongs for the campsite (and crossing streams); extra poncho(s) in order to fish in the rain without taking the groundcloth out from under the tent; and a small towel. Remember that even damp towels are heavy. Take only one and share it.

After that you're on your own. If something gives you particular pleasure—a washcloth or party hat, a tallis or a cummerbund—take it. A couple of years ago, we were startled to see, across a wilderness lake, a woman standing on a rock, dressed in a full karate outfit with a *kendo* stick in hand. Colored by the setting sun, she was an unexpected and picturesque sight. Her whim had cost extra weight, but was worth it in charm, and, we suppose, in self-satisfaction.

## *Layering: Defense Against Heat, Cold and Rain*

Temperatures in the mountains often vary radically, from 80 to 90 degrees at noon to subfreezing at dawn. Your body temperature, however, needs to stay constant, so dressing right is critical.

Loose, absorbent clothing allows air to flow next to the skin in hot weather, and keeps you cool and dry. Natural fibers like cotton and wool insulate best against the heat.

As the air cools, add layers of clothing. Wickable synthetic underwear is the space-age answer to long johns—lighter, more comfortable and "breathable." Skiers and mountaineers use underwear made of polyester and polypropylene fabrics such as

Polypro®, Capilene® and Coolmax®
(though Hal won't wear anything
he can't spell). Synthetic multi-layer,
multi-fabric underwear, complete
with venting panels under your
arms and around your thighs, has
recently catapulted old-fashioned
undies into the 21st century. Next
come pants and a shirt. Cotton and
wool are the oldies but goodies—
durable, sweat-absorbing staples. If,
however, you expect to wash and
dry a pair of pants on the trail, do
cotton. Hal once washed a pair of
woolen pants in the Salmon Mountains and the damn things took two
days to dry, ending up feeling like
felt. You know, the stuff that Mon-
golian nomads use to construct
their yurts? We're still fond of
cotton shirts and wool sweaters, but
recognize that the new layered
garments made of modern
"miracle" fibers may do as good or
better a job of keeping you warm
and comfortable. Their names are
as endearing as a bureaucracy—
Cordura®, Supplex® and Polartec®,
for example—and their price tags
are suitable for the average BMW
owner, but they work.

    As the sun sets, add a light-
weight insulated parka against the
cold, filled with goosedown, duck
feathers or a synthetic fiber. Most
parkas are rated for weight and warmth. Down is the lightest,
most efficient and most expensive. Synthetics are non-allergenic
and mildew-resistant, and they dry faster when wet. If it's going to
be damp as well as cold, you might want to treat your parka with a
liquid or spray water repellent.

*Layering* *is important to trap air
and create layers of insulation around
the body. The basic layers are:
underwear, clothing, insulation and
outer shell.*

OUTER

INSULATION

CLOTHING

UNDERWEAR

Finally, if it's wet, you'll need an outer layer of protection—anything from a plastic garbage bag to the latest "breathable" fabrics such as Gore-Tex®, which permit sweat to escape but are impermeable to rain. Top-of-the-line gear, featuring sealed needle holes on the seams, guarantees to keep your powder dry in a three-inch-per-hour rainstorm. It costs, but it is worth it on Mount Ararat and other storm centers. Short of that, go plastic. You'll sweat but stay dry (if that's not a contradiction) and debt-free. Canoeists, incidentally, do better in rainsuits or garbage bags than in ponchos, which transform them into human sails in a high wind.

Whatever your mother may have told you, too many layers can cause as many problems as too few. Your body sweats constantly, even on cold days. Inner layers of cotton or wool will soak up the moisture and become damp, heavy and uncomfortable. Inner layers of synthetic and polyester materials work better because they "wick" the moisture out.

Even if your outer garment allows sweat to escape in the form of water vapor, it's still going to leave you damp inside if that garment's ice-cold. Why? Because water vapor condenses—turns into liquid—when it hits a cold surface. To counter such cold weather condensation, wear baggy outer clothes, perhaps with zippered "pit vents" to permit greater ventilation. So if you find your inner layers wet, it doesn't necessarily mean your outerwear is leaking. It may mean you've dressed in too many layers. Take some off, stay dry. Just don't tell Mom. (See also "Vapor Barrier Clothing" on pages 89-90).

Clothing manufacturers continue to produce miracle garments; the newest trend is to combine several layers in one. For example, shirts can wick moisture but also keep out the wind; waterproof shells can prevent condensation with good ventilation. As you might expect, these garments are more expensive than traditional fabrics, but they save weight and are designed with active campers in mind.

Be sure to follow manufacturers' instructions on the care and feeding of miracle fabrics. Gore-Tex® is actually a thin membrane with zillions of tiny holes, sandwiched between layers of nylon or other fabrics. Extensive exposure to salt-water spray can clog the holes with salt crystals, thus hurting its ability to "breathe." Some manufacturers recommend special liquid detergents for washing

Gore-Tex® garments, on the theory that powdered soaps may also clog the pores. They also recommend ironing Gore-Tex® garments with a warm steam iron after each washing. Or treating the fabric with sprays or wash-cycle additives to revitalize their wonder properties.

Sweat, above all, is a pain in the foot. Dry feet don't burn or blister; sweat-soaked feet do. Changing socks is a form of layering, and it can save your day. Carry three pairs, one to wash (and dry on your pack while hiking), one to wear, and one to change into as your feet get hot and wet. Some hikers wear a light silk or polypropylene sock next to the skin. This transports the sweat into the woolen hiking sock, keeping the foot dry. And for those who are both technophiles and foot-fetishists, new ultra-light, multilayered socks—made with up to five different materials—are just the ticket.

Layer at night as well. Wear long johns and a shirt to bed if your sleeping bag is too light: Hell, wear *all* your clothes if need be. And if you're stuck in a bag that's too efficient, wear a thin layer of clothing to absorb the sweat and avoid a clammy wake-up call. Wear a wool hat when it's cold. It'll prevent major heat loss, something that skiers know and hikers ought to.

If it starts to rain on the trail or in camp, make sure that you and your clothes and your sleeping bag are protected. Some people, like canoeists, carry an extra set of clothes in a plastic bag, especially if they're camping in rain country. Remember also that synthetic fibers dry faster than down and, like wool, they keep you warm when wet. If you fall in a river, take time to dry your clothing or hang it from your pack as you hike. If you're sleeping in the open, keep tomorrow's clothes in your sleeping bag, or in a stuff sack which can double as a pillow. It's not exactly wash 'n wear, but remember that a combination of wet, cold and wind can cause hypothermia (lowered body temperature), which can be fatal (see Chapter 7 under "Hiking in the Rain").

## Vapor Barrier Clothing

After a long hot hike, your socks are soaking wet, as are the insides of your boots. In most cases, that's not a problem. As long as you have a fresh pair of socks and your boots can dry out overnight, you'll be fine in the morning. But what if you spent the day hiking in the snow? Wet boots will freeze solid overnight.

During World War II, cold weather troops solved this problem by creating a vapor barrier with a plastic baggie worn between the thin inner sock and the heavy outer sock. Once the inner sock hit 100% humidity, their skin would stop sweating. Results? Inner sock and foot wet, outer sock and boot dry.

In cold weather, much the same process goes on in your sleeping bag. As you sweat overnight, moisture leaves your body and condenses in the bag and on the inside of your tent. In the morning, the bag is as much as four pounds heavier, and the inside surfaces of your tent may be frozen solid. It may sound strange that you'll stay warmer if you wrap yourself in a plastic bag, but essentially it's true. Once the thin layer between you and the plastic reaches 100% humidity, your body stops sweating. The sleeping bag maintains its dry loft and you stay warm.

Modern-day vapor barrier fabrics are a far cry from a plastic bag. Some feel like nylon; others feel fuzzy. All are waterproof. Vapor barrier systems are essentially the opposite of Gore-Tex®. As you sweat under a Gore-Tex® outer layer, all your clothes get slightly damp as the moisture works its way out. But if you've got a waterproof vapor barrier in place, the moisture *can't* get out. The layer next to your body gets wet, but the layers beyond the vapor barrier stay dry and warm. In cold weather, that counts for a lot.

## Keeping Clean

One year, four of us were climbing down a steep bowl to Dead Man's Lake, several miles off the trail. Rick looked, as usual, like a peddler from the lower East Side, socks and pots dangling from his pack and belt, his Levis caked with sweat and dirt. First-timer Essie's clothes, new three days before, would have been rejected by Goodwill and the Salvation Army. Karen resembled a misplaced bedouin, swathed in tattered gauzes of her own devising to shield her sensitive skin from the sun. Hal brought up the rear, the Pigpen of the group and living proof that there is a difference between dirt (what humans create) and earth (what nature creates).

We weren't alone. Coming from the other side of the bowl was another party of four. When we eventually met, we were astounded. They were a nice nuclear family: Mom, Dad and twin boys, aged 11. They were clean and tidy. In fact, they were fastidious! Mom's hair looked as if it had just been set; Dad was ready for church; the boys were exemplary behind the ears and, one supposes, everywhere else. Their clothes fit well and were spotless. We still remember Mom's lipstick, make-up and manicure. Yet these were no fancy dude ranchers. They were experienced backpackers, had been over this arduous terrain before, carried plain efficient packs and wore modest clothes that never saw the inside of a posh sporting goods shop.

The point is, you can be as clean or as "casual" as you want. One is not better than the other. Just be sensitive to the preferences of others in your party.

If you intend to keep your clothes washed, take precautions to keep the wilderness clean, too. Don't wash clothes in a lake or stream. Don't use soap: It's the sweat you want out; dirt can wait for the laundromat. Even without soap, clothes often contain detergents from previous washes. They also spew dirt into the water. Wash in pots and discard the laundry water at least 300 feet from the water source. Otherwise seepage will carry suds and dirt back to the stream or lakebed.

Clean freaks rejoice! No longer do you have to haul the dreadnought enamel bathtub into the wilderness to bathe in comfort. Lightweight "solar" showers are available for campers who place cleanliness on a par with godliness. Backpackers may wish to forgo the added one-pound privilege, but car campers, canoeists, or horse/llama packers are in luck. These showers consist of a plastic bag specially coated to retain heat, with a small tube and shower nozzle attached at the bottom. Fill the bag with water, let it sit in the sun for a few hours (or mix in some heated water), hang it on a nearby tree branch and you're ready for a quick shower. Take care to keep the suds (if you insist on using soap) well away from the lake or stream, and rinse off fanatically. Otherwise, the next time you take a plunge, you'll leave soap bubbles on the lake.

## Odds 'n Ends

Individual precautions are vital. Karen is allergic to the sun. A long-sleeved cotton shirt, lightweight long pants, a visor and lots of super sunscreen are necessities to keep her on the trail and in the canoe. Hal's thinning hair recently reached the point of no return; after a blazing sunburn on his balding head, he now wears a cap instead of a visor. Our friend Don, who carries baby Julia, the hair-pulling champ, has discovered a foreign legionnaire's hat with a neck piece that protects what's left of his locks from the dreaded one-year-old cling and jerk.

If you have special needs or the area you're headed for has unusual conditions, you'll find an incredible variety of specialized clothes available. From lycra biking shorts to desert headware which reflects (and hence deflects away from you) the sun's heat, from gloves that shed moisture to rain outfits which zip all the way up the sides, your local camping store should be able to outfit you for almost any adventure or climate.

We always leave a clean shirt and underwear, fresh socks and pants in the car while we hike. They do wonders for morale when we're driving through 95-degree heat toward home. And we need hardly mention what they'll do for the staff of the roadside beanerie where you stop for your first indoor meal in a week.

## Sleeping Bags

A sleeping bag is nothing more than a heat-retaining sack to keep you warm while horizontal and snoozing. It needs to be efficient: the temperature of the body drops when it's at rest, and the higher the elevation, the colder both the air and the ground will be. But a sleeping bag doesn't need to be so efficient that it would keep a climber cozy on Everest; it doesn't need to be so expensive that it would make a night at the Ritz a bargain by comparison. It should be light (five pounds or less; ultralight for summer cyclists), warm and affordable.

Sleeping bags are generally filled with either down (goose or duck) or synthetic fiber. Down is warmer, lighter and more expensive. But when wet, it loses its insulating abilities. Fibers—Quallofil®, Hollofil®, PolarGuard®, Polysoft®—come out of the test tube, are cheaper, and increasingly challenge down's warmth/weight ratio. Combined with heat-reflecting bag liners, fiber bags are becoming lighter than ever. These fibers dry faster than down and are warmer when wet, because they maintain their loft. Unless you're off to Annapurna, a down/fiber mix or a 100 percent fiber bag will easily suffice.

Sleeping bag ratings indicate the lowest temperatures at which they'll keep you warm. Going to be in high alpine country? Use a bag rated at 10-plus or 20-plus degrees Fahrenheit. Camping on the bayou? A thin shell should do. Remember, however, that the rating system isn't exact science. We heard one story about a group that rented 20 identical "zero degree" bags and slept in temperatures near freezing. Some folks were hot, some cold, and others just right. Remember too that the temperature rating assumes you're sleeping in motionless air: no wind. If you like to sleep out under the stars, you'll likely need a bag rated 10 to 15 degrees cooler.

Want the best of all possible worlds? Buy a lightweight bag along with a snap-in liner and/or an "overbag" for colder trips. The liner has another advantage. After a week or two in the outback, when everything begins to smell like a locker room, a lightweight fabric liner is a lot easier to wash and dry than a down bag.

**Sleeping bag and pad**

Now consider the construction of the bag. As always, quality costs. You pay more for better nylon, closer stitching, high-quality zippers, and fancier insulation systems which promise to stay in place over the years. To reduce weight, newer bags concentrate the insulation over your head, chest and feet, where you need it the most. Another innovative design has no bottom insulation at all, providing instead a slot for a sleeping pad which thus becomes part of the bag. As a bonus, the pad stays under you all night!

The sleeping bag is only one part of the "sandwich of warmth" you need to create. If other parts of the sandwich are missing, you'll be in exactly the kind of trouble one encounters trying to eat peanut butter and jelly without any bread. Think layers. On the bottom is a groundcloth, poncho or reinforced tent floor.

Then comes a thin sleeping pad, available in a wide range of materials, lengths and thicknesses. The old standby is Ensolite, a blue foam roll-up pad. The latest and lightest, such as Ridge Rest, are made of closed-cell foam, molded into a series of ridges (for comfort) and valleys (for trapped-air warmth), making them flexible (for packing ease). Direct from aerospace comes a remarkable self-inflating pad called Therm-A-Rest. It's a foam mattress that refused to grow up. Covered in a nylon fabric with a valve at one corner, it deflates as you roll it up, squeezing the air out of the foam pockets, and inflates as you unroll it, the air seeping back into the foam. Car campers and canoeists can use the $3^1/_2$-pound model or regular $1^1/_4$-pound or $2^1/_{16}$-pound (long) pads; cyclists and backpackers the ultralight models ($1^1/_{16}$ pounds and $1^1/_4$ pounds). They're not cheap, and it's easy to slide off them, so if you're a restless sleeper, go for something simpler.

Next up is the sleeping bag. Inside that is a clothed body, if the bag is not very warm—the warmer the bag, the fewer the clothes. The older Hal's bargain-basement bag got, the more clothes he wore. Finally, he was forced to make a choice: Get a raccoon coat or a new bag.

Finally comes the roof of the tent, with a rainfly as another layer just above. Properly arranged, this sandwich is guaranteed to keep you warm and dry.

Unless you have the habits of a nocturnal arctic animal, a cold, sleepless night isn't much fun. And a wet sleeping bag almost assures a grouchy morning. If it does get wet, however, you have several options, depending on how soaked the bag is and what it's made of. If you're sleeping out in the open and wake up with a dew-drenched bag, it'll often dry out an hour or two after the sun rises. If a thunderstorm catches you en route and your bag gets partially wet before you batten down the hatches, you can usually get through the night comfortably: the wet spots will be on the surface and won't penetrate the fill. If a sleeping bag really gets soaked, you've got troubles. A hot sun will dry out any bag eventually, though down takes considerably longer than fiber. But bad weather may cut off that option and the only alternative may be to share the other bags in shifts or pack up and head out. So take every precaution to keep the middle layer of your sandwich of warmth dry.

When it's time to wash your down bag, take it to a commercial cleaner who specializes in down garments. Alternatively, use Cold Water Woolite® in a commercial front-loading machine. The top loader at home may be hard on the fabric and the stitching.

Take care lifting the wet bag out of the washer; there may be enough water inside to tear it as you lift. Then dry on low heat in your laundromat's big dryer.

## Sleeping Bag Tips

- Some sleeping bags can be zipped together to make one double bag. When buying or borrowing bags, make sure that you come away with both a left-hand and a right-hand zipper. Otherwise, even if you're with your mate, you'll be sleeping alone.

- A cheaper way to sleep two in warmer weather is a "coupler" kit. An unzipped rectangular (*not* a mummy) bag zips onto a piece of cotton fabric which has a bottom slot to accommodate two sleeping pads.

- Children's sleeping bags are available everywhere, but kids grow and bags don't. One new solution is a "modular" bag, which starts out the right size for a five- or six-year-old. As your child grows, you simply zip on extensions to make the bag longer.

- Carry a couple of repair patches. Nothing is quite so discouraging as free-flying goose or duck down. Band-Aids or adhesive tape will also do the trick in a pinch.

- Be sure the stuff sack you use actually accommodates the bag. In fact, if the sack is a bit bigger, you can fit a down jacket, wool hat and flashlight—all your nighttime gear—with the sleeping bag in one convenient place.

- Follow cleaning directions carefully or you may end up with a ruined sleeping bag. Hang bags on hangers or keep them on shelves when not in use. Kept in stuff sacks, they lose their loft.

- Expect to spend anywhere from $80 to $260 for a good sleeping bag. Warmer, lighter bags with better zippers, materials and construction cost more; it pays to shop around.

- To avoid sliding off a slippery sleeping pad, apply a hold-fast spray available at most outdoor stores.

- In cold weather, wear a wool hat to bed. You lose as much as 80% of your body heat through your head.

- Finally, be patient when trying to unsnag the edge of the sleeping bag if it's caught in the zipper. It will get caught often, especially when you need to zip up or down in a hurry. To unsnag, pry apart gently in a horizontal motion. The thumbs do most of the work as they move away from each other. Don't try to unzip the snag. You'll only snag it further or rip the material.

*When trying to unsnag the sleeping bag from the zipper, pry apart gently in a horizontal motion, letting the thumbs do most of the work.*

## Tents

On the afternoon of the fifth day at North Lake, it began to rain. Our old, two-person, A-frame tent was set under a tree on a slight incline. By 9 p.m. water was seeping through the tent floor. Rain was dripping through the makeshift rainfly we'd rigged from two ponchos, then through the roof of the tent. Add two wet and affectionate dogs atop our sleeping bags, and by morning, our tent would have made even Buffalo attractive to W.C. Fields.

The rain continued for the rest of the next day and all that night. Though wet, we kept warm and active, and by nightfall we were steeled for another eight hours of marine life inside the tent. We finally dozed off around dawn. Later, we peeked out. It had stopped raining. Now it was snowing! We made a quick decision. Forty-eight hours in a wet tent, half-frozen as well, was enough. We headed out. In fact, we headed straight for the tent section of the camping store, determined never to be evicted again.

Tents, like sleeping bags, come in many varieties. But there are three basic variables: utility, weight and cost. A tent does two things: It keeps out the weather and keeps out the bugs. If it accomplishes both those tasks but weighs in the neighborhood of Barnum and Bailey's Big Top, it's fine for the county campground but next to useless on the trail. And if it's the right weight (no more than seven pounds, about three-and-a-half pounds per person), but costs as much as the bridal suite at Claridge's, it'll never leave the display window. You can spend as little as $40 or as much as $200 for a two-person tent (see Chapter 2 for catalogs which rate and compare tents).

The hottest new tents, now arriving at a showroom near you but too expensive for most mortals, are "self-pitching" tents. The poles or "spines" are internal to the design: almost no tent assembly necessary! A miniature version of the "pop-up" tent is now made for infants—perfect for naps along the trail and as a tent-within-a-tent at night, allowing Mom and Pop to get some sleep while little Julia has a room of her own just a cuddle away. It comes with a pad for the tent bottom.

Of the affordable designs, the freestanding dome or geodesic tent is one of the best. It can be erected effortlessly without pounding stakes or poles. The dome is suspended on two or more spines made up of collapsible fiberglass or aluminum poles, and unless there's a high wind, the tent doesn't have to be staked. That means you can pick up the whole tent, with sleeping bags inside, and move it into the shade for a mid-afternoon nap, then return it to its original site for the night. Also, you can sit up and even kneel in it comfortably, a decided advance from the old horizontal squirm required in the A-frame.

Even lighter and more compact than a dome is the "tunnel" or covered-wagon tent. It also uses "spines" to give the tent its shape. This design creates the most usable floor space in relation to tent size, but is usually not free-standing and must be staked.

Make sure you've got enough tent pegs to secure the tent and rainfly. Plastic tent pegs are useless in the high granite country; we prefer to carry metal ones. Often a tent peg is useless no matter

**Tents** *are available in a variety of styles and sizes. With the application of modern materials and engineering, the A-frame tent has gone the way of the dinosaur.*

what it's made of. Don't fret: Wrap the tent line around a heavy rock or tree trunk instead.

Be careful of fiberglass tent "spines." While lighter and less expensive than aluminum, they get brittle with age and may break. The break is often "clean" and hard to splint; and replacements cost as much as the tent itself. Aluminum poles seem to last forever, bend when they fail, and are much easier to fix.

Most tent roofs are *not* waterproof. Made of breathable ripstop nylon, they allow the moisture in your sweat and breath to evaporate. That means you *need a rainfly*. It *is* waterproof, fits over the roof of the tent and is meant to carry rainwater off and away from the tent sides. Beware of rainflies which can't be extended several inches beyond the lower tent walls: A steady downpour will seep through the tiny seam holes of the "waterproof" sidewall. Everything will be soaked. It's a good idea to apply a "seam sealer" at home to fill the needle holes and seam openings in your tent floor, sidewall, and rainfly. Some people simply use the "plastic rubber" compounds sold in hardware stores; others prefer more expensive and specialized compounds (Seam Grip® by McNett is the preferred brand). A soldering brush works well to slather it on. Do the work in a well ventilated area. Above all, give the seal time to dry. It may take 12 to 24 hours. If you re-stuff your tent in its sack too soon after sealing, you're likely to have folds of tent permanently bonded together.

The rainfly makes the tent hot. Many people leave the rainfly off until they sense rain. But sudden storms have a way of sneaking into camp unannounced. So give yourself a break and leave the rainfly in place even on clear nights. You won't regret it. As a bonus, it will protect the tent nylon from overexposure to the sun and hence prolong the life of the tent. The rainfly thus doubles as a sunfly.

Tents are often rated as "three season" or "four season," depending on the wind- or snow-load they will bear. A tent rated for a heavy winter storm will be stronger, heavier, and more expensive than a summer-rated tent of the same size. Also, remember that tent sizes mean different things in different situations. A "two person" tent might be cozy on a spring night, with your hiking boots and pack sitting outside. But it might quickly become a "one person" tent in a blizzard with all your gear inside. Plan on at least 15 square feet per person in the tent for sleeping bag and stuff sack(s). Get a tent big enough for your needs.

If you expect wet weather or muddy conditions, a tent with a "vestibule" is a big plus. It provides a protected space where you can stow your gear and remove your boots before entering the tent. Some tents even have a porch roof (called a "tentwing") providing additional sheltered space outside the tent. As these extras are detachable, they can be left behind if you need to cut down on weight.

**Tent with vestibule and tentwing**

The newest, lightest and strongest tents are designed with either "breathable" high-tech fabrics or completely waterproof materials and sophisticated ventilation systems that allow moist air to escape. Neither type requires a rainfly (hence the light weight), but the miracle fabrics and fancy design drive the cost up to nearly $500 for a two-person tent.

Interested in both light weight and low cost? There are several tepee-style tents on the market made out of waterproof fabric. They have no floor at all, and they set up with several inches of open ventilation space between the tepee hem and the ground.

**Tepee-style tent uses a shock-corded pole for support or hangs from a tree limb**

Devotees claim that the mosquitos which fly in through the lower ventilation space buzz up to the top of the tent and stay there. (Hal is not yet a devotee.) No food is allowed inside, as all kinds of critters large and small can squeeze under the lower opening. On the other hand, these tents weigh under four pounds, allow you to stand up inside, and can be purchased for under $100. And the basic design has been around since the Ice Age.

For the tent-less ultra-light packer, a bivy sack is just the ticket. A big Gore-Tex® bag, it slips over a sleeping bag, weighs less than two pounds, and keeps out the rain. Unfortunately there's almost no ventilation. On cold nights, water vapor from your sweat can rise through your sleeping bag, hit the ice-cold Gore-Tex® and condense before it passes through the fabric. The result is a wet, clammy or even frozen sleeping bag and bivy. If you experiment, you can wear just the right clothes to minimize sweating and vent your breath away from the inside of the bivy. Or try a "vapor barrier" sleeping bag liner if you can tolerate truly "clammy" sleeping conditions. (See "Vapor Barrier Clothing" on pages 89-90.) Since a bivy is quite expensive, we'd recommend renting one first to see how well it fits your camping and sleeping habits.

Tents are susceptible to fish hooks, knife blades, sharp edges, red-hot pans, burning cigarettes and importunate dogs wanting in. The more holes in your tent, the more moisture and bugs, so it's useful to keep some patches on hand to repair damage immediately. At home, the tent should be thoroughly dried, then brushed or shaken clean and stored on a shelf or a hanger, rather than in its stuff sack. A pre-trip zipper treatment with silicone or WD-40 will keep the zips from sticking on those stormy days.

One final word of advice. Make sure everybody who's using the tent knows how to set it up. Let everyone take a turn at it on sunny days, so they're ready during that sudden hailstorm. Manufacturer's directions usually get lost, so learn the tricks yourself and pass them on by the old show-and-tell method.

## The Versatile Garbage Bag

One more item that'll keep you dry is the garbage bag—the big garden-sized plastic sack that you stuff fallen leaves into once or twice a year. No longer does a backpack or food stash have to be crammed into your tent during the rain; the garbage bag is a perfect protective fit. It is the functional equivalent of an inverted canoe! Take along as many bags as there are packs on your trip. In a pinch, if you run short of rain gear, punch some holes in one to wear for upper body protection. We always buy ours as thick as they come (they're measured in "mils"). Special backpack covers are also available for very wet climates.

# Boots

When our London friend, Brian, arrived for a quick trip to the Yosemite backcountry on his way to Alaska, we were not surprised that he had no boots. He'd just come from hiking all over Europe—*sans* boots. And he was too broke to even think about getting some. We tried to convert him: he could use good boots in Alaska. He agreed to think it over, even went out and tried on a pair. And a day before we were to leave, he came back all smiles from a shopping spree. He'd made the plunge. Out of a huge box he pulled a beautiful, pristine white pair of high-top basketball sneakers. He was ready for the Himalayas.

Brian made a Class 2 ascent of an 11,600-foot peak ("Class 2" is mountaineering for moderately difficult), took two rough cross-country trips, went off on a four-hour solo adventure down a tributary of the local river, carried a heavy pack, and got nary a blister or sore foot from his high-tops. Hal's daughter, Annika, did a five-day trip in a pair of boots meant for city wear in the snow. And her friend Kelly, loath to shell out too much money before she knew if she'd really like backpacking, hiked comfortably in tennis shoes.

It's possible to hike seriously in rough terrain in almost any kind of comfortable footwear that has some sort of rubberized sole and a modicum of support. Good mountaineering boots are used—and useful—because they're sturdier than other kinds of shoes, last better under the punishing treatment they receive in mountain terrain, give support to ankles and feet that are subjected to heavy loads and unexpected twists and turns, prevent frostbite and falls during freak snowstorms, and provide better traction on steep rock faces and other quirks of nature not found on Main Street. Brian, for all his agility, came out of the mountains minus those new sneakers—they'd been ripped to shreds. Kelly will never play tennis again in her tennies, and Annika is hard put to keep the snow out of those poor over-abused boots.

The message is this: Don't be intimidated if you don't have and can't afford a pair of super-ace Mountain Goat expedition boots. Don't stay at home just because you feel unshod. However, if you can afford decent hiking boots, you won't be throwing away mutilated sneakers every year after five days in the wilderness. You'll be more confident in off-trail situations where traction is vital, safer in inclement weather, and probably more secure with a heavy pack. Cared for properly, good boots will last a long time—often five to ten years, depending on how hard you and the terrain are on them.

### Boots, *a glossary:*

**Full grain** is the outermost part of the cow's hide; it is the stiffest, most waterproof type of leather. It is sometimes turned inside-out (rough-out) so the smooth, outer layer won't get nicked or scratched. The **upper** part of the boot should have as few seams as possible. A one-piece upper is more water resistant. A **gusset** is a thin piece of flexible leather sewn to both the tongue and the upper. It keeps out water and stones. A "bellows" tongue has wide gussets, allowing it to open further so it is easy to put on. Some boots have two "overlapping" tongues, each connected to one side. The **back-stay** is a strip of leather sewn over the back seam. If it gets torn or chafed, it is almost impossible to replace. For

that reason, it should be as narrow as possible. A **welt** is the stitch which connects the upper sole. A Norwegian welt is double-stitched, strong and stiff. Other welts (Good-year, McKay, etc.) are not as strong but allow more flexibility. A **rand** is a wide rubber strip protecting the stitching that holds the upper to the sole. The **sole** has three parts: a padded "footbed" just below your foot, an "insole" below the footbed and an "outsole" on the bottom. The insole can be soft and flexible for light

hiking, or it can be stiffened with a half- or full-length "shank" (sheet) of plastic or steel for added support. The sole is made of rubber (Vibram is a type of stiff, hard rubber) with a "lug" pattern designed for gripping the path. Deep lugs are best for steep, rugged terrain, while shallow lug patterns are lighter and more flexible.

If you've won the lottery or inherited an oil well, you may want to look into the new high-tech hiking boots just coming on the market. Some people are calling them revolutionary. But that's what they called Lenin, and look what it got him. Anyway, remarkable new advances have been made and you can have fun checking 'em out in the boot department before you buy a second hand pair of loafers. Many of the innovations have been made by snow-boot manufacturers who have adapted their technologies to hiking and mountaineering. Among the new features: external, adjustable plastic cuffs which control lateral movement and thus reduce the chances of ankle sprains; dust and mud covers which zip and Velcro over the laces; internal mesh fittings which keep the foot from sliding forward when hiking downhill, and thus fight the good fight against jammed toes; new, improved grip soles which may in the future replace the still-trusty old Vibram soles; air cushioned heels; even air pumps. Yes, air pumps! To cradle the heel and cushion the sole. Duuude! Check out the wrap-around high-carbon rubber outer soles on the new trekking boots, which also feature inner Gore-Tex® bootie liners which let your foot breathe and stay dry at the same time. And if you can only afford one pair of boots for walking the streets and the trails, there is now a whole line of "cross-over" lightweights, which work wonders in both environments. (Window) shop till you drop.

## On the Trail of a Good Boot

It's one thing to "talk" boots, another to buy them. Consider the following:

- Leather or lightweight? Leather is strong, tough, durable and heavy. Great for serious mountaineering. Lightweights are made of plastics, nylon and other synthetics. They literally take a burden off your feet. Sturdy, flexible, and comfortable, they are perfect for hiking and most backpacking.

- Soles. The thicker the Vibram rubber sole and the deeper the treads or "lugs," the greater the traction but the heavier the boot. Likewise, the stiffer the "mid-sole" layer above the rubber sole, the stronger but less pliable and comfortable the boot. Day hikers don't need steel/plastic mid-soles; mountaineers do.

- Welts. Welts are stitching systems that join boot to sole. The better the welts, the stronger the join. Hence welts make shoes that are more water-tight, more durable, though perhaps less flexible.

Lighter shoes use bonding-cement joins.

- Cycling shoes. Try touring in soft running shoes. Your toes will go numb. Cycling shoes with stiff soles distribute pressure evenly over more of your foot, preventing numbness, encouraging comfort. But at a price. Weigh cost and comfort in the balance.

- Canoeing shoes. No such thing. Wear whatever pleases, short of high-heel stillettos or baseball cleats, as long as they're tied to your feet. Otherwise you'll lose 'em during a spill. Cutting several holes in old sneakers provides instant drainage.

- Sandals. A new generation of snug-fitting, high-tech sandals has many hikers and backpackers risking stubbed toes and twisted ankles for the feel of the wind between their toes. They swear these sandals are lighter and more comfortable than any hiking boots and work great for hiking along smooth trails, even with a pack. They also wear 'em while wading, fishing, or crossing streams.

Aside from the appropriateness of the boot (you don't want technical mountaineering boots, unless of course you are a technical mountaineer) and the cost, the all-important consideration is size. Get it right. You and your hiking mates will regret it if you don't. Seek out a reputable store and an experienced salesperson to find the best fit. Wear the same socks (or inner and outer socks) you'll be wearing on the trail. Unless you're replacing a specific size and model, exercise extreme care with mail order purchases or discount-mall shopping. There are too many variations in the human foot and body to take chances. Someone who's flat-footed and 240 pounds won't be comfortable in the same boot as someone who has a high arch and weighs 145, even though both may have size 10 feet.

Like a podiatrist, a knowledgeable salesperson will consider several measurements: heel to toe, heel to ball-of-foot, width at various spots, and overall shape. She or he will check how you walk—do your ankles roll in or out?—and ask about things like bunions and bone spurs as well as your hiking habits before recommending a boot for your foot and your needs. Don't be surprised if you discover in the process that your left and right feet differ in size, especially when "weighted."

Boots are one of the few items that are hard to rent. So the money you spend—not less than $80 and more likely over $125— is a long-term investment. Plunge wisely, watch for sales, and see if the salesperson will bargain.

Install fresh, strong laces before your trip. If a lace breaks on the trail, knot it and carry on. If the whole thing shrivels and dies, rig up a lace out of a length of that nylon cord you're carrying.

When you get home from each trip, clean your boots and treat them with a conditioner. Be careful: leather boots need oil- or wax-based conditioners; composite boots (fabric plus leather) need silicon-based conditioners. Store in a cool, dry place with crumpled up newspapers inside to absorb any moisture. Before going out on the next trip, treat them again with conditioner and perhaps coat the seams with seam-sealant to protect the stitches from mud and rain.

Never dry your boots by a fire, stove or heater. Excessive heat cracks leather, destroys cement, and generally shortens the life of boots. Let them dry gradually in warm, dry air.

The subject of boots inevitably leads to the subject of blisters. No matter how perfect the fit of the shoe or how expert the wearer, blisters can strike anyone, anytime. New boots, an extra-long day of hiking, a continuous downhill stretch, wet or dirty socks, an inadvertent abrasion on the heel or toe—the causes of blisters are endless. To be prepared, carry enough Moleskin (the trade name of a lightly-padded adhesive plaster) to service everyone on the trip. One pack of several strips per person is generous. To cut Moleskin to the desired shapes, a scissors far surpasses a knife. Some people prefer their Moleskin doughnut-shaped, with the blister in the center. Others use Band-Aids, or gauze and tape.

A recent innovation on the blister-busting front is Second Skin® by Spenco, a protective coating which helps *after* you get a blister. It's a thick, cellophane-like product applied to the sensitive skin after the blister has popped. It keeps the sore spot from being chafed any further, and it can be used alone or underneath a Band-Aid or piece of Moleskin.

## Packs

You can day hike with a gunnysack or a Gucci bag over your shoulder. You can't backpack that way. That requires a pack on the back. To do this efficiently and with reasonable comfort, you need al frame pack. Such a pack consists of a lightweight frame, usually made of aluminum or an aluminum alloy, from which is suspended a large nylon bag, often divided into compartments and pouches. The frame goes on you, via padded shoulder straps and waistbands. The load, packed in the bag, goes on the frame and is separated from you by a back band. No part of the load should touch any part of you. The principle is to distribute weight evenly between shoulders and hips, and a good pack will permit you, by adjusting the straps, to shift weight from your shoulders to your hips in varying degrees.

External-frame packs put the weight over your hips and let the load sway slightly as you walk. But if you try to climb or ski with such a rigging, you'll be thrown off balance. Look up as you climb? Your head hits the back of the pack. Shift your weight? The pack may shift it too far.

Internal-frame packs, by comparison, lower the center of gravity of the pack and "hug" your body. All gear is stowed snugly inside the pack. You can turn around and maneuver without losing balance. But hiking long distances with heavy loads in an internal-frame pack will be hard on your back.

Outfitters stock a bewildering variety of packs: top-

*External frame packs consist of a rigid frame made of aluminum or aluminum alloy, from which the bag is suspended. Sleeping bags are strapped to the frame.*

PADDED SHOULDER STRAPS

ADJUSTABLE PADDED BACK-BANDS

PADDED HIP-BELT

TOPLOAD CAPACITY

SIDE POCKETS

TWIN COMPARTMENTS

BOTTOM LOAD CAPACITY

*Internal frame packs* employ a semi-rigid support system. All gear, including a sleeping bag, is stowed inside the pack.

LOAD LIFTER
STRAPS

FIXED
LUMBAR PAD

PADDED
HIP BELT

PADDED
HIP BELT

TOP LOAD
COMPARTMENT

LOWER
COMPARTMENT

VERTICAL LOAD
COMPRESSION
STRAPS

loading and back-loading backpacks with single compartments, divided compartments, adjustable hip arms, quick-release compression straps, and on and on; babypacks with canopies and windshields (!) to protect the sole heir from inclemencies; travel packs, rucksacks, daypacks, fanny packs; duffels; packs that convert to luggage. Know what you'll use the pack for. Be guided by weight, utility, comfort and cost. Research and shop carefully. Most adult packs weigh from $4^{1}/_{2}$ to $5^{1}/_{2}$ pounds. (The latest models, barely in the stores, are constructed of super-light fabrics—Spectra, for example, a bullet-proofing synthetic—and titanium stays, resulting in expedition-size packs weighing only a little over three pounds! If you're a rich, class-one climber, you'll be able to afford one.) With ordinary materials, however, anything lighter means either the frame will be weak (poor welds, cheap alloys), or the pack will be made of material too fragile to sustain a heavy load. Anything much heavier you won't want to carry.

Try on several packs. Frame sizes differ. It's important to get the frame that's made for your height and build. Most packs come small, medium, large or extra large. Make sure the frame has room below or above the pack for strapping on a sleeping bag, tent, ground pad and other gear. Think also about how much you plan to carry. A three-day trip requires a pack capacity of 3,000 to 3,300 cubic inches on an external frame. For the same purpose, an internal frame needs 4,000 cubic inches to accommodate a sleeping bag stowed inside.

Weight also counts. It won't make sense to buy a huge 5,000-cubic-inch pack if you can only handle the weight that would fit into a 2,500-cubic-inch pack. Ask the salesperson to load up the pack so you can test it for weight. See how it feels on your shoulders. Check out the number of compartments and side pouches. A single-compartment top-loading bag may be the one you like, but if it doesn't have a back-loading zipper panel as well, every time you want something stashed down at the bottom, you'll be pulling everything out. If you plan to "live" out of your pack, you'll appreciate multiple storage compartments. Some manufacturers have expandable packs. They increase their capacity through the use of zip-on or fold-out compartments. Others have built-in daypacks which unzip from the main pack and strap to your hips or shoulders on day hikes.

Look at the suspension system, how the bag is hung on the frame. Can the bag be moved for body adjustments? Can the hip or waistbands be altered? Can a missing part (pin, bolt or back band) be fixed or replaced? Check for soft padding on shoulder straps and hip belts. Most manufacturers also make specially designed packs for women, with narrower frames and better fitting straps than in comparable men's models.

Unless you rent, expect to pay $100 and up for a good pack. Among the brand names you can trust are Kelty, Camp Trails, Jansport and REI.

Wear and tear on packs show first in the fastenings. Zippers and their fittings fray; D-rings and tie-cord loops disappear; key wires work loose from clevis pins; nylon bags rip. With some care, however, a good backpack should last for years. Hal's 19-year-old loaner looks forlorn and much amended, but there it is, on his back, on the trail, hauling and carting as bravely as ever.

Necessary repairs can be made cheaply. A little WD-40 lubricant (or a silicon-spray equivalent), available in auto parts stores, should be applied to all zippers before leaving home. Frayed nylon strands that get caught in zippers can be trimmed with scissors. Rings and wires can be fashioned out of everything from bailing wire to paper clips. Bags can be patched and sewn. Weakened or broken frames can be rewelded ("heliarced" with aluminum alloys); on the trail they can be patched together with cord, fishing line and ingenuity.

## Packs for the Pooch

Let your dog do its part of the work when backpacking. If weight is evenly distributed over its sides, most dogs can and will pack a modest amount, at least as much as they'll eat. Mature dogs will carry 20 to 25 percent of their body weight, younger dogs at least 15 percent. Setting out, they'll carry their own food. As that diminishes, they can take on your supplies, such as cups, socks, shoes—whatever can be symmetrically distributed. Dog packs cost from $40 to $200, depending on size and padding. They consist of two oblong carrying sacks made of treated nylon with a tough canvas or leather underside fixed to a strong nylon "saddle" that fits on the dog's back. The sacks are suspended over the dog's flanks in a manner that will not chafe its legs or sides while on the trail. Straps fit around the chest and under the belly.

**Dog Packs**

We use homemade versions of the commercial model for our small dogs. Two rubberized canvas sacks or small reinforced stuff sacks from an army surplus store, two lengths of strap and four large safety pins are all that's needed, plus the patience to sew the parts together with heavy carpet thread. The safety pins are used to close the sack openings.

Rover doesn't need special training to carry a pack, though a dry run helps get the pooch used to that strange unseen burden. Remember to keep the dog on a leash whenever the pack is on, even when you are stopping to rest. Otherwise, on the first scent of a deer or a chipmunk, dog and pack will disappear. Dog will most likely return, but pack almost assuredly will not. If it does, it may be minus its contents: rocks and brush can rip it to shreds. Off the trail, remove the dog packs and carry them yourself. And unless your pooch's pack is watertight, expect the bottom of the pack and its contents to get wet when crossing shallow streams and rivulets.

## Bike Packs: Panniers

A bicycle is more stable if its pack weight is low and evenly distributed. With a sleeping bag and tent strapped *above* the rear wheel, the bike may start to shimmy uncontrollably while braking. Panniers keep everything close to the ground and allow even weight balance. If you plan to tour on a bike, you'll need at least two, and probably four, panniers.

High-quality (and expensive) models have better rain protection systems (flaps or special covers), better or quicker attachment systems (remember that panniers tend to fly up each time your bike goes over a bump), more pockets, and interior straps to keep the load from shifting around inside the pannier.

Loaded panniers require a strong bike frame and carrier racks to take the extra weight stress. After investing a lot in the former, be sure you've invested enough in the latter. Otherwise *you'll* be carrying the panniers *and* the bike.

Once your panniers are full, there are a number of further load-carrying options available for your bike. Handlebar packs allow easy access while moving. Small seat packs and triangular frame packs (which mount just below your seat in the frame) are handy storage areas for tools and repair kits.

If you like to combine biking and hiking, consider investing in convertible panniers. They quickly and easily convert to daypacks. Leave your bike at camp and take a hike. Leave the added bulk of your own daypack at home.

*Bicycle panniers*

**Bicycle with seat packs and frame packs**

Bike packs demand the same care and feeding as backpacks. Mend the tears, lubricate the zippers and patch the holes. Also, add reflective striping if the panniers don't come with it. And while you're loading up with equipment, think about adding headlights to your bike. Over the last few years, battery and bulb quality has improved to the point that riding in the evening is an option you might want to consider.

## Canoe Packs and Racks

The great canoe pack controversy was resolved 1,500 years ago when someone observed, "The canoe *is* your pack." A sensible argument if not absolutely watertight. As a concession to inept paddlers, card-carrying splashers, rain and wind, stow your gear in "dry bags." Use that old rubberized duffel in the attic, wrap and tie your gear in a heavy-duty garbage bag, or buy a spiffy polyurethane duffel designed specially for water sports. They're oval top-loading bags that come in all sizes and designs. You'll find them with duffel straps, shoulder straps, hip straps and load-compression straps. You'll spend from $40 to $60 for a bag big enough to hold a sleeping bag, tent, clothing and food.

All these packs have to be portaged, often several times a day, so it's important that you get the right shape and fit. Experienced portagers swear that the key to comfort and efficiency is the tumpline, a padded strap that harnesses you at the forehead or around the chest. It acts to keep you and your pack wedded to each other. Remember, portage packs don't come with fancy frames and suspension systems the way backpacks do. In their place, the tumpline keeps a tight fit and takes some of the weight off your back.

As for other criteria, ask the experts how they feel about "flat-sided" vs. "box-sided" packs, rigid packs for schlepping heavy metal—cooking gear, fishing reels, the lawn mower—and packs with or without zippered pouches and with long or short flaps. Don't expect unanimity here. There's a partisan for every pack. In the end you may have to trust your judgement and take some chances with home-fashioned containers rigged with makeshift straps.

The canoe as a luggage carrier on water is matched by its facility on a car rack. Lash all your gear inside the canoe, load it on the rack upside down and there you have it—a rainproof, space-efficient packing system.

## Bicycles

Remember when running was easy? Put on a pair of high tops, old shorts, and place one foot in front of the other quickly? Then the marketing boys took over and now we have therapists to see us through the ardors of shoe selection. Cycling's the same. Cycling's worse.

Confused about the kind, make, efficiency and cost of cycles and accessories? Don't know the difference between racers, all-terrain bikes and hybrid touring models? Between chromoly steel, titanium, carbon fibers and aluminum? Beween 17 kinds of gearing and braking systems? Getting the answers to these and other arcane cycling trivia is easy. Adopt your local bike store staff. Get to know them on a first-name basis. Their wheels may cost a few bucks more but they'll pay you back in knowledge and guidance. They'll help you select the right bike for the right occasion, make adjustments and modifications, and service your machine like a pit crew.

If you're buying, do some homework. Rent and test-ride several kinds of bikes. Ask questions of experts. Tell them what you want it for: day touring, casual tour camping, group touring where you don't have to schlep any gear, serious long-distance touring and camping, or trail and off-road riding.

Bike shops tend to specialize in two or three brands. Few carry them all. Shop around. And when you do, remember that bike "sizes" measure only one part of the frame; two "25 inch" frames from different manufacturers may fit quite differently.

Recently, the hottest trend in mountain bikes has been the addition of suspension systems. Shock absorbers have been added to the front fork, and sometimes to the rear wheel as well. These make those pounding mountain trails much easier on your body.

If you do most of your riding with a close friend or mate, consider a tandem, the post-modern version of the old bicycle built for two. They cost more, but you can talk while pedaling, share the effort pumping up those hills, and never have to worry about your friend falling behind.

And for something entirely different, try a "recumbent" bike. These strange-looking contraptions have chair-type seats and pedals out in front. The handle bars usually are below the seat. While they take some getting used to and aren't recommended for rough, off-road trails, recumbent bikes are comfortable, easy on your body, and have lots of devoted fans.

As with other expensive camping equipment, start modestly. Test the fit and feel on rented bikes, and if you opt for a used bike, make sure you get the right size. Your local bike store can put together an infinite variety of frames, tire sizes, handle bar sets, and gear ratios to fit your needs. You won't have much choice at your neighbor's garage sale, so be careful.

Once you determine how bikes and camping fit together, you'll begin to understand the possible trade-offs in weight, strength, cost and reliability. By the time you're hooked, you'll know exactly what you want. That's the time to plunk down $1800 for the full-suspension Hell's Fury of your dreams. In the meantime, see Chapter 2 and the Book List for assigned reading on cycling, bikes and buying.

## Bikes on the Net

How do you prevent saddle sores? Pantyhose, of course. How do you make a bikestand for under $5? Hang two padded hooks on rope from a beam in your garage. Where can a woman find bike seats that aren't made for men? Who's in the lead of the Tour de France? The Internet is full of forums, chat groups, home pages and bulletin boards on biking. Whether you want the latest article on frame design, a 40-page treatise on bicycle seats and human anatomy, or the answer to your questions about kid-seats and trailers, you'll find the answers you need somewhere on the Net. See Chapter 3 for operating instructions and the relevant Web addresses (URLs).

# Canoes

Boats are bigger than bikes and even more expensive. If you're prepared to walk in and buy a canoe before you've ever been water camping, you're reading the wrong book. Don't kid yourself. First of all, these things are big—averaging 15 to 17 feet—and expensive. And once you own one you need a car rack, tie-down material ($^1/_4$-inch nylon rope), paddles, PFDs (personal flotation devices—lifejackets to you), kneeling pads, towing or tracking line, perhaps a carrying yoke for portages, and (you forgot?) a place to store it! Rent, borrow, or join a club outing first. And second. Then perhaps invest in a used canoe. Tinker with it and your camping technique for a couple of seasons. Then go get a new one. It'll cost between $850 and $2,000.

Length, weight, width, capacity, stability, maneuverability, construction and design will vary according to performance need and cost. Whitewater canoeists and duck hunters speak different languages and paddle different canoes. Lake campers require good tracking (straight-line) ability and load-carrying capacity. River campers need moderate speed and maneuverability. Both need their craft to be durable, especially if heading for remote wilderness waters. Most manufacturers offer both versatile (multi-purpose) and specialist craft, and choices are no more (or less) complicated than buying boots.

## *Buying a Canoe? What to Consider*

- Solo or partnered canoeing?
- River or lake? Both?
- Day trips or camping trips?
- Durability or light weight? Both?

- Versatility?

- Maneuverability? Speed? Stability?

- Capacity?

- Easy maintenance?

The aerospace industry has touched canoeing as it has camping and biking with lightweight, durable plastics and bonding agents. At the top of the line are Kevlar (grandson of fiberglass) and the hybrid laminates which draw on miracle resins, airex foam, high-tech fibers and gel-coats. Heavier are Royalex, ABS plastic and fiberglass, all also tough in the crunch. (See Chapter 2 for explanatory catalogs and reliable manufacturers.) Weightier still is aluminum, whose most fetching quality is its indestructability. You could enter a demolition derby and still sail away. But not quietly. Aluminum's noisy, an irritation to some. Advanced flotation chambers make canoes buoyant, stable and safe. Inflatable craft may be the wave of the future, so to speak. New models, constructed of heavy-duty hypalon-coated synthetics, make for easy stream and lake paddling and are convertible into kayaks for whitewater running.

PFDs are *legally mandatory*. You need at least one lifejacket in the canoe, preferably one for each passenger. They come in five U.S. Coast Guard-approved types, rated according to buoyancy and function (floating conscious or unconscious persons; use in watersports, etc.). Your local canoeing expert and the Red Cross will recommend the most appropriate for you—probably Type III,

*Personal flotation devices* are available in five U.S. Coast Guard-approved types. One PFD per person is mandatory.

the kind waterskiers wear, though the very young (five and under) may be more secure in a Type II with neck collar and step-in leg straps.

Paddle selection depends on the level of skill and the water conditions you expect to encounter (think of the unhappy marriage between a long paddle and shallow water), but almost anything reasonable will do. Cheap is beautiful. Here's the old standard measure: place the paddle on the ground; the grip should come to eye level. Should you carry a spare? Probably, though your chances of losing a paddle in the water are less than it falling off the top of the car. Figure costs and take it from there. And if you're canoeing with a five-year old, bring along a kiddy paddle, around 36 inches long. They're cheap and fun, and that's what counts.

Kneepads are a blessing. So are cushions for the kids. Make 'em at home out of old lawn chair cushions or cut down ensolite pads. Or bring along a child's booster seat.or one of those folding, legless backpacking chairs. And the golfing umbrella for those moments paddling in the rain. If you need anything else, call your banker. Anchors aweigh!

## *Canoes on the Net*

Want to get into the politics of clean water? Get the address of every local paddling club in the U.S. and Canada? Read a learned disquisition on the portage pack? Learn how to fit a canoe with oarlocks and row it? Hook up with a crowd in Boise for a weekend river trip? Browse a photo gallery of river and lake scenes? One site on the Web announces 31 sources on the Internet for paddle sports. There's a river of promise on the Internet and no one yet knows how many tributaries there are. For launching instructions and Web sites, see Chapter 3.

# Stoves and Fuel

Among the several basic types of backpacking stoves, white gas, kerosene and bottled gas (propane or butane) are the most popular. Alcohol stoves are cheap, but so inefficient they're not worth it, and Sterno, which is light, is impossible to control. Since there's a wide and technical range to choose from, we suggest you study the literature, get face-to-face advice from someone who has actually used these stoves, then check them out in person. If possible, rent and use one before buying. Some questions to consider:

- What kind of fuel?
- What kind of fuel's available? (Attention international campers!)
- How complicated is it to use?
- Can you trim it to a low flame for simmering?
- Does the stove include a windscreen? Is one available?
- How much fuel does it consume?
- How much does it weigh?
- What is likely to go wrong?
- Can you fix and clean it with the tool(s) you have along?

The best news for campers is the new generation of multi-fuel stoves. They burn white gas, kerosene, even diesel and gasoline! The fuel tank is external to the stove, doubling as the pump and carrying bottle, thus eliminating messy and dangerous fuel transfers. Priming, which we explain below, is easy and doesn't require separate primer fuels. Most of them come with efficiency-enhancing wind baffles. Drawbacks? They're next to impossible to control for simmering, as they burn at only one intensity. To overcome that defect, slip a coffee can lid between burner and pot to disperse the heat, thus lowering it.

White-gas stoves are popular because the fuel ignites fast and burns hot. They're easy to use. Many require no pumping to vaporize the fuel, which can be carried in easy-to-pack aluminum or plastic containers. The disadvantages? White gas is volatile, which is what makes it ignite so easily. It needs to be handled with care so it doesn't burn unexpectedly, and fuel containers need to be vented periodically so that pressure doesn't build up. Also, white gas may be difficult to find, though hardware and camping stores stock it or a substitute called camping or Coleman fuel, known also at gas stations as "Blazo."

Kerosene ignites more slowly but burns hotter. It's thus potentially safer and more efficient. It is also almost universally available and cheap. On the minus side, it stinks, it stains and it's hard to start in the cold. Furthermore, it usually requires another

**Stoves** *are available in many styles and burn a variety of fuels. Here are some typical examples.*

**Optimus 111B**
*(white gas)*

**Bleuet S200S**
*(butane)*

**MSR WhisperLite**
*(multi-fuel)*

fuel, such as denatured alcohol, for priming, and it needs to be pumped up to obtain vaporizing pressure in the fuel tank. In short, kerosene stoves are rarely worth the hassle.

Many white-gas and all kerosene stoves need to be primed to start. This means that the stove must be pre-heated with some extra fuel so the gas in the tank will vaporize, expand and force its way into the burner in a steady flow. To prime a stove, extract some fuel from the fuel container—*not the stove's tank*—with an eyedropper or plastic tube. Place it in the bowl of the stove beneath the vaporizer. Light it and, as it burns, open the control valve. This starts up the burner—or it's supposed to. If it doesn't, begin the whole operation over again. Don't overfill the bowl. And remember, cold weather inhibits vaporizing, so it may be harder to start your stove in the mountains than in your backyard.

Bottled-gas stoves are so easy to use that you'd think they'd have long since replaced all the others. The fuel—propane, butane or a mix of the two—is purchased in a pressurized cartridge. When it's attached to the stove, all you do is turn on the valve, light up and cook. No pumping, no priming, no muss, no fuss. The flame is more finely adjustable than on the liquid-gas stoves. However, the fuel can be hard to find and is more expensive. It doesn't burn as hot, which means you need more of it to get the same amount of work done, and the stove's efficiency decreases in direct proportion to the amount of fuel left in the cartridge. Four days into the mountains, you'll have to cook longer and longer to get a meal done. Propane and butane also have an embarrassing tendency to revert to liquids when it's cold, or freeze solid if the temperature really hits bottom. Butane liquifies at 10 degrees Fahrenheit, propane at minus 45 degrees Fahrenheit. If the weather threatens to turn you blue, it will turn your gas blue, too. Take a fuel cartridge to bed; sleeping-bag warmth will help keep it in firing condition. The recent propane/butane mixes overcome a lot of these problems and work well at high altitudes and in extremely cold weather. Two final things: Once a butane fuel cartridge is attached to the stove, it can't be removed until it's empty; a puncture hole in the cartridge allows the gas to escape into the stove. It will escape all over the environment if you remove it. Yet hiking on with a half-empty cartridge attached to the stove can be cumbersome. And, of course, you have to pack out the used cylinders.

Your actual "mileage" may vary, but with a little basic math you can get a ballpark estimate of how much fuel you'll need. First, count the meals. Say you're going for seven days. On the first and last days you'll need only one hot meal, on the other five, you'll need two—altogether twelve hot meals. Assume you use half an hour of fuel for each meal. That's extravagant, as at least some of your meals will be those "add-hot-water-and-serve" affairs. But better to have more fuel than less, especially for that last unforeseen banquet of six big trout with all the trimmings. So in all, six hours of cooking. If you're using a small multi-fuel stove, say an MSR X-GK which burns very hot, the pump/fuel bottle will hold 22 fluid ounces, enough for the entire trip. Say, on the other hand, that you're using a butane-burning Bleuet Gaz C-206. Six hours will use most (or all) of two cartridges.

Ever notice that the people in those rosy-hued camping stove ads are always smiling? That's because their stoves work! It'll be cold comfort in the mountains if you can't get your Promethean Mountain Model going when you need that hot cup of brew to get *you* going. Know how your stove works. Practice starting it at home. Take it completely apart and put it together again. Bring along the tools you might need to tinker and clean. Stove repair people say that over 50 percent of "defective" units work just fine—the problem is the camper and not the stove.

Purchase the cleanest fuel available. And if you're really fastidious, use a small strainer or a piece of old pantyhose stretched across a funnel while filling the fuel bottle. This latter method may wreck your sister's junior prom, but it'll help minimize fuel-line clogging. Always rinse the crud from the bottom of your fuel bottle before refilling it. Just swirl a little fuel around in the container and empty it out. *Don't* use water.

Remember that you want a blue flame. If it burns yellow, turn the flame down for a few minutes. That'll warm up the combustion area and vaporize the fuel better. Clean the fuel jet often, every day or two if you use it for all your meals. If you use a liquid-fuel stove, turn it off each time by turning the flame down low, then blowing it out. That keeps the fuel flowing through the nozzle till the end and makes for less carbon deposits. Make "Stove Check-up" a part of each pre-trip list, and if your stove uses rubber "O" rings, throw a spare package in the repair kit just in case.

Learn to save fuel. Wind and misguided enthusiasm are the great gas guzzlers. Wind scatters the flame, increasing fuel consumption. Overzealousness misreads operating and cooking directions, increasing fuel consumption. To combat the wind, use a baffle, screen, rocks, or set the stove in a protected hollow.

CUTAWAY VIEW

**Adding a screen** *around your camp stove*

**MSR's Heat Exchanger**
*serves as an efficient heat retainer and can be used without a windscreen.*

To overcome "the dumbs," read recipes carefully. If the recipe calls for a cup of water, don't boil two cups "just for good measure." The most efficient and brilliant menu in the world won't warm the cockles of anybody's heart if you can't heat the pot. And don't fire up till you see the whites of their eggs!

Finally, welcome to the latest gimmick, the electric-fan stove. Remember the blacksmith's forge, with its leather bellows? Blowing air over a fire increases its heat output quickly and efficiently. Well, there's a product out there that borrows this concept. It uses a battery-operated electric fan to heat small pieces of wood, pine cones, bark, even "buffalo chips"!

This is the lazy camper's kitchen helper. Out of breath? Don't want to blow on the fire? Crank this little doggie up, sit back and wait. It weighs less than a pound and its AA batteries will power the fan for nearly three hours. Considering it only takes about five minutes to boil a liter of water, it's a reasonably low-impact and efficient tool. It does, however, create a lot of soot. You'll need to pack it in a plastic bag. And however tempting, it's *verboten* where fires are not permitted.

**Electric fan stove**

## Ovens

Years ago, Hal tried to impress a raven-haired friend named "Blondie" (go figure) while car camping in the King Range in Northern California during the height of the ollalie season. (Ollalies are the heavyweights of the blackberry family.) He picked a potfull, and with a what-the-hell attitude, set out to "bake" a pie on the two-burner propane stove. It was gorgeous. It was inedible. You can't bake over an open flame. Or can you?

The answer depends on the ability to convert flames into hot air. Those old, boilerplate reflector ovens did that for campfires, and with a couple of piano mover pals you could still get one into the wilderness. Not as heavy but just as metal are those box-like convection ovens which fit over two-burner Coleman stoves. You could prepare an entire Thanksgiving dinner in them, and if you happen to be in a campsite in November, give us a call. More

THERMOMETER/ KNOB

CONVECTION DOME

COVER

TEFLON PAN

RISER BARS

DIFFUSER PLATES

REFLECTOR COLLAR

STOVE (NOT INCLUDED)

**The Outback Oven**
*allows you to bake over a camping stove.*

elegant and ingenious is a 10-ounce device called an Outback Oven™, clearly invented by one of those unsung geniuses who sit around dreaming up better mouse traps.

The Outback Oven works like this. Over the flame of even the smallest mountain stove, you place a round stainless steel heat diffuser plate, which is surmounted by metal "risers." Your covered pot sits on those risers, the heat from the gas flame is forced out and around the diffuser plate, and a snazzy heat-retaining "skirt," grandly called a Convection Dome, allows the hot air to circulate up and around the pot. Voilà! Instant oven. And it works. We've tried all our baking recipes on it with three-star results. Best of all, it is fuel efficient. In fact, the operating manual warns against running your stove at full tilt. The deluxe kit comes with a lidded teflon pan but any pot with a lid will do just fine.

## Essential Stove Lore

- Fuel contaminates food. Pack it separately from edibles. Wrap the fuel container in a plastic bag or two. Then if it seeps, or cracks when your pack drops on the ground, the food stays safe.

- Fuel is volatile. Keep it away from extraneous heat sources. Release the vapor pressure in fuel containers and the stove's tank occasionally as you hike. Never refuel a stove while it is hot.

- Stoves need ventilation; give them air. A large pot on a small stove may prevent proper ventilation and cause overheating. So can cooking in a closed space.

- Be careful while cooking in a tent. Many tents are flammable;

only recently have laws required that tents be made of flame-resistant materials. Make sure yours has been treated before cooking inside it. Even then, open tent flaps and keep the stove near an exit. Check out the new hanging stoves for tent use; they're designed to prevent spills.

- Stoves work best when set on a flat surface and protected from the wind. Cook on a flat rock or smooth ground in the lee of a tree or boulder, or make a wind baffle out of a circle of rocks or aluminum foil fashioned into a cylinder that fits around the stove leaving enough ventilation space.

- Oh, and one more thing. Don't forget your matches.

# Water Purifiers

The question is no longer, "Should you treat water?" but "How to treat water?" Disease-bearing microorganisms thrive in "pure" mountain lakes and streams, and the cramps, vomiting and diarrhea they visit on the system are enough to strike fear in the bowels of any camper.

Treatment systems vary in method and effectiveness. Iodine crystals or tablets are light and easy to use. They kill microorganisms, though not all forms of Giardia. They also take from 20

*A scanning electron micrograph of a Giardia. Not a nice sojourner in your intestinal tract.*

minutes to an hour to work, a long time if you're thirsty, and make the water taste worse than the stuff you left behind in the city. If you do use iodine tablets, drop a tablet of vitamin C into your canteen or jug after the iodine has done its work. The ascorbic acid of the vitamin converts iodine to "iodide," and gets rid of most of the "chlorine" taste. Also before leaving home find out if anyone in your party is allergic to iodine. (If they're allergic to shellfish, that may be a telltale sign.) The reaction can be sudden and strong.

A recent development in water treatment makes use of a special resin which releases the iodine only when it comes in contact with a contaminant. The more pure the water, the less it tastes like Camp Chawanga's swimming pool. Some systems combine this kind of demand-release system with filtration.

Boiling water—a full, rolling boil for three to four minutes—is another alternative, but doesn't eliminate debris, takes forever to cool, uses up fuel and may taste odd.

Filtration systems are expensive and heavy. But they're quick, safe and nonintrusive. The water tastes as if it actually came from a mountain stream. You pay in increasing weight as the filter retains liquid and clogs with use. Ceramic filters can be cleaned and reused, but they cost $180 and may crack if dropped. Paper-type elements are cheaper, about $35, but not renewable after clogging. They can, however, be back flushed (pumped in reverse) with a supply of pure water and reused for a total life of about 400 quarts.

**Water filters** *are a wise investment since all wilderness water should be considered contaminated. Any stream can be infested with Giardia or bacteria. Boiling and chemical treatments can be effective but are not always convenient—filters are compact and reusable.*

Plan ahead for your drinking-water needs. Mix and match. Cook with boiled water, use the filter till it clogs, and keep a tiny bottle of pills in reserve for emergencies. Crystal clear river and lake water can sometimes turn into a muddy soup overnight, depending on terrain, wind and weather. In that case let the sand and debris in the water pot settle before filtering, and fashion a pre-filter out of a piece of coffee filter secured with a rubber band to the inlet hose. In the end, however, a spare water filter at the bottom of the pack may be the trip-saver.

## Adaptive Equipment for the Disabled

The number and types of adaptive aids for disabled campers are growing exponentially. So are the prices. But everything from adapted fishing rod holders and electric reels to swimming frames, all-terrain wheelchairs, accessible rafts, kayaks, canoes and hand-powered bikes are out there. Availability is often haphazard and geographically limited, but resources and references are varied and plentiful. See Chapter 2 for listings.

## Fixing Things and Mending Bodies

### Repairs

If all that expensive gear breaks down on the trail, the one-year guarantees won't be worth their proverbial paper. You either live with the problem or fix it. We've never seen or heard of a camping trip where everything worked right; something invariably breaks, tears, rips or malfunctions. A good repair kit is essential.

- Small Vise Grips
- 2 needles, with thread to match (One of each should be "heavy duty")
- Safety pins
- Spare clevis pins and key wires (for the backpack)
- Spare flashlight batteries and bulbs
- 50 feet of nylon cord
- Nylon "ripstop" repair tape
- Swiss Army knife ("Tinker" model)
- Tweezers, razor blade and a roll of half-inch adhesive tape from the "medicine chest" will also help repair things

Patience and ingenuity are also required to make adequate repairs; these are both a matter of attitude. Make the job challenging and fun. Sit in a shady place, unpack the repair kit and ponder the problem. Take frequent breaks if the job is tedious. Once Hal's boot sole started to come apart. He got out the large needle, pushed it through the rubber and leather with a rock, then pulled it the rest of the way with the vise grips. On another trip, a backpack frame broke in two. We trimmed a tree branch to fit inside the hollow tubes, butted the broken pieces against each other with the branch acting as a reinforcing rod, then taped and tied the frame back together. Another time, a low-hanging branch snapped Rick's fishing rod in half. He found that one section of the hollow fiberglass tubing slid right into the other. So he looped the thick carpet thread around the break to keep the pieces together. Using only the Swiss Army knife and vise grips, we've even disassembled and reassembled our backpacking stove. Ripped packs, broken sunglasses, sticky fishing reels all have been repaired. Finally, don't worry if you make something worse by trying to fix it. Even the most ingenious Jack- or Jill-of-all-trades occasionally packs out a broken article. If, however, you work slowly and carefully and have some basic tools and supplies, you can usually do an adequate job.

## Bike Maintenance and Repairs

Like any machine that gets regular use, your bike needs periodic maintenance. If you're a mechanical klutz, have the local bike shop "tune-up" your bike regularly. They'll clean and lube the gears and chain, check and adjust the brakes and cables, tweak the spokes, and generally give it a once-over.

If you only ride on well-traveled roads during the summers, one tune-up a year should be enough. But if you plan to ride out of a mechanic's orbit—especially out in the mud, dirt, sand or rain—you'll need to take a more active role in keeping your bike alive and well. If your fishing reel jams or your stove conks out, you don't have to pack up and go home. If your bike breaks down miles from the nearest shop and you don't know how to fix it, you may not be *able* to get home. The moral? Learn how to troubleshoot and make simple repairs. Carry a basic tool kit in a seat pack. Attach or tape a pump and spare spokes to the bike frame. Or else!

Unless you're a mechanic or a genius, you're not going to repair any bike but your own and maybe your partner's. Take a maintenance course at a local bike clinic. Buy a maintenance manual written a couple of years *after* your bike was built. That way it's liable to cover the new systems which are actually on your bike: derailleur, freewheel removal, brake and gear adjustment. Buy the tools which *your* bike requires: the laser widget for Greg LeMond may be useless for you (see the Appendix for a clip-out tool list).

What are your basic maintenance and repair needs on a trip? You should regularly clean and lube the gears and chain, especially after riding off-road. Mud and sand particles can work like tiny grinding wheels to wear and damage moving parts. Water washes off lubricants and causes parts to rust. Know how to check and adjust the chain, brakes, and derailleurs. Give the bike a once-over in camp each morning or evening.

You'll also want to do some repairs on the road. Chains break, spokes snap, tires go flat. These repairs require practice and the right tools (listed in Chapter 6). None are so hard that you can't do them yourself. Practicing at home or in a bike maintenance class will make you a more confident, less frustrated rider. And save you some long, long walks.

## Bike Repair Hints

- Tube and tire repair. Make sure the pump fits the tire valves. Dust the spare tube with talcum; carry in a plastic bag. Use duct tape to reinforce torn tubes and to wrap cut tires.

- Broken spokes. Improvise: Loosen the brake to provide clearance for the wobbly wheel. Use the brake on the one good wheel. Slow down and carry on till you're in camp. Then replace the spokes. A "pocket vise" (see Chapter 6, third list) provides the best leverage to remove the freewheel nut. Spare spokes can be taped to the bike frame.

- Broken chain. Be sure spare links fit *your* chain. Know how to use the chain tool to remove and install the pin.

- Cable repair. Carry spare rear brake and derailleur cables with one head removed to allow threading through the housing. Front cable breaks: coil excess cable and trim later.

## Canoe Repairs

Bikers need wrenches. Canoeists need glue, or a facsimile thereof. The best all-purpose facsimile is ordinary heating-duct tape. In an emergency, it'll patch and fill till you get to camp. Then haul out the canoe and make a mend with the epoxy kit you've brought along. Use a torn-up kerchief as stuffing. Serious repairs—of dents, splits, loose rivets or damaged fiberglass—can be made at home or in the shop. A little seepage never hurt anyone; a lot could sink your trip.

## First Aid Kit

Our first aid kit has never really been tested. We've never had a major medical or first aid problem on a trip. All we can tell you is what we take and what we've used. There are good books on outdoor and wilderness first aid which you may want to look at (see the Book List on pages 381-386). Beyond that, we suggest you get in touch with local authorities regarding any special medical precautions you should consider for your trip (for example, preventive measures against Lyme disease or against contaminated water).

We routinely use lots of aspirin on hiking trips. It relieves headaches caused by sun, lack of salt, altitude or fatigue. It also helps aching muscles. Band-Aids and Moleskin, both of which may be found liberally attached to our feet, are the other two items always in high demand from the first aid kit.

The rest of our first aid supplies are rarely touched but they're there, just in case. We bring several square gauze bandages; strong tweezers for splinters, ticks and porcupine quills in the dog's nose; adhesive tape and needle (from the repair kit), codeine or its equivalent for serious pain, decongestant, Lomotil for diarrhea, antacid for upset stomachs and antibiotic pills in case of strep throat. A salve, first aid cream or disinfectant is also useful. Some people bring Ace bandages for strained or swollen ankles or knees. When backpacking alone, add a mirror in case something gets in your eye. Mountain bikers, who live more dangerously, should add butterfly bandages and hydrogen peroxide for the inevitable scrapes and cuts, and an "instant cold" pack to use for swelling in the first 30 minutes after a

**Fold-out first aid kit**

sprain. We've been told by international travelers that "electrolyte replacement" tablets help recovery from digestive problems. And your list of Kid Stuff should include children's Tylenol, ipecac syrup and chewable amoxicillin tablets.

If you don't want to put your own emergency medical kit together, try one of the excellent kits on the market, ranging in price from $20 to $120. True, it's an added expense, but there are advantages too. First, you can actually find the first aid kit when you need it. The brightly colored fold-out nylon pack has a big red cross on it, so you won't confuse it with the other 26 Ziploc baggies in your pack. Each item in the kit is clearly labeled, so that you, or anyone else in your group, can find what you need in an emergency. Special kits are tailored to the specific needs of canoe-ists, rafters and mountain cyclists. And most kits include a small first aid reference book full of sound advice and important medical information.

Sunscreen is a must, even if you plan to wear a hat and visor most of the time. Mosquito repellents are also a godsend when the breed is in full swing, but they contain pesticides, so use at your own discretion. The strongest, such as DEET, are absorbed through the skin into the bloodstream, and should *never* be used on children. If you must, daub it on your clothes and boot tops to defend against ticks, Dracula, and mosquitos. There are now on the market so-called low-pesticide repellents and a number of pesticide-free repellents. Mosquitos have yet to be polled as to their effectiveness, but these repellents may be safer for children than the full bore varities.

Individuals should carry whatever medicines they need. Karen wouldn't be caught in Carlsbad Caverns without a good sunscreen, while Hal would sooner go into the mountains without boots than leave his back pills behind. Mary brings sulfa drugs in case of a urinary infection and Rick is addicted to Vitamin C. Don't skimp on what's necessary for you.

There are two other necessary items: lip balm and hand lotion. Hot weather, cold winds and constant exposure to the elements really dry out the face, hands and lips. A nightly applica-tion of lotion goes a long way toward preventing loss of moisture, as does a daily dose of Chap-Stick. After one trip when it becomes painful to move your hands or lips, you'll never forget either of these items again.

The great snakebite question inevitably arises. We can give you a few hints. In 25 years of backpacking in California, the Rockies, the Ouintas and the Southwest, we've never seen a poisonous snake nor heard one rattle. Snakes are as terrified of you as you may be of them. Statistically, the number of fatalities from snake bites in the U.S. is so small as to be almost negligible: about 15 people, mostly small children, die each year from snake venom.

The snakebite kit itself (razor blade, tourniquet and disinfectant) is a double-edged sword. "Authorities generally advise carrying a snakebite kit, but in unpracticed hands of semi-hysterical first-aiders, the kit can be more dangerous than the bite; the rule is to seek instruction before entering an area where it may be needed." (Harvey Manning, *Backpacking, One Step at a Time*, pg. 52). We used to carry a bite kit, but it seems to have disappeared in recent years and we haven't replaced it. There are very few snakes over 7,000 feet (where we backpack), but rattlesnakes might be a danger in other areas. Check before you go. If you're in snake country, be sure to wear long pants and heavy boots.

Likewise, in deer tick country, wear long pants tucked into hiking socks or taped closed against disease-carrying ticks (see also Mosquitos and Ticks, page 182). Wear long sleeved, light-colored clothing (the better to see the ticks, my dear), and rub a little DEET insecticide on cuffs and sleeves.

What about serious injuries exceeding CPR and first aid skills, such as setting a broken leg, handling a near drowning, or suturing a wound? In the first place, these are most dangerous when alone. If you and your gear fall into an icy river late one rainy, windy afternoon, there is a real danger of hypothermia. Alone, you're in the same fix as a solo climber who falls and breaks a leg. Anytime you go off by yourself, whether exploring or cycling, be sure someone knows exactly what your plans are and where you'll be. And come back on time, even if that means not making it to your destination.

The second rule is not to move seriously injured victims. Set up a campsite that is as warm and dry as possible. Then go for help. Canoeists can often make good time to a trailhead and help. Most ranger stations have helicopters available in case of life-threatening emergencies. Rangers are rarely more than two or three slow hiking days away (one long hiking day without a pack).

If the injured person can be left in comfortable surroundings, you can usually have a doctor there within 24 hours. Don't try to carry anyone out over rough terrain.

## Weight (and the Gear You Left Behind)

Weight watchers—cyclists and backpackers—need to fuss. If all that nicely assembled gear is too heavy to move out of the living room, you might as well stay home. Just how much you can carry depends on your own weight, height, physical condition and state of mind, and on the facilities you have for carrying a load: a strong and big pack, a strong and little pack, two or four panniers. It also depends on how long the trip is and how many people will be sharing the load. Putting all these ingredients in the hopper and shaking, we've come up with the "average load" for an "average adult" for a four-person hiking trip for six days, door to door: 34 pounds. Of this, food will weigh about $7^1/_4$ pounds per person ($1^1/_2$ pounds per person per day, excluding the first and last travel days). Non-food weight—clothing, equipment and personal accessories—will be about $26^3/_4$ pounds, including water and the weight of the empty pack itself. As trips get longer, food takes up a greater percentage of total pack weight, and other things, like the inflatable raft, 35mm camera or the *Shorter Oxford Dictionary* may have to go.

But take heart. Our hyperventilated consumer society keeps coming up with lightweight, portable versions of all your needs, imagined or real. Some even do double duty. You can get a flexible camping chair which doubles as a sleeping pad or a walking stick which doubles as a camera "monopod." From fishing gear to inflatable boats, from binoculars to solar-charged flashlights, you can probably find a light backpacking version and take it camping. That's what we usually do.

At the other end of the outdoor spectrum is a new breed of "fastpackers" who've shaved down the weight of their fully-loaded packs to less than 12 pounds, not counting food or water. By lightening their pack frames, modifying shortened sleeping bags to double as down parkas, and using multiple layers of "miracle" garments, these folks routinely cover 20 to 30 miles a day. But they don't bring the frying pan.

If you do take along something extravagant, each person will need to add a little more weight to the pack load. That doesn't mean everyone will carry equal weight. On a four-person excursion, somebody will haul nearly 45 pounds and someone else closer to 25 pounds. That's okay. If there are only two of you, you'll each carry a lot more (excluding the raft), for a minimum total of just over 39 pounds.

How much can one person carry? A good guide is to begin with 20 percent of your body weight. If you're in good shape, you can raise that to 25 percent. A group of 160-pound joggers can easily carry 40 pounds each. But if three of your four-person group weigh less than 120 pounds, you might have to start cutting corners to reduce their packs to 25 pounds or so.

Much the same applies to cyclists. When push comes to shove, you have to be able to lift the bike off the ground if it falls over! Figure 40 pounds maximum for four fully-loaded panniers; figure a lot less for your biking pleasure. Unlike backpackers, you can always replenish supplies *en route*.

## Anticipation

With equipment in order and maps and permits in hand (see Chapter 2), you're ready to head for the market. The following chapter will get you there.

# CHAPTER 5

# Food

---

## Food Weights and Planning

Our friend Lowell used to be an ace backcountry hiker. Then he became a letter carrier on the hills of San Francisco. He soon grew weary of his busman's holidays and retired from backpacking because he hiked so much in his work. But on the trail he was good, and often did things his own way. Where others wore the latest hiking boots, he'd lead the way down rock falls in a pair of battered basketball hightops. When others pressed grimly toward the destination in the afternoon's hottest sunshine, he'd find the deepest shade available, unroll his Ensolite pad and sleep out the heat, often arriving at the campsite by flashlight. And where the rest of us were satisfied with dried foods and soup packets, he insisted on packing in fresh onions, potatoes, carrots, turnips and other weighty produce for his cherished stews.

Then there's Rob, who lives on rice and oatmeal cooked in a coffee can, raisins, seeds and other bird food so he can carry along his camera and telephoto lenses. The message? If you really want to bring something badly enough, you'll bring it and enjoy it, even though it seems to defy all the logic of backpacking. This logic insists that food is heavy. Especially food with a high water content. If you filled your pack with onions, you'd need a forklift to get it up on your back. Food is also bulky and packs have just so much space.

Car campers and canoeists need not attend class today. Unless planning a multi-day hiking trip from the campground, take your granny's entire larder for all we care. Cyclists, like backpackers, however, need to be minimalists or plan to shop on a daily basis.

Unless you pump iron for a living or are related to a pack mule, weight and space will dictate how much and what kind of food you can take on a camping trip. So will distance and taste. When all the variables are considered and combined, the figures work out something like this. An average pack loaded with everything except food will weigh in the neighborhood of 27 pounds. To this will be added about 1.5 pounds of food per person per day, the accepted median limit of food weight in most backpacking circles. Jewish mothers, a stable of sumo wrestlers, and Lowell with his stews may insist on two pounds per day, but any more than that and you'd better start pumping iron for a living or take a burro with you.

Actually, we begin with the goal of a pound a day and grudgingly go up the extra half pound when we can't part with the Kahlua or matzoh meal. If you go exclusively with freeze-dried foods, of course, your cooking utensils will be cut to one pot, plus stove and fuel, which permits greater food weight. Anything much below a pound a day verges on nuts and berries—the school of caloric deprivation.

For the sake of argument and a contented after-dinner glow, let's take 1.5 pounds and see how it adds up. A five-day trip will mean a 37.5-pound pack; an eight-day trip, a 42-pound pack and two weeks, a 51-pound pack. That's a lot to haul up a hill. Beyond that, plan to cache some food or get resupplied. If you don't believe us, put 50 pounds of rocks (or onions, we're not fussy) in a backpack and walk up two flights of stairs. Welcome to the reality of weight watching.

Those 1.5 pounds a day include everything you'll ingest—staples, ready-to-eat foods, spices, cooking oil—as well as the packaging containers. Thus, another law of backpacking logic is: the lighter the container, the more food you can carry. Check out the *net* weights on food packets when you shop. That gives you the amount of actual food in a package, as distinct from total shelf weight, which includes wrapping, cardboard, plastic and puffed-up space. With few exceptions, everything will need to be repacked in the lightest wrapping anyway, so the net weight becomes the operative figure in calculating those 1.5 pounds.

Before going to the market or camping store, figure out how

many meals you'll be having and where you'll be having them; on the trail (simple and quick) or in camp (complex and leisurely). You needn't know precisely what you'll be eating for every meal, just what will be available for as many hot meals as you'll need. Of course, if you like to plan menus, do so; lots of suggested meal plans appear in the literature. Since we're never sure if we'll want minestrone on Tuesday or lunch (at all) on Wednesday, we fudge on the menus and prepare with an eye toward improvising. That, however, does not mean we're completely spur-of-the-moment.

To illustrate the food-planning process, we show you how we planned two six-day trips, each with four people. For both trips, the total *on trail* food weight was about 30 pounds (i.e. 1.5 pounds per person per day, *not including* car meals). But that does not mean that each group carried the same food.

A couple of years ago, we went on one of those literally breathtaking trips in the high Sierra—five days at about 11,000 feet, above the tree line where no fires are permitted. The four of us were (and still are) what can only be called "competition eaters." We intended to eat well and nutritiously with a one-burner MSR X-GK stove and a 22-ounce fuel bottle—enough gas to cook two hot meals a day for five days for a small bar mitzvah party of 30, though light enough to justify the extravagance. We didn't even contemplate taking freeze-dried foods. We brought fishing rods for day hikes at lower altitudes, but didn't like our prospects and, anyway, knew better than to count our fishes before they're caught. So, our 1.5 pounds-per-day specs didn't include the *trout flambée des Alpes Maritimes.*

Take a look at the Food Planning Table that follows. Let your eye run down the first column. There is enough variety to provide for quick but filling meals (an important consideration at that altitude) and a few improvisational licks. (See Chapter 9 for recipes for all the dishes described here.) We ate strawberry pancakes, having dried plenty of strawberries at home and let them soak in cold water overnight to rehydrate; also fruit crêpes, the mixed home-dried fruits reconstituting quickly in water boiled at high heat for a few minutes. Nobody could face the instant oatmeal plain, so we concocted a pan-fried "polenta," mixing the oatmeal with cornmeal, margarine, sugar and eggs.

Suppers were super. Pasta with homemade spaghetti sauce, dried and reconstituted, topped with parmesan cheese, which is one of the best hiking cheeses because it's hard and doesn't spoil. Homemade minestrone, also dried and reconstituted in a few minutes; Indian fried rice with raisins, nuts, coconut, sprouts and chicken, spiced with *garam masala*. And three providential trout caught on the last day sautéed with almonds, and served with stir-fried veggies. Karen insisted as a finale that we have her famous chocolate mousse à la Red Peak Pass, and she used up enough of the remaining fuel to lighten the packs for the hike out. On day six, we ate a quick oatmeal breakfast and hot chocolate, snacks for lunch and reached the car with just enough left over for an emergency that never happened.

The second trip couldn't have been more different: Rick, Hal and two ravenous adolescents, intent on several days of hiking, fishing, cooking and general relaxation. We camped at three successive lakes, all well stocked with small brown trout. Firewood was plentiful. Most afternoons, while the girls were swimming or reading—or noshing on the snack food—we invented new ways to bake breads, cake, pizza and the thousand and one other recipes you'll find in Chapter 10. A couple of things went wrong. Stanya decided after catching her second fish that she was a vegetarian, and Annika stunned us with the announcement that she loathed cheese. Rick, ever resourceful, said, "Let them eat cake." They did. And loved it. We ate the fish and cheese, and loved it.

## Food Planning for Two Six-Day Trips

| | Trip One Min. Cooking (weight=lbs.) | Trip Two Max. Cooking | Weight Difference (2nd trip) |
|---|---|---|---|
| Ready to Eat Foods: | | | |
| Dried fruit, Raisins | 3.0 | 3.0 | |
| Chicken/Beef Jerky | 1.8 | 1.8 | |
| Dried Vegetables | 1.5 | 1.0 | 0.5 less |
| Cheese | 3.5 | 2.5 | 1.0 less |
| Nuts | 0.8 | 0.5 | 0.3 less |
| Cookies | 1.5 | 1.5 | |
| Crackers | 1.5 | 1.5 | |
| Chocolate | 2.0 | 2.0 | |
| Granola and Coconut | 0.8 | 0.5 | 0.3 less |
| Sprouts | 0.1 | 0.1 | |

| Rice, Pasta, Soups: | | | |
|---|---|---|---|
| Minute Rice | 1.0 | 0.7 | 0.3 less |
| Dried Minestrone | 0.8 | 0.8 | |
| Dried Pea Soup | 0.8 | 0.0 | 0.8 less |
| Spaghetti Sauce | 0.8 | 0.8 | |
| Spaghetti and Ramen | 1.2 | 1.0 | 0.2 less |
| Flour, Sugar, Cereals: | | | |
| Instant Oatmeal | 0.4 | 0.0 | 0.4 less |
| Flour | 1.5 | 3.0 | 1.5 more |
| Yeast, Baking Powder | 0.0 | 0.3 | 0.3 more |
| Cornmeal | 0.3 | 0.3 | |
| Sugar | 0.5 | 1.0 | 0.5 more |
| Dairy, Oils, Spices: | | | |
| Powdered Milk | 0.5 | 0.8 | 0.3 more |
| Eggs | 1.0 | 1.7 | 0.7 more |
| Hot Chocolate | 1.5 | 1.5 | |
| Tea/Coffee | 0.2 | 0.2 | |
| Cooking Oil | 0.0 | 0.5 | 0.5 more |
| Margarine | 0.5 | 0.5 | |
| Spices, Condiments, Syrup | 2.5 | 2.5 | |
| Total Weight | 30.0 | 30.0 | |

The interesting thing about these two radically different trips is the similarity in their food lists. Most of the items are exactly the same. They diverge—in quantities—where considerations of fuel use and food-preparation time are paramount. Neither of these factors appears on the food lists, but they cannot be ignored when planning a trip.

One last piece of advice: many wilderness hikers recommend having extra quantities of emergency high-protein food, like milk powder, soup or bouillon cubes. Should you get caught in an early snowstorm for two unexpected days, that could be vital to pull you through.

The more you know about your appetites, abilities and the conditions at your destination, the better you can plan a food inventory. You're already familiar with the first two: you know what and how much you like to eat, and can gauge your physical ability to carry weight. Conditions, however, are likely to change. Someone may get sick and may not be able to eat what's available. The fishing may be lousy. The salami may be left in the fridge at home by mistake. The bears may get to dinner #3 before you do. By assessing the knowables, and expecting the variables, you're better prepared to improvise.

## Food Planning: What You Need to Know

- Fires permitted? Check *before* you go.

- Fishing prospects? *Never* assume you'll catch fish. Accept them as a bonus.

- Dietary considerations? Check likes and dislikes before you go. Likewise special needs. Vegetarians won't eat jerky; carnivores won't eat just vegetables.

- Taking the dog? Plan food weight for the pooch as carefully as you would for yourself. The size and weight of your dog make a difference. Average: two packets of moist food per day. Plan to carry dog food over rough terrain.

- Fuel consumption? Stove campers: Learn the cooking capacity of your particular stove before you go. Fire builders: Leave axes at home. Use only free-fall wood.

- Low-impact camping? One hot meal per day rather than two. Take more snacks, less cooking food.

- Plan car meals separately, but *don't forget them*. The fried chicken, macaroni salad, fresh fruit and juice to be taken in the cooler go on your shopping list. Likewise the small juice packets for the ride home.

# What To Bring?

It's finally time to shop. You've discussed likes and dislikes, determined how much or how little cooking you'll do, how much money you can spend, what kind of hot meals you want, what munchies are absolutely indispensable. You've made a preliminary shopping list, then checked off what items you already have at home. Your first target is the supermarket. It's cheaper than specialty stores and carries all kinds of heat-and-serve foods. If there's a bulk-food store in town, you'll probably shop there for grains, flours, dried fruits, nuts and the like. If there's a camping store, you may head there for the latest in freeze-dried foods. If you do, bring along a shopping bag full of money.

You won't be Ace Market's favorite customer if you ask for "one pound and 11.5 ounces of cookies, please, and throw in 7.5

ounces of flour, will you?" Weigh out the amounts at home after you've done the shopping (see Weighing Food in this section). If you buy too much, save it; it won't spoil.

## Cooking and Eating Utensils: What We Bring

Spartan backpackers hell-bent for distance can make do with a pot and a spoon. Add a pocket knife to skin a bear or fell a tree and they are content and at peace with the world. Cooking in the wilderness, after all, is no exercise in elegance. However, if you prefer Athens to Sparta, you may want to add just a couple more pots and maybe even a fry pan. The goal is to keep things few and light, but as you'll see from our recipes (Chapter 10), it's possible to satisfy most hedonistic impulses with a minimum of hardware. Here's what we take for two to eight people on our longer trips.

- A set of three nested pots and tops with capacities of one quart, two quarts, and two-and-a-half quarts. Weight: 1 pound, 13 ounces.

- A flex-grip metal pot holder, a pliers-like tool that grips the rim of a pot, one tong fitting under the lip of the rim, the other fitting over it. Weight: 2 ounces. If the pots have bails (wire handles), use a heavy pair of gloves instead. Steadier and more efficient than the flex-grip.

- An 8.5-inch teflon-coated aluminum fry pan. It's old enough so that we don't worry about scratching the surface. Otherwise, use a spatula made of wood or plastic instead of metal. A teflon-coated pan requires less shortening, saving weight in the cooking oil department. And it's easy to clean in case of burning on uneven heat. Weight: 1 pound.

- A small aluminum spatula. Weight: 3 ounces.

- A lightweight three-pronged backpacking grill in its own protective sack (to keep soot off other things in the pack). Weight: 4.5 ounces. If we're going where the fish are, we often take along a 14" x 10" wire-mesh grill (a cake rack works fine) which makes grilling fish a breeze. Weight: 7 ounces.

- A plastic egg container (one dozen). Weight: 5.5 ounces.

- A small wire whisk. Weight: 3 ounces. Alternatively, a small spring-loaded swizzle stick (like an egg beater). Weight: 3.5 ounces.

- Pocket knives, one each person. We use Tinker-model Swiss Army knives, which substitute a Phillips screwdriver for the more common corkscrew. Weight: 3 ounces.

- Two boxes of sulphur kitchen matches packed separately in watertight Ziploc bags. Weight: 4 ounces (both boxes).

- Two small plastic garbage bags for packing the pots and fry pan— for soot containment.

- Extra Ziploc bags for food storage: Weight: 1 ounce.

- Eating utensils: 1 Sierra cup (3.5 ounces), 1 tin plate (3.5 ounces), 1 fork (1.5 ounces), and 1 spoon (1.5 ounces) per person. The forks are optional; chopsticks are lighter. The pocket knife completes the set.

- An MSR X-GK multi-fuel stove. Weight: 1 pound. Plus 22-ounce fuel bottle/pump (need not be filled to capacity). Alternatively, a Bleuet C206 camping stove plus one butane cartridge. Weight: 1 pound, 7.5 oz. Take these only if campfires are not permitted.

The total weight (not including the stove equipment) is 5 pounds, 14 ounces. The MSR stove and its accessories add 2 pounds, for a grand total of 7 pounds, 14 ounces. Clearly there are expendable items here. Consider how much time you want to spend, and what kind of cooking you plan to do. Then adjust the utensils accordingly.

# Shopping

## *Light and Quick Foods*

In the above trip plans, freeze-dried foods are conspicuous by their absence. After many years of sampling, we found we didn't really need them. First and foremost, our budget never allowed it. Freeze-dried foods aren't cheap. Second, we prefer to dry our own. Third, we don't need their convenience. With a fire, our rice, beans and dried veggies do just fine. Where a stove is required, home-dried meals, soups and noodles work as well and are a lot cheaper.

Nevertheless, freeze-dried foods *are* remarkably convenient. Light in both bulk and weight, they're quick and easy to prepare. Supermarkets carry some, but the largest selections are found in camping or specialty stores. And many people find them quite palatable.

## Bulk Foods

Bulk foods include rice, beans, pasta, lentils and peas, nuts, raisins, and dried fruits. They're cheaper than packaged varieties, are bought in just the weights you want, rather than what the processor wants to sell you, and exist in enough varieties to satisfy just about everyone. Brown sugar, brown rice, rye or soy flour, 57 varieties of noodles—most bulk food stores have what you need.

## Alternative Foods

A world of other possibilities exists out there in the marketplace. One friend, after spending nearly 10 years as a reporter in Tokyo, relies almost exclusively on Japanese food products. He takes Japanese buckwheat noodles (*soba*); he also carries seaweed (*nori*), which he wraps together in a flexible bamboo square used in rolling rice for Japanese sushi (raw fish and rice delicacy). He also relies on soybean soup bases (*miso*), dried fish, and, unaccountably, popcorn. Others carry falafel mix, a practical and delicious Middle Eastern grain and chick pea combination. And for the sentimental mid-Americanist, there are always instant mashed potatoes and Rice-a-Roni.

Don't forget about your local import/gourmet store, the place where you usually go for wall-hangings and affordable ceramics. It also carries a wide variety of cheap, dried imported foods. One recent trip to ours netted the following improbable haul:

- No less than 15 different varieties of trail mix, from Tex-Mex and Cajun to traditional granola-raisin.

- Numerous varieties of dried Japanese mushrooms, such as shiitake, matsutake, enokitake.

- Powdered gourmet sauce and glaze mixes, including béarnaise sauce, white sauce and fruit glazes.

- A seemingly endless supply of just-add-water meals, including refried beans, black beans, sweet corn chowder, pasta and sauce, vegetarian chili, snowpeas and rice, you name it. Many are packaged in just-add-hot-water paper cups for office microwaves. But fear not. Just pour the contents into plastic bags, and voilà! you've got inexpensive camping food. (We know a guy who took his microwave on a canoe trip, but that's another story.)

- Vacuum-packed ravioli, tortellini and gnocchi (Italian potato dumplings), which don't require refrigeration. These packages include a little moisture, which adds to their weight, but one of them can be stretched to feed two in a pinch.

- Hummus mix. Hummus is another one of those Middle Eastern snack foods, and like falafel seems almost addictive. It's a chick pea mash made into a paste with oil, garlic, lemon, and tahini. However, these mixes are not light, so weigh things in the balance before deciding on them.

- Pesto in a tube. Think about it. They got toothpaste in a tube, didn't they? Note however that pesto's heavy, and if you're going to pack it in, why not make your own and put it in a squeeze tube?

The great thing about import stores as sources for camping food is that they buy in huge quantities from countries where food—and alas labor—is cheap. Furthermore, they're basically wholesalers to the general public, rather than specialty camping retailers. The result is a large variety of cheap, wholesome and interesting camping food.

## Extravagances

If backpacking were a science, there'd be no room for frills. We'd have to leave fresh eggs at home, along with mustard powder and sesame oil. But backpacking's an art, subject to (some) whim and a (little) fancy, and that allows for incorporation of particular idiosyncrasies into the overall weight limit. If you absolutely cannot do without some Granny Smith apples or a watermelon, pare down the weight elsewhere. Your extravagance becomes a working part of your inventory. You have turned a frill into a necessity.

## Dog Food

Dry dog food is too bulky to take on a mountain trip. Canned dog food is full of water *and* prohibitively expensive. That leaves moist dog food, which is not as bulky as the dry, nor quite as expensive or heavy as the canned. And, according to the makers' claims, it's more nutritional per unit of weight. It's also conveniently packaged. We always allow our pooches a little more than the minimum requirements, but never so much that they can't carry most of it. For our (medium-sized) dogs, eight packets are sufficient for a four-day trip, 12 packets for a seven-day trip. The

only other thing to remember is that dogs, like humans, can carry
only so much weight. Make appropriate allowances for your
dog's size.

# Weighing, Packing, Transporting and Caching Food

## *Weighing Food*

Virgil, a fanatical solo backpacker who goes out for six weeks
at a time without resupplying, refuses to weigh his food. He just
eyeballs the amount, tests the "feel" of his pack, and goes off. He
hasn't starved or expired of muscle fatigue yet. The rest of us
mortals need reassurance that we have the right amount of food
for the finite number of days we'll be on the trail. It need not be
exact. If you've gone rigid with anxiety over our fine-tuned weighing in those food lists above, relax. You needn't be a charter
member of the U.S. Bureau of Standards to camp, hike or backpack. The important number is the total weight—that's what
you'll carry. To determine this, a bathroom scale will work fine.

When you get the food home from the market, eliminate all
extraneous packaging. The aim is to get as close to the net weight
as possible without sacrificing freshness or protection against
breakage and spillage. You may want to keep the Ry Krisp in its
cardboard box to prevent crumbling, the soup powder in its packet
to save cooking instructions, or the baking chocolate in its box for
shelter against the sun. But as a rule, repack almost everything in
plastic bags. Then fetch the bathroom scale. Weigh yourself. Now
weigh yourself holding all the food in a cardboard box or brown
paper bag. Don't forget the eggs, cheese, salami and other things
stashed in the fridge. You won't be able to read the scale because
the food box will be in the way. Ask a friend to read it for you.
That's what friends are for. You now have an idea of the total net
weight. If it much exceeds your expectations (1.5 to 2 pounds per
person per day), start cutting and paring. Some of the flour can go.
Put some of the maple syrup back in the cupboard. On second
thought, who needs that many almonds? Now get back on the
scale. If you're a couple pounds over or under, it's close enough.
When you reach the trailhead, you can cut or add again.

If you own a small postal scale, the kind that weighs packages up to about four pounds, you can fine-tune by weighing individual items. If you're a classic anal compulsive, you can even get a letter scale that is calibrated to half-ounces. That way you can be content in the knowledge that exactly 3.5 ounces of cinnamon and sugar are nestled against the 1.5 ounces of nutmeg and cloves. Authors of camping books somehow always feel obliged to know such things; no one else we've ever met on the trail has known or cared.

## Packing and Transporting Food

Don't knock plastic. The Ziploc bag just may be the most important advance in hiking since the invention of the foot. We sympathize with those who hate Ziplocs; we often can't get them closed either. If you're a Zipophobe, pack your food in sturdy plastic bags and secure them with wire ties. If you can deal with Ziploc technology, buy several boxes and use them liberally. So liberally, in fact, that you'll double-bag many items. Always carry out the used bags with you. Burning plastic is a foul(ing) deed.

In the off-season, collect plastic bottles. Small ones are perfect for vinegar, sesame oil and hot sauce; large ones for cooking oil, maple syrup and brandy. Compartmentalized pill boxes, obtainable in drug stores, are great for carrying spices. On the trail, carry extra plastic bags. They'll come in handy to replace torn ones, or to store caught fish, map cases and garbage bags.

Individual foods should be packed separately. Cookies, nuts, dried fruit, etc. get their own bags. Liquids such as syrups and oils should be kept in well-sealed containers and carried upright. Don't put them vertically in a backpack which you then lay on its side for a five-hour drive to the trailhead; you may find a syrup-soaked pack when you arrive. Keep liquids upright in a box in the car and transfer them to the pack before you start to hike.

Eggs should be placed in plastic containers you can buy at camping stores. They come in half-dozen and dozen sizes and keep the eggs from breaking even if the pack gets dropped or slammed around. Some people prefer to keep breakfast, lunch and dinner foods separately, each in their own section of the pack. Others, like ourselves, prefer to organize the staples apart from the ready-to-eat (trail) foods. Whichever system you use, what's important is that it works for you.

Once everything is swathed in plastic or secured in containers and bags, you need to get it into the packs. It's common to pack at home and transport the filled packs in your car to the trailhead. But loaded backpacks take up lots of space in a car. Especially if you drive a compact, you could leave the final packing for the trailhead and transport the dry food in boxes and the perishables in a cooler. Then tie the empty backpacks on the roofrack, or under the canoe.

Be sure you know where in the pack your food is. If you dive in searching for gorp and cheese for lunch and can only come out with cornmeal, you might be nettled. So do a little planning. Someone might carry the lunch foods; someone else the staples, liquids and dinners. If you're a large party, two people can carry the ready-to-eats and two the staples. Within any pack, try to be consistent, so nuts and raisins are in the same place every day and are not crushed by, say, that watermelon you couldn't leave behind. And while in camp, where most cooking, baking and eating are going on, system becomes crucial. We try to arrange the packs in camp so all the baking gear is in one place, all the condiments and spices in another, the jerky, salami, cheese and crackers in the left upper pocket, the chocolate in the fridge, the cookies in the cupboard, and so on. If two packs will accommodate all the food in camp, it becomes more efficient. Only those two packs have to be moved periodically to keep up with the shade.

## Caching Food

We'd never made a food cache until we met an old-timer some years ago who convinced us that it was easy and efficient. The simplicity was at first unbelievable. He took the food he wanted to stash, stored it in plastic containers stuffed in a green plastic garbage bag and thrown on the floor of the forest. Nothing more. He insisted that bears and other cognoscenti rarely disturbed the sack. Were we being taken? We'll probably never know, because we take a few more precautions with our own cache.

Old coffee cans and plastic half-gallon ice cream containers with tight lids make up our inner defenses, in which we pack and tightly seal 10 pounds of extra food. We then stuff them in a garbage bag, and bury the stash under a canopy of rocks under a low-spreading tree high in a mountain meadow. We've never retrieved a cache in less than perfect condition.

A couple of hints: Store relatively dispensable food, such as extra flour, dog food and supplementary sweets. Make sure the cache is out of the sun. Make even surer you can find it again. That particular tree might not look so particular from a mile away. Or the meadow may be shin-deep in water when you get back and look very different from your last view. Sight your cache from different angles. You don't need a compass, just a sense of proportion and a good memory.

Allow space in your pack for the cache food and its large containers when you leave the trailhead. You may have to hang the empty containers from your pack until you get to the cache site, or stow them in the pack already filled, if there's space.

Finally, grin and bear it if the bears or squirrels get what you've squirreled away. Besides, you may catch enough extra fish to compensate for your losses. Anyway, it's not that awful to hike out a day or two early.

# CHAPTER 6

# Lists:
# A Schlepper's Guide
# to the Universe

Out there somewhere may be a monster of total recall who can keep in mind everything necessary for a camping trip. But that's not us. We keep lists. Lots of lists. Lists for food and equipment. Replacement items within the equipment list (such as the first-aid kit and repair kit). We even make a list of the lists we need to make. That sounds like a lot of trouble, but since our requirements don't vary much from trip to trip or year to year, once one is made it can be used almost forever. Just keep a master list in reasonably good shape in your map drawer. Lists will grow and shrink occasionally, according to group size, needs, new discoveries or tastes and discarded or obsolete items. It's a good idea to keep a spare list handy to jot down details as you think of them before, during and after your trips.

The lists in this chapter should make it possible for you to create a set of master lists—combinations which work best for the particular kind of trip you have in mind. Tear the copies out of the Appendix, apply scissors and tape, mix and match. Then, when you've got the right package, xerox it in multiple copies. That way you won't have to start from scratch two years from now when you set out on a similar camping trip. Never mind that you no longer need the baby wipes or tire patch kit or that you no longer "do" sugar and polished rice. Cross out what's obsolete—the ear spoon and foghorn, the training wheels and fire axe. Pen in the sketch pad, bird book and mosquito net, copy again and you're ready for the last half of the last decade of the twentieth century. Use three copies of the list for each trip, the first while assembling gear, the second when loading the car, the third at the trailhead. After that, it's best to forget what you forgot.

We begin with the car and proceed through canoes and bicycles, ending with the kinds of planning lists which multi-day hikers and backpackers need to get them well-provisioned on the trail. The Food Planning List for Two Six-Day Trips (Chapter 5) is not reproduced here; however, all lists are reproduced in the Appendix for your clip-out convenience. Note that some items are duplicated as we try to make each list comprehensive in itself.)

## *List of Lists:*

# The Before-Leaving-Home-Did-I-Turn-Off-the-Gas Checklist

❑ Leave a schedule/map/
itinerary with someone to
call out the Mounties if you
don't return on time. Include
name and phone number of
nearest ranger station.

❑ Get neighbor to watch the
house and take in newspa-
pers, take out garbage, feed
the pets.

❑ Leave written instructions on
plant care.

❑ Leave adequate pet food,
and name and phone
number of the vet. Alternatively, take pets to the
boarding kennel.

❑ Camping equipment:
 ❑ Lubricate all zippers—on
 tents, sleeping bags, packs—
 with silicone lube or a light
 oil (WD-40).
 ❑ Waterproof boots. Use only
 recommended agent for
 your particular footwear.
 ❑ Repair/replace damaged or
 missing parts. *(A leaking
 inflatable raft can ruin a fishing
 trip. So can a missing tent pole.)*

❑ Check car:
 ❑ Tires, belts, hoses and
 battery cables
 ❑ Wiper blades. Fill windshield
 washer reservoir with a
 mixture of Windex and
 water.

❑ Vital fluids: gas, oil, automatic transmission fluid,
brake fluid, coolant
❑ Tire-changing equipment:
jack, lug wrench, spare tire
❑ Roof rack: All parts present?

❑ In car:
 ❑ License and car registration
 ❑ Credit cards and cash on
 board
 ❑ Fire/wilderness permits,
 fishing licenses
 ❑ Road maps and directions to
 trailhead or campground
 ❑ Ranger station address and
 telephone number
 ❑ Sunglasses
 ❑ Accessible rain gear
 ❑ Cooler/ice chest with
 perishable foods
 ❑ Car meals and snacks
 ❑ Drinking water
 ❑ Dog food and water bowl
 ❑ Litter bag
 ❑ Games, toys, stuffed
 animals, books, distractions
 ❑ Personal needs: music/story
 tapes, Walkman, pencil,
 paper
 ❑ Clean clothes for return
 drive home

❑ Did I leave the gas on, the
toilet running?

# Bicycle Touring/Mountain Bike List

- ❑ Bicycle in top running order
- ❑ Cycling shorts
- ❑ Helmet *(with built-in visor for intense sun)*
- ❑ Cycling shoes
- ❑ Shoe covers
- ❑ Cycling gloves
- ❑ Rain gear
- ❑ Sunglasses *(shield type)*
- ❑ Safety glasses *(for mountain biking)*
- ❑ Shoulder strap *(for carrying a mountain bike up or over rough terrain)*
- ❑ Rear-view mirror
- ❑ Horn/bell
- ❑ Panniers
- ❑ Pannier rain covers *(or plastic garbage bags in which all gear is stowed)*
- ❑ Lock
- ❑ Headlamp plus extra batteries
- ❑ Fold-up reflective triangle
- ❑ Water bottle(s)
- ❑ Litter bag
- ❑ Talcum powder *(for saddle sores and flat tires)*
- ❑ Optional: *(for high-tech cycling)*
  - ❑ Small radio *(for weather reports)*
  - ❑ Cyclometer *(indicates speed, distance traveled, etc.)*
  - ❑ Two-way radio that fits in helmet *(lets you chat with a partner while biking)*

- ❑ Tool and Repair Kit
  - ❑ 6" crescent wrench
  - ❑ Folding Allen wrench set *(metric / standard)*
  - ❑ 2 four-way cone wrenches *(metric / standard)*
  - ❑ Small vise-grips with wire-cutter built in
  - ❑ Swiss Army knife *(Tinker model includes Phillips and standard screwdrivers)*
  - ❑ Paper towels and hand cleaner
  - ❑ Pump *(does it fit your tire valve?)*
  - ❑ Spare tube *(right size?)*
  - ❑ Talcum powder *(to dust spare tube before wrapping in a plastic bag)*
  - ❑ Plastic bag
  - ❑ Patch kit: fresh, unopened tube of glue plus several patches in a plastic bag
  - ❑ 2-3 tire irons *(plastic, aluminum or steel)*
  - ❑ Duct tape
  - ❑ Pocket vise
  - ❑ Spoke wrench *(does it fit your spokes?)*
  - ❑ 3-4 extra spokes taped to frame
  - ❑ Chain tool
  - ❑ 4 spare chain links
  - ❑ Chain lube
  - ❑ Extra rear brake cable *(cut off one end)*
  - ❑ Extra derailleur cable *(cut off one end)*
  - ❑ Extra nuts and bolts *(for all-purpose emergencies)*
  - ❑ Safety wire
  - ❑ 2-3 $CO_2$ cartridges *(will save lots of tire-pumping)*

# Canoeing List

☐ Canoe *(a very hard item to forget, but we know people who've had to go back for it)*

☐ Roof rack and tie-down line

☐ Paddles and one spare

☐ Personal Flotation Device: one per person

☐ Dry sacks *(or duffels lined with plastic garbage bags)*

☐ Waterproof map case *(or a large Ziploc bag)*

☐ Portage harnesses, tumpline *(to convert duffels, sacks into carrying packs)*

☐ Knee pads plus cushions for children

☐ 50-foot length of 3/8" line: one per multi-canoe party *(for rescue, etc.) Note*: Plastic lines float.

☐ Two 15-foot end lines *(bow and stern)*, 3/8" diameter

☐ Foul-weather gear

☐ Sneakers with drainage holes cut in them

☐ Watertight food containers

☐ Large sponge *(your handy "bilge pump")*

☐ Bailer

☐ Portaging yoke *(if required)*

☐ Optional
  ☐ Extra flotation *(styrofoam inserts)*
  ☐ Booster seat *(for children)*
  ☐ Legless, folding backpacking chair
  ☐ Rowing seat
  ☐ Golf umbrella *(or tarp for paddling in rain)*
  ☐ Thigh straps
  ☐ Extra tie-down straps
  ☐ Spray skirt

☐ Repair kit
  ☐ Duct tape
  ☐ Patch material *(appropriate to canoe-type, e.g., epoxy plus glass cloth scraps)*
  ☐ Swiss Army knife *(with scissors, sharp blades)*
  ☐ Small putty knife
  ☐ Sandpaper
  ☐ Paper towels
  ☐ Lacquer thinner
  ☐ Small paint brush

# Group Accessories, Individual Needs, Optionals

## Group Accessories

So many things on a camping trip can be shared that they become group accessories rather than private necessities. Some things everyone should have while other things individual members of the party may want. Here's a list of items which we take as shared goods on backpacking trips:

- Maps and permits
- Compass
- GPS *(global positioning system)* device
- Star chart
- Tree guide/bird book/ wildflower guide
- 2 boxes kitchen matches with sulphur heads (strike any- where). Everyone carries some in a Ziploc bag.
- First-aid kit
- Drugs and medicines
- Repair kit *(see itemized list)*
- Toothpaste, dental floss
- Small towel
- Liquid (biodegradable) dish soap and pot scrubber
- Lantern *(car/canoe/horse camping only)*

- Mosquito repellent *(two bottles)*
- Plastic spade *(to bury human waste)*
- Paper and pencil
- Camera, film, extra battery
- Extra pack straps
- Garbage bags *(one for each member of the party)*
- Extra Ziploc bags *(10-12)*
- Extra tent pegs
- Extra ground cloths/ ponchos *(one for each tent)*
- Backpacking (Sven) saw
- Book for reading aloud
- 2-person inflatable back- packing raft plus paddles *(when other weight considerations permit)*

## How Much Toilet Paper

This is the most poignant question of all. The answer is, "enough to satisfy everybody's expected needs." This includes cleaning pots, polishing glasses, sometimes lighting a fire, as well as the manufacturer's recommended use. We've found that two rolls are adequate for a six-day trip for two. Others require two or three times as much. This is a touchy point. Don't argue. Nobody's right; everybody's right.

## Individual Needs

Everyone should have the following:

- ❑ Pocket knife
- ❑ Sunglasses *(in hard case)*
- ❑ Matches *(from Group Accessories list)*
- ❑ Flashlight *(such as a Mallory AA compact flashlight or another weighing about three ounces with batteries, and which can be held in the mouth when both hands are needed)*

*Caution:* Remove batteries before storing for winter. This will avoid a corroded, ruined flashlight six months later.

## Optionals

Other things are optional in the eyes of some, but essential in the eyes of others:

- ❑ Ring clip to carry the car keys
- ❑ Fishing license
- ❑ Camera and tripod
- ❑ Binoculars
- ❑ Paperback book
- ❑ Toothbrush, toothpaste, comb, barrettes, ponytail bands
- ❑ Towel and bar of (biodegradable) soap
- ❑ Sanitary napkins, tampons, etc.
- ❑ Birth control devices
- ❑ Glasses case and extra glasses
- ❑ Contact lens solution
- ❑ Personal medications or prescriptions
- ❑ Nail clippers
- ❑ Playing cards, chess set, etc.
- ❑ Security blanket, stuffed animal, etc. *(Rick's daughter Sherri does not travel without her miniature pink plastic ponies and a generous selection of bath toys. They're always necessary.)*
- ❑ Walking stick

## *Tips on Sunglasses*

- Ultraviolet rays (UVA/UVB/UVC) are dangerous. Protect your eyes in strong light.

- General-use sunglasses should pass no more than five-percent UVB and eight-percent UVA. Check labels; ask questions.

- Sports sunglasses should pass no more than one-percent UVB plus equal amount UVA and visible light. Check labels; ask questions.

- Cyclists should wear shield-type glasses; *never* wraparounds which impair peripheral vision.

- High-altitude hikers (in bright sun/snow) should wear very dark wrap-arounds for full protection.

- Lens color: neutral gray or green yield the least color distortion.

- Use retainer straps if engaged in strenuous activity. *Canoeists note*: some retainer straps float and will prevent glasses from being deep-sixed.

## *Leave-at-Homes*

Some things, however desirable, should not be brought into the wilderness:

- deodorants, perfumes and other scented cosmetics, which all attract insects and some of which attract bears

- cassette recorders and other machines which don't come with headphones (why disturb other campers' searches for solitude?)

- guns, which are not permitted in designated wilderness areas and which can be dangerous in the close quarters of a camping trip

# Backpacking List: Equipment

## Tent and Sleeping Gear:

❑ Sleeping bags

❑ Ensolite, Ridge Rest, or Therm-A-Rest pads

❑ Tent, rainfly, stakes, poles (*Note: a two-person tent will not sleep three. Add another tent, rainfly, etc.*)

❑ Spare tent stakes

❑ Ground tarps/ponchos: one per tent

## Packs and Protection:

❑ Backpacks

❑ 4 straps per pack

❑ 4 extra pack straps

❑ Bear-proof storage canister (*for bear-infested parks*)

❑ Large green garbage bags (*or pack covers*)

❑ Ponchos/tarps (*as rain gear in addition to ground tarp for tent*)

❑ Stuff sacks for clothes and personals

❑ Day-pack (*or a strap-rigged stuff-sack to double as day-pack*)

❑ Flashlights plus new batteries and bulbs

❑ Dog packs, as necessary

❑ Child carrier, as necessary

## Cooking, Fire, Water Gear:

❑ 3 nested pots and lids

❑ Sierra cups

❑ Tin plates

❑ Spatula

❑ Forks and spoons (*or chopsticks*)

❑ Frypan

❑ Backpack grill

❑ Camp stove plus fuel and funnel

❑ Matches (*2-plus boxes; strike-anywhere type*)

❑ Lighter fluid/fire starter paste in tube or cubes

❑ Candle

❑ Scouring pad/sponge

❑ Aluminum foil (*2 folded sheets for baking*)

❑ Light mesh bag (*as dish drainer, suspended from tree*)

❑ Pair of garden gloves (*for cooking, wood gathering*)

❑ Sven saw (*for gathering dead wood*)

❑ Canteens/water bottles

❑ Collapsible water container

❑ Water-purifier system

❑ Food storage:

　❑ Plastic egg carton (*half-dozen or one dozen sizes*)

　❑ Plastic pill box (*as "spice rack"*)

　❑ Plastic bottles, jars (*as condiment, syrup, oil, margarine containers*)

　❑ Spare Ziploc bags (*10 each, small & large*)

# Backpacking List: Clothing, Boots

*For high-altitude temperatures: 20s-90s Fahrenheit*

- ❏ 1 pair pants *(jeans or cotton/canvas)*
- ❏ 1 pair shorts *(lightweight; doubles as swimsuit)*
- ❏ 3 pair socks *(inner and outer)*
- ❏ 3 underwear
- ❏ 2 cotton shirts *(one long-sleeved, one short)*
- ❏ Long johns *(cotton/polypropylene/wool)*
- ❏ 1 sweater or sweatshirt
- ❏ Down parka *(or Gore-Tex shell and layered sweaters)*
- ❏ Baseball cap or sun visor
- ❏ Wool (ski) hat
- ❏ Sunglasses *(with UV protection)*
- ❏ Boots

- ❏ Moccasins/tennies/reef slippers *(for stream crossings, fishing, in camp)*
- ❏ Mosquito-netting "hat" *(slips over visor; indispensable for "that" time of year)*
- ❏ Pocket knife
- ❏ Personal toiletries: *(mandatory)*
  - ❏ toothbrush
  - ❏ toothpaste, dental floss *(Group Accessory)*
  - ❏ toilet paper *(Group Accessory)*
- ❏ Personal toiletries: *(optional)*
  - ❏ comb/brush
  - ❏ barrettes/ponytail bands
  - ❏ razor
  - ❏ glasses case
  - ❏ small towel *(share)*
  - ❏ birth control devices
  - ❏ contact lens solution
  - ❏ nail clippers *(Group Accessory)*

# First Aid and Medicines

*Quantities for Four-Person Trip*

## *First Aid:*

❏ Moleskin *(1 or 2 packets)*

❏ Adhesive tape *(1 small half-inch roll)*

❏ Band-Aids *(12 assorted sizes)*

❏ Gauze pads *(6 assorted sizes)*

❏ Ace bandage *(1)*

❏ Butterfly bandages *(4)* *(Attention: mountain bikers)*

❏ Hydrogen peroxide *(Attention: mountain bikers)*

❏ Instant cold pack *(Attention: mountain bikers)*

❏ Tweezers/surgical locking hemostat *(1)*

❏ Small mirror *(for shaving, inspecting eyes, signaling)*

❏ Baby-wipes or similar "dry washes" *(4, unless there's a baby aboard, in which case thousands!)*

## *Drugs and Medicines:*

❏ Aspirin or its equivalent

❏ Mosquito repellent *(2 bottles for four people; look for "reduced DEET" on the label)*

❏ Sunscreen

❏ Lip balm

❏ Hand lotion

❏ Optional:
  ❏ Vitamins
  ❏ Neosporin/Bacitracin *(first-aid ointment)*
  ❏ Caladryl itching lotion
  ❏ Antacid pills
  ❏ Snakebite kit
  ❏ Aspirin with codeine
  ❏ Lomotil diarrhea medicine
  ❏ Electrolyte replacement tablets
  ❏ Athlete's-foot treatment
  ❏ Desitin/Zinc ointment
  ❏ Talcum powder *(Attention: cyclists)*

# Repair Kit

- ❑ Swiss Army knife
- ❑ 50-foot length of nylon rope
- ❑ Small vise-grips
- ❑ Heavy duty *("carpet")* thread plus two large needles
- ❑ Light nylon thread plus two small needles
- ❑ Nylon patch material *(called "ripstop" tape)*

- ❑ Patch kit for rubber raft
- ❑ Extra flashlight bulb(s) plus batteries *(two per flashlight)*
- ❑ Safety pins
- ❑ Spare clevis pins and key wires for backpacks
- ❑ Roll of half-inch adhesive tape *(see First Aid and Medicine List)*

# Maps and Permits

- ❑ Spare change for phone call
- ❑ Campsite reservation
- ❑ Fire permit
- ❑ Wilderness permit
- ❑ Fishing license
- ❑ Driver's license
- ❑ Automobile registration
- ❑ Road map

- ❑ Trail map
- ❑ Topo map
- ❑ Sea chart *(Attention: canoeists)*
- ❑ Waterproof map pouch or Ziploc bag
- ❑ Compass
- ❑ Star chart

# Traveling with a Dog

- ❑ Check that dogs are permitted at your hiking venue
- ❑ Dog pack
- ❑ Dog food *(minimum two packets moist food per day)*
- ❑ Leash
- ❑ Flea collar

- ❑ Name tag with address, phone number
- ❑ Water bowl for car
- ❑ Extra food for car
- ❑ Tweezers/hemostat *(to extract porcupine quills, etc.)*

# Kiddy List: For Babies and the Very Young

❑ Whistle *(hang a loud one around child's neck)*

❑ Extra clothes: *(depending on ages and affinity for dirt)* 4 pairs of pants, 3 shirts, 4 pairs of socks for one-week trip

❑ Diapers: *(mix of cloth and disposable)* one dozen each for one-week trip, cloth for sunny weather and disposables for inclement weather

❑ Diaper-washing gear: 2 plastic buckets, biodegradable soap, clothes line

❑ Baby wipes

❑ Tie-on hat

❑ Rain suit *(for use at meals as well)*

❑ Plastic bags as "outer" socks *(quart/gallon size depending on size of foot)*

❑ Life jacket *(for swimming, boating, canoeing)*

❑ Syrup of ipecac *(induces vomiting)*

❑ Fever-scan forehead-type thermometer

❑ Baby Tylenol and chewable amoxicillan

❑ Zinc oxide/Desitin

❑ Games

❑ Books

❑ Favorite toys

❑ Comforters: stuffed animal, favorite blanket, etc.

❑ Edible hiking incentives!

# Fun and Games

❑ Paper and pencil

❑ Playing cards

❑ Star chart

❑ Tree guide

❑ Wildflower guide

❑ Bird book

❑ Binoculars

❑ Books

❑ Camera, including extra battery and film

❑ Musical instruments

❑ Pocket chess/checkers

❑ Lightweight games

❑ Frisbee

# Fishing List

*Quantities for 2 Anglers, 5-Day Trip: Spinning Tackle Only*

❑ Fishing license
❑ Telescoping rod
❑ Rod case *(to prevent snapping in backpack)*
❑ Spinning reel, lubricated and in good working order
❑ Fresh 4-pound test monofilament line on reel
❑ Spare 4-pound test line *(one small spool)*
❑ Spare 2-pound test line *(one small spool)*
❑ 6 bubbles
❑ 8 flies
❑ 10 lures *(vary by weight, size, color)*

❑ 2 bottle corks *(to carry lures, five per cork)*
❑ 8 snap swivels
❑ 2 packets No. 12 hooks (six per packet), for 8"-15" fish
❑ 1 packet No. 14 hooks (six per packet), for 8"-12" fish
❑ 8 weights: split shot, egg sinkers *(vary in size, weight)*
❑ Bait *(bottled salmon eggs; power bait; cheese; worms)*
❑ Worm threader *(optional)*
❑ Net
❑ Large Ziploc bags *(the "tackle box")*
❑ Swiss Army knife

# Food Shopping List

*No quantities given here. See Food Planning list in Chapter 5.*
*If drying food at home, purchase fresh fruit and vegetables up to a month in advance of trip; purchase meat and poultry no more than a week before trip.*

❑ Flour
❑ Cornmeal
❑ Sugar
❑ Yeast
❑ Baking powder
❑ Baking soda

❑ Powdered milk
❑ Semi-sweet baking chocolate
❑ German sweet baking chocolate
❑ Instant hot chocolate
❑ Tea

- ❏ Coffee
- ❏ Rice
- ❏ Beans
- ❏ Mung beans
- ❏ Pasta: spaghetti
- ❏ Soba
- ❏ Instant ramen
- ❏ Chinese noodles
- ❏ Nori (Japanese seaweed)
- ❏ Raisin cookies
- ❏ Ginger snaps
- ❏ Ak-Mak crackers
- ❏ Saltines
- ❏ Instant soups
- ❏ Instant oatmeal
- ❏ Cooking oil
- ❏ Sesame oil
- ❏ Rice vinegar
- ❏ Soy sauce
- ❏ Maple syrup
- ❏ Brandy
- ❏ Hot sauce
- ❏ Lemon/lime juice
- ❏ Salami
- ❏ Cheese
- ❏ Margarine
- ❏ Dried fruit/fresh fruit for drying
- ❏ Vegetables for drying

- ❏ Dried meat (jerky) or turkey/chicken for drying
- ❏ Nuts: almonds, cashews, filberts
- ❏ Eggs/powdered eggs
- ❏ Raisins
- ❏ Powdered ginger
- ❏ Garlic
- ❏ Cinnamon
- ❏ Cayenne
- ❏ Paprika
- ❏ Tarragon
- ❏ Basil
- ❏ Thyme
- ❏ Curry powder/*garam masala* (pepper, cumin, cinnamon, cardamom, coriander, cloves, mace, nutmeg)
- ❏ Salt
- ❏ Pepper
- ❏ Car food
- ❏ Chicken
- ❏ Salad stuff
- ❏ French bread
- ❏ Cheese
- ❏ Juices
- ❏ Fresh fruit
- ❏ Dog food
- ❏ Baby food

# Your Master List

- Select from the lists only those appropriate for your trip. (See Appendix, pages 401 to 455 for clip-out lists.)

- Eliminate duplications.

- Add individualized items.

- Combine into handy packet. Our own master list for backpacking trips consists of three pages:

## *Equipment:*

❑ Cooking Equipment (page 155)

❑ Camping Equipment (pages 155, 158, 159)

❑ Dog Equipment (page 158)

❑ In the Car (pages 149, 152-154)

## *First Aid, Clothing and Fishing:*

❑ First Aid & Repair (pages 152-154, 157, 158)

❑ Clothing (pages 156, 159)

❑ Fishing (page 160)

## *Food:*

❑ Food Planning and Shopping (pages 136-137, 160-161)

# CHAPTER 7

# Getting There

## Packing Your Car

Six hours in a car headed for that dream wilderness vacation can be hell on wheels. You know the feeling: too many bodies, not enough space, sticky buns melting down the dashboard, maps misplaced, a couple of wrong turns and a flat at high noon. Welcome to the Great American Highway.

Is there any relief in sight? Yes, as a matter of fact, if you plan the car ride the way you would the rest of your trip. For one thing, if you pack that old Ford Fairlane right, you'll save a lot of grief. The cooler with lunch and snacks belongs right there within hand's reach—especially little hands. Stowed in the trunk, it's useless. So are the water bottles, several of which you have frozen the night before. At hand they're terrific in that Olds steam bath. They'll melt slowly, giving you hours of cool, thirst-slaking drink, while heading down Interstate 5. The maps need to be in the navigator's general vicinity, not on the kitchen table or in the duffel lashed to the canoe on the roof.

A little foresight goes all the way to the ranger station. Got cash for tolls and the last roadside hash house in northern Minnesota? Credit cards for the tow truck? Games and books for the kids? A big litter bag? It all seems obvious, but we've found over the years that a car checklist gets us off with most of the Absolutely Indispensable Items on board. (See Chapter 6.) It's amazing how comforting it is to know that the car jack is in the trunk and actually works, that the dog has a water bowl which can be filled at gas stations and rest areas, that stick-on window shades will protect the sunward passenger(s) from drowning in a sea of sweat before the last K-mart passes from sight, and that a small pillow, strategic seating and sensible packing may let someone actually get a bit of sleep.

Okay, that's the inside of the car, where cabin fever and expectations of the wide open spaces vie for attention over the long haul. What about the other places? Up on the car rack is the gear that can't fit in the trunk and that you don't need until you arrive at the final carpark. Once off the main highway, it's going to get coated with an archaeological layer of dust if it's not covered with a tarp. Once it starts to rain....Obvious, isn't it? But one piece of advice. Secure the tarp carefully before heading out of the driveway. Loose ends or edges soon begin to flap maddeningly on the freeway, sounding like an awning shop in a hurricane.

In the trunk will be the other stowables, including most of the food for your camping trip. All of the liquids—cooking oil, soy sauce, syrup and hot sauce—will stand upright in their containers, packed securely against leakage. Otherwise they'll come up empty by the time you pack the backpacks at the trailhead. And since it'll get colder as you gain altitude and night falls, warm clothing should be easily available.

A car packed properly is a lean, mean pleasure machine. Enjoy it. But don't make the trip into an endurance contest. Rarely are wilderness trips tied to deadlines. If you need to make 14 pit stops rather than the planned three, because someone wants out of the car, make 'em. And let the dog out each time. Instead of eating lunch in the broiling sun on some highway turnout, check out the local park in the little town just off the road. (A good travel guide should have that kind of information. Take one along.) A 10-minute detour may rescue nerves and flagging humor. Lunch under an old New England elm at midday in early August will soothe a savage breast, or at least let the driver snooze in the shade. Properly rested and fed, the car crew will waltz through those final dusty miles up the old logging road to the trailhead or put-in point along the river.

## Packing Your Pack

We usually arrive at the trailhead after dark. We crawl into our sleeping bags, and the next thing we know, the sun is coming up. Time to hit the trail. Half awake, we squint mournfully at the little Datsun station wagon that brought the four of us here. The seats are piled with coats and parkas, the back is full of food boxes, and strapped to the roof rack is a monstrous heap of packs, ponchos and stuffsacks. How will we ever fit all that gear into our packs? And how much can we possibly pack into the backcountry on our backs?

Everything seems so disorganized the first morning that it's a miracle when we square things away. But somehow it all fits into the packs, and somehow we contrive to pack it into the mountains. We just keep telling ourselves that the packs are always heaviest and the hike always hardest this first morning. And each day, as we hike farther away from civilization, the load gets lighter, our bodies get stronger and the packing gets easier.

How should you pack a backpack? First decide what you'll need during the day. What does the weather look like? Will you need easy access to rain ponchos and plastic garbage bags to cover the packs? Or will you want to change into shorts at midday? A change of clothes, along with sunglasses, suntan lotion, maps, candy bars, and other small essentials need to be within easy reach. Lunch and munch food should also be easily accessible. Plan to take pictures at every scenic point? If so, keep your camera in a handy pouch.

After the small, reachable pockets have been filled, the main compartments can be packed. It may sound obvious, but keep in mind that whatever goes into the pack first will come out last. Also, heavy items should go next to your back and as high in the pack (between shoulders and waist) as you can get them. (The latest packs have compression straps which allow the load to be pressed toward that ideal carrying point on the back.) The pots and pans, stove and fuel go in first. Heavy food packages, such as flour, rice and beans, go next. That two-pound block of cheddar cheese (less some for lunch) falls in the "heavy" category too, as does the collected works of Charles Dickens.

Once those are packed, separate the rest by function. We usually make one compartment the "drug store/emergency room." Another is the "hardware/fix-it shop." You might designate a "candy store" as well. Save the lightest items—ponchos and Ensolite pads—to strap onto the top of the packs.

Organizing by function lends itself to packing as a group.

One person may have the cheese, another the utensils and spices, and a third might end up with two sleeping bags and an inflatable raft. One person could be responsible for all liquid containers: cooking oil, maple syrup, vinegar, etc. Make sure this pack always stays upright. No one carries more than he or she feels capable of. And if a shoulder or neck begins to ache after two miles, we reorganize, trading a heavy sleeping bag for a lighter Ensolite pad.

There's room to strap things on the top and bottom of most packs. A stuffed sleeping bag, rolled-up poncho, tent or stuffsack full of clothes are easy to trade if one person's pack is too much for weak knees or a bad back. But be careful. A rule of thumb is that anything hanging below your waist "feels" about 50 percent heavier than it would up next to the middle of your back. Anything strapped to the top of the pack feels about 75 percent heavier than it really is. And whatever hangs behind you in the middle of the pack gains a good 100 percent because it is so far behind, swinging as you walk.

When strapping on pads, tents and stuffsacks, it's important to double-knot everything. Each stuffsack gets tied into a double-bow. Each strap gets wrapped back around itself, then knotted. Never leave anything that might work loose as you hike. This is especially important if you're the last person in line. We've had a few instances where things fell out of stuffsacks or off packs, but usually the person immediately behind noticed. If you're last, the wool sweater you drop will probably stay lost. And when you're shivering at night, you'll become a lifelong convert to the double knot.

A couple of other tips from the school of hard knocks. Don't keep your maps or permits in your pants pockets. They'll invariably get wet from sweat, fog or rain. Once that happens, and the colors and lines start to run together, they become difficult to use at all. In fact, most books recommend keeping maps in a plastic bag inside the pack so they won't get wet in a sudden downpour (or if they're below a cracked bottle of vinegar, a leaky tube of suntan oil or a broken egg).

Take care packing your fishing rod, too. On Rick's first backpacking trip, the rod stuck out a good 18 inches above his pack. While he managed to avoid low overhanging branches for the first two days, he accidentally knocked his pack over during a rest stop on the third day, and the top 18 inches of his rod snapped

**Packing the pack**

MAP IN MAP POUCH

PONCHO, TARP, SLEEPING PAD

STOVE POTS, WATER FILTER, FISHING GEAR

FUEL CONTAINER REPAIR KITS

MEDICINE KIT

CLOTHES

HEAVY FOOD (RICE, BEANS, ETC.)

LUNCH, SNACKS

WATER BOTTLE

SUNGLASSES, CAMERA

SLEEPING BAG, TENT

off. The rest of the trip he fished with a "splinted" fishing pole.

Most "backpacking" rods come apart in small sections or collapse ("telescope") to a small size. They can simply be placed in the main compartment of your pack. But many spinning and fly-fishing rods don't break down small enough to be protected inside the pack. They need to be secured to the outside of your pack, enclosed in a hard case or tube.

If the weather's been wet, try to keep the waterlogged rainflies and ponchos separate from the tents and sleeping bags when heading out the next day. The tents and sleeping bags may be damp in the morning, but they won't be nearly as wet as the rainflies. Pack them separately, even if it means breaking up a logical pair, such as tent and rainfly or sleeping bag and ground-cloth. You need not pack everything in the same manner each day, or even from morning to afternoon. Also, remember that your backpack is a natural drying platform. Wet socks? Dripping poncho? Hang them securely from the pack as you hike, rotate them occasionally to get the sun on all sides, and by the end of the day, they'll not only be dry, but fresh and aired, too.

Finally, your belt or belt loops can act as an extension of your pack, though don't forget to secure things on your belt—knives, gorp pouches and compass—with the same care you take with things hanging off your pack.

# Adjusting the Pack to You

Three things connect you to the pack: two shoulder straps and a hip strap. All three should be padded. Unpadded straps tend to cut into clothes or skin. It's best to have someone help you with the initial adjustment. Then, when the straps are right, you might want to put in a safety pin or tie a knot to prevent them slipping as you walk.

Adjust the hip belt first, with someone holding the pack against your back. The belt should rest on your hip bones tightly enough to hold the pack there. Then, tighten the shoulder straps so the pack is held upright but doesn't pull on your shoulders. The pack should actually ride on your hips, which support most of the weight. The shoulder straps are meant to take very little weight. They mainly keep the pack in position, straight up and centered over your hips. As you hike, the pack should not cut into your back. Sometimes a misplaced belt buckle or stove piece will protrude and become a pain. Sometimes shoulder straps cut into shoulder bones. They can usually be shifted sideways to get a better fit and temporary relief. Also, the spots on each hip where the pack makes contact might get a little sore.

**Fitting the pack**

SHOULDER STRAPS LEVEL WITH, OR AN INCH OR TWO ABOVE THE SHOULDER

BACK BANDS SHOULD BE TIGHT AND POSITIONED FOR MAXIMUM COMFORT

HIP BELT SHOULD RIDE ON THE PELVIS

If you choose an internal frame pack, be sure all the straps are loose while fastening on the hip belt. Then tighten the shoulder straps to get a snug fit. Most of the weight should be on your hips. Finally, tighten the two "load lifter" straps just enough to keep the pack from falling away from your back.

Occasionally you'll want to shift weight to rest your hips. Simply loosen or release your hip belt. The pack will drop about an inch, your shoulder straps will tighten and the weight will now be on your shoulders. Experiment as you walk—more weight on the hips or shoulders—until you find the right distribution. After a day or so, pack, back and hips all seem to mesh comfortably into an incredible walking machine.

## Packing Your Bike

Load panniers bottom to top, heavy to light. Whether you have two or four panniers, they need to be symmetrically balanced. To get this right, weigh each pannier load and make fine adjustments. No sense falling into the canyon because your port side panniers are hauling you off the track.

The front-to-rear load should be balanced as well. One way to do this is to set the bike on two bathroom scales, one under each tire. Lean the bike against the wall, load the panniers, then climb on. Have a friend read the two scales, then make weight adjustments between rear and front till the readings on the two scales are close.

Some mountain bikers prefer to use a tight-fitting, internal-frame backpack rather than panniers. That results in a higher center of gravity, but you'll be less likely to snag, rip or tear the pack on rocks or logs.

## Packing Your Canoe

Like bicycles and dogs, canoes yearn for low, even weight displacement. If you lean the old Philco radio against one gunwale, lean the laundry hamper against the other. Steady as she goes. Pack the dry sacks or duffels as you would panniers—vertically, heavy to light. Set them, balanced like panniers, at midships, offset by passenger weight. The aim is to trim the canoe so that neither bow nor stern are too high out of the water. Weight displacement figures, telling you how much the canoe will safely carry, vary according to size and design of the craft, and you should know them.

As with backpacks, stow stuff you'll need while paddling in easy-to-reach places, and keep the map and compass (and your

**Packing and loading the canoe.** *All items should be packed in waterproof dry sacks or plastic garbage sacks. Heavy items should be centered on the bottom of the canoe with lighter items stowed above and around them. Necessity items should be stowed on top for easy access.*

powder) dry. Tie fishing rods and other non-floatables securely to the canoe, and spare paddles lightly to same. You may need them in a hurry. *Bon voyage.*

## Tips on Getting Acclimated

The week before your trip, you run around like the proverbial headless chicken, lists in hand, trying to arrange every detail while working an eight-hour day. You're up half the last night trying to finish packing. You leave early the next morning, drive hours to the trailhead and immediately begin to hike. You're at 7,000 feet, walking uphill, with the pack at its maximum weight. Your body is not accustomed to so much strain. All day you feel dizzy, nauseous and achy. That night your brain feels like it's trying to come out of your ears. You're camped at a beautiful lake at the top of the world, and all you want to do is crawl head first into your sleeping bag until the pain goes away.

Luckily this isn't inevitable. It needn't happen to you. With a little forethought and a few precautions, you can avoid Early Trip Discomfort (ETD). Here's how:

- Even if you have only a week for your trip, plan a whole day to drive to and sleep at the trailhead. That first night in the thin air will help acclimate your body to the first hard day on the trail.

- Eat breakfast. Anything which gives you some protein, fat and carbohydrate is adequate. Cheese and crackers, a granola bar, or peanut butter and jelly make a fine beginning. Most of your initial hiking will usually be over by early afternoon, so breakfast is the main source of energy for the day's challenges.

- You might want to use salt and aspirin. (This applies only to people not adversely affected by either of these substances. Salt can cause nausea; aspirin can upset the stomach.) The salt can be in food, such as salami, jerky or crackers. Some people take it in pill form or direct from the container. We also often take one or two aspirin first thing on the morning of a long hike.

- Start early. This is hard for the leisurely breakfast junkies, but that's invariably the most pleasant time to hike. The cool air is refreshing and you don't lose a lot of water through sweating. The sun isn't blinding, the rocks aren't hot, and by the time the afternoon thundershowers begin, you've arrived at your destination and set up camp.

- Wear sunglasses and a hat or visor. You've heard of snow blindness, caused by the intense glare of the sun off a white snowfield. The same problems can be caused by reflections of sunlight from gray granite boulder fields. The mountain air is thin and the mountain sun is bright. While hiking, it's best to keep your eyes and face covered, especially for the first few days.

- Drink plenty of water. Stop on the trail when you get thirsty. Drink a few cups before steep uphill climbs. We carry a minimum of a quart of water for every two people, but it's not a bad idea to start with even more. You can always pour it out if you're sure that the streams you expect to cross are running full, and you have the time to filter or purify the water. Several times we planned to fill the canteens at a stream which was running on the map but dry as a bone on the trail. That meant several miles of dry throats. In the spring, there's water everywhere. In the fall, however, be careful. Extra water is heavy, but it's much more uncomfortable to hike when you're thirsty.

- Don't be afraid to stop and rest, or vary your pace, which often accomplishes the same thing. The destination is rarely over that next rise. A steady pace will get you there with fewer problems and less pain than the sprint-and-collapse method. Cyclists know all about problems of pace and can teach hikers a thing or two. They shift gears, we shift legs. Remember the tortoise and the hare.

- A walking stick enhances balance and takes weight off the feet and knees. An old cross-country ski pole will do, though spendthrifts will want the "telescoping" variety for uphill and downhill shifting.

- Keep the carbohydrates coming. Stop for energy food about mid-morning, or carry a pouch of gorp to munch as you hike. We like semi-sweet baking chocolate, raisin cookies and ginger snaps. Sweets give you that instant pick-up you can use along the trail. If you know your limits and don't push too far beyond them, and if you're not afraid to stop and relax, you'll do just fine. Two days into the trip, you'll be hiking farther, breathing easier, resting as often as you like without fear that you won't get "there," and carbo-loading like a champ.

# Crossing Streams

Many trails are constructed so that horses can cross streams. The trail crosses a stream at a level, wide area with a rocky bottom. A horse doesn't care about stepping stones. A horse also doesn't care if the water is one or five feet deep. Unfortunately, it's not as easy for a human to wade across in three feet of freezing, rushing water. A stream is always a wise place to take a break. Make it a point to ponder before you ford. Make it another point to scout the stream up and down for the best crossing.

One spring, Rick and a friend were among the first backpackers on the trail after a wet winter. About halfway to their destination, they came to a stream running high, fast and cold. Sam, a first-time backpacker, took one look and decided that wading was not part of the original contract. So they renegotiated. Rick would wade across with both packs, one at a time. Sam would head a few yards upstream to a stretch of water which was deeper, but strewn with enough high boulders to let him step across. Sam balanced gingerly on the first boulder. He hopped to the next, then the third. Two more to go. The second-to-last boulder was unsteady. So was Sam. With arms flailing and eyes wide, he plunged into the foaming torrent. Luckily, he only got a few bruises and soaked his clothing. Had he decided to boulder-hop with his pack on—including his sleeping bag and all his extra clothes—it would have been a lot worse.

Late in the summer, when there's not much water flowing, you can hop from boulder to boulder without much trouble or danger of getting everything wet. But early in the spring, it's better to wade. You'll have to get wet. It's that simple.

Well, hopefully it's that simple. A pair of sneakers or tennies, which you've brought along to use in camp, come in handy here. The water is usually so glacial and the bottom of the stream so rocky that going barefoot is painful and dangerous. Just remove your socks, sling your boots around your neck, don the Converses and head in. If you didn't bring any sneakers, wear your boots, *sans* socks. Once across, drain your boots and put on a pair of dry socks, which will soak up most of the moisture as you hike on. At your next rest break, change into a second pair of dry socks, and by the time you get to camp, your boots will be dry.

During the spring, the level of a stream rises noticeably during the day as the sun melts snowfields high above, and it falls again each night as snow refreezes after sundown. The best time to cross a stream is early in the morning; the worst time is late in the afternoon.

Be especially careful of stream depth: *do not* confuse clear water with shallow water. Mountain streams are often so crystal clear that what looks like a two-foot bottom might actually be six feet deep. It's a good idea to cross once without a pack to be sure you won't encounter any dangerous flows or depths. It's much easier to bail out and turn back with nothing weighing you down. Caution is the key.

It helps to carry a big stick or wading staff when crossing. You can distribute weight more evenly on three points than on two. As long as you walk slowly and carefully, with the staff downstream, and don't mind numb feet and legs, you'll get across safely.

What about using a rope? It's possible, of course, and sometimes necessary. But our own rule of thumb is this: If a crossing is so dangerous that it *requires* using a rope, don't do it unless it's *more* dangerous to stay where you are. In an emergency, a two-person party with about 150 feet of five-millimeter climbing rope can ford a stream, as follows.

• Step one. The rope is tied to a tree, wrapped once around the forder, then held by the anchor person who stands downstream of the forder and pays out rope from the coil. The anchor person is *not* tied to the rope. The forder always faces upstream while crossing. If she/he falls, the anchor person hauls her/him in. Once across, the forder waits while the anchor person unties the rope from the tree. The length of free rope is then hauled over and tied to a tree on the far side.

• Step two. The rope extends from the tree to the original anchor person, who wraps it once around the waist and then tosses the remaining coil to the first forder. The first forder walks downstream of the second forder and pulls in slack as the second forder, also facing upstream, makes her/his way across.

It may take two trips to get a single backpack load across a stream, because the stuffsacks which hang from the pack can't be left in place if the water is deeper than about two feet. When you're wading with a pack on, it's advisable to unbuckle the hip strap. That way, if you fall, you can release the pack easily and not

**Crossing a stream with two people**

**Crossing a stream with three people**

get swept under or downstream by it. Once you've safely negoti-
ated the stream and carried all the gear over, dry off, take another
rest, repack, put the return crossing out of mind, and head up
the trail.

If a log happens to be across the stream just where you want
it, don't let such luck go to your head. Take your time. Log walking above a rushing stream can feel like walking a tightrope. And
like tightrope walkers, you may want to use along stick or staff as a
balance rod. Ideally it should be longer than you are tall, but it
doesn't have to be. Hold it even with your waist as you cross the
log. Also, beforehand, come to terms with everybody's sense of
balance in your party. The surest-footed member should take the
packs over. The unsurest should sit, straddle the log and inch
across. And if you're traveling with dogs, one of you may have to
wade across with them on a leash. We've never been able to
persuade our pooches to walk the log.

Summing up, when wading across a stream: 1) Wear sneakers
or boots but not socks; 2) Check depth; 3) Use a big branch as a
wading staff; 4) Face upstream when crossing; and 5) Unbuckle
your hip belt.

## Hiking in the Rain

We once made a list of "Things to Do When it Rains," and
hiking was at the top. That's because huddling in a tent or under a
poncho can get awfully boring, and keeping everything in a
campsite dry *without* cramming it all into the tent with you is a
practically unattainable goal. If you can keep dry, hiking in the
rain is fun, pretty, and actually easier than hiking in very hot
conditions.

There are many "systems" for keeping yourself and your
pack dry in the rain. We prefer to wear short ponchos designed to
cover a person without a pack on. These can be used around
camp without dragging in the mud, and while fishing in the rain.
The special ponchos designed to cover you and your pack are so
long they can be unwieldy. If the weather is warm, a short poncho
and a pair of hiking shorts are ideal for a walk in the rain. So are
plastic bags as foot protection for very young children who don't
wear boots. They go over the socks and into tennies, cheap protection against soaked socks and feet.

Special backpack covers are sold at outdoor stores, but garbage bags are a lot cheaper and just as light. Punch two holes and feed the shoulder straps through before hoisting the pack onto your back. The garbage bags flap a little in the wind, but they keep the packs very dry. Buy the thickest ones you can find and carry one or two extras.

Sometimes there may be no getting away from a prolonged spell of foul weather. However, many summer rains are of the "afternoon thundershowers" variety. They come on fast, last a short time, then move off. Often, the mornings are gorgeous, and at 2 p.m. there's not a cloud in the sky. But by 4 p.m. you find yourself huddled in a forest as the thunder crashes around you and huge hailstones bounce off your head.

From the comfort of a cottage, a thundershower can be spectacular; at 8,000 feet, near the timberline, however, it can be terrifying and dangerous. You need to keep dry and stay safe—if possible among the smaller trees. Easy access to the plastic garbage bag and a poncho will let you stay dry and cover ground at the same time. Or, if you prefer to sit it out, protect your pack while you watch the thunder and lightning roll across the mountain tops. The poncho will keep most of you dry, and while you end up with wet boots, socks and maybe pant legs, it's rarely enough to worry about.

However, when it rains, beware of hypothermia! It needn't be cold out—even wind and rain at 60 degrees Fahrenheit can make you dangerously chilled. The symptoms are uncontrolled shivering, followed by the inability to think clearly. Don't wait to reach your destination to deal with this. Get out of the wind and your wet clothes. Start a fire or crawl into a protected sleeping bag. Drink something hot. Huddle close to others who are dry. Rest and get warm.

If you're going to an area where it rains hard or for days at a time, this may require serious preparation. Foul weather gear (like that used on sailboats), special backpack covers, boot covers, Gore-Tex® wool parkas (which ingeniously keep the rain out while letting your sweat escape)—all or some may be necessary. Check out the weather conditions before you leave home. Most camping trips, however, are predicated on sunny weather, and wet ponchos or socks can usually be dried out in the warm morning sunshine.

# Mud and Snow

From the hillside above, a lush Sierra meadow looks like a golfing green. But trying to hike across it in the first few weeks after snow melt is like trying to run through tapioca. Each step is an effort. Your boots get stuck in the mud. We've known people to lose their boots entirely in the slimy goo, pulling up their feet to find nothing but a sock on. If there's an alternative trail which skirts the springtime meadow, take it. It will save time, physical effort and mental exhaustion. It will also save the ecologically fragile meadowland.

Snow is normally considered a problem for winter backpackers, but it can stay on the ground long into the spring and summer. The trouble is, snow can be hard or soft, icy or slushy, sticky or slippery. It can be a pleasant stroll or a dangerous slide, and you need to be careful on it.

Mornings, snow is usually icy and slick. A very slight gradient can throw your feet out from under you. Even worse, it might start you sliding down an icy slope into a freezing river or lake. As the day progresses, the snow begins to melt. By late afternoon, it may have turned into sticky slush. Like mud, this kind of snow is a disheartening inconvenience. It slows you down but isn't likely to hurt you. Beware, however, of "snow bridges" which may collapse during hot afternoons. A snow bridge is a layer of snow—perhaps a foot or more in depth—over a large hole caused by flowing water (from melted snow) underneath. Step on the bridge in the morning, and it will hold you. Do so in the afternoon and you'll fall through. A likely spot for snow bridges is next to large rocks, which absorb heat and melt snow from below at the same time the sun melts it from above. The result is a sort of ice cavern whose sides are prone to collapse when weight is put on them.

Our advice is to try to avoid hiking over more than short stretches of snow. If you must, hike early. When you get to the snow line, don't plan to go much farther. If you know in advance that there will be a lot of unmelted snow on the trail, bring a pair of crampons to strap onto your boots. These are spikes which allow you to walk on icy or slippery snow without much danger of falling. They won't help in very soft, powdery snow, for which you need snowshoes or cross-country skis, but they will get you safely through most springtime snow conditions with a minimum of bruises and sore muscles.

The other thing to consider before you tromp off above the snow line is that firewood up there is probably buried beneath a foot or two of wet slush. That makes cooking and warming a great deal more time-consuming and complicated. If you have to be up there, bring a good camping stove and fuel that works efficiently in cold weather. (See Chapter 4 for tips.)

# Biking Tips: On Road and Off Trail

Cyclists need rest breaks, carbohydrates, liquids and common sense, just as hikers do. Biking with a heavy load, even on flat, well-paved stretches, is a lot more strenuous than the day-biking you may be used to. Take a break. It can be short and sweet (if you let the chocolate melt in your mouth, not in your pannier). It's also restorative. Toes, hands and butt go numb if you're too long in the saddle. Stop and walk some circulation back into these useful body parts. In fact, walk the bike up steep grades when the going gets too hard. Nobody's timing you. You can't come in last.

Like hikers, bikers need to have warm clothes and foul weather gear close at hand. The speed of a bike increases the wind-chill factor impressively. A 15-mile-per-hour wind blowing in the face of a bicyclist traveling at 25 miles per hour downhill is the equivalent of a 40-mile-per-hour wind chill. Lesson? Dress warm in these conditions. And remember, as wind causes a bike to yaw with a heavy load, rain makes brakes less efficient. Steering feels sluggish, and sudden stops on steep grades can be dangerous. Hard weather makes a bike hard to control. It also cuts down visibility—yours and passing motorists'. Take it easy. Stay warm, dry, keep a helmet on and, where appropriate—such as on mountain trails or dusty roads—use safety glasses to protect against dirt, twigs and bugs.

# Up the Creek with a Paddle

Unlike most hikers and bikers, canoeists can arrange to go in one direction only. Downstream, for example, or (with a streak of masochism) upstream, or across a lake or inlet. With a car pickup at the end of the route, the work load can be regulated more easily, or at least predicted with more certainty.

Predictability goes only so far, however, and you need to take

basic precautions whether headed
down the Grand Canal or across the
local duck pond.

- Boarding and exiting the canoe
  are the choicest times for tipovers.
  Learn the proper techniques
  before entering the mill race.

- Prepare for rough water even if
  you don't expect to encounter any.
  When the wind comes up on a
  lake, things can get dicey. You can
  get swamped. Pull into shore,
  paddle in the lee of the land, take
  time out on an island. Turn *into*
  swells rather than taking them
  broadside.

- Learn (from a Red Cross course, a
  guide or an experienced partner)
  how to "read" a river. The
  current usually flows faster in
  midstream and does tricks (which
  only physicists understand) at
  sharp bends. Stick to the inside
  rather than the outside of a big
  bend for safer, easier handling.
  Ledges, rocks, "holes" and falls all
  create flow problems which can
  be solved by proper handling
  techniques. We are not talking
  about *The African Queen* or riding
  Niagara in a barrel, but foreknowledge is a useful "hiking"
  tool on the river. Even then, be
  prepared to get lost on occasion.
  The current is not always the
  surest guide to the main channel.
  Rain-water may obliterate a
  familiar river bank; drought may

**Boarding a canoe**

turn a navigable passage into marshland. When you dead-end up
the Blackstone River, take a nosh break, scratch your head, mull
over the situation, sigh, backtrack, and be comforted by the fact
that your second cousin Rudy and a lot of other experienced
deckhands have been here before you.

- Use your ears as eyes. You can often hear a waterfall long before you can see it. At that point, be prepared to pull in and portage around the fall. Unless you're Humphrey Bogart or Katherine Hepburn.

- Island hop at high tide. You don't want to return to shore when the tide's out for the simple reason that you'll have to schlep the canoe over hundreds of feet of mudflats.

- A rain poncho worn in high wind becomes a sail. Beware!

- As backpackers need to learn how to cross a stream, canoeists need to know how to walk a canoe through passages too rough or swift for paddling. You may have to use end lines attached to bow and stern to "track" a canoe upstream (or "line" it downstream) around obstacles. This can be done from shore, if not too impassable, or in wading water along the shore.

- Portaging engages the same techniques and attitudes as backpacking: slow and easy, lots of rest breaks, have a bite to eat. A portaging yoke allows one person to portage a canoe, but beware of neck injuries if you don't know how to use one. Two persons can easily carry a 70-pound canoe over the portage. You may have to go back for the packs if the load is too heavy, but call it a day-hike and enjoy. Local up-to-date printed guides may indicate portage trails, while older trails may still be marked by blazes. If you're unsure of where you are, take five and reconnoiter. Land bridges between bodies of water are usually accessible and short. Get a fix on the easiest route first and then heft the canoe and packs.

**Lining a canoe**

TWO MAN LINING

ONE MAN LINING

# Dealing with Fears and Phobias

As we noted earlier, you take all of yourself into the mountains when you go backpacking. It's impossible to leave the bad parts behind. This means that your whole party has to deal with anyone's particular hang-ups, and you should know what they are before you go. But you should not let them stop you from going. Hal, for example, is scared of heights. Really scared. He learned it to his surprise about 20 years ago when he was halfway up a Mayan temple pyramid in the Yucatan. Convinced that he was about to pitch backwards into space, he clung for dear life to the safety chain, inched to the top, sat down in a cold sweat, fantasized helicopter rescues and other humiliations, and eventually invented one of mountaineering's newest and most useful (if less graceful) techniques: "rappaporting."

Rappaporting is a play on the word "rapelling" and·has nothing in common with it. To rappaport is to get from Point A to Point B *very carefully*. That's it. Any way you can do it, do it. It usually involves a good bit of frantic caution, inelegant clambering, and the use of the "sidle," as you inch your bottom and those jellied appendages called legs over the loose shale toward the haven of a firm root or branch or a six-million-year-old boulder. You can tell you're rappaporting when other members of the party, no more experienced than you, move confidently, even nimbly, on two sure feet over the same terrifying terrain.

In short, it's perfectly possible to live with a fear of heights in the mountains and enjoy the trip thoroughly. It's okay to laugh *with* the person who makes fun of his or her own phobia. It's *not* okay to laugh at them. A foreknowledge of the problem, a helping hand, plus a whole lot of support and common sense gets one, and therefore everyone, through.

The same is true in camp. One of our friends has an abiding fear of spiders. It means taking extra care that tent flaps and mosquito nettings are *always* tightly secured. And it means doing a careful spider search for that friend whenever the request is made. A little extra effort and support makes enjoying the outdoors both possible and fun for someone whose fears might otherwise preclude it.

Support for somebody's fears doesn't mean going gooey with concern or "manly" with false bravado. The person who is scared of heights more often than not doesn't need your hand, just a little more time. And the person who's scared of the dark or of mountain thunder doesn't need to be surrounded by firm shoulders to rest on. Unaffected presence is usually enough. In any case, let people know before you set out what may bother you; let other people know also that it's all right to have their own bothers.

## Mosquitos and Ticks

In late spring, mosquitos can literally drive a hiker crazy. It's not so bad when you're camped, as you can escape into your tent and close it up. But when you're hiking through a meadow with a cloud of mosquitos buzzing around your ears and eyes, and sometimes up your nose or into your mouth, you will devoutly wish to be anywhere else on earth. Repellents, such as Cutter's or one of the war-surplus "jungle juices," will stop the little critters from biting, but it's the humming and buzzing that makes you want to throw yourself off the nearest cliff. Rest stops are pure purgatory, and it's not unusual for you to hike twice as fast and far as planned on total insane energy.

Two suggestions besides the repellent: mosquitos like grass, forest, water and deep shade. So when you stop to rest, pick a spot as high, barren, rocky and windy as you can find. Second, if you hear rumors in advance of a particularly bad mosquito plague in the area you're headed for, you can get lightweight mosquito-net hats which drop a circular netting from a round hat to your shoulders. This will keep the mind-wrenching buzzing away from your ears, eyes and nose. A long-sleeved shirt and some repellent on your clothes will allow you to hike through even the worst mosquito-infested marshes.

Mosquitos aren't the only varmints out there. Deer ticks carry Lyme disease and something called HGE *(human granulocytic ehrlichiosis*—glad you asked). These aren't your familiar swollen blood-suckers but rather nearly invisible nymphs about the size of the dot over this "i." They get into the bloodstream and go quietly to work. Lyme disease may take months or even years before serious symptoms (aches, pains, fatigue, fevers) appear. HGE comes on like a monster flu. Both are serious. What to do? Cover up. (See page 130 for instructions.)

# Maps

In Chapter 2, we showed you how to obtain up-to-date Forest and Park Service and topographical maps. The first kind, which show distance and direction but not elevation, are fairly easy to read. Trails are marked by broken lines, roads by unbroken lines, unimproved dirt roads by double hash marks, marshes by grass clusters, that sort of thing. The symbols are standardized and you can learn them fast. Best of all, the symbols lie on a flat-plane surface (hence the technical name of the maps: planimetric) and are easy to locate and follow. Topographical maps, which show distance, direction and elevation, require some explanation.

A topographical ("topo") map does for the backcountry traveler what a street map does for the urban visitor. It helps in the planning of your trip: what's the safest and most convenient route between the trailhead and final destination, how far you want to hike each day, how high you want to climb, which day trips are possible and which aren't worth the effort, what kind of scenery you're likely to encounter—shale and rocks, long vistas, lakes and streams, high mountain meadows or granite passes. They're a little harder to read than the handy street plan of the South Bronx, but you won't, repeat won't, want to be without one in the wilderness.

## How To Read a Topo Map

The most noticeable things on a topographical map are the thin brown lines running in circles and arcs and squiggles all over the place. These are contour lines, lines corresponding to a specific elevation above sea level. Here's how they work. Imagine a small island in the ocean. At low tide, we might draw a line around the island where the water meets the shore. At high tide, we might draw another line around the island. Perhaps high tide is 10 feet above low tide. So we now have two contour lines, one drawn at low tide, one 10 feet higher drawn at high tide. Imagine next a super high tide, 10 feet above normal high tide. We draw another contour line around the island. And then a fourth, fifth and sixth line each where the water meets the shore if the water level keeps rising at 10-foot intervals.

If the lines were large and distinct enough, we could draw the island as it looks from an airplane. Six lines, each representing the shape of the island at a specific height above sea level, would be visible from the air. Now, suppose one side of the island is a sheer 50-foot cliff. All the contour lines will converge on this side when viewed from above, because they are nearly on top of each other. The opposite side of the island might be a wide sandy beach. Our first contour line rings the beach at low tide. Much of the beach is underwater at high tide. So our high tide line (10 feet above sea level) appears far from the first line, nearly at the edge of the jungle. And our line 20 feet above sea level does not touch the beach at all; it's a line through jungle and rocky cliffs.

The lines are widely spaced on the beach area of the island and close together where there are cliffs. This is our first clue to reading topo maps. Two or more lines very close together mean a very steep grade or cliff. Two or more lines wide apart mean a gentle slope or relatively flat area. Thus, for example, a trail that crosses contour lines is a steep trail and one that runs parallel to the lines is level.

Our illustration below demonstrates this. There are places where the lines form U's, V's and figure-eights. Whenever the contour lines form U's or V's, they indicate either a ridge or a gulley/streambed. A ridge is indicated on the map by a set of U-

or V-shaped lines pointing toward lower elevations. A streambed or gulley is marked by a set of U- or V-shaped lines pointing toward higher elevations. On the illustration, our ridge ends in a cliff overlooking the sea, and our streambed/gulley begins high up, at the 60-foot line, and descends to the sea in a series of inverted V's. Imagine the view from the air. When the 60-foot line describes an inverted V—facing into the island center—it is traveling along the walls of a streambed. So are the other, lower lines. When the lines describe a V pointing out to sea, they are running along the slopes of a ridge. The figure-eights, observed from above, describe two mountain peaks separated by a fairly gentle slope in one direction (east-west on our illustration) and by fairly steep gulleys in the other direction (north-south). This gives the contours a kind of pinched waist effect which translates into a figure-eight. (If you want some practice reading contour lines, see Bjorn Kjellstrom's *Be Expert with Map and Compass.* He even provides a couple of quizzes.)

The following four simple rules explain the contour lines on a topo map:

- Lines close together mean steep gradients.

- Lines farther apart mean gentle gradients.

- V-shaped sets of lines pointing to higher elevations mean gulleys or streambeds.

- V-shaped sets of lines pointing to lower elevations mean ridges.

## Scales and Distances

A topographical map has two scales shown at the bottom margin of the map. One indicates distance as the crow flies, the other elevation between contour lines. The distance scale is called "SCALE," and is represented by a ratio number, such as 1:24,000, meaning one inch on the map represents 24,000 inches (or 2,000 feet) in real linear space. Under that notation are usually three calibrated line figures which represent distance in miles, feet and kilometers. The elevation scale is called "Contour Interval" and tells you the vertical distance between the contour lines, such as "Contour Interval 40 Feet." To make all these squiggles easier to follow, most topographical maps give real elevation readings along darker-brown contour lines every 100 or 500 hundred feet. Thus, for example, 7,500 will be marked along a dark brown line. There will then be several light brown contour lines and then another dark brown line with an 8,000 on it. You can figure out how hard or easy it'll be to climb up or down those 500 feet by reading the contour lines in between. Close together means tough going; far apart, it's a piece of cake. In either case, it'll certainly take you longer than walking 500 horizontal feet along a dry meadow. By interpreting distance and elevation readings, you can plan how long and how far you can go in a day.

Topo maps come in different scales. If you see a map with a scale of 1:250,000, (meaning one inch on the map represents 250,000 inches or 20,833 feet in real linear space), a large distance can be crammed onto it—a whole national park, for example. That's great for a panoramic view of where you are in relation to the rest of the world, but it won't have the kind of detail you want for backpacking. Thus it is called a "small-scale map"—it contains a large amount of space but a small amount of detail. Always try to get the map with the most enlarged detail. Even if you have to carry two or three high-detail, large-scale maps to cover the distance you want to go, it'll be worth it. They foretell all the nooks and crannies, spurs and outcroppings, feeder streams and marshes you'll encounter, something to be thankful for.

## How to Interpret Map Dates, Colors and Symbols

Many maps, as we've noted, are outdated. Topo maps, mostly made in the 1950s from aerial photographs, then verified by survey teams, are great on permanent features such as mountains, but often not so great on impermanent roads and trails. Check along the lower border for the date of the map, and if necessary, try to locate a more up-to-date Forest or Park Service map to use in conjunction with it.

The picture from which a topo map is made was supposedly taken in a year of average rainfall during the dry season—late autumn in most parts of the country. The map should show all lakes and rivers at their driest stage. Still, there's no guarantee they'll be the same size or shape when you arrive. Much depends on the season and the latest annual rainfall. When you hike in the spring, that small creek marked on the map by a dotted blue line may be a raging torrent, too tough to cross. That same creek in the fall may be bone dry just when you were planning to stop for some fresh water. On the other hand, large lakes, rivers, meadows and most physical contours on the map will be just as they're supposed to be. Occasionally a flood or avalanche will have rearranged the topography, but on the whole you can rely on the topo map for contour accuracy.

Maps also show structures visible from the air when the area was photographed. Some are houses, cabins, ranger huts or run-down old barns. Some may have rotted away completely. Take care not to depend on the topo map to find shelter from a storm. Those structures—even bridges—may no longer exist.

Finally, map colors are important. Gray represents treeless, rocky areas. White signifies snow or glacier. Green means forest. Mottled green or green-white shows meadowland. These colors help you hike by describing the terrain. Thus, when you plan to leave a marked, manicured trail, it's important to consider not only contour and streams but also the kind of terrain you're heading into. A nearly flat manzanita forest is impassable. But the next hillside, while steeper, may be a pine forest crisscrossed with deer trails. Rocky areas are the easiest to cross but may take some climbing to get to. They're found mainly above the treeline at higher altitudes. Some terrain must be analyzed on the spot, but a great deal can be learned from the topo map's colors and symbols.

## Bicyclists' Maps and Routes

Most people who tour on bicycles use automobile road maps and bike tour guides which include maps, elevation changes, distances and campgrounds. Here are a few hints if you are planning a bike tour without a guidebook.

- Try to stay on the smallest rather than the newest or widest roadways. Local county roads are quieter, safer and more interesting than state highways (interstates don't permit bicycle traffic). Color- or letter-coded maps distinguish road size, paving and jurisdiction.

- If there are no elevation markings on your map, look for mountain peaks and rivers. Once you determine which way a river's flowing, you can usually figure out how the road will run, uphill or down.

- Topo maps allow you to plan routes and adventures much more accurately than road maps. Large-scale, 1:250,000 topo maps of National Park or Forest Service lands are great supplements to up-to-date road maps.

- It is as important for a mountain biker to learn to use a compass and topo map as it is for a hiker or backpacker. Covering ground is one thing, knowing where you are is another. Get lost once and you'll become a convert to orienteering, the art of reading maps and a compass.

## Canoeing with Map and Sea Chart

Canoeists use topo maps, too. The larger the scale (1:24,000 is a larger ratio than 1:240,000) the better, for what's at stake is the ability to pinpoint bends in the river, inlets, shoals, eddies, falls, flats, swamps and marshes. The curse of the backpacker is shared by the canoeist: a topo map seems never to be new enough, even if printed yesterday. Nevertheless a river- or lake-borne camper without a topo map is a camper in trouble. Streams can degenerate over the years into swamps. Small lakes can dry up. In tandem with a good, current local canoe guide, a topo map and the ability to read it will get you in and out of the wilderness in high fashion rather than high agitation.

What the topo map is to land, the sea chart is to water. In fact, a sea chart is nothing but a topo map turned on its head. It reads the elevations and declensions under water. Coastal and island canoeing, large-lake canoeing require some ability to read sea charts and usually tide charts, too. The big problem here is fog. It's the great disorienter, and without a compass and sea chart, you may be in the pea soup longer than is healthy. Get your bearings before the fog rolls in. Fix your destination on the compass and chart. Stay calm, take frequent readings, and trust the needle, not your nose.

# Trails

A trail is constructed to certain specifications. It must be a certain width and level across its span. It must have drainage ditches or gutters to channel runoff rain water. Tree branches have to be cleared to a certain height above the trail to allow horseback riders to pass unimpeded. Also, a trail is allowed only a limited angle of inclination. If the grade is too steep, the trail must switch back and forth (hence "switchbacks") so it doesn't exceed the angle at which a horse can comfortably walk up or down. Of course, not all trails comply at all points with all rules. But the vast majority of park trails were built with these standards in mind.

Trails are also maintained regularly. Trees are cleared, brush is trimmed, paths are rerouted on a regular basis in areas of flood damage or avalanche. Trail crews are hired or volunteer to bring the original trail back up to specifications and are paid by the mile. The work is checked by rangers who simply hike the trail behind them, and most parks keep records of trail maintenance. Occasionally a park will abandon a specific trail because it is used so rarely, or to give that particular sector of the backcountry an opportunity to regenerate. Sections of an unmaintained trail will disappear almost completely in three to five years. If you're planning to take what looks like an "out of the way" trail, it might be a good idea to check that it's being maintained before you begin. Any trail shown on the topo map but not on the more up-to-date Forest Service map should be regarded with suspicion. It may not be there any more.

## Don't Cut Corners: They'll Wash Away!

It's difficult to construct switchback trails which won't wash out in the rain. To do this, the trail needs to have drains and runoffs in fixed places. When hikers decide it'll be faster to avoid the switchbacks by going straight up or down the slope, their footsteps tend to dig new drains across the switchbacks. When the rain begins to follow those new, irregular paths downward, the trail quickly erodes. The message, therefore, is clear and simple. When hiking switchbacks, don't cut corners. It'll be easier on your knees and feet to avoid a steep descent with a heavy pack and, more important, it saves the trail for those who come later.

# Losing a Trail

### Shortcuts

Shortcuts are highly unpredictable. The terrain can be tricky or thick with vegetation. There's also the danger of getting lost. Shortcuts often take longer than the route you're "cutting short."

On one of our first mountain trips we decided to take a shortcut. It looked easy on the map: half a mile saved and all downhill. When we started out, we immediately ran into almost impenetrable brush—six-foot-high manzanita—solid and prickly. We couldn't see where our feet were landing. We got poked in the eyes. At points it was so steep we had to hang by the nearest branch, then slip and slide our way down. When the grade leveled off, we found ourselves over our heads in bush grass. The going was muddy, hot, slow, frustrating and just plain dumb. We reached our destination more exhausted and tattered than if we had stuck to the trail. Luckily, we weren't hurt or lost.

## Lost and Found

Even if you avoid shortcuts and have the right maps and a compass, it's still not hard to lose a trail. Trail markers may have been destroyed, junctions and turn-offs may be indistinct, or the trail may simply peter out at points. Finely- crafted drainage ditches or dry streambeds might look more like the trail than the trail itself. Deer paths in the woods may seem to be the main one until they cross others that look exactly alike, at which point you begin to wonder where your partners went.

On a recent four-person trip, we found ourselves lagging while our two companions wanted to hike faster. It was decided that they'd wait for us at the signpost to "Silver Lake" or at a trail junction. They bounded off without any maps, while we plodded slowly. About an hour later, we realized that there'd been neither a sign nor a trail junction, and that we were well beyond Silver Lake. Doubling back, we found the signpost, broken off and obscured by brush, next to the junction, which was in an area too rocky and sandy to be seen. Meanwhile, we had no idea if our companions had found the lake or not. So Hal sat at the junction with the packs while Rick hiked a mile to the lake, found no one there, and returned. Then Rick sat with the packs while Hal hiked down the main trail until he found our friends drying off after a trailside swim in a tiny lake they assumed was Silver Lake. Soon we were back together, but not without relearning a couple of lessons. First, never assume trails or crossroads are well-marked or marked at all. And second, never split up in unfamiliar territory.

There are several other things to keep in mind, too. The most important is that as long as you have drinking water, food and the shelter you carry on your back, you can make camp almost any-where. If you can't find the trail, simply hunker down, take time to mull things over and meanwhile, enjoy your surroundings. Also, never let that pack out of your sight as you wander around in the woods looking for Route 66. And, for that matter, instead of plunging blindly ahead into the unknown, try to backtrack; that'll usually return you to square one and get you safely on your way again.

Often even a well-maintained trail can disappear as it crosses granite faces or other rocky terrain. There are no trees with blaze marks or ribbon markers to keep you on course, no boot prints in the dust. No dust! Only rock. You've stopped without a clue. Go back to where the trail is last visible. Check on your map how far you'll be walking over the rock face. Maybe it doesn't make any difference exactly where you walk if you can key in on your destination, and if the terrain is equally safe in the approximate vicinity of the trail. Above all, look for cairns (sometimes called "trail ducks"): three rocks set one on top of the other by some thoughtful hiker who knows the route. They are usually at regular intervals along the rock face or through an open, trackless meadow. Anyone who has ever lost a trail will be grateful to those anonymous friends who took the time to stop and build a cairn.

**Trail ducks**

Other hikers will not only sometimes mark the trail, but will also have advice that keeps you on course. Ask lots of questions of those coming from the opposite direction. Where are they coming from? How far is the nearest lake, campsite or watering spot? Where's the best fishing? Does the trail become hard to follow or is it well-marked all the way to your destination? Then offer information. Sit down, pull out maps and go over routes. Tell them which way to go. Remind them that a trail marker a mile back was hit by lightning and is no longer visible. They'll be as grateful to you as you are to them.

If, after all your efforts, you can't find a decent, well-marked trail, turn back. You may be on an unmaintained track. An alternative may have been constructed since your map was made. If you go on, assume that things may get worse and that for all practical purposes you will be doing a "cross-country"—that is, an off-trail hike.

# Off-Trail Hiking

Slow and careful are the keys to cross-country or off-trail hiking. Cross-country hiking never works out exactly as planned, and you need plenty of time to stop, figure and rest—off-trail "bushwhacking" tires you out faster than on-trail hiking. Give yourself as much time to hike cross-country as you can. To do this, stay on the trail as long as possible before leaving it for the off-trail leg of your trip. Never start out late in the day if you have to be somewhere by nightfall. You might need a whole day to negotiate the rock fall or steep ravine that stands between you and fabled Lake Mooselookmeeguntuk. Reaching your destination is always very slow; the return trip over now-familiar terrain will be much faster.

We usually average a quarter mile per hour off the trail in the high Sierra or Rockies, half a mile or more in the Alaskan tundra or the high desert of Nevada. We never plan to cover more than one or two miles in a day. To start as early as possible, we camp near the point where we leave the trail. We always lay out our route in advance using the topo map, which is not difficult for such short daily distances. Just look for a route between two points that involves the least change in elevation. Try to avoid places where contour lines run close together. Even if only two lines seem to converge, that's a sheer 40-foot cliff—too steep to climb without experience, confidence and the proper gear. Keep the contour lines as far apart as possible when you plan a cross-country trek.

You must be careful with every step when off the trail. You can't let your mind wander to the scenery or to the snows of yesteryear. Eyes must stay on the ground just ahead, checking every footfall. There's lots of balancing to do, especially when hiking through brush. It saps strength, tears stuffsacks, snags fishing rods and anything else not properly battened down on your pack. If you have to go through brush, make sure all ties are double-knotted, and all zippers are fully zipped. Fishing and tent poles must not stick up above your pack or they will be broken by low-hanging branches. You might fall. If you do, fragile objects inside your pack—camera lenses, eggs—may break unless they are properly cushioned. Liquids not tightly contained and encased in plastic will run all over everything.

Keep your hands free to clear brush or grasp at branches to pull yourself along. Mark your route if possible with bits of colored cloth or rope tied to branches so you don't get turned around or lost. And stay together! It's too easy to get separated and lost in thick growth.

Hiking over boulder fields is more common in the high mountains than crashing through brush. It helps to wear hiking boots (rather than tennis or jogging shoes)—the soles are not torn up by walking and balancing on the corners of large boulders, and the ankles aren't twisted by the precarious angles. Again, keep your hands free; use them to hold on when you can. Try to test each rock or boulder with light foot pressure before putting all your weight on it. If the rock is wobbly, be careful. It can send you and your 40-pound pack tumbling down a field of granite boulders.

It's generally easier to hike uphill than downhill when you're making your way off the trail. You can plan an uphill route from below, with a good view of the entire hillside. Going down, you're likely to come to a steep gradient you couldn't see from above. Suddenly you're staring down at what seems like a sheer cliff.

Never assume a straight line is the safest or easiest way from here to there. Use the topo map wisely. Once you figure out the best route, try to stick to it closely so long as it proves safe and feels right. The important thing is not to walk yourself into a place you can't return from.

If the going gets too tough, you can stop, turn or go back. There's no requirement to get anywhere by any time. Never feel pressured to continue even your own pre-planned route. Stay flexible, stay cool and don't be afraid to change plans and routes. There are other lakes to fish, other streams to camp along, other routes to the same place. There's no need to do something you're afraid of off-trail. Knowing that is the difference between a novice and an old-timer.

## Getting Your Bearings Off-Trail

How do you prevent getting lost off the trail? Plan well, stay highly alert and observant, and keep track of both what's ahead and what's behind you.

First, pre-plot your route carefully. Know, for example, that it will take you over a ridge, along the flank of a 10,000-foot peak, down a granite field, then up a stream and through a meadow toward the lake. Keep these features in the forefront of your mind. Before you leave the trail, take a hard look around for all distinctive landmarks: a strange rock outcropping, a tall barren tree once struck by lightning and thus black against the green forest, a distant mountain peak. Note what lies in the direction you're headed. Think how the appearance of these landmarks will change as you hike cross-country. And look for features you know are on your route.

You may or may not plan to return by the same route. Nevertheless, you may need to get back to the trail at this same spot, especially if your route proves impassable and you must turn around. Thus, you might want to mark your trail. Cairns, colored ribbons strung on branches and retrieved if you return, green vegetation hung on a barren branch—all give you a sense of confidence that is more than worth the additional time you spend doing it. Also, if you do intend to come back the way you went in, a marked course will save you one final embarrassment—walking right past the maintained trail. It's surprisingly easy to miss an "obvious" trail, and frustrating, doubling back till you do find it. If you mark everything from the start, you can avoid that problem on a day when you may have to hike out, drive home and get to work.

More precise than sighted landmarks or marked routes is a combined use of the topo map and a compass. They can help you decide where you are and where your destination is relative to you. There are whole books on the use of compass and maps (see the Book List on pages 381-386); what we give you here is a quick digest of the main points.

Whether you have a compass or not, practice with the topo map on the trail, before you really need it. When you reach open places, try to locate where you are on the map by observation alone. Do this by orienting the map to two or more observable landmarks, then draw imaginary (or real) lines from them back toward "yourself." Where the lines intersect is approximately where you are.

### *Plotting position by observation*

Now do the same thing with your compass. First orient the map. That means getting it aligned with the real world out there. Set the map on a flat rock, placing the edge of your compass on the magnetic north (MN) declination line marked on the bottom margin of the map, and twist map and compass together until the north-pointing needle is lined up with the 360 or 0 degrees mark on the compass. (See page 196.) Now your map is properly aligned and you're ready to go to work. Take sightings on two or more identifiable landmarks, the farther away (though still represented on your map) the better.

Here's how you take a sighting. Hold the compass in your hand. Point the Direction-of-Travel arrow toward the landmark. (The assumption here is that you have an "orienteering" compass; see page 194.) Now twist the compass housing till the north-pointing needle is lined up with the orienting arrow at the bottom of the housing. That's all. Just read the number of degrees which come up on the edge of the housing facing the landmark.

If you don't have an orienteering

### *The compass*

compass, face the landmark, holding the compass in front of you. Slowly rotate the compass until its north-pointing needle lines up with the N on the housing. Don't rotate yourself! Now read the number of degrees facing the landmark.

Say the reading is 330 degrees. Once you have a first reading, take a second or third on other landmarks, the farther from each other the better. In the illustration below, the second reading is 32 degrees. Now go back to your oriented map, set one edge of the compass on the first landmark and then rotate the compass, still keeping the edge in contact with the landmark, until the north-pointing needle again lines up with the orienting arrow, giving you a 330-degrees reading on the map. Draw a line along the compass

### Map orientation with a compass

2. Extend magnetic declination line with pencil. Place edge of compass on magnetic line.

3. Rotate map & compass until needle points to 360° or 0° "DIRECTION OF TRAVEL."

1. Place map on flat rock or ground away from metal objects. (set compass at 360° or 0° "DIRECTION OF TRAVEL")

Anchor map down before removing compass.

### Triangulating position with a compass

POSITIVELY IDENTIFIED PEAKS

ORIENTED MAP

330° MAG

32° MAG

330° M

32° M

WRITE DOWN BEARINGS & DRAW THOSE BEARINGS ON MAP

YOUR POSITION IS WHERE PENCIL LINES CROSS

edge back toward yourself. Repeat for the second landmark and maybe a third. Where the lines intersect is where you are. You can now determine from the map how much farther it is and how rough the terrain will be between your present location and your destination.

*For more help reading maps and using a compass, you can go straight to the U.S. Geological Survey on the Internet.*

A final word of caution. Your sightings, readings and orientings may be correct but there is still a chance you'll end up with approximate, rather than pinpoint, locations. You may trudge on for an hour, reach the top of a rise and expect to see the promised lake. Instead, you see another rise, like the bear that went over the mountain. You take more readings and bearings and come up with the same results. You have moved, but those distant peaks on which you sighted are so far and so high that to them you haven't moved at all. Keep the faith, check your progress vis-a-vis closer landmarks, and take it slow and easy. The lake is there, over one or two more rises, and if your footing is sure and the sun is up, you'll arrive in time to unpack, set up camp, drop a line and cook a fine trout supper.

*Chapter Seven*

## The Global Positioning System (GPS)

You're hopelessly lost. The trail you thought you were following has turned into a prickly thicket unfit for Br'er Rabbit. Not to worry. You reach into your pack and draw out a small walkman-sized electronic gizmo. You push a few buttons. Within moments, the screen lights up and tells you exactly where you are, how far you've come, how far you have to go, and in which direction. It will direct you to the nearest lake, the closest ranger station, or back to camp. The choice is yours.

Since December 1993, a multi-billion-dollar system of geographical location satellites has been available for use by anglers, aviators, and anyone else who doesn't want to get lost. Called the Global Positioning System (GPS), these satellites beam down signals year-round, day and night, rain or shine. If you can catch those beams, you can find your position within around 300 feet horizontally and about 500 feet in altitude. All you need is a clear shot at the sky and a GPS receiver. Once as expensive as $1500 and as heavy as three to four pounds, today they cost less than $300 and weight about nine ounces, including a couple of AA batteries which keep 'em running for five to ten hours. They're also completely waterproof. In years to come they're sure to get smaller, cheaper and more sophisticated. Before you purchase one from a camping store, check marine supply catalogs for the lowest prices.

A GPS unit works anywhere you have a straight shot at a broad chunk of sky. Trees don't seem to cause signal problems, but mountains, cliffs and tall buildings may block or reflect signals, causing "shadows" and errors. The lightweight units are sometimes slow and may take as long as 10 minutes to check the sky for satellites and calculate your position when first turned on. But when checked again, they remember which satellites were up there and find the signals faster.

How sophisticated will these things get? Today, lightweight GPS units display longitude and latitude; you have to find your position on a topo map. In a few years, the screen will be large enough to display the map. The GPS will plug into your home computer to load in the road and topo maps for the trip. While you're still in your car, the GPS will help you find that dirt road only the locals know. And once on the trail, it will keep tabs on your rate of speed and figure your estimated time of arrival at

camp each night. It will
consider both altitude and
distance in plotting the best
route off-trail to Long Lost
Lake for a day of fishing; then
guide you back to camp that
evening with a maximum
error of about 100 yards. The
expensive GPS devices used
today by power boaters already
can do all those things.

QUAD·HELIX
ANTENNA

DOT·MATRIX
DISPLAY

Will GPS devices also get more
accurate in the next few years? Not exactly. The satellites
belong to the Department of Defense, which purposely messes
with the signals to foil spies and other Enemies of the State.
However, they do promise you a location within 100 yards of
reality 95 percent of the time, and within 300 yards 99 percent
of the time. Unlike compass reading errors, which have a
tendency to compound as you walk onward in a slightly
skewed direction, GPS readings will never err by more than a
few hundred yards. As much fun as we have fiddling with our
map and compass, they may soon become technological
artifacts. In another decade, all anyone will need in the wilderness will be a GPS and a few extra batteries!

CHAPTER 8

# Setting Up Camp

## Choosing a Campsite

A campsite must meet two minimum requirements to provide the kind of comfort you've promised yourself after all those miles on the trail. It has to have access to water and offer a sheltered place to sleep. You usually find those essentials where the trail crosses a stream or meets a lake. Ideally what you want is a level, sheltered area, complete with fire ring and tent sites. Often you'll get just that, because the people who build or maintain trails have been there first and know that people and pack animals require these amenities. Try to stop at a site that's been used before rather than hew out a new one from scratch. You'll do less harm to the environment and work a lot less hard as well.

Canoeists want the same sort of deal—convenience, shelter, comfort and a great view. But they need one other thing as well: access *from* water. It's hard as hell to haul a 70-pound canoe up a vertical incline to Pocahontas' Boudoir, and you may have to settle for Joe Sixpack's favorite inlet and pool hall. Nose around and ask questions beforehand.

Be forewarned that campsites vary with the season. That babbling brook you had your heart set on may have withered away late in the season, leaving you with a waterless gully. Mapmakers draw stream lines to conform to springtime reality. Check water sources as you hike. If the map shows blue and you find sere dust or a mud flat, suspect that other streams in the same area will be dry as well. Ask the local rangers about drought (or flood) conditions before heading into the backcountry. Choose your campsites accordingly.

Our favorite campsites are high mountain lakes, full of fish but not full of campers. Most picture-postcard lakes—the kind you see on the cover of *Sunset* magazine—have wide and well-maintained trails to them. They're accessible to large groups, either on foot or horseback. The crowds at these lakes can get oppressive, especially on weekends and holidays. We like to get off privately to swim, sun and have fun. Usually this means scouring the map for a mountain lake off the trail, one we can call our own, if only for a few days.

We also love to catch, cook and eat trout—another consideration when seeking an off-trail lake on the map. Trout require a lake deep enough so that it won't freeze solid during the winter. Lakes at or near the tree line get colder sooner, remain frozen longer and cannot support the insect life that fish need to survive. In addition, the higher the lake, the less firewood there is for our cooking projects. You'll find the best fishing at a lower-elevation lake with water flowing through it. If it's surrounded by meadows, don't plan on catching anything but mosquitos. In fact, you might find nothing but mud if you get there late in the year. Steep cliffs and sheer rock walls rising from one bank are an indication of a deep section, which may contain fish.

At times, you'll want to spend a night on a ridge or peak—without access to running water. There's nothing so spectacular as the night sky seen from a summit. Sunsets and sunrises alone make it well worth the inconvenience of carrying water up there. We figure about a quart per person will get us through dinner and a morning hike down without doing any dishes. We wash them later when we get to the next water source (though never in it).

Once you've arrived at fabled Lake Whitefish, choose a campsite with care. A free-running stream or wilderness lake requires a light touch and distance. Foul it and the whole idea of backcountry camping goes down the drain. Locate tent, fire ring and washing-up areas at least 100 feet away from the water, and even farther if it's safe and convenient. That way, spills will be filtered somewhat should they get back into the water. Remember, too, that any water you drink should be treated, boiled or filtered first: Giardia stalks even the clearest springs.

Many hikers bring a collapsible, two-gallon container for storing water at the campsite. This is especially convenient if your camp is some distance from your source—for example, if the mosquitos are swarming down near the lake. In the absence of such a container, make do by filling all your pots and canteens, then covering them with lids or metal plates. Do this before dark. It's hard to carry two pots of water and hold a flashlight as you scamper up a steep grade to your campsite.

# Tentsite

The sole requirement for a tentsite is that you can sleep there. This means different things to different people. We knew one old-timer who never carried an Ensolite pad. Instead, he'd stop early in the afternoon and work for at least two hours preparing his sleeping site. He'd meticulously smooth the earth, pick out all the rocks and twigs, then lay down a soft bed of pine needles and fallen leaves. Finally he would spread his sleeping bag down on the soft bed just in time to go fishing.

Before you choose a tentsite, look carefully at the drainage system of the surrounding hills. More than once we've set up in a likely looking area, flat and sandy, near a lake, only to discover it turned into a large mud puddle in the rain. Mountain rains often come suddenly and hard. Flat sandy areas can become Lake Superior in 20 or 30 minutes, putting you and your tent under two or three inches of water.

Another consideration in choosing a tentsite is the ability to stake your tent. While newer dome-type tents do not require stakes, most small tents need secure staking in the ground. This makes them difficult to set up in granite or sandy areas. In such spots, lay the stake flat on the ground and pile rocks on top of it, or wedge it in a granite rift. Sometimes you can tie the tent ropes to boulders or tree branches instead of to stakes. Sandy campsites present similar problems: the stakes shift easily or pull out. Every time the tent is bumped, the stakes slip a little and pretty soon the tent sags like a suspension bridge. Both rocky and sandy areas require extra care when you enter or leave the tent.

In foul weather, stake both rainfly and tent. The rainfly should completely cover the tent in order to shed water several inches away from the base of the tent, beyond tarp or groundcloth. Even then, you may still be in trouble if the uphill side of the rainfly funnels the water against the tent side or onto the groundcloth. The telltale sign will be a puddle inching across the floor of the tent in mid-storm. At that point, your options are cut to the bone. Use the small towel or sponge you've brought along to sop up the water. Wring out and repeat. This will keep you busy and your mind off murder. Get out and fix the rainfly's drain-off system. Or slosh around till the rain passes, make do as well as you can for the rest of the night, and hope for warm sunshine in the morning to dry you out. Next time, site the tent farther from that potential Victoria Falls.

A rainfly should also be stretched or staked so that it clears at least an inch of the tent itself. If the rainfly simply lies on top of the tent, internal moisture from breath and sweat won't be able to escape, and by morning, you'll be cold and clammy even if it's warm and dry outside.

Finally, one word about digging drainage ditches around your tent: *Don't.* They scar the land and, when filled with runoff water, erode the earth. You can literally diminish the wilderness.

Many people camp with only a sleeping bag and poncho or tarp. The poncho can be rigged up between or under trees or bushes to form a roof and keep you out of the rain. A turned-over canoe can shelter you from a light rain, and rigged with a tarp, it can provide adequate protection if the wind is not up. If you use a tarp, carry some light nylon cord to secure the ends. Some tarps have grommets or reinforced holes; otherwise use Visclamps (purchased separately) which act as portable grommets. Also useful are four metal tent stakes, which can anchor a tarp to the ground.

As long as the ground stays fairly dry, such shelter is adequate for most summer showers. A tentless pack is that much lighter, but it takes a fair amount of ingenuity to stay dry in really stormy weather (to say nothing of mosquito-proofing). And a wet sleeping bag can take days to dry out. Even if you plan to sleep under the stars, put up your tent (or tarp) as a precaution. Nothing changes faster in the mountains than the weather.

## Campfires

Campfires have a magic all their own. Staring into the fire late at night gives you a sense of peace and security that is hard to match at home. Our trips into the mountains center around hot meals, which invariably center around the campfire. Cooking, baking, sipping hot chocolate, heating water for dishes and washing all require a well-tended hearth.

Wilderness campfires consume tremendous quantities of wood, however. In many areas of the mountains, that wood is becoming very scarce, and fires are not permitted. This is particularly true at high elevations and along well-traveled trails. Even where it's legal to gather wood for a campfire, follow your conscience rather than the letter of the law. If you see that there's little deadfall wood left, leave it. Give nature a breather. Sacrifice the fire. Use the stove instead and cook your meals quickly. Or eat cold food on evenings when you camp in impacted areas. You may be rewarded for your fireless evening by a host of interesting sights and sounds usually obscured by the light and crackle of the fire.

Let's assume, though, that you're camped at a lower elevation lake or stream, a couple of miles off the trail. There's plenty of dry wood on the ground. You plan to stay here a couple of days and your mouth is already watering with culinary intentions. First you need a fireplace.

A backcountry fireplace is nothing more than a circle of rocks with earth in the middle. Fires feed a constant shower of sparks into the air. While there's little wind, these are entirely harmless. But a sudden gust can blow the sparks toward combustible material, and you can quickly have a forest fire on your hands. If your campsite already has a fireplace, use it. Just be sure to clear the ground for four or five feet in all directions and check for dead, dry branches hanging less than 10 feet directly over the fire area.

For cooking and baking, we usually modify existing fireplaces, or construct new ones of our own design from scratch. The back of the fireplace is made narrow to support a small camp grill. The front of the fireplace has one or two rocks that are easy to remove. We clear an additional area in front of these rocks for baking, and surround this area with a ring of stones. At baking time, we remove both rocks and rake hot coals into this ring. Meanwhile, we can heat dishwater or stir-fry vegetables on the back grill.

As you construct different campsites, you'll get different ideas on how to modify the basic fireplace to meet your needs. If a wobbly rock sends a full pot of water tumbling into the fire, you won't let that happen the next night. You'll firm up the rocks to make a more stable base for the impending soufflé. Next you may discover there isn't enough draft the way this fireplace is constructed, and you'll need to build the back higher than the sides. And you'll doubtless find that the artistic fireplace you come across at the Arcadian lake of your dreams is just too big for your one pot. It would be fine for U.S. Steel or a party of 30 with mules, but... So you hack and haul, sculpting a new, smaller, lighter and more efficient version on the same site.

It's useful to collect firewood in a variety of sizes. Small dry twigs are great for starting fires, but they burn too quickly for cooking. Large, long logs burn for hours, but won't fit under the grill for heating a pot of water. We bring a camp saw to cut large logs into shorter, easy-to-use lengths, which can last longer. The saw is lightweight, folds into itself for safety, and can be sharpened at a saw shop between trips. It is *never, ever* used on living trees, only on uprooted deadfall wood.

If you have to go far to gather the wood, bring a poncho to carry extra smaller pieces back to camp in fewer trips. But don't use it as a sack; it's guaranteed to tear. Rather, wrap the wood in the poncho and cradle the whole load in your arms. We also take a pair of garden gloves which help save our hands when we gather firewood. They also double as pot-holder mittens. In Chapter 10, we tell you how to use the fire most efficiently.

## Starting a Fire

Late in the summer, at a forested campsite, you'll find plenty of dry kindling. If you can bend a twig back against itself without breaking it, it's too wet for kindling. The best kindling will snap in two with a loud crack as soon as you bend it.

Start with the smallest, driest kindling you have. Keep a pile of it in reserve to add to the first flames. Remember that fires need lots of air. Too much fuel creates too much smoke which keeps the air away, so the fire goes out. Start your fire with a small, well-ventilated flame at the bottom, a space for air, then another layer of wood. You can shape this like a tepee, a lean-to, or a log cabin. Make sure the kindling is burning well before adding larger pieces of wood.

So far so good. It's easy to start a fire with good dry kindling. But what if it's wet? Old-timers may tell you to break lower branches off live trees for kindling. These lowest limbs are actually deadwood and, if they fan out into small twigs, they are fine for starting a fire even in rain or snow. But the idea of breaking dead branches from living trees is ecologically repugnant. Most camp-

## Camp fireplace and baking pit

sites are surrounded by stripped trees for a 100 yards in all directions. It looks like the area was bombed from the bottom up. Don't
break branches off trees *except in an emergency.*

We often use the pages of our paperbacks to start fires. We
usually read 30 to 70 pages a day, between trailside rest stops and
afternoon cooking sessions, so we have plenty to burn. Paper or
cardboard from food containers is also great for starting fires.

Another easy way to start fires is to use a flammable liquid or
gel. If you have a kerosene or alcohol stove, the fuel can start wood
burning in wet conditions. Some people bring a small can of
lighter fluid for emergency fire starting. If you do use a flammable
liquid, *never* pour any onto a fire that is already lit or smoldering. It
may ignite the can you're pouring from! You can also buy fire
starter in a tube, like toothpaste.

Okay. The kindling is burning, whether it's dry or wet. Now
for the larger pieces. The point is to build a fire gradually. Onto
the kindling go larger dry branches. When they're well lit and
flaming (not smoking), place a log or two gently on top, leaving
plenty of air space between the pieces of fuel. Larger logs are likely
to be dry inside. Once you get them burning, they'll keep burning
even in a drizzle or mist. If there's protection above them, they'll
burn in the rain. We often place a layer of rain-dampened logs
about three feet above the fire between two piles of rocks. This
wooden roof protects the fire from rain and dries the logs at the
same time. When these logs get dry enough to burn, they can be
pushed into the fire and replaced. With a little ingenuity, you can
cook and eat in the rain without much trouble.

One last word on fire-starting frustrations. The fire has
started. The cardboard is burning. You add some more wood, but

it's wet and the fire starts to go out. Frantically, you squeeze some fire starter onto a stick and throw it into the embers. It flares up, flames for a minute, then dies again. What now? Our advice is to stop, let it go out and start over from the beginning. We've seen novices waste reams of paper and tubes of fire starter trying to burn wet wood. Remember, a good fire starts with good kindling. For the second attempt, gather drier twigs and branches, even if you have to walk deeper into the forest or desert to find them. Keep a larger supply of dry twigs to add to the fire as it starts to burn. It will work—guaranteed! And at the next campsite, you'll gather the right combination of wood sizes and dryness to start the fire easily the first time.

# Food Storage

## Little Critters

The squirrel family is undeniably cute. All of them: chipmunks, prairie dogs and ground squirrels. They are positively Disney Worldish in their lovability. They'll approach fairly close, stand up on their hind legs, rub their front paws together and chirp. It's tempting to reward them with a morsel or two. Squirrels are also smart and voracious. They're world-class experts at stealing your stash. Chewing through a pack and several layers of plastic and cardboard is child's play for them, leaving you with a shortfall of precious food.

A cardinal rule of backpacking is *never feed the animals*. It is unfair *and* dangerous. Instead of applying themselves to gathering their natural food, they've discovered an easier, tastier way to fill up. If you feed them, or leave leftover food behind, it makes them dependent and renders them less able to survive in their natural habitat. That's the danger to them. The danger to you, aside from the loss of some closely budgeted food, is a possible bite, which can be painful and sometimes septic.

A family or two of rodents living in or near any well-used campground is inevitable. They come out mostly at night and look for food. They are so used to finding food in backpacks that they will often chew through your pack even when all food has been removed and hung high in a stuffsack. All edibles should be hung up at night, if possible (see illustration, page 211). Should you find rodent toothmarks on your cheese, just cut off the chewed portion and eat the rest. We've never heard of anyone getting sick by eating the untouched part. And a nibble-sized hole in a pack or pouch is easily sewn up.

We react similarly to ants and bees, brushing off those in the packets and eating the food. These insects can be kept out by packing food in tightly sealed plastic bags. Another common problem is food spilled inside the pack. The pack was set flat on the ground rather than upright, and the maple syrup, like flowing water, sought and found its natural level. Clean up as you might, the ants and bees will love that pack even when it's empty. But they never seem to do any harm.

## The Long Hot Summer

Our worst problem with food is storage on hot days. Keeping your stash out of the midsummer sun at a rocky campsite can be a 14-hour struggle. Not all food is harmed by excessive heat, but such things as cheese, eggs and chocolate are. At the beginning of the trip, you tend to throw chocolate bars into the nooks and crannies of the pack to save space. But if they're not double-bagged in plastic, and if you set your pack down in the blazing afternoon sun, a melted chocolate mess will be oozing through your pack. If you're in the desert or there are no deep-shade trees around your camp, you have to figure out other ways of keeping food out of the sun. Don't try leaving food in the tent all day. Tent fabric is so thin it works more like a greenhouse than a refrigerator. Sometimes the side of an old tree trunk or a rock ledge may have a shady spot at its base. Or you might rig a poncho or tarp to block the sun from the food pack.

## Bears

We've heard lots of bear stories: bears ripping open automobile trunks with powerful paws; mama-and-cub teams getting into "bear-proof" bags hanging high on guy wires strung between trees; bears strolling on trails; and even campers "playing dead," hoping that a bear wouldn't maul them after it ate all their food several feet away. We even have a few stories of our own, but like taxi stories—driver *and* passenger!—enough is enough. The point is that if you take a few precautions, you can share the wilderness safely even with the big critters.

The most important rule for dealing with bears is to be forewarned. Find out about them and plan a strategy before you reach bear country. Ask the ranger when you apply for your permit. Consult with the guard at the park entrance. Try to plan your trip to avoid campsites that have a reputation for bear troubles, such as Troublesome Creek Campground in Denali State Park, which was named for bear encounters!

## Bear-Proofing the Food Stash

If you'll be camping in problem areas, learn if there are "bear boxes" (large steel containers literally bolted to the ground) available, as in some of the national parks, or bear-proof wires at any of the campsites. These are steel cables, about three-eighths of an inch thick, strung about 20 feet off the ground between two stout tree trunks. If there are wires, you only need 50 feet of rope and two stuffsacks. Here's what you do.

Divide your food between the stuffsacks. Throw one end of the rope over the wire (tying a rock to it will help). Tie a stuffsack to the other end. Hoist the stuffsack about 20 feet into the air. Tie your other stuffsack to the rope as high as you can reach. The two sacks should roughly balance each other, one about six feet off the ground, the other about 20 feet up. Don't leave any extra rope hanging; stuff it inside the sack. With a long stick, raise the bottom sack as high as you can. Raising it to about 15 feet will lower the other sack to about the same height. And there you have it: two food-laden stuffsacks suspended about 15 feet off the ground. The wire is too thick for a bear to cut or tear and the sacks are too high for mom or her cubs to reach. You can sleep soundly. In the morning, you'll need a pole long enough to push one sack up until the other is low enough to grab. Usually such a pole sits next to the wire and is easy to recognize.

If rangers or other campers tell you of a bear problem and there are no bear-proof wires in the area, you have several options. The first is to camp elsewhere. Bears don't *naturally* bother people or eat their food. But they learn over time, like squirrels, that it's easier than foraging. They tend to have a territory that they regularly patrol in search of campers, foodsacks and garbage. If you're on their route, they'll try their luck with your goods. The farther away you get, the less likely they'll come to your campsite. An extra afternoon of hiking will often give you enough room that you needn't worry. Hiking three miles from that scenic lake and camping along a stream might save a week's food.

A second option is to rig up your own bear-proof system of hanging food sacks. Getting a tight line 20 feet off the ground between two trees isn't easy, but it is possible if you persevere. Or you might just hoist the food 15 feet up by looping it over a single high branch. Another plan is to use a cliff ledge. While bears can climb trees, they cannot climb rock faces. If you find a cliff or ledge 12 to 15 feet up, and if you can reach it, the bear won't be able to.

### *Hanging foodstuffs*

A new twist is a bear-proof storage canister, an oval-shaped plastic gizmo you carry in your pack which requires a screwdriver or coin to pry open. It comes in two sizes and can be rented or purchased. The smaller size weighs nearly three pounds and stores about 12 pounds of food; the larger size weighs five pounds and stores nearly 25 pounds of food. While this adds significant weight to your load, bears have yet to figure out how to get into them. They're now required equipment in the backcountry of Denali Park in Alaska.

HARD PLASTIC CANISTER

ZIPPERED NYLON CARRIER

LID

**Bear-proof food canister**

STRAPS

TWIST LOCKS

The canisters are genuinely "bear-proof," but that doesn't mean bears won't try to open them up. If you use a canister, hang it in a tree or place it on level ground, some distance from your campsite. When bears find it, they'll bump, kick or otherwise move it around before leaving in frustration. They may even send it rolling down a granite slope. But it's visible, retrievable and durable. Take a hike, recover your food and, if it's a rental, your deposit.

The final choice is just to leave the food in your pack or in a stuffsack on the ground. You might fasten some cups or forks or spoons onto the drawstrings. Then go to sleep and hope that: 1) no bear appears; 2) failing that, you hear it beginning to rustle your food; and 3) you are in the presence of one timid enough to be scared away by a furless, clawless and fangless human banging pots and throwing rocks, something *never* to be tried in grizzly terrain. Remember: It's better to lose your food or your pack than to tangle with an angry bear.

## Grizzlies

Outside Glacier and Yellowstone National Parks and Alaska, most of the bears you'll encounter in the wilderness are black bears. They're interested in your food, but they aren't intent on doing you any harm. What if you meet such a bear on the trail? If you remain calm and back off, the bear will probably do the same. Never get between a mama and her cub though. Don't surprise or scare a bear. And never back one into a corner. If you're worried about bumping into bears on the trail, make a lot of noise as you hike. Forewarned, the bear will avoid you.

Grizzly bears (and their relatives, brown bears) are something else. The only major grizzly populations in the Lower 48 are in Glacier and Yellowstone. Here the bears are very dangerous, being garbage-fed and unpredictable. They have been known to hurt people, seemingly for no reason. When antagonized (and just entering their territory can be antagonistic), it's possible they'll attack instead of waddling off. If you're entering grizzly country, you have to be much more careful. One veteran put together these rules:

- Make a lot of noise as you walk, especially when you're in thick forest or tall brush where visibility is limited.

- Try to hike with others. Numbers sometimes discourage bears.

- Leave the dogs at home. They can rouse a grizzly to a fright and fury.

- Camp, when possible, near a climbable tree. (Grizzlies don't climb trees. Though they can shake the hell out of 'em!)

- Try to cook (and hang your food at night) 200 to 300 yards downwind of your sleeping area. Have a separate set of "cooking clothes" and hang them up also with your food at night.

- Never bang a pot or throw a rock at a grizzly.

- Carry a spare stuff sack. If the grizzly gets your food, you'll still have a sack for your sleeping bag.

## Stormy Weather

Most first-time backpackers have a negative attitude about rain, considering it "bad" weather. At home, you don't go out into the rain or cold for fun. You stay indoors, turn the thermostat up and watch TV. The backpacking equivalent of that attitude is to set up the tent, put on the rainfly, and curl up in your sleeping bag until the sun comes out. But it doesn't take long to realize the quarters are a lot more cramped in a pup tent than in your living room. You get claustrophobic. You want to stretch. Every time you go out for a snack, you track water back into the tent. Soon, you start to get depressed about the weather.

There is a different attitude toward stormy weather, however, one worth cultivating. The rain is another mood of the mountains, creating a unique beauty in altered sounds, smells and perspectives. Get out of your tent and enjoy it. In fact, we often take our tent down when it starts to rain and use the groundcloth and rainfly to make a porch and covered cooking area. We store the packs under plastic garbage bags. Once the clothes and sleeping bags are secure, we can go about our business. We read in the rain, cook in the rain, fish in the rain (often the best fishing), and sometimes just sit and watch the lightning in the distance, listen to the thunder as it rolls closer, and view the rain-washed lake and mountains.

Then the storm is past and the skies begin to clear. As long as you stay warm with several layers of clothes, and dry with a poncho on you or strung up above you, you can weather bad weather in good spirits.

There is no such thing as "normal" mountain weather. The hottest days often come in September. July thundershowers can turn to hail and snow at upper elevations. A clear morning can be followed by a wet, miserable afternoon. You have to be prepared for it all. Our guidelines are:

- A poncho for every person.

- A rainfly and groundcloth for every tent.

- A garbage bag for every pack.

These are admittedly conservative. Many people do it with less. The more experience you have, the better you can manage with less protection. It's frustrating to pack rain gear around for nine or ten days and never use it. On the other hand, people who pack in less rain gear often plan to do a lot of hiking each day. Since it's more likely to rain in the afternoon in the mountains, they plan to hike through the storm and need only keep themselves and their packs dry. Our idea of backpacking, however, stations us at a campsite most afternoons, either because we hike only in the morning or because we stay in one place for two or three days at a time. So when we see that first hailstone bounce off the ground, the extra gear is suddenly worth its weight in gold.

# Washing Up

Pollution in the high country is disheartening and unnecessary. If you find a gum wrapper on the trail, you can pick it up and carry it out yourself. But if you see soapsuds along the shore of a lake, it's too late to do anything about it. Don't let detergent get into the water in the first place—that's the only time to stop it.

The single best way to avoid adding to the growing mess is to leave all soap at home! All. Ask yourself, "Do I really need this?" At worst you're going to get sweaty and dusty, and clean un-soaped water gets rid of sweat and dirt just fine. Try the following experiment: Take a clean pair of jeans, right out of the washer and dryer. Fill your bathtub. Soak the jeans, rubbing as if you were washing 'em. Notice anything? Right, a hint of soap film or even suds. That's what happens in the wilderness. Now try the same thing on yourself. Wash your hair and bod. Rinse clean. Go about your work or play. Later in the day fill the tub again and soak in it. No soap. Scrub hair, body and soul. Voilá. More soap film or suds. You can't get all that goop out, and Lake Purewater is going to suffer even if you don't use soap. If you do insist on the Great American Fetish, here's how to keep things to a minimum:

Never wash dishes in a lake or stream. Carry them and a pot of hot water at least 100 feet away into the woods or sage. Put two drops of biodegradable liquid soap in a small pot, then add about a third of the hot water. Wash each dish or pot with this until the food particles are gone. Rinse out the sponge, then rinse each dish with the clean sponge and the remaining hot water. One pot is plenty for all the washing up after a four-person meal. If even that amount of soap offends you, do without it. A good scrubbing with a steel wool pad or even pine needles gets utensils clean. Use the same washing spot for several days, 20 or 30 yards from camp. Though it will attract flies and bees, it will impact the environment less and make campsite clean-up easier and more thorough.

Do your laundry the same way. One pot for soapy water and one for rinse water are enough for two people to wash shirts, socks and underwear. Often, a good rinse without soap will get socks or a shirt ready for a morning hike. Even then, the dirty water shouldn't go into the lake or stream. Dump it onto the ground.

Cleaning yourself should also be done away from the stream or lake. Heat a pot to a comfortable temperature. Find a scenic spot back in the forest, away from the lake. Then soap and rinse. You can even do a fine job of washing your hair. Just have some-one help you with the rinse.

Don't soap up and jump into the lake or stream to rinse off.

Even if the label says "biodegradable," the suds will be around killing fish and insects until next spring. Rinse yourself thoroughly so the soap soaks into the ground. When you go for a swim, leave the water as unpolluted as you found it.

Finally, there's the matter of a toilet. The rule of thumb is 100 *yards* from any water; the farther, the better. Dig a hole at least five inches deep. Cover thoroughly when you're finished. Pack it down. Don't bury toilet paper. While organic waste will decompose quickly, toilet paper may take years. Bring it back to camp and throw it into the fire (if lit), or put it in the garbage bag to burn later. The same rules apply to tampons and sanitary napkins: burn or pack along, but don't bury.

## Breaking Camp: The Low-Impact Way

A "low-impact" wilderness ethic has developed in recent years, which is typified by the motto, "Take only pictures, leave only footprints." The wilderness is a fragile place and visitors, however careful, leave a permanent imprint. When you break camp, clean up. Repair any damage you've done. Take apart fireplace additions and thoroughly douse the fire. Comb the area for scraps of paper or plastic which may have blown into the brush while you were cooking or eating. Pack out found garbage as well as your own.

If you camp at a pristine, never-before-used site, leave it as you found it, without a fireplace or stacked kindling, a path to the lake, a naked patch of earth where the tent was sited, or that overturned stump you made into a chair.

And in return for the joy you get from the wilderness, put some energy into its maintenance and preservation after you get home. Spend a weekend on a local cleanup crew or trail maintenance work group. Join environmental and outdoor organizations. Become involved in the legislative process that helps preserve and protect the wilderness.

# CHAPTER 9

# Home Cooking:
# Using a Dehydrator

## Two Cooking Strategies

Our friends know us as "discriminating fressers." (To "fress" means to "eat like a pig.") If that conjures up an image of a couple of slobs shoveling ballpark franks washed down by a chilled Chateau Lafite Rothschild, forget it. We can't tell Ripple from Manischewitz. But we like—we love—to eat, and on a camping trip, we have the best of both possible worlds: great food and world-class outdoor living. And as everybody knows, great food tastes even better outdoors. That's why you're here, to rip out the recipes in the back of the book and to learn to live without them at the same time.

We operate on two levels here, careful home preparation of foods that can be pre-dried, and carefree improvisation around the campfire or stove out in the wilderness. In this chapter, we introduce the versatile dehydrator, essentially a blowdryer for food. We assume you understand or have access to the lore of the kitchen—measurements, proportions, definitions and directions.

In the next chapter, we show you how to play riffs on the available food in your pack. We assume you have nothing at hand except your imagination and a couple of pots and pans. Hence we explain a few basics and show you how to free yourself from the iron law of precision. Either way is right. Both are easy and fun. Neither has the remotest resemblance to institutional cooking or assembly-line freeze-drying. (Though check our suggestions for new and interesting vacuum-packed, add-water-and-serve international foods, Chapter 5, pages 141-142.) Stop, look and listen to the cries of joy emanating from the kitchen.

# The Dehydrator: How It Works, What It Does

Hal recently came upon four old-timers in a wilderness campsite stocked with three cases of beer, countless cans of beans and spaghetti sauce, an old iron reflector oven, sacks of flour and cornmeal, and two cast iron skillets. They didn't appear to be weight conscious, probably because they'd used two llamas to haul in all that stuff. Most of us, however, have to watch our pack weight, and that's where dehydrated food comes in.

There are lots of ways to preserve food. You can pickle it, conserve it in sugar in airtight jars, salt it, freeze or vacuum-dry it, or dehydrate it by the application of slow heat. The last three of these methods remove the water content of food, leaving a dry shell which can be reconstituted by those three immortal words, "Just add water." And while modern technology has made it possible to freeze and vacuum dry food at home, it still has the feel (and expense) of a physics experiment. That leaves the modest fan-driven dehydrator as the best home companion for wilderness cookery since Irma Rombauer stopped making air drops.

The home dehydrator is no industrial-strength giant. Its five or six stacked, slotted trays sit on a base, also slotted, which houses a small electric motor. This motor drives a fan which forces air over a heating coil—sort of like a four-sided toaster coil—and thence up through the trays encased in a perforated plastic cover. Some of the air recirculates down and over the trays, as the rest escapes to maintain an even temperature. Food placed on the trays loses much of its moisture within 24 to 48 hours. The electric motor is energy inefficient but it gets the work done and saves on camp stove and natural fuels in the wilderness. Some models have temperature settings, but ours doesn't, and we've never missed them.

**Typical home dehydrators**

If you don't have or want a dehydrator or can't afford one (it costs between $60 and $90 at camping stores and whole food outlets), you can use the kitchen oven as a drier. To achieve the slow, circulating air effect of a dehydrator, run your oven at its lowest temperature setting and keep the oven door propped open. Don't look too closely at your next gas or electric bill. That's the price you pay for "saving" on a dehydrator.

There's another inexpensive, energy-efficient way of drying fruits and veggies, the only requirement being that you live in the sun belt. A solar drier is nature's way of extracting moisture from fresh produce. The principle is to collect the sun's heat, not its direct rays, and circulate it over the produce at a temperature of about 110 degrees Fahrenheit until most of the moisture is gone. Our surfer friend Jane, a sun worshipper, found the directions for a home-made model which should run you less than $50, and we pass on the basics here. Essentially what you're looking at is a plywood box inset with screen-covered trays, a couple of air circulation vents cut in the top and bottom ends, and the whole thing topped by an old window under which is set a black sheet metal collector. You attach a couple of legs at one end to tilt it toward the sun at the proper angle (five degrees less than your local latitude).

To get a full set of instructions, write or call the *San Jose Mercury News* in San Jose, California, citing "Utility Bills Update No. 527" from their June 26, 1993 issue.

**Homemade solar drier**

PLYWOOD BOX

DRYING SHELVES

OLD STORM WINDOW

AIR CIRCULATION VENTS

PRINTING PLATE OR SHEET METAL

## Endless Possibilities

About a month before our backpacking trips, we crank up the dehydrator and keep it running 24 hours a day until there's enough camping food to feed us and several waves of hungry in-laws or bears, whichever show up first. It's possible to dry food much farther in advance—in late winter or early spring, for example—and pack and store it securely till needed in summer. Dried thoroughly and double-bagged in airtight Ziploc bags, stored in cool, dry, dark containers (again the trusty black garbage bag will do in a pinch), most fruits and vegetables will be edible for half a year or more. Meals containing meats and other perishables—such as milk, eggs and cheese—can be similarly packed and stored in the freezer. But summer fruits and vegetables are too good to miss, so we wait till the first bloom is off the peaches, and the apricots and eggplants are in the markets and then get to work.

Home drying allows hikers and campers to do two things: prepare in advance lightweight snack foods and full-course hot meals. Fresh fruit and veggies dehydrated become instant *nosherei* (snacks and trail food) as well as potential ingredients for hot meals made in camp. Soups, stews, sauces, ragouts, desserts allow for one-pot cooking in the wilderness and more free time to catch the fish or bake the bread that will accompany them on day three up the Housatonic.

## Food Drying Tips

- Dehydrator trays should be washed and dried before beginning the drying season and when it's over.
- Line the dehydrator base with aluminum foil or plastic wrap to catch drips from the trays. *Don't* cover the air slots in the base.
- Spray a light coating of Pam or any of its anti-stick relatives on the trays before each drying. More things stick than don't, and to pry dried watermelon off a dehydrator rack requires the patience of an archaeologist.
- The thinner the fresh food slice, the faster the drying process, but often the less satisfactory the eating. Experiment with the thickness of slices. Medium cuts seem best. Example: slice a medium-sized peach into eighths, a small plum into quarters, a large banana or zucchini into 10 to 15 slices.
- Food is done when it feels leathery. Don't expect to match the commercial driers. You're going to end up with chewy banana

slices, not banana chips. Apricots will shrivel but never look like those sun-dried or sulphur-treated beauties in the produce store.

- Dried fruit will be as sweet as the fresh product you started with. Dehydrating concentrates natural sugars; it doesn't supply them. A tart pineapple is going to taste tart, dry or moist; sour grapes will stay that way.

- Line trays with plastic wrap or aluminum foil when drying liquids such as sauces, soups and stews. Spray the lining with Pam, too! Some dehydrators come with one or two plastic inserts as liners for trays. Spray those as well.

- All uncooked fruits and vegetables dry well. But some do not reconstitute well. Carrots and (fresh) tofu, avocados and eggplants end up hard as coprolites and don't take kindly to water. Broccoli disintegrates into green dust. Citrus fruit is a bust: it's made up essentially of water and tough fiber. You end up with fiber.

- Almost anything you cooked in thickened liquid form—sauces and soups, for example—will dry *and* reconstitute well.

- Unless marinated fresh meats (jerkys) are thoroughly dried, they will deteriorate faster than other foods. Dehydrate them last, closer to departure time, and give them 48 hours on the drier.

- No need to turn food over, despite directions to do that in other books.

# Recipes

## Fresh Fruit

Ripe summer fruits are the best candidates for drying. The following are among our favorites:

| | |
|---|---|
| Mangoes | Cantaloupe |
| Nectarines | Strawberries |
| Papayas | Bananas |
| Peaches | Blackberries |
| Pineapple | Apples |
| Plums | Raspberries |
| Watermelon | Apricots |
| Figs | |

Slice six to eight pounds of summer fruit into moderate sections. Remove papaya and watermelon seeds. Peel mangoes. Core apples and pare at your discretion (we don't). Spread directly on lightly "Pammed" trays. Dry for 12 to 24 hours. Pack in large Ziploc bags. Yield: about 3.5 pounds of dried fruit.

CAMPING USES
- Eat as is.
- Filling for fruit crêpes. See recipe, Chapter 10, page 285.
- Chutney for Indian meals. See recipe, Chapter 10, page 310.
- Filling for chocolate cake. See recipe, Chapter 10, pages 303-304.

## Fresh Vegetables

All veggies contain water and hence can lose it through dehydration. But like fruit, some rehydrate better than others, a consideration for the campfire cook. Some first need to be blanched (plunged into boiling water for a minute or two, no more). Others require thorough cooking before dehydrating. Some can be treated like fruit and tossed directly onto the drying trays.

• No preparation required:

| | |
|---|---|
| Onions | Leeks |
| Summer Squash | Mushrooms |
| Zucchini | Bell Peppers |

Tomatoes *(Okay, they're fruit, so sue us.)*

• Blanching helps:

| | |
|---|---|
| Cauliflower | Broccoli |
| Green Beans | Eggplant |

• Cooking required *(see dinner recipes below):*

| | |
|---|---|
| Potatoes | Beans (dried) |
| Tofu | Carrots |

Cut four pounds of fresh vegetables into medium slices. Blanch those requiring it. Place directly on lightly "Pammed" trays. Dry for 12 to 24 hours.

*Note*: Onions *smell* while drying. Place dehydrator outdoors on an extension cord in good weather to keep the smell out of the house.

*Note*: Marinate fresh tofu in soy sauce/tamari and rice vinegar and only partially dehydrate, on Pam-treated plastic lining, for about six hours. It's done when chewy and overdone when rock-hard. This will *only* keep a few days. Dehydrate two days before your trip; eat on the first day.

CAMPING USES:

- Eat as is. Peppers, tomatoes and onions are sweet, delicious snacks.
- Reconstitute for in-camp recipe or sauces.

# Soups

The single requirement for any backcountry soup is that it fill you up. It is *the* meal, not a foretaste of things to come. It must be hearty, thick, tasty and even nourishing. If successful, it evokes images of great cauldrons bubbling over fires in open hearths: Breughel and barons, late autumn chill and a hint of snow. There's no room at the campfire for a delicate clarified consommé, a thin, consumptive chicken soup. Make a big soup or no soup at all. The following recipes are some of our favorites. The point is that you can make any of yours, too.

## Black Bean Soup

This is a great Brazilian recipe that delivers on its promise of being a meal within a meal. No known life form has ever eaten a second course after this one, not even the legendary John Israel, a *gourmand* in gourmet's clothing.

*1 lb. black turtle beans*
*¹/₄ c. olive oil*
*¹/₄ lb. raw cured ham (Smithfield/country) cut into ¹/₂" cubes*
*¹/₄ lb. salt pork cut into ¹/₂" cubes*
*4 c. finely chopped onions*
*¹/₃ c. finely minced garlic*
*14 c. fresh or canned beef broth plus salt (optional) & pepper to taste*
*¹/₄ tsp. cayenne pepper to taste*
*2 Tbs. wine vinegar*
*¹/₄ c. dry sherry*

Soak beans in cold water overnight. Render salt pork of its fat; discard fat. Cook the onions in oil in a deep kettle till translucent. Add the cubed ham, salt pork, garlic and continue cooking, about five minutes. Drain beans, add to kettle. Add broth, bring to boil. Add salt, pepper and cayenne. Partly cover and cook, stirring occasionally, about four hours. Put half the soup with beans through a sieve or use a blender. Return to the kettle, stir to blend with remaining soup and beans. Add vinegar and dry sherry.

Ladle onto lined "Pammed" drying trays. Each tray should be just covered with soup. Dry for 12 hours or until thoroughly dry. The texture, when done, will be crumbly, resembling a thin, loosely structured peanut brittle. Store in Ziploc bags. Figure three trays for four adults. Reconstitute by adding water to cover and bringing to boil. Serve very thick over cooked rice, with flaked dried onions and a dash of lemon or lime juice. Expire with pleasure.

VEGETARIAN VERSION:

In place of salt pork and ham, substitute two cakes of tofu, cubed and sautéed in oil till lightly browned. Add to kettle with onions and garlic. May need more salt to replace that in the salt pork.

## *Dutch Split Pea Soup*

Don't plan any strenuous paddling or cycling after this one. Dutch burghers have infarcted just reaching for their pipes after two helpings.

*1 lb. split peas*
*2¹/₂ qts. water*
*¹/₄ c. diced salt pork*
*¹/₂ c. chopped leeks*
*¹/₂ c. chopped celery*
*¹/₂ c. celery root*
*¹/₂ c. chopped onions*
*¹/₂ bay leaf*
*2 tsp. salt (optional)*
*1 pig's knuckle*
*1 smoked Dutch ring sausage sliced, or 1 c. sliced Polish sausage*
*chopped parsley*

Soak the peas overnight in a large kettle. Do not drain. Sauté the salt pork in a large pan for about seven minutes or until rendered of fat. Add the vegetables and cook till tender. Add the salt pork and veggies to the peas with a bay leaf, salt (optional), and the pig's knuckle. Bring to a boil, reduce heat to simmer, cover and cook for about two hours or until meat on the pig's knuckle falls from the bone. (If foam forms on the top of the soup during cooking, remove with a slotted spoon.) Take the pig's knuckle from the pot, dice the meat and reserve. Discard bone and bay leaf. Purée veggies in a blender. Return them and the meat to the soup, add the sliced sausages and simmer five minutes longer.

Ladle onto "Pammed" lined trays. Dry 7 to 12 hours or until dry and flaky. Store in airtight bags.

VEGETARIAN VERSION:
Omit salt pork, pig's knuckle, sausage. Flavor with ¹/₄ cup sherry, three tablespoons hot sauce, lots of black pepper to taste.

## *Minestrone*

An Italian regiment in the Val d'Aosta on the Swiss alpine frontier mutinied when they couldn't get their promised rations of this great vegetable soup. We don't blame them; it's cold up there. Don't worry about the long list of ingredients. It's easy to assemble, inexpensive and worth the effort.

*¹/₂ lb. dry white beans soaked overnight in water*
*3 qts. water*
*1 tsp. olive oil*
*¹/₈ lb. salt pork, diced (vegetarians omit)*
*1 clove garlic, chopped fine*
*1 small onion, chopped*
*1 leek, diced & washed*
*1 tsp. fresh chopped parsley*
*1 tsp. fresh chopped basil*
*1 Tbs. tomato paste*
*3 tomatoes, peeled, seeded, chopped*
*3 stalks celery, chopped*
*2 carrots, sliced*
*2 potatoes, diced*
*1 small turnip, peeled, diced*
*¹/₄ small cabbage, shredded*
*2 zucchini, diced*
*1 ¹/₂ qts. water or soup stock*
*salt (optional)*

*ground black pepper to taste*
*1 c. elbow macaroni*

Drain the beans then boil about 1 hour or till tender. Drain.
In a large kettle, render the salt pork for about 10 minutes, then
add olive oil and brown the following: salt pork, garlic, onion, leek,
parsley, basil. Add tomato paste and a little water to thin it. Cook
five minutes. Add tomatoes, celery, carrots, potatoes, turnip,
cabbage, zucchini, water, salt (optional) and pepper. Simmer
slowly about 45 minutes to one hour. Add the beans. Add the
elbow macaroni and cook 10 minutes more or until tender.

Ladle onto lightly "Pammed" lined trays. Dehydrate 7 to 12
hours or until thoroughly dry. Seal in airtight plastic bags. Three
trays serves four adults. Four trays serves four adults in the Val
d'Aosta. Reconstitute by covering with water and boiling. Serve
topped with lots of grated (or finely sliced) parmesan cheese, a
great backpacking cheese: it's hard, good on its own or in dishes,
and it won't spoil.

## Leek and Mushroom Soup

Make this soup as thick as a vegetable purée. Eat it with fresh
bread baked at the campsite (see recipes, Chapter 10, pages 285-
300).

*2+ lbs. leeks, sliced, washed, drained*
*3 large celery stalks with leaves, chopped*
*2 large carrots, sliced*
*1 small summer squash or zucchini*
*4 Tbs. olive oil*
*1 1/2 qts. vegetable stock*
*6 fresh basil leaves in season or 4 sprigs parsley*
*2 Tbs. flour*
*1/2 lb. mushrooms, chopped*
*3 Tbs. margarine or butter*
*lemon juice*
*salt (optional) plus ground pepper to taste*

Sauté the celery, carrots, squash and leeks in the olive oil until
just tender (five to seven minutes). Sprinkle with flour and cook for
three minutes more. Add chopped basil or parsley, pepper and
salt. Barely cover with some of the vegetable stock, lower to simmer, cover and cook 15 to 20 minutes till soft. In the meantime,

sauté the mushrooms in the butter or margarine till barely soft, about three minutes. Drain on paper towels. Place the leek and vegetable mixture in a blender. Add the mushrooms. Add a ladle of vegetable stock and blend till puréed. Return to clean pot and add just enough of the vegetable stock to make a thick soup to serve four. Add lemon juice and pepper to taste. The thicker the soup, the better it will dehydrate.

Ladle onto prepared, lined trays. Dehydrate 7 to 12 hours or until thoroughly dry. Reconstitute by covering with water and bringing to a boil.

VARIATION WITH TOFU:

Cut a half-cake of tofu into small cubes. It can be either hard or soft, Chinese or Japanese. Brown on all sides in peanut oil with a dash of sesame oil. Add ground black pepper to taste. When ready to purée other ingredients in blender, add the cooked tofu. Run the blender at high speed for at least two minutes. Otherwise the tofu will give the soup a grainy texture. Blended properly, the tofu adds a rich, creamy taste and texture to the soup.

## Vegetable Stock

You're not going to dehydrate vegetable stock, but you *are* going to use it in a lot of the recipes which follow, which *will* be dehydrated.

Stores used to sell soup greens, basically a little of this and a little of that—a collection of celery leaves, spinach, chard, turnip or carrot tops. They don't anymore, so you have to buy whole vegetables and make do. Vegetable stock is the generic home of leftovers. Don't worry about proportions or niceties. All you need is a big stock pot and lots of vegetables which have seen better days. If you need to clean out your fridge, you're on schedule for a great vegetable stock. Here's a recent one we managed out of necessity—it was either make a soup stock or appear at a hearing before the health inspector. The proportions below are arbitrary.

*1 large onion, left whole*
*4 scallions, chopped*
*4 garlic cloves, crushed*
*2 leeks, washed, chopped, including green tops*
*2 large carrots, sliced*
*3 large celery stalks, with leaves, chopped*

*1 small turnip, with top, left whole*
*¹/₂ bunch spinach*
*¹/₂ lettuce head*
*mixed fresh herbs: bay leaves, oregano, parsley, basil, thyme, tarragon*
*10 peppercorns, whole or slightly crushed*
*olive oil or butter*

Lightly brown the vegetables in olive oil. Then season and cover with cold water in a large stock pot or kettle. Bring to boil, lower heat and simmer for two hours. Strain through a colander. Discard vegetables. Return soup stock to pot, reduce under high heat to concentrate flavor. Cool in pot. Freeze in airtight containers till ready to use. Keeps for months if properly frozen.

# Vegetable Purées

We used to think purées were baby food for adults. Were we wrong! They're the perfect camping fare, easy to make, easy to dry and pack, easy on the eye, nose and throat, easy on the wallet, nutritious as hell, light as a fare-thee-well, and, if you didn't quite catch the point, terrific. The concept is too simple to belabor: a mix of veggies is lightly cooked, bound with butter, cheese, sour cream, potatoes or the veggies themselves, puréed in a blender, spread on drying trays, reconstituted on the trail, and celebrated in legend and lore. Almost any combination will do. Try one.

### Leek and Potato Purée

*1 bunch of leeks, washed, drained, sliced into ¹/₄" rounds*
*1 small potato, peeled and diced*
*3 stalks celery, diced*
*4 Tbs. margarine or butter*
*2 c. vegetable or chicken stock*
*salt & pepper to taste*
*2 tsp. dried mint leaves, crushed, or 1 Tbs. fresh mint*

Melt butter in a saucepan, sauté the celery, potato and leeks for about 10 minutes. Add mint leaves, salt and pepper, and the stock. Cover and simmer slowly for about 15 to 20 minutes, till the leeks are tender. Remove to a blender or food processor, and purée till smooth. Check seasonings.

Spread on lightly "Pammed" foil- or plastic-lined trays, dry
for 12 to 15 hours or until hard and crumbly. Store in freezer till
ready for the trail. To rehydrate, pour the dried mix into a pot,
add small increments of water while reheating, stirring constantly.
This can easily serve as a meal in itself, or as an accompaniment to
a fresh trout.

For a variation, leave out the potato.

## Carrot and Squash Purée

Two of our favorite cooks, Julee Rosso and Sheila Lukins, are
apparently no longer talking to each other, but in their great *The
New Basics Cookbook,* they put a lock on veggie purées, and in
exchange for this improv combination of three of their recipes,
we'll take 'em to Lac Gastronome anytime.

*5 carrots, sliced 1/4" thick*
*2 yellow summer squash, sliced 1/2" thick*
*1 small onion, chopped fine*
*4 Tbs. butter or margarine*
*2 Tbs. orange juice*
*1 tsp. cinnamon and sugar mix*
*salt & pepper to taste*

Boil the carrots in water until just soft, about 10 minutes.
Remove from pot, run under cold water and reserve. Meanwhile,
sauté the squash and onion in the butter till the squash is just soft
(but not mushy), about 10 minutes. Now toss in the carrots, orange
juice, cinnamon and sugar. Glaze the veggies with this mix and
continue until things begin to thicken a bit, say four to five minutes. Salt and pepper to taste.

Toss in the blender or food processor, purée till smooth. Dry
and reconstitute as above.

VARIATIONS:
- Add slivered almonds for three minutes at the end of the cooking.
- Cook carrots in veggie or chicken stock.
- Flavor with cardamom.
- Flavor with chives, ginger and coriander.
- Omit the onion.

## Purée Variations

Crank up the imagination, mix and match, experiment. For example:

- Make a mix of carrot and beet purées. It'll match that Smokey Mountain sunset and taste even better.
- Purée together broccoli, spinach, and Swiss chard.
- Celery and pears! (Sauté 8-10 stalks of celery, sliced into 1/2" pieces, in 5 Tbs. butter, add barely ripe pears, a pinch of powdered cloves, 1 Tbs. chopped fresh parsley, cover with a blend of white wine and chicken stock, simmer till celery is soft, about 10 minutes, add salt and pepper to taste, purée as above.
- Cauliflower, potatoes, water cress, lemon or lime juice.
- Eggplant, mushrooms and Swiss cheese. (Prick 2 eggplants with a fork, roast in a 400-degree oven till soft. Scoop out the eggplant, reserve. Sauté 1/2 lb. sliced mushrooms in 4 Tbs. butter or margarine with 2 cloves minced garlic. Place eggplant, mushrooms, garlic and 1/2 c. grated Swiss cheese in blender and purée. Dry and rehydrate as above.
- Your turn…

# Stews

Anything thick enough to stick to your ribs can be precooked and dehydrated, then reconstituted in a single pot by adding water, thus becoming a homemade entrée away from home. It will be as good as the ingredients you use to make it. That's its advantage over commercial freeze-dried dinners. You don't have any control over them, just faith, which is probably misplaced, but that's our particular axe. Like the soups, the following recipes are meant to inspire your imagination, not exhaust it. Add to the list, send us your ideas, and we'll add them to the next edition.

## Chicken Casserole

A confession is in order here. We've never actually tasted this dish reconstituted. That's because it's so good dried that we ate all of it as trail nosh before we ever got it to the dinner pot. What can we say? We've eaten it often at home and guarantee it's a winner. If not, tear out the recipe and send it with an irate letter to our publisher.

*4 lbs. chicken, cut up as for frying*
*$1/4$ c. seasoned flour (flour mixed with finely sifted breadcrumbs and mixed*
  *herbs: savory, chervil, chives, basil, tarragon, pepper, salt, paprika)*
*$1/4$ c. olive oil*
*1 small onion, sliced*
*1 clove garlic, sliced*
*3-4 celery stalks, chopped*
*1 medium carrot, sliced*
*$1 1/2$ c. hot chicken broth*
*1 c. sliced, sautéed mushrooms*
*12 stuffed olives, sliced*

Dust the chicken parts with the seasoned flour, then brown chicken in olive oil in a large Dutch oven or fireproof casserole. Remove. Brown the onion, garlic, celery and carrot in the oil. Return chicken to pot with vegetables, pour the broth over all, barely to cover. Bake covered in 350-degree oven $1 1/2$ hours or till tender. Five minutes before it is done, add the sautéed mushrooms and olives. Allow to cool.

When cool remove and debone the chicken parts, discard bones and return chicken to pot. Mix with vegetables. Spoon onto lightly "Pammed" plastic sheets covering the dehydrator trays. Dry for 12 to 20 hours. The texture will be crumbly, with chicken pieces dried like jerky. Pack in Ziploc bags as air-free as possible. Reconstitute by adding water barely to cover and bringing to boil. Serve over boiled rice.

## Burgundy Beef

This famous dish (Boeuf Bourguignon) started as a peasant stew and graduated to the high table by the kind of culinary magic only known to the French. The first thing you're going to say is, "Why go to all the trouble?" The second thing, "Oh man, am I glad I went to all the trouble." It's one of the best stews you'll ever eat, which is more than you can say for Ranger Ron's freeze-dried Mulligatawny.

*$1/2$ lb. bacon, diced*
*3 lbs. lean beef chuck, cut into 1" cubes*
*1 c. chopped onion*
*salt (optional) & pepper to taste*
*3 Tbs. flour*
*3 c. dry red wine, burgundy if possible*

3 c. beef broth
2 Tbs. tomato paste
1 Tbs. chopped fresh rosemary leaves
3 carrots, sliced
2 c. small pearl onions
1 Tbs. butter/margarine
1 c. mushrooms, sautéed
1 Tbs. red currant jelly

In a big flameproof pot, sauté bacon till crisp, then remove and drain on paper towels. Brown the cubed beef on all sides in the bacon fat, then remove. Brown the chopped onion and carrots in the fat, then return the bacon and beef to the pot. Add the flour, stirring to coat all ingredients and continue browning for about five minutes. Add wine, broth, tomato paste, rosemary, salt and pepper. Bring to a boil. Cover and place in a 325-degree oven. Bake till meat is tender, about two-and-one-half hours. Boil the pearl onions till just tender, and when cool, peel and reserve. Sauté the mushrooms in the butter or margarine. Reserve. When meat is done, transfer casserole to stove top, add the onions, mushrooms and currant jelly. Mix in very gently. Cook till hot, about five minutes.

Spread on dryer trays lined with plastic wrap and lightly "Pammed." Dehydrate 12 to 24 hours, till thoroughly dry. Pack tightly against air. Rehydrate by barely covering with water and bringing to boil. Serve over rice.

## Squash Stew with Chilies and Almonds

This is a vegetarian stew created by the famous Greens Restaurant in San Francisco. We simplify and corrupt it here for plainer, easier cooking, and no doubt they would disown the whole thing. That's okay, they're not going camping; we are.

3 Tbs. sesame seeds, toasted in a dry pan till lightly browned
2 dozen whole almonds, toasted in a dry pan till browned, then coarsely
    chopped
2 Tbs. chili powder (less or more to taste)
1 $^1/_2$ tsp. ground cumin
2 tsp. dried oregano
2 Tbs. olive oil
2 onions, roughly chopped ($^1/_2$" squares)

*2 cloves garlic, finely chopped*
*3 c. squash (winter / summer) cut into large chunks*
*¹/₂ lb. mushrooms, halved or quartered*
*salt (optional)*
*3-4 c. vegetable stock, heated*
*¹/₂ cauliflower, broken into florets*
*1 small can hominy, drained*
*2 lbs. tomatoes, fresh or canned, seeded, puréed*
*1 c. peas, fresh or frozen*
*2 Tbs. chopped cilantro leaves*

Grind the toasted almonds and sesame to a fine meal in a coffee grinder. Heat oil in flameproof casserole. Cook onions till just soft, then cook another minute with the garlic, cumin, oregano and chili powder. Add squash, mushrooms, salt (optional) and stock. Bring to boil, lower heat, simmer till squash is tender, 15 to 20 minutes. Add more liquid as necessary. Add the ground almonds and sesame seeds, cauliflower, hominy, puréed tomatoes. Continue cooking until cauliflower is almost tender, then add peas and chopped cilantro. Let cook a few more minutes.

Spread on "Pammed" and lined dryer trays. Dry 7 to 12 hours. As this dissipates most of the liquid, the remaining ingredients will look pitifully few. Don't worry. Pack all five trays' worth. Reconstitute by adding water barely to cover, boil and serve over rice or with fresh baked camp bread (see recipes, Chapter 10, pages 285-300).

VARIATION:
To cooked stew, add 2 to 3 large tablespoons sour cream or yogurt. Mix. Dehydrate and rehydrate as above. Remember that sour cream and yogurt are perishables, so make this variation no more than a week before leaving. Pack tightly and keep in shade.

## Pepper, Squash, Chard & Hominy Stew
We found this recipe in a newspaper, and like free software, share it with you. A great campsite dinner!

*1 onion, diced*
*4 cloves garlic, chopped*

*¹/₂ lb. banana squash, peeled, chopped into ¹/₂" pieces*
*2 Tbs. olive oil*
*1 tsp. dried oregano*
*1 green pepper, diced*
*1 red bell pepper, diced*
*1 Tbs. flour*
*2 Tbs. chili powder*
*¹/₂ tsp. cumin*
*1 c. dry white wine*
*2 c. broth of choice (or half broth, half water)*
*3 tomatoes, seeded & diced*
*¹/₂ bunch chard, blanched and cut into ribbons. Discard the tough main stem.*
*1 can hominy (29 oz.), drained, rinsed*
*chopped cilantro*
*¹/₂ - ³/₄ c. sour cream or yogurt (if camping with a cooler)*

Sauté the onion, garlic and squash very lightly in an oven-proof pan. Add oregano, peppers, flour, chili powder, and cumin. Stir and cook several minutes. Add wine, broth to cover, and tomatoes. Cover and simmer 30 to 45 minutes. Add chard and hominy, and cook another 15 to 20 minutes. Stew should be reasonably thick. If too thin, pour off some of the liquid and boil down till reduced.

Spread on "Pammed" lined trays and dry till brittle, about 15 hours. Rehydrate at campsite by adding water to the stewpot, and heat while stirring. If camping with a cooler, serve with sour cream or yogurt and fresh cilantro as a garnish.

## Four-Wheel Drive Vegetarian Chili

We put this recipe in Chapter 10 for the avid car and canoe campers, but it dehydrates perfectly and comes back saucy and strong with a little water at your wilderness retreat. See page 279.

## Eggplant and Tomato Casserole

This recipe is brought to you directly from a hippie commune, vintage 1972. The flower children did a lot of nice things, and this is one of them. It reconstitutes more as a stew than as a casserole, but who's going to quibble about niceties on a soft rainy evening deep in the Boundary Waters Wilderness?

*1 large eggplant*
*1 tsp. salt (optional)*
*2 eggs, beaten*
*2 Tbs. melted margarine / butter*
*fresh ground pepper*
*2-3 Tbs. chopped onion (or more!)*
*$1/2$ tsp. dried oregano*
*$1/2$ c. bread crumbs*
*2 large tomatoes, sliced in thin rounds*
*2 oz. grated cheddar or Edam cheese*
*$1/4$ c. grated parmesan cheese*
*paprika to taste*

Peel and slice eggplant. Place in pot with salt and cover with about one inch of water. Cover and cook about 10 minutes or until eggplant is soft. Drain and mash with potato masher. Add the beaten eggs, melted butter, pepper, onion, oregano, bread-crumbs. Butter a $1^1/2$-quart baking dish or casserole. Cover bottom with half the sliced tomatoes. Spread in all of the eggplant mixture. Put rest of tomato slices on top. Mix together the grated cheeses and sprinkle on top. Then sprinkle with paprika. Bake in 375-degree oven about 45 minutes.

Spread on drying trays lined with plastic wrap and lightly "Pammed." Dehydrate 7 to 12 hours. Texture will be dry, crumbly. Pack in Ziploc bags. Eggs and cheese are perishable, so store in cool, dry place; keep out of direct sunlight while in camp. Rehydrate by adding water to moisten. Reheat slowly to prevent burning. Serves two fressers or four courteous adults.

# Risottos

In our tireless search for one-stop campsite fressing, we've stumbled upon the secret of Pavarotti's girth. Forget the pasta and pizza, the spuds and spoonbread. It's risotto first to the waistline! One of the glories of Italian cuisine, risotto is the camper's dream come true: a carbo-loaded, knockout delicious banquet in a pot. The principle is simple, the variations endless. Rice absorbs liquid. Italian risotto absorbs liquid almost infinitely. It's called "arborio," and having a rounder, fatter grain than our long-grained varieties, it retains more water (or stock or wine) than a Wagnerian soprano. Add veggies, seafood, cheese and meats in endless combinations and you've got a full dress dinner for the entire European Common Market.

Risotto is labor intensive. It takes constant stirring. And lots of care in adding the liquid, for the idea is not to stew the rice but to let it sop up the liquid instead. The end result can either be creamy in texture or thick and sticky. In Venice, they like it creamy, in Milan sticky. We've noticed that in rehydrating risotto, it often comes out sticky. Welcome to Milan.

For camping purposes, we follow two strategies: 1) Slightly undercook the risotto before dehydrating, thereby allowing a more generous addition of liquid at the campsite when rehydrating; 2) Store all dehydrated risottos in the freezer till ready to hit the trail. That's because they all include oil in the making, and oil can go off. We're going to give you a couple of basic recipes and then suggest how you can tinker and fiddle with them to add variety to your life.

## Basic White Risotto

This is your risotto training wheels. Master this and you're ready for roller blades. Remember that like the other recipes here, this will produce two large adult servings. Attention vegetarians: Wherever chicken or beef broths are called for, you can substitute vegetable stocks at will. There will be *no* loss of flavor.

*1 large, heavy (preferably enamel-lined) pot*
*wooden spoon or fork for stirring*
*2 Tbs. olive oil (or butter)*
*1 small onion, chopped fine*
*1 c. arborio rice (UNRINSED!!)*
*3-4 c. chicken bouillon (or water), simmering*
*salt & pepper to taste*

Bring the bouillon or water to a simmer in a separate pot and keep it that way throughout the cooking. In the heavy pot, sauté the chopped onion in the oil or butter till just golden. (The oil/butter controversy divides Italy along North/South doctrinal lines. We have no intention of trying to resolve it.) Then add the rice and cook, stirring, for about three minutes, until the rice is well coated with the oil. Okay, now for the liquid. Start with a cup of the bouillon or water and slowly add. Stir it and let it simmer. The rice will absorb this dosage quickly. When just about fully absorbed, repeat with the next cup, adding it *very* slowly—maybe half a cup at a time—stirring. Remember, wait till the liquid is mostly absorbed before continuing. Keep this up until you've used all of the liquid. This may take 15 minutes or more. The texture should be slightly creamy, yet the rice should be sort of chewy, like *al dente* pasta. The important thing is that *you* like the taste and texture. That's when it's really done. And if you back off just before that point, leaving it slightly undercooked, then dehydrate it, you'll be able to add more water or other liquid at the campsite to bring it back to life. Salt and pepper to taste.

Spread the risotto on drying trays lined with plastic wrap or aluminum foil. No need to "Pam." The oil in the risotto will suffice. Dry overnight. The texture will be crumbly. It's edible as is, though somewhat hard. Store in Ziploc bags and place in freezer till ready to go. To rehydrate, bring a Sierra cup of water to a simmer in a camping pot, add the risotto, stir, and continue to add water (or soup, or wine) till soft. A filling meal on its own.

VARIATIONS:

- Just before the risotto is done, stir in a tablespoon of butter and $^1/_2$ cup grated parmesan cheese.
- Substitute $^1/_2$ cup white wine for an equivalent of the bouillon or water. Add the wine first.
- Add your favorite spices: rosemary, thyme, Italian parsley, fresh chopped cilantro.
- At campsite, add rehydrated veggies or jerkys or other cheeses or all three in any combination.

## Risotto alla Milanese

Almost every cookbook has a recipe for this, yet you'd be surprised how many variations exist. Here's ours.

*1 small onion, chopped fine*
*1 clove garlic, minced*
*2 Tbs. olive oil (or butter)*
*1 c. arborio rice, unrinsed*
*$^1/_2$ c. white wine*
*3-4 c. chicken stock, simmering*
*pinch of saffron, crushed and steeped in $^1/_2$ c. of stock*
*salt & pepper to taste*
*parmesan cheese, grated*

Sauté the onion and garlic in the oil till just golden. Add the rice and cook for three minutes. Add wine, stir and let the rice absorb it. Then add in slow increments most of the stock, stirring, till absorbed. Reserve $^1/_2$ cup stock, in which to steep the saffron. Add the saffron colored stock, salt and pepper to taste, and stir till the rice is crunchy to the taste. Stir in grated parmesan cheese, or reserve this step till you get to the campsite.

Dehydrate and reconstitute as above.

## Risotto with Fresh Veggies

The possibilities are virtually endless, the colors glorious, the taste sublime. Here's merely one in a million, followed by enough variations on a theme to keep even Chopin or Thelonius happy.

*1 small onion, chopped fine*
*2 small summer squash, one yellow, one green, diced*
*$^1/_2$ red bell pepper, diced*
*1 handful snow peas, trimmed*
*1-2 ripe Italian tomatoes, seeded, diced*
*1 Tbs. chopped parsley (Italian or regular)*
*3 Tbs. olive oil (or butter)*
*1 c. arborio rice, unrinsed*
*3-4 c. chicken or vegetable stock, simmering*
*salt & pepper to taste*

Sauté in the oil the onion, summer squash and red pepper. Add rice and cook, stirring to coat, for three minutes. Meanwhile, blanch the snow peas in water just until they become bright green, maybe 20 to 30 seconds. Remove and reserve. Add 1 cup of the stock, stir lightly till absorbed, then add the remaining stock in $^1/_2$ cup increments. When the rice is almost done (about 15 minutes) add the snow peas, tomatoes and parsley. Continue stirring and if necessary add more liquid. (The blanching water from the snow peas will be perfect.) Cook about three minutes longer. Salt and pepper to taste.

Dry and reconstitute as above.

## Green Party Risotto

Ever see a piece of Derby Sage cheese? It's got nothing to do with this recipe, but its marbled green and white coloring is a nice analogue to this beautiful risotto. Rad!

*1 small onion, chopped fine*
*2 cloves minced garlic*
*3 Tbs. olive oil*
*1 bunch fresh spinach, washed, drained, chopped*
*5 Tbs. fresh cilantro, finely chopped*
*2 Tbs. fresh chives, finely chopped*
*1 tsp. fresh rosemary, finely chopped*
*1 Tbs. fresh basil leaves, finely chopped*
*1 c. arborio rice, unrinsed*
*3-4 c. vegetable or chicken stock, simmering*
*grated parmesan cheese to taste*
*salt & pepper to taste*

Sauté the onion and garlic, add rice and stir to coat for three minutes. Slowly add most of the stock till it is absorbed. Then add all the veggies: spinach, cilantro, chives, rosemary and basil, and the rest of the liquid slowly. Cook till slightly underdone, then add salt and pepper and parmesan.

Dry and rehydrate as above.

VARIATIONS ON A RISOTTO THEME:
- Combine sun-dried tomatoes, fresh tomatoes, basil and wine.
- Sauté Japanese or Chinese eggplant and add at the end. Combine with grated sheep's milk cheese or feta, and chopped parsley.
- Parboil leeks and broccoli, combine and add at end with pine nuts or coarsely chopped almonds.
- Soak dried mushrooms (the Italian ones are called "porcini") in simmering red wine, cook up a batch of bacon separately, then add the mushrooms and bacon near the end of the cooking process.
- Steam clams or mussels in white wine and water, remove from shell, use the cooking liquid for the rice and add the clams or mussels at the end. To this you can also add fresh, shelled prawns (they cook in a few minutes right in the rice mixture), even pieces of steamed sea bass. Flavor with rosemary or dill or a combination thereof, and a tablespoon of capers. Remember to store in freezer after drying.
- Combine pesto, parmesan and chopped nuts.
- Make a combination of three or four cheeses.
- Use frozen corn, peas and other veggies. They'll thaw in the final cooking.

# Indian Cooking

For reasons we can't explain, almost all wilderness campers and canoeists we've met like their food highly spiced. Maybe it's a reaction to years of bland camp cooking, watery soups, peanut butter 'n jelly on Wonder Bread, K rations. Maybe it's a function of hard exercise, cold nights, and a need for a jolt and a kick from the menu. Whatever the reason, we've perfected the art of spicing over the years, though the only other person able to match Rick's tolerance for hot sauce is a Dravidian wise man we once met in southern India. He was impressed. Here are some of our favorites.

## *Zucchini Curry (Goodhi bhajji)*

*2 $^1/_2$ lbs. zucchini (or summer squash), sliced into $^1/_4"$ rounds*
*$^1/_4$ c. sesame oil*
*1 tsp. mustard seeds*
*1 tsp. ground turmeric*
*$^1/_2$ tsp. chili powder*
*$^1/_2$ tsp. black pepper*
*1 tsp. onion seeds (optional)*
*1 large onion, sliced into thin rounds*
*4+ oz. raw, unsweetened coconut*
*1 tsp. garam masala*
*$^1/_2$ tsp. salt (optional)*

Heat the sesame oil in a deep sauce pan or flameproof casserole. Add mustard seeds, which will sputter and pop. Add turmeric, chili powder, pepper and onion seeds. Stir over gentle heat for two minutes, then add sliced onions and sauté till just soft. Add zucchini, turning gently, cooking five minutes. Add coconut, garam masala, salt. Cover pan and simmer gently about 10 minutes or till zucchini is soft. Add a little water if zucchini is sticking to bottom of pan while simmering. That's it. Simple. Superb. Promise.

Spread on lightly "Pammed" and lined drying trays. Dehydrate 7 to 12 hours or till dry. Pack in Ziploc bags. Rehydrate by adding water to moisten. Heat and serve with rice (basmati rice is great here; so is brown rice). A great complement to this dish is a campground chutney (see recipe, Chapter 10, page 310).

## Garam Masala #1

*Garam masala* literally means "hot spice" and is your basic homemade curry powder. There are as many varieties as there are Indian dialects, so you can tinker according to your own tastes. It's so simple to make that we bet you never go back to store-bought curry powder. Here are two variants, the first "hotter" than the second.

*4 oz. coriander seeds*
*5 bay leaves*
*4 oz. white cumin seeds*
*1 oz. cardamom seeds*
*1 oz. cloves*
*2" stick cinnamon*
*2 oz. chili powder*
*2 oz. black pepper*
*1 tsp. grated nutmeg*

Mix and spread on a cookie tin or baking pan the coriander seeds, bay leaves, cumin seeds, cardamoms, cloves and cinnamon stick. Roast in a hot, 400-degree oven for 20 minutes. Remove and place in coffee or food grinder. Grind to a fine powder. Mix with the chili powder, pepper and nutmeg. Store in an airtight jar. Will keep for months. On camping trips, put a few teaspoons in a Ziploc bag, small plastic bottle or a plastic pill box.

## Garam Masala #2

Follow same procedure for Garam Masala #1 but omit the chili powder and black pepper. This makes a lighter curry powder, more aromatic than spicy. In both cases, add the *garam masala* to recipes close to the end of the cooking. This brings out the flavors and kicks in the spicing just before it hits the back of your throat. It'll bring tears to your eyes, a delicate emotion as you scarf down a third helping the night before the ascent of that 13,000-foot pass you promised yourself.

## Spiced Cauliflower (Gobi Musallum)

Read this one and weep. Well, eat it and weep.

*1 large cauliflower*
*1 Tbs. tamarind extract*

1 c. boiling water
2 oz. cooking oil
2 tsp. chili powder
2 tsp. ground coriander
2 tsp. ground cumin
2 tsp. ground turmeric
2 tsp. black pepper
1 Tbs. vinegar
1 tsp. salt (optional)

Break the cauliflower into florets, discarding the central stalk.
Heat the oil, add the chili powder, coriander, cumin, turmeric and
pepper. Stir two minutes, then add cauliflower, turning to coat
with the spices. Add tamarind extract and the boiling water, then
the vinegar and salt. Continue to cook over moderate-low heat
about 15 minutes or until cauliflower is just tender.

Spread on prepared, lined trays, and dry for 7 to 12 hours.
Pack in airtight bags. Rehydrate by adding water to moisten over
moderate heat. Serve with cooked rice.

## Lentils with Cauliflower (Gobi Dal)

If there is a vegetarian heaven, this dish is served there every
other day. It's to die for.

$^1/_2$ lb. pink split lentils (masoor dal)
1 small cauliflower, broken into florets
2  medium onions
4 oz. cooking oil
1 tsp. chili powder
2 tsp. black pepper
$^1/_2$ Tbs. ground cumin
$^1/_2$ Tbs. ground coriander
2 tsp. ground turmeric
$^1/_2$ lemon
2 c. chicken stock
2+ oz. raw, unsweetened coconut
$^1/_2$ Tbs. flour
$^1/_4$ lb. cashew nuts

Wash and drain lentils; peel and finely chop onions. Heat oil
in a large saucepan or flameproof casserole and sauté onions till
translucent. Add chili powder, black pepper, cumin, coriander and

turmeric. Stir and cook for another 30 seconds. Add lentils. Stir
vigorously. Add lemon juice, then cauliflower florets. Pour chicken
stock over all, sprinkle on the coconut. Bring to boil, lower heat
and simmer 20 minutes. Mix flour with small amount of the
cooking liquid to make a smooth paste. Add to pot. Now toss in
the salt and cashews. Cook 5 to 10 minutes longer until lentils
form a thick sauce and cauliflower is tender.

Spread on "Pammed" lined drying trays, and dry for 12
hours or until thoroughly dehydrated. Pack in airtight bags.
Rehydrate by adding water barely to cover; heat to boiling. Serve
with plain cooked rice and a campground chutney (see Chapter
10, page 310).

## Steamed Yams (Dum Arvi)

Once you eat this dish you may never go back to Granny's
Thanksgiving candied yams. Tough luck, Granny. See ya down at
Man Eatin' Lake. A great filler-upper.

*2+ lbs. yams, peeled and cut into large (1¹/₂") chunks*
*³/₄ c. cooking oil*
*1 large onion, thinly sliced into rounds*
*3" piece fresh ginger peeled and cut into thin strips*
*2 tsp. ground coriander*
*2 tsp. garam masala*
*1 tsp. chili powder*
*1 tsp. black pepper*
*2 tsp. ground turmeric*
*2 tsp. salt (optional)*
*4 green chilies, topped and tailed*

Heat oil in large ovenproof saucepan or fireproof casserole
and brown the yams gently. Remove and set aside. Sauté the onion
with the ginger; add, stir in well, and cook for two minutes the
coriander, *garam masala,* chili powder, pepper, turmeric. Now add
the yams and salt, and stir to coat. Cover casserole and place in
350-degree oven. After 30 minutes add chilies. Bake another 30
minutes or until yams are tender.

Spread on "Pammed" lined trays. Dry 12 hours or till yams
are thoroughly dehydrated. Pack in Ziplocs. To rehydrate, add
water to moisten, and stir while heating. Serve with campsite
chutney (see Chapter 10, page 310).

## *Indian Lentils (Masoor Dal)*

Take the lowly lentil, dress it up with aromatics and coconut, serve it with rice, and watch contentedly as the hikers in the next campsite fumble with the library paste they've made out of their Space Shuttle Beef Stroganoff.

*$^1$/$_2$ lb. pink split lentils, washed, drained, boiled gently with water to cover, till soft*
*1 medium onion, sliced thin*
*2 cloves garlic, chopped fine*
*$^1$/$_4$ c. cooking oil*
*2 tsp. ground coriander*
*2 tsp. ground cumin*
*2 tsp. ground turmeric*
*1 tsp. chili powder*
*4 cardamom seeds*
*4 cloves*
*2" stick cinnamon*
*1 tsp. salt (optional)*
*4 oz. raw, unsweetened coconut*
*$^1$/$_2$ c. water or coconut milk*

Heat oil in pan, sauté onions and garlic, then add coriander, cumin, turmeric and chili powder, stirring well. Cook two minutes, then add cardamoms, cloves, and the cinnamon stick. Add to the cooked lentils (and their liquid), mix well, sprinkle with salt, cook for five more minutes, adding a little water if necessary. In a blender, mix the raw coconut with $^1$/$_2$ cup water or coconut milk till smooth, then add to lentils and stir.

Ladle lentils onto "Pammed" plastic-lined drying trays and dehydrate 12 hours or until dry. To reconstitute, add water to cover, boil down till thick. Top with dried tomato bits, and serve with rice.

# Spaghetti Sauces

It's inevitable that you're going to eat pasta for one of your camping meals, so you might as well enjoy it. It doesn't make sense to haul whole tomato sauce into the backcountry if you have to carry it in panniers or backpacks. It makes a whole lot of sense to prepare your own favorite sauces at home, dry them and carry the lightened load into the mountains. They reconstitute perfectly and really taste like home cooking because they are!

## Tomato Sauce

*1 large can whole tomatoes*
*1 small can tomato paste*
*2+ Tbs. sun dried tomatoes*
*$1/2$ lb. mushrooms, halved or quartered*
*1 bay leaf*
*3 sprigs parsley*
*ground black pepper to taste*
*6-8 fresh basil leaves, finely chopped, or 2 tsp. dried basil*
*1 c. boiling water*
*1 c. dry red wine*
*3 Tbs. olive oil*
*1 large onion, chopped fine*
*1 large clove garlic, chopped fine*
*$1/2$ lb. ground country sausage, or $1/2$ lb. fresh Italian sausage*

In a large saucepan, put the tomatoes, tomato paste, sun-dried tomatoes, chopped mushrooms, bay leaf, parsley, pepper, basil leaves, boiling water and wine. Bring to a simmer, cover and cook while preparing other ingredients. In a frying pan, sauté the garlic and onions till translucent. Add to tomato pot. Sauté the sausage over medium heat, drawing off the fat as it accumulates. Add the sausage to the tomato pot. Simmer for two to four hours, adding wine/boiling water as necessary. Stir occasionally. Adjust seasonings. The sauce should be thick when done.

Spoon or ladle onto "Pammed" lined trays. Dehydrate 12 to 24 hours until a dark-red tomato "leather" has been formed. Peel off the plastic tray liners and store in airtight bags. Two full trays will yield enough sauce for four; three trays will feed two adolescents.

To rehydrate, add water to cover, heat, stir, and if it's too watery, boil down. Serve with spaghetti or any other pasta and top with finely sliced or grated parmesan cheese.

## Eggplant and Walnut Sauce

This is so good that you may want to retire the more familiar tomato sauces you've grown up with. The combination of tomato,

eggplant and walnuts is surprising only to us outlanders. The
Sicilians have known and loved it for centuries.

*2-3 large eggplants*
*3 eggs*
*15 walnut kernels*
*Quick Tomato Sauce (recipe follows)*
*salt and pepper to taste*
*olive oil*

Place the eggplants whole on a cookie sheet or baking pan in
a hot 425-degree oven, and roast for about 35 minutes. You'll
know they're done when they're wrinkled and soft. Meanwhile
make the tomato sauce and hard boil the eggs till the yolks are
firm and creamy, not hard, about four to five minutes. Run the
eggs under cold water, shell and separate the yolks from the whites.
Reserve. Grind the walnuts in a coffee or food grinder. Cut the
roasted eggplants in half, scoop out the pulp and mix with the
walnuts. Add the egg yolks and mix thoroughly. Now add the
tomato sauce, salt and pepper to taste and a few drops of olive oil.

Spoon onto "Pammed" lined trays and dry for 12 hours or
until thoroughly dry. Store in Ziploc bags. To reconstitute, add
water barely to cover, stir while heating. Serve over pasta of your
choice.

## Quick Tomato Sauce

*2 Tbs. olive oil*
*1 medium onion, chopped*
*2 cloves garlic, chopped*
*1 large (14 oz.) can whole tomatoes*
*1 tsp. sugar*
*salt and pepper to taste*

Sauté the chopped onion and garlic in the olive oil till soft.
Add tomatoes with their juice, sugar, salt and pepper. Cook over
moderate-high heat uncovered for 20 minutes, stirring occasionally. When thickened, purée in an electric blender. Finito. Use by
itself with pasta or in other recipes.

Spoon onto treated plastic wrap on the drying trays and
dehydrate 12 to 24 hours till a tomato "leather" is formed. It will
feel like a fruit leather. Peel off and store in Ziploc bags. To

rehydrate, add water to cover, heat and stir till hot and thick. Serve over pasta topped with parmesan cheese.

## Other Sauces

White and brown sauces and gravies can all be made in advance at home like spaghetti sauces, and successfully dehydrated. Follow your own recipes and remember that any sauce or gravy that contains butter, milk or eggs should be carefully packed and stored after thorough drying to prevent spoilage. Try to avoid storing them in direct sunlight while in camp.

And if, after all of this, you just want to go down to the neighborhood Mom 'n Pop store, buy a jar of spaghetti sauce and dehydrate it, that's okay, too. It works. We'll be busy for dinner that night, but we sure would've liked to be there. Bon appetit.

# Desserts

If the super incredible, once-in-a-lifetime on-site campfire baking offer made in Chapter 10 isn't enough for your sweet tooth; if the semi-sweet baking chocolate, raisin cookies, ginger snaps, lemon drops and hard candy aren't enough on the trail; if honey drips and you don't "do" plain sugar—then here are a couple of ideas for the kitchen and dehydrator. Forget the cakes and homemade cookies. They'll be too heavy and bulky to carry, quickly go stale, and disintegrate under the pressure of a compressed backpack. On the other hand, call a pudding by any other name—"mousse," "flan," or "crème brulée"—and you'll transform the canoe ride, even if it's up the sewer outlet, into a gourmet tour of the old country.

## Indian Pudding

What more appropriate dessert to eat around the campfire on a moonlit night, even if you aren't in New England? We didn't promise you sugarless, but this comes pretty close.

*1 qt. milk*
*¹/₂ c. yellow cornmeal*
*2 Tbs. melted butter or margarine*
*¹/₂ c. molasses*
*1 tsp. salt (optional)*

*1 tsp. cinnamon*
*¹/₄ tsp. powdered ginger*
*2 eggs*

Scald the milk and pour over cornmeal, stirring constantly. Cook over hot water in the top of a double boiler for 20 minutes. Combine butter, molasses, salt, cinnamon, ginger, and add to well-beaten eggs. Add all to the cornmeal mixture. Pour into greased baking dish. Place the baking dish in a larger pan of hot water. Bake in a 350-degree oven for one hour.

Spread on "Pammed" plastic-lined trays. Dry 7 to 12 hours. Store in cool dry place in airtight containers till you're ready to hit the trail. Rehydrate by adding a spoon of dry, powdered milk to water to moisten. Heat slowly. Serve plain or with stewed-fruit compote (see Chapter 10, page 285, under Fruit Crêpes.)

## Rice Pudding

You're going to want rice one way or another on a camping trip, so why not in its sweetest, most inviting form?

*1 qt. milk*
*4 c. uncooked long-grain rice*
*¹/₂ c. sugar*
*¹/₂ tsp. salt*
*¹/₂ c. raisins (optional)*
*1 tsp. vanilla or rum*
*¹/₄ tsp. nutmeg*

Mix the milk, rice, sugar and salt in a buttered casserole. Bake at 300 degrees uncovered for two hours, nice and slow. If you use raisins, soak then in water (or rum!) to soften; drain and add with the vanilla (or rum) and nutmeg to pudding after the two hours and bake another half-hour without stirring. The rice should be very tender. If not, bake on.

Spread on "Pammed" lined trays and dry thoroughly, about 7 to 12 hours. Pack tightly against air and keep in cool, dry place. Rehydrate by adding a spoon of dry milk powder to water to moisten. Heat slowly or eat cold.

## Chocolate Pudding

When we're backpacking, we fake a chocolate pudding by doing this and that with a couple of leftover ingredients (see Chapter 10, page 304 for slightly more precise directions). Everybody (except Jessie, who's allergic to chocolate) loves it, so we decided, why not make it at home? As the Chinese would say, "Shuo shi chi, na shi kuai!" —no sooner said than done.

*¹/₂ c. sugar*
*1 egg, beaten till light*
*1 c. coffee*
*1 Tbs. melted butter or margarine*
*1 ¹/₂ oz. melted semi-sweet baking chocolate*
*1 ¹/₂ c. flour*
*¹/₄ tsp. salt*
*1.¹/₂ tsp. baking powder*
*¹/₂ tsp. vanilla*

Gradually stir sugar into the beaten egg; then stir in the coffee, butter and melted chocolate. Sift together the flour, salt, baking powder and add to egg mixture. Add the vanilla. At this point you're supposed to place the batter in greased custard cups, but since we're going to dehydrate the pudding, there's no need. Just pour it all in a well-greased baking dish. Cover with foil and steam for half an hour in a 350-degree oven by setting the dish in a pan of hot water.

Spread over "Pammed" lined trays. Dry for 7 to 12 hours. Seal tightly in Ziploc bags, keep cool. (Keep the pudding cool, too.) To reconstitute, moisten with some hot coffee or milk from powdered milk. Reheat and slosh down. If necessary, grab your partner by the throat to prevent total consumption before you get a whack at it.

VARIATIONS:
- For vanilla pudding, omit the melted chocolate and substitute milk for the coffee. Use one teaspoon vanilla.
- For a fruit "flan," make the vanilla pudding and before dehydrating stir in four heaping tablespoons of stewed fruits or berries. Dry and rehydrate accordingly.

## Trail Snacks

We are not going to teach you how to make gorp here. Anybody who can throw together in a bag any combination of raisins, nuts, sunflower seeds, granola, chopped dried apricots, chocolate chips and whatever else suits a nosher's fancy can make gorp. You've just done it. What you get here is something entirely different, beef and chicken/turkey jerky, and fruit leathers.

## Jerky

We can almost hear the gnashing of old-time game-hunters' teeth when they contemplate the namby-pamby methods of "jerking" beef these days—using commercial dryers and shovel loads of preservatives. "There's nothing complicated about making jerky," wrote a genuine Hudson's Bay outdoorsman 30 years ago, reminiscing about a better—a truer—age. "You cut lean deer, moose, elk, caribou, buffalo...into long strips about one-half inch thick. These you hang apart from one another in the sun, in the attic, or some other place where...they will gradually lose most of their water content. At the same time, they'll become hard, dry, black and, incidentally, both nourishing and tasty...Good? Friends of ours...jerk a deer or so a year in this fashion just for their own personal eating." (Bradford Angier, in *Wilderness Cookery*, pages 87-88. Stackpole Books, Harrisburg, PA, 1961.)

That's a hard act to follow. We don't jerk no deer here. But Bradford was right. Jerky can be good, and it's simple to make.

## Beef Jerky

*1¹/₂ lbs. lean beef (the better the beef, the better the jerky: flank or round steak, and up from there)*
*soy sauce, sesame oil, rice vinegar, honey, red wine as marinade*
*fresh ground pepper to taste*
*fresh grated ginger*
*powdered mustard to taste*

Either have the butcher slice the beef into quarter-inch slices or freeze the meat and slice it while just beginning to thaw, so you can get the blade through. The slices can be as long or short as you wish. Marinate in two parts soy sauce to one part other liquid ingredients, thoroughly mixed together with a wire whisk. Add pepper, ginger and mustard to taste. Marinate in fridge overnight.

Apply a liberal coating of Pam directly on the dryer trays; lay the beef strips on the trays and dry for 24 to 36 hours, until very dry, blackened, hard. Pack in airtight Ziploc bags and keep out of sun in camp. We try to make all our jerky the last week before a camping trip. High-powered commercial driers get more of the moisture out than our Model T, so we dry late and eat early.

### Chicken / Turkey Jerky

Follow directions for *Beef Jerky*. Use the breast of the chicken or turkey for tenderest meat. Have the butcher slice it thin for you, or do same at home, partially frozen—it, not you. Try other marinades. Here are two that are great with poultry.

RECIPE 1:
*¹/₂ c. olive oil*
*1 ¹/₂ c. corn oil*
*7 cloves garlic*
*4 sprigs fresh thyme*
*4 sprigs fresh rosemary*
*ground pepper to taste*

Mix thoroughly with a wire whisk. Spread on chicken/turkey slices. Refrigerate overnight.

RECIPE 2:
*²/₃ c. olive oil*
*¹/₃ c. tarragon vinegar*
*¹/₄ tsp. dry mustard*
*1 tsp. dry tarragon*
*ground pepper to taste*

Mix thoroughly with a wire whisk. Spread on chicken/turkey slices. Marinate overnight in fridge.

# Fruit Leathers

Any fruit you can stew you can dry as a fruit leather, too. The leather is intensely sweet, as the sugar gets concentrated, and in our opinion better than almost any other sweet we carry with us. There are two problems, however. One is that they're heavy. Made properly, they come off the dehydrator almost thin enough to see through yet concentrated with some moisture and lots of sugar to give them heft. You can't carry as much as you'd like unless you're willing to sacrifice that Dickens novel you've scheduled for the vacation. The second problem is they're popular. Ours lasted one day during a recent five-day trip. Now you see 'em, now you don't. Plan accordingly.

# Rhubarb and Strawberry Leather

2 lbs. rhubarb
1 $^1/_2$ c. water
2 pints strawberries
2 c. sugar
lemon juice

Wash and slice the rhubarb crosswise. Place in a large enamel pan. Add water. (Rhubarb is loaded with water, so don't fret if it looks like there's not enough). Bring to a slow boil, then lower heat to simmer. Add one cup of sugar. Stir very gently once during cooking to immerse top pieces in the boiling water. Slice strawberries and add just before the rhubarb begins to get soft. The whole process will only take 10 or 15 minutes. Near the end, add the other cup of sugar to taste. Rhubarb is tart and usually takes more sugar than you'd like. When soft, it's done. Remove from heat. Squeeze half a lemon onto the mixture and adjust taste.

Spoon onto thoroughly "Pammed" and lined trays. Heavy aluminum foil works well here, as does plastic wrap. Dry for 12 to 24 hours. Peel off and store in airtight bags. That's the time to reduce the weight by eating more than you store. Enjoy.

## Peach and Apricot Leather

2 lbs. ripe peaches
2 lbs. ripe apricots
1 $^1/_2$ c. sugar
2 c. water
lemon juice

Slice peaches and apricots, remove pits, place in an enamel pan. Add sugar and mix thoroughly till all slices are amply coated and the mixture begins to "sweat." Add water, bring to boil, keep heat moderately high, stir occasionally to prevent sticking. When the fruit mixture begins to thicken, in about 20 minutes, it's done. Remove from heat and add the juice of half a lemon to taste.

Spoon onto "Pammed" and lined trays. Dry for 12 to 24 hours. Peel off and store in airtight bags.

CHAPTER 10

# Campsite Cooking:
# Using the Imagination

## Hidden Lake Soufflé

"Catch, clean and poach three to five small (7" to 9") trout taken from a crystalline wilderness lake at 8,000 feet." Thus reads the first sentence of our original recipe for Hidden Lake Soufflé. "Remove and discard bones and skin. Set aside the flaked meat in the tent to protect from flies, bees and larger predators. Over a low fire, prepare about a Sierra cup-and-a-half of white sauce in the smallest of a set of three nested pots. Do not eat ingredients halfway through. Assuage munchies or lingering hunger with dried fruit, nuts, candy, whatever, thus preserving the fish, cheese and eggs for the soufflé. Add flaked fish to sauce, season well, and pour into a greased, two-quart pot. Fold in egg whites which have been beaten stiff with the trusty spring-loaded swizzle stick. Cover pot and bake in coals until done. Cooking time: one chapter of *Huckleberry Finn* read aloud. Eat at once. Bask in the glow of self-congratulation. Groan with pleasure."

We made up these directions one glorious morning in a remote campsite deep in the mountains. We'd planned the soufflé as a late brunch, but the project built slowly and turned into an early dinner. That didn't matter. We had all the time in the world. This wasn't survival; it was hedonism, like a day trip, a long nap, or an hour of fly-casting at sundown. After dinner, we revised the recipe, wrote it out, and then, the next day, left it in a cairn atop an unnamed peak in the mountains. We don't know if anyone ever found it or tried to use it. We were told later, however, by friends who did try, that they needed something a bit more specific, and in the following pages we will take you step-by-step through this recipe (poaching, making a sauce and baking) as well as through others that have kept us fat and happy during long days in the mountains.

At the same time, though, we're trying to hook you on a general philosophy of backcountry cooking. Namely, that with some basic knowledge and ingredients, you can concoct master-pieces in the wilderness. If you don't have a home dehydrator and arrive at your campsite with bundles of flour, sugar, beans and rice; if you've got time on your hands and a song on your lips; if you have a fired-up imagination and a fire on the hearth—you're in the right place. Recipes are fine in the beginning. You can jot some down in indelible ink on a few notecards covered with plastic wrap that will fit into your map pouch, or you can tear out the ones in the Appendix. But the fact is, you don't need any. Now we show how to improvise, how to play variations on simple themes, how to work from the general to the specific: how to have your cake and eat it too!

# Food Preparation Fundamentals

In Chapter 9, we assumed you knew all. Some wise old kitchen sage was just a phone call away. Here we assume you know naught. And that you can't get advice without hiking 13 miles to the nearest car phone. A few pages of basic training, then, and you'll be off on another adventure.

You'll be preparing food in one of five ways: boiling, baking, frying, grilling and poaching. Purists will insist that some of these are actually broiling, sautéing, wrap cooking and roasting, but this is not the Culinary Institute of America, and the fine points can be skipped.

## Definitions

*Boiling:* Cooking in a liquid at its boiling point. Remember that the higher the altitude, the lower the temperature at which this occurs. That's the good news, because it takes less time to get the water bubbling. The bad news is that the lower boiling tem-perature means you have to cook the food longer than at sea level. The following chart indicates the differences:

| Altitude | Boiling Point of Water | |
|---|---|---|
| | *Fahr* | *Cent* |
| Sea Level | 212 | 100 |
| 2,000 ft. | 208 | 98 |
| 5,000 ft. | 203 | 95 |
| 7,500 ft. | 198 | 92 |
| 10,000 ft. | 194 | 90 |
| 15,000 ft. | 185 | 85 |

*Baking:* Cooking in enclosed heat. At home, this means using an oven. In the wilderness, it means nesting a covered pot in coals. For best results, the pot is *not* set directly on top of the coals, but on a cleared spot in the middle of the ashes of a fire. It is then *surrounded* by the hot coals. Foil-wrapped food placed on or under coals (or both) is also "baked."

*Frying:* Cooking in fat over direct heat. The fat may be any cooking oil—vegetable, corn, peanut, canola, safflower or sesame—or vegetable shortenings like Crisco, Spry, etc. Margarine works too, if you keep it cool and in a tightly lidded container. Butter and olive oil spoil too rapidly to be practical. Bacon drippings are fine for frying, but bacon doesn't last much longer than butter. We travel with a plastic bottle of vegetable oil and several sticks of margarine in a small plastic container.

*Grilling:* Cooking over direct heat on a rack, a grill or a stick, a.k.a. broiling or barbecuing. Backpacking grills are lightweight and small. Sticks, if used, should be pointed at one end, green so they don't burn, and long, so your hand doesn't cook along with the food. If the stick is big enough, it's called a spit, and if the food on it is rotated while cooking, this is known as roasting, a technique best left to Tudor kings with very large fireplaces.

*Poaching:* Cooking by simmering gently in just enough water to cover. Simmering describes what water does just below the boiling point: rather than bubble actively, it moves only slightly. This point is hard to maintain on an open fire, but happily it doesn't matter. Boiling works fine instead of poaching.

## Practical Suggestions

So much for theory. Practice is more rewarding. In getting started, you should take the following into account:

*Measurements*: Our motto is "more or less." You won't have

measuring spoons or cups and you don't need them. Approximations, guesses and tasting will suffice. In the following recipes, all of which make enough for two hungry adults, we try to keep quantities approximate. Where we use measures, they mean the following:

- *Spoonful*: A standard camping-kit spoon, about soup-spoon size.
- *Cup*: A Sierra-type cup, actually about a cup and a quarter by normal measurements. Sierra cups are light-weight, stack easily, and are less likely to burn your lips when drinking hot liquids than ordinary metal cups, because the rim is made of a heat-resistant alloy. They are available at all camping supply stores.
- *Handful*: Just that, an average adult handful.
- *Pots*: Our small one holds 4 cups, our medium one holds 8 cups, and our large one holds 12 cups.

## Other Helpful Hints

*Meal size*: Camp cooking is cooking in miniature; i.e., a little goes a long way. Be prepared to scale down your normal at-home expectations as to how much you need. You don't want leftovers. Most are hard to store without attracting strange visitors. Plan meals with this in mind. If necessary, feed the last spoonful to the fire or the dogs.

*Utensils*: Pots and pans should be reasonably clean. Make sure the handles don't burn. If you have to stir something on the fire, lengthen your stirring spoon by tying on a stick. Garden gloves also work well to keep your hands protected.

*Water*: Have enough on hand for both cooking and cleaning up as you go. A dirty mixing pot often is needed for baking a few minutes later. Lids keep dirt and ashes out. Whenever you remove a pot top, set it on a clean rock or plate. Before replacing, check to be sure you won't be adding any unwanted twigs or leaves.

*Fire*: You want coals more than flame. A blaze burns rather than cooks. It also consumes a lot of fuel.

*Fire Area*: A fire requires a flat, cleared area, free of brush and clear of any overhanging branches. Don't put it too near your tent, or a slight wind may fill it with smoke. If the fire area is near some natural "chairs" (a big log will do) or "tables" (like a large flat rock), life is easier.

*Ingredients*: Keep them at hand. You don't want to run all over the campsite for garlic or soy sauce.

*White or Wheat Flour?* We use unbleached white flour in all the recipes, but whole wheat works just as well.

*Shade*: Keep all food in the shade while you're in camp. You may need to move the food stash several times a day, but it's so little trouble, especially if you keep the perishables together, and so sensible it should become part of your daily routine. If you leave for the day, place the perishables somewhere out of the arc of the sun.

*Tent*: A veritable kitchen cabinet—use it. If there are several stages to your food preparation and you need to put something aside, store it in the tent beyond the reach of flies, bees and mosquitos. Make sure, however, that you don't burn a hole in the tent floor with a hot pot. Feel the bottom of the pot, place it on a stone or a plate if necessary, and keep it away from sleeping bags and Ensolite pads. Don't forget to zip the mosquito flap all the way. Also, be careful of smelly spills. A tent reeking of raw fish or dried white sauce is likely to attract unwanted guests, such as ants or bears. If you have a spare poncho, spread it in the tent before storing food inside. If you do spill anything on the tent floor, wash it thoroughly before dark.

*Covering Food*: Foods you cook uncovered at home may need to be covered over an open fire to keep out ash and dirt. In such cases, set the lid on loosely and watch that the contents don't burn.

*Washing Up*: Make a wash-up area at the very edge of your campsite so as not to attract insects and animals. Carry water to the wash-up site rather than carrying dirty utensils to a lake or stream. Be sure any detergent, even "biodegradable" varieties, goes into the ground. Those bubbles that you see more and more of these days, even in the remotest wilderness areas, won't be going away. We usually wash pots with no soap at all: a little hot water and a good scrubber do fine. If you want to use soap, do so sparingly. A few drops are enough.

*When to Eat What?* One hot meal a day usually suffices. Two are sometimes essential. The hot-breakfast fanatic has to be fed; there's no getting around it. The hot-dinner fanatic also has to be fed. Now, if they're the same person...Don't try to convert anyone to anything while out on the trail. If you're a minimalist, cut back your own rations, but don't force your partner the carbo-loader to abstain on your account. Just remember that there is no fixed order to meals in the mountains, hot or cold. If you want nothing but desserts for breakfast, enjoy. One day we made and ate a chocolate cake with chocolate icing, a cherry pie and a loaf of sweet sourdough nut bread. The next day roots and grubs looked great. There's no accounting for the suddenness or strangeness of an attack of the munchies, so you might as well not fight it.

*Invidious Comparisons*: Whatever you cook in the wilderness won't be the same as what you make at home. The aim is not to duplicate what you can do seated at the controls of a 21st-century kitchen, but to make do with what you've got. The soufflé you bake at 9,000 feet might fall flat. It might not even warrant the name you give it. But it will be full of eggs, cheese and trout and will taste at least as good as an omelet. So if you're a hot shot chef in the lowlands, don't despair when things turn out differently from what you think is "right." Hopefully, you'll enjoy the cooking as much as the eating.

KEYS AND SYMBOLS USED IN RECIPES:

| | |
|---|---|
| ❖ | = Can be prepared on camp stove or campfire |
| ✱ | = Can be prepared with campfire or camping oven (see illustration, page 122) |
| ✿ | = Can be prepared only with campfire |
| c. | = Sierra cupful |
| hfl. | = Handful(s) |
| sp. | = Camping kit spoonful |

POTS

| | | |
|---|---|---|
| small | = | 4 cups |
| medium | = | 8 cups |
| large | = | 12 cups |

# Fish

## Cleaning and Storing Fish

Unless you're a pelican or a down-at-the-heels samurai, you'll want to clean your fish before eating it—an easy task. Ideally, you should do it as soon after your catch as possible, but that's often impossible. You may be on a day hike or out in the raft or too busy catching more to get far enough away from the lake to clean the one you've just caught. In those cases, stow the fish in a Ziploc bag or a pot, or thread it on a stick. Try to keep the fish out of the sun.

Fish are easy to clean, but it's also easy to foul the environment while doing it. While floating on a pristine backcountry lake, nothing is more depressing than to look down and see fish entrails floating in the water. Always clean fish far from all freshwater sources—and from your campsite. And don't even begin to clean them until you've found a spot with soft soil or sand and have dug a hole or trench at least four or five inches deep with your heel or a cup. That's going to be your Dispose-All.

To clean a fish, you need a sharp knife and some rinse water. Hold the fish in your hand, belly up. Slit the belly from the vent (the small hole just in front of the back fin) to just behind the head. If you plan to cut off the head (lots of folks leave it on), do it now. Cut on a diagonal line from just behind the front fins through to the spinal column. The fish is going to be slippery; hold on tight. But that backbone is tough, so be careful you don't take your hand off along with the head as the sharp knife severs the bone.

The fish is now opened. Most of the entrails will spill out on their own (into the hole you've dug). Remove the remainder with your hand, scraping away the tissue along the backbone with a thumbnail or knife. That's all there is to it! Rinse out the cavity, put the fish in a bag or pot, clean your knife and hands, pour out the dirty rinse water, cover up the hole and head for supper.

**Basic method of cleaning a fish:** *1) Slit belly from anal vent to gills. 2) Sever lower junctions of gills. 3) Pull out innards and gills. 4) Run thumbnail along cavity to clean out dark matter.*

Fish are best cooked and eaten immediately after catching and cleaning. But this too is not always possible. To store the cleaned fish overnight, keep them in a plastic bag inside a pot. You don't need to use any water. Cover the pot and set a heavy rock on it to discourage late four-legged diners. The cold night air will preserve the fish and breakfast will be great.

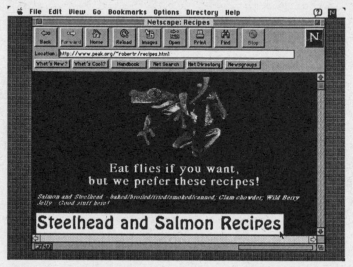

*Outdoor recipes are easy to find on the Internet.*

## Cooking Fish Without a Pan

You've bagged a couple rainbows and your partner has taken the required snapshot. The fish are fresh and cleaned; a feast is in order. There are many ways to cook fish: frying or poaching in a pan, stewing or baking in a pot, or grilling or broiling over an open flame. For starters, let's say you've left your frying pan in the car—at the time it seemed too heavy. The pot lids are too small and light to use as substitutes. The fish are biting on everything from hand-tied flies to matzoh balls, and the idea of one more fish stew palls. What to do? Go primitive. Use a stick, a rock, the flame or coals as your pan or oven. Here's how.

## Primitive Trout Cooking

A lot of ink is spilled these days over such concepts as "back to basics," "less is more," and "smaller is better." Well, here are several ways of putting theory into practice.

## *Trout on the Coals* ✳

2 rainbow trout
1 campfire, flames low, coals just cooling
pepper / hot sauce to taste
lemon / lime juice

Toss the fish in the coals! Honest. It works. If you were squeamish about ashes in your food, you wouldn't be here anyway. The worst that'll happen is the fish will be charred beyond recognition. So who needs recognition? Extricate the blackened trout after three to five minutes (depending on the heat of the coals). Use a spare plate to scrape away the charred skin. The flesh will be fine and flaky. Add pepper / hot sauce and a squirt of lemon juice from the miniature plastic bottle. Make Neanderthal noises while eating.

## *Trout on a Stick* ✳

Anybody who can roast a marshmallow can roast a trout on a stick too. And if that's all you've got by way of kitchen-ware, use it.

2 rainbow trout
1 campfire, moderate flames, coals red hot
1 green, sharpened hardwood stick
cooking oil
pepper, salt to taste
lemon / lime juice

Strictly speaking, this is a way to grill, not roast, fish. But the chances of dropping the fish into the fire are good, so you get the best of both techniques. Rub oil on the sharpened stick, lay the oiled part in the cleaned, open belly of the fish, poke the point of the stick into the head to secure it. Truss the fish by poking twigs through one side of the belly, over the stick, and through the other side of the belly. Season it to taste and grill over red-hot coals. The smaller the fish, the less time it takes: an 8-inch trout should be ready

**Trout on
a stick**

in about six to seven minutes. Check flesh with a fork or knife (or your fingers, if you've lost the cutlery, too). If it flakes easily, it's ready to eat.

### Trout on a Rock ❋

Okay, we've never done this, but others have. If a highly selective bear makes off with all your gear except a fishing line, three matches, and some oil, you too can get dinner.

*2 rainbow trout*
*1 campfire, very hot*
*1 big, flat rock*
*Cooking oil*

Heat the rock in the fire. Work it to the edge of the fire ring, oil the fish, set it on the flat face of the rock, turning once during the cooking. No utensils? Gather round the rock and eat with your hands. Incoherent Cro-Magnon grunting is appropriate here.

## Grilling Fish

There must be a word for people who hate fish: fishogonists? fishophobes? They're the ones who catch a fish and then go to elaborate lengths to disguise its taste by PO (Preparation Overkill). Grilling is not one of their strong suits. Grilling is simple, direct and honest: a tribute to the noble creature that gave you such a good fight.

### Grilled Trout ❋

*2 freshly caught small trout*
*cooking oil*
*soy sauce / tamari*
*rice vinegar / lemon juice*
*1 campfire, red-hot coals*
*1 lightweight, wire-mesh grill or 3-pronged backpacking grill*

Oil the grill to prevent the fish from sticking. Set it about five inches above the coals. Let the grill get very hot before it receives the trout. Sprinkle cavity with soy sauce and rice vinegar, also a light coat of same on the trout's skin. Toss on grill. (If using a three-pronged grill, set the fish on it gently. Otherwise it'll end up in the fire.) After about five minutes, turn the fish. A small spatula is useful for this, though chopsticks or a knife and fork will do as well. Use the flake test for doneness: that is, with a fork pry up a piece; if is flakes off easily, the fish is finished, and you've just begun to eat. It will remind you of that great Japanese restaurant you went to last year.

## Baked Trout

One of the best and easiest ways to cook fish without a pan is to wrap it in aluminum foil, set it on a bed of hot coals, and cover it with another bed of coals, or use a camping oven for a similar effect. As the recipes below show, there are endless variations to this way of cooking. We carry enough foil for at least one meal made this way. About two-and-a-half feet can be folded small and tucked inconspicuously in a pack pouch. It's usable only once. And remember, foil doesn't burn, so pack out the remains with your other non-organic garbage.

You can either wrap the fish individually or fashion a flat "oven pan." First, crimp the edges up on all sides so the juices won't spill out. Second, keep the "lid" opening toward you and not the fire; that way you can open the foil with a minimum of movement when the baking is done, without losing the juices.

## Foil-Baked Trout &#42;

*2 ten-inch trout*
*rosemary / tarragon*
*salt, pepper to taste*
*1 clove garlic, sliced thin*
*small dab of margarine*
*hot coals*
*1 to 2$^1$/$_2$ ft. heavy aluminum foil*

Rub the cavity with the margarine, then season it with the herbs and garlic. Foil-wrap the fish tightly and place on a bed of coals. Cover with hot coals. Note: coals have a habit of cooling, so expect the fish to take about 15 minutes to bake. You may need to add fresh coals if the originals lose a lot of their heat along the way. If you get good at it, you can test for doneness by poking a fork through the foil, while the fish are cooking. If the fork slides in and out easily, meeting little resistance, dinner is done. Or take the whole shmeer out of the fire, open, check, eat, or return for a little more cooking.

VARIATIONS ON FOIL-BAKED TROUT:

- Bake in soy sauce, garlic, ginger and sesame oil.

- Stuff the fish with finely chopped nuts and prunes soaked for an hour or so in brandy and warm water. Add a dash of sesame oil.

- Lay the fish on a bed of cooked rice; add a mixture of chopped nuts and cut-up dried fruits (apricots, raisins, apples, prunes), salt, curry powder and lemon juice.

- If you find any roe (fish eggs) when cleaning the fish, save them. Put the roe back in the cavity with whatever else strikes your fancy and bake.

- Cajun Red. This calls for bread crumbs, but a mixture of flour and cracker crumbs will do. To the mixture add paprika, oregano, salt (optional), red pepper flakes (or cayenne). Beat an egg with a little milk powder and water. Dip trout first into egg mixture, then into "crumb" mixture. Bake in foil as directed.

## Pan-Fried Fish ❖

If you carry a cast-iron frying pan into the mountains, you'll develop very strong calf muscles but you won't get too far. If, however, you bring a lightweight, teflon-coated pan, the slight increment in weight will be repaid many times over in versatility and pleasure. You can't cook a pancake on a stick, and it's hell to fry a fish without a pan.

Pan-fried trout are so easy and satisfying that you may not get beyond them in a week in the mountains. Small lake or stream trout are tender, cook fast and need almost nothing to enhance their flavor. A pan, lightly greased and set on a grill or nestled between rocks about four to five inches above a bed of coals, and a string of cleaned, lightly seasoned trout are all you need for a first-rate meal. The oil should be hot before you add the fish. Turn them over after about four or five minutes (sooner if they're small or if the fire is very hot) and cook for another four or five minutes. Sprinkle generously with lemon juice. That's all, folks.

As soon as the flesh flakes with a fork, it's done. Be careful at this stage; an overcooked fish loses a lot of flavor. When in doubt, take the fish off the fire sooner rather than later. You can always put it back, but you can't reverse a burn-out. All our suggestions for minutes per side are approximate. We don't wear watches in the wilderness. It's better to feel for doneness, following the clock in your head, than to put a stopwatch on the food in your pan.

One other precaution: make sure the oil doesn't burn. It starts to smoke and turns black if it gets too hot. At the smoking stage, add more oil to the pan to reduce the temperature. By experimenting with the heat of the fire and the height of the pan above it, you'll soon get the right combination and the fish will cook to perfection.

## Pan-Fried Trout ❖

*4 eight-inch trout, cleaned, with heads left on*
*cooking oil/margarine*
*salt, pepper to taste*
*lemon juice*

Heat a mixture of oil and margarine if you can spare them; otherwise one or the other. Brown the trout on one side, about 4 minutes; turn and finish cooking. Salt and pepper to taste. Test for doneness by flaking. Turn out on plate, pour the cooking oils over fish, add a dash of lemon juice.

## Trout Amandine #1 (Trout with almonds) ❖

Prepare as Pan-Fried Trout. Add a handful of chopped almonds to the pan after you have removed the cooked fish. Brown the almonds quickly in the cooking oils. Do not burn. Spread almonds over the trout and the juices over all. This is simple and elegant, maybe the best of all ways to prepare a freshly caught small trout. Don't worry if you only have peanuts or cashews. It'll taste just as good, and Escoffier is not likely to pop out from behind a tree to point an accusing finger.

## Trout Amandine #2 ❖

Dust the fish with a handful of seasoned flour. To season flour add any combination of spices to it and mix: pepper, rosemary, tarragon, basil, ginger. Prepare as per Trout Amandine #1.

## Trout Meunière (Flour-dipped, Pan-Fried Trout) ❖

"Meunière" means a miller, someone who grinds grain to make flour. This is one of the classic ways of preparing fresh whole trout. Note that "sp." here means "spoon," as in mess-kit spoon. Quantities are not important. Not to worry.

*4 fresh, cleaned trout, with heads left on*
*2-4 sp. margarine / cooking oil*
*2 sp. flour*
*salt, pepper to taste*
*lemon / lime juice*

Dip the trout in flour to coat. Heat oils—a mix of the two is great—and add fish. Season to taste. Brown on one side, about four minutes. Turn and complete cooking. Add a dash of lemon juice. Serve. Why leave the head on in these recipes? For both taste and style. The cheek meat on a fish is the tenderest of all. Why give it to the scavengers? And a whole cooked trout is beautiful. That's reason enough.

TROUT MEUNIÈRE VARIATIONS:

- Prepare as per recipe, but use a mixture of flour and cornmeal. Some old-timers put the flour-cornmeal mixture in a bag, drop in the fish, shake and fry.

- Make a small cup of milk with instant powdered milk and water, dip the fish into the milk, then the flour or flour/cornmeal mixture. Cook as in recipe.

- Substitute an egg for the milk. Crack it into a pot lid and beat lightly with a fork. To make it go farther, add a spoonful of water or milk to the egg. Dip the fish into the egg and then into the seasoned flour.

- Suppose you run out of flour and cornmeal and still want to coat the fish? Crush a couple of RyKrisps (or whatever other crackers you have) between a plate and your Sierra cup. Using this coarse meal, proceed with or without egg or milk.

- A piece of stale bread or biscuit can also replace flour or corn-meal. Just make a fine layer of crumbs by rubbing the bread between your hands. Ground-up nuts, seeds, left-over rice—almost anything'll do. Use your imagination.

## Cajun Blackened Trout ❖

Mardi Gras at the campground. Ideally this calls for an iron skillet, but you don't have one. Teflon will do in Little N'orleans. This one's simple and will set your socks on fire.

*2 fresh, cleaned trout (optional: filet the trout)*
*3 sp. cooking oil*
*paprika to taste*
*onion and garlic powder to taste (or dried onion flakes and minced fresh garlic)*
*pepper, cayenne, chili powder to taste*

Get that pan as hot as you dare without wrecking the Teflon coating. Season the trout inside and out (or, if fileted, top and bottom). Fry till blackened—right, *blackened*—on both sides. Eat by the light of your flaming socks.

## Trout Flambé ❖

Plan to serve this spectacular dish after dark for best effect. Prepare as in any of the pan-fried recipes. Just before eating, pour a little brandy in a Sierra cup, hold it over the fire until it's warm to the touch and light it with a match. As the brandy catches fire, pour it over the trout. A soft blue flame will dance over and around the trout for up to half a minute and will add another delicate flavor to the dish.

## Poaching

We've noticed on camping trips that we often crave rib-sticking foods, the kind that even in small quantities make us feel full. This may be a genuine physiological need: to replenish bodies that have worked abnormally hard over two or three days. Or it may be all in the mind—a need to eat a lot when there isn't a lot to eat. Whatever the cause, the consequence is either to eat everything in one sitting and then go home, or devise ways of making hearty, bulky meals with what you've got. We prefer the latter. That's where poaching comes in.

If you want a thick stew, curry, trout in white sauce, soufflé, or crêpes, you won't want to pick bones and skin out of them. To remove these beforehand, simply poach the fish. This leaves the flesh tender and ready to eat; the rest is disposable. Here's how.

## Poached Trout ❖

A poached fish is a finished product. Seasoned well and not over-cooked, it's as tender as you'll get a trout. But a poached fish is also part of a process that involves other methods of cooking. The six recipes following this one will show you how to combine several methods of preparing fish in order to end up with something definitely more than the sum of its parts.

*2 fresh, cleaned trout*
*seasonings to taste: pepper, Italian herbs*
*lemon juice*
*frying pan filled with boiling water*

Put enough water in your frying pan to barely cover the fish. Season it with salt and herbs to taste. Place the pan over the fire and let the water come to a slight boil. The fish will curl up. That's all right. There's also no need to turn the fish over. It's done when the skin peels off easily, and the flesh has lost its "transparent" look and comes off the bone at a nod and beckon. This takes about 10 minutes from the time the water begins to boil.

Remove the pan from the heat, the fish from the pan, and then with fork, knife or fingers peel off the skin and flake the flesh from the bones. Ideally, the backbone will come off in one piece, taking most of the skeleton and leaving you with a simple mop-up operation close to the fins. It's simple, but work fast or you'll end up wearing a halo of flies and other airborne participants. When finished, place the fish in the tent until ready to use and go bury the skin and bones. If you won't be using the poaching water (see Trout in Curried Sauce, Fried Rice Chinese Style or Hidden Lake Soufflé for possibilities), throw it out far from both your living area and the lake or stream.

## Trout Tandoori ❖

This is a curry dish, filling and fiery. Eat it, and you'll find the rainbow at the end of the pot. (Note: hfl. = handfuls)

*3 small rainbow trout, cleaned and poached*
*2 hfl. rice, boiled*
*assorted chopped nuts, dried fruits, about a small dishful*
*chopped dried onion, as much as you like*
*cooking oil*
*2-3 large pinches garam masala to taste*
*cayenne pepper (optional)*
*lemon / lime juice (optional)*

Heat up just enough oil to cover the bottom of your frying pan. Toss in the poached fish, rice, nuts and fruit. Season with garam masala and cayenne to taste. Add a dash of lime juice. Stir frequently. Done when hot. Serve with a Campground Chutney (page 310). Guaranteed to warm whatever in you is not.

## Trout in Curried Sauce ❖

The ingredients are the same as for Trout Tandoori. Add the poached trout to a cup of white sauce made with the poaching liquid, and flavored with *garam masala* and cayenne. Serve over boiled rice with nuts and fruits on the side, and a big helping of chutney (page 310).

## Fried Rice Chinese Style ❖

*3 small trout, cleaned and poached*
*2 hfl. rice, boiled*
*2+ cloves garlic, chopped*
*sesame oil/peanut oil/cooking oil*
*powdered ginger*
*dry mustard*
*black pepper*
*soy sauce*

Heat oils (a mixture is desirable but not necessary) in frying pan. Add poached trout, rice and spices. Fry, stirring, till hot. Then add soy sauce to taste and stir thoroughly. *Note:* The soy sauce provides all the salt you'll need. The Chinese have a saying: Chinese food doesn't taste good unless you use chopsticks. You have now been warned.

## Hidden Lake Soufflé ✴

A soufflé is a concoction made by putting cooked food—in this case, poached trout—into a sauce, pumping it up with air provided by beaten egg whites and baking. This definition may not satisfy the cognoscenti, and our methods will probably plunge them into a deep culinary depression, but they work, and the results are unspeakably good.

A soufflé is a three-stage affair: poaching the fish, making a white sauce with the poaching liquid, and folding in beaten egg whites before baking. (Note: "c." = Sierra cup) Here are the instructions:

*2-4 small (8") trout, cleaned and poached (pages 267-268)*
*1/2 c. thick white sauce (page 273)*

*1-2 eggs, separated*
*salt, pepper to taste*

Never separated egg whites from yolks? Crack the egg in half gently against the side of a pot, or strike a knife against the shell. Hold half the shell in each hand. Most of the white will drool into the container by itself. Help the rest by moving the yolk back and forth between the shell halves. Don't kill yourself to get all the white. It's okay if a little yolk stays along.

After separating the eggs, mix a spoonful of the cooked sauce into the yolks so they won't hard-boil, then add them to the sauce to make it thicker and richer. Now toss in the poached fish and seasonings. Stir and remove sauce from heat. Reserve (in tent if there are flies).

Beat egg whites with the spring-loaded swizzle stick or a wire whisk. (If you can spare two eggs, all the better, but one will do, too.) The idea is to get them stiff but not dry. Out here in the wilderness, this isn't always possible or necessary. Basically you're trying to whip air into them. The bigger the pot and the more you agitate the egg whites, the better your chances of ending up with the right product. We've tried to use forks as beaters with little luck. Our trusty swizzle stick was just the ticket until it finally broke down this past year. It seems irreplaceable. (Try some old bar or kitchen-supply stores.) A miniature wire whisk works okay.

Fold the beaten egg whites into the sauce, gently as she goes. Just turn the sauce over on the whites with a spoon till they're pretty thoroughly incorporated. Lose their air and the soufflé will end up with a specific gravity close to that of lead.

Now grease and lightly flour the middle-sized pot (even if you have to do some dish washing and pot juggling to get it free and clean), and pour in the soufflé mixture. It should come about one-third of the way up the pot, depending on how much fish you have. Cover and bake.

You've already got a fire going (to poach and thicken the sauce) so by now the coals are glowing red. Scoop out a pot-sized depression in the ashes near the front of the fire and set the pot down—not on the coals, but on the cleared ground or warm ashes. With a heavy stick, pile coals around the pot until it's nestled up to its lid in heat. If the coals are too hot, the soufflé will burn. If they're too cool, it'll take ages to cook and you'll do a slow burn with it. Ideally, the coals should have lost their most intense heat; the fiery red glare should be going out of them. Baking time will be about 20 to 30 minutes, or a chapter from a good book. You may need to add coals to the pile to keep its warmth constant.

It's permissible to peek but be careful not to knock everything awry or get ashes in the pot. Don't worry if the outside of the soufflé is slightly burned; the inside will be as tasty as promised. The soufflé *will* actually rise, to almost double its bulk, and will look spectacular. Savor it quickly, however, for it deflates rapidly after taken off the heat. But by then, appetite will take over from aesthetics. Tuck in, eat up.

## Trout Crêpes ❖

Once you can poach a fish and prepare a sauce, you also have the makings of the filling for crêpes.

*2-3 fresh trout, cleaned and poached*
*1 ¹/₂ c. thick white sauce, made with poaching liquid*
*seasonings to taste*
*2 c. crêpe batter (pages 284-285)*

Crêpes are made with eggs, so you don't need any in the sauce. Keep the sauce warm, near the fire, and covered while you make the crêpes. It's neither easy nor necessary to make all the crêpes at once, so eat them in turns as they come off the fire. Put a crêpe on a plate, spoon sauce into it, wrap and eat. Then let your partner(s) follow suit.

## Trout, Rice and Bean Salad ❖

Here's another use of poached trout, especially if you've had an abundance of luck on the lake. Take the leftover poached, flaked trout and add it to our famous Bean and Rice Salad (page 280).

## Sashimi (Japanese-style Raw Fish)

This book does not aim at conversions. If the idea of eating raw fish turns you green, move on to sauces. But if you like *sashimi*, learn how to prepare it, because you'll never have fresher fish than the ones you catch. Here are some important facts about preparing *sashimi* in the wilderness:

## *Raw Trout*

- The fish must be absolutely fresh. They can't sit around for a couple hours in a pot, even cleaned. You need to eat them soon after catching or keep them alive until you have enough (say, four or five 8" trout) for a meal. Incidentally, if you're fishing near a snowfield, you can pack your catch in snow immediately, and have them as iced as your local fishmonger's.

- There's not much flesh on a small trout. Some is also lost in skinning and boning. Don't expect a filling meal, but *sashimi* is a perfect lunch snack.

- There are two ways to prepare it. For both, clean the fish thoroughly. For the first method, skin it and peel the flesh from the bones. To skin a fish, begin by cutting under the fins and yanking them toward the head. Then slice along the backbone from head to tail. With your knife, loosen the skin around the gills. Now work your fingers, the knife or both, under the skin at the head and strip it back toward the tail. Once the fish is skinned, cut away the flesh, beginning at the backbone and working down. Toward the end, fingers work better than a knife. Place the raw fish in a Sierra cup.

- For the second method, bone the fish first, then remove the skin. Spread open the cleaned and beheaded fish, gutted side facing you. With your knife, cut gently along one side of the backbone from top to tail. Do the same on the other side. This severs the spine from the skeletal bones or ribs, and it can be pulled out, working from neck to tail. Last, get the skeletal bones out. Starting from the tail, work your blade under the bones gently toward the neck, turn the knife around, and then come back toward the tail. Starting from the neck, lift the bones away. This leaves a whole, flat, boned fish with the skin still on the "under" side. You can now remove the flesh from the skin by working your blade under the flesh and scraping it away. Start at the tail, which you can grasp for leverage, and move up. You'll have the fish in one piece this way. Again put it into a Sierra cup.

- One word of caution. All this boning and skinning tends to draw flies. Unless you're fast, you may want to do it in your tent. If so, spread a poncho on the floor so the tent will stay clean even if you're messy.

- You need a spicy condiment with your *sashimi*, as well as some soy sauce. The Japanese use a fiery green horseradish called *wasabi*. This comes in powdered form. You add enough water to make a paste, which is then added to the soy sauce. The fish is dipped into it and eaten straight away. You needn't carry a packet of dried *wasabi*. Dry mustard, particularly the good hot kind, will do just as well and is, frankly, more functional, since you can use it in many other dishes. Either way, *sashimi* is great! Give it a try.

# Sauces

You've been in the mountains eight days and are low on supplies. You have some RyKrisps left, a lump of degenerating cheese, a few spoonfuls of flour, some oil that looks like it came from a crank case and a handful of milk powder. The prospects of catching a trout are dim. You want a hot meal. Not to worry! If you know how to make a sauce, you're in business. A combination of oil, flour, milk powder and water will give you a base for the cheese and whatever spices you have left. When it's all melted, thick and steaming hot, you've got yourself a kind of rarebit which can be eaten on the crackers for a filling, hearty meal.

This kind of sauce, practically a meal in itself, can also stretch other foods far and in many directions. It has almost as many names as uses: cream sauce, white sauce, bechamel. It's basically equal parts shortening (usually butter) and flour, which are heated for a few minutes before you slowly add liquid (usually milk or the stock with which you've been cooking). That's it. Some seasonings, cheese, perhaps an egg yolk give you sauce thick enough to eat alone or use in a soufflé, crêpes, curry or cream soup.

At home, you'd use real butter and whole milk. Over an open fire and with neither on hand, the technique changes a bit, but the principle is the same.

*White Sauce* ❖
*3 sp. margarine / shortening / oil*
*3 sp. flour*
*1-2 c. poaching liquid, or 1-2+ c. water*
*1 sp. milk powder*
*salt, pepper, curry powder, nutmeg, paprika to taste*

In a small pot, melt the margarine (or, in descending order of preference, shortening or oil: they all work). Add an equal amount of flour (heaping spoonfuls if a very thick sauce is desired). Stir this mixture over the heat for a minute or two to kill the taste of the raw flour. In your kitchen you'd use a low flame. At a campfire, that isn't so easy; alternate the pan on and off the heat to prevent the sauce from burning. If you are using the poaching liquid from the fish, add this a little at a time, stirring. If you are using the milk powder and water, add the milk powder to the mixture, then add the water a little at a time, stirring. The mixture will thicken almost instantly. Continue to add liquid slowly. By the time you've added a cupful or more, the sauce will have thinned out, much to the relief of anyone who thought they were being conned into making kindergarten paste. Keep stirring till smooth. Add seasonings to taste. The sauce is done when reasonably thick and smooth. Don't lose heart if the flour and milk powder aren't completely absorbed by the liquid. It'll still be hot, filling and delicious. When done, add whatever else you want: poached fish, crushed biscuits, cheese, cooked rice, noodles.

## United Nations Rarebit ❖

It would be an insult to the Welsh to call this by its conventional name, so we'll let the National Security Council decide its provenance. Anyway, it'll stick to more than ribs and keep you fat and happy.

*3 c. white sauce*
*3-4+ sp. sliced cheese*
*1 egg (optional)*
*hot sauce*
*brandy*

Add as much sliced cheese as you can spare to the completed white sauce. If you have an extra egg, beat it well and add. Continue to stir till cheese is melted. Season with hot sauce to taste and a dash of brandy from the medicine kit. Serve on crackers, boiled rice or fresh baked bread.

If the sauce is too thick or pasty, keep adding liquid till you get the right consistency. If it's too thin, either let the sauce boil down while stirring, or in a pot lid, make five or six marble-sized balls of dough from flour and shortening or oil. Drop these into the sauce and stir. They'll thicken the sauce without leaving it filled with lumps of unabsorbed flour, which you'd get if you added flour alone to the sauce.

## *Tomato Sauce* ❖

Here is the stripped-down fighting version of the homemade sauce (page 245) you weren't able to dehydrate this year. As long as you have some dried tomatoes and onions, perhaps some dried mushrooms and jerky, you're in business. You'll use this sauce for pasta and for the pizza (page 300) you can't live without.

*1 lg hfl. dehydrated tomatoes*
*1 hfl. dehydrated onions*
*1 clove garlic, sliced*
*1 hfl. dehydrated mushrooms*
*2 sp. sliced or diced jerky (optional)*
*mixed Italian spices*
*salt, pepper to taste*
*water*

Cover the tomatoes with twice their volume of water. Bring to boil and stir frequently while the tomatoes are rehydrating. Add water as necessary. The tomatoes will not completely transform into a sauce, but enough so to give a first-rate illusion of same, in about 20 minutes. About half way through the cooking, add the onions, mushrooms, garlic, jerky and spices. Continue to cook till the ingredients absorb most of the water and become saucy. Adjust seasonings. Ta da!

*Note*: If this is going to be the base of your pizza, omit the onions, mushrooms and jerky, as they'll go on separately.

# Rice, Noodles and Beans

You can't always count on catching fish, but you can always count on a hot and filling meal if you have any of these great staples of backpacking. They can be eaten alone, hot or cold (though cooked), in stews and soups, in freeze-dried dinners to add bulk and a little real taste, in puddings, salads, omelets and a thousand other dishes. Their only drawback is that they're heavy, so you need to limit the amounts you take and make do with what you can sensibly carry.

## *Rice*

Put two generous handfuls of white rice in the medium pot with a pinch of salt. Add enough water to come up to just below the middle knuckle of your forefinger. This is enough rice for two adults. We can't explain the knuckle measure. It was taught to us years ago, and for reasons that are still mysterious, it's invariably correct. Neither the size of the finger nor the size of the hand nor the size pot seem to matter. Remember: the water will boil faster in the mountains than at sea level. Thus the knuckle measure will give you more water to start off with than you'd use for a good fluffy rice at home.

White rice cooks in about 10 to 15 minutes, depending on the heat of the fire. Brown rice requires more water, to about the middle of the knuckle, and more time to cook. Allow about 25 minutes. To make the pot easier to clean, pour water in it immediately after you've spooned out the rice, and keep it warm near the fire. By wash-up time, the pot almost cleans itself!

## Fried Rice With Vegetables & Chicken ❖

This joins Trout Tandoori and Fried Rice Chinese Style in the fried rice repertoire.

*2 hfl. boiled rice*
*1 c. mixed dried vegetables, rehydrated in water to cover*
*1 hfl. chopped nuts*
*sliced/diced chicken jerky (optional)*
*1 clove garlic, sliced*
*cooking oil*
*hot sauce, spices to taste*

Heat the oil in the frying pan, add garlic and nuts till just turning brown, then veggies and spices. Stir and saute till done; add cooked rice, stir till thoroughly mixed. Adjust seasonings.

## Risottos

If you've got plenty of fuel and patience—risottos require constant stirring—you can make any of the risotto recipes in Chapter 9, pages 235-239, on a camp stove or fire.

## Rice Pudding ✹

This can be a meal in itself—dessert and main course combined. Seem like too many ingredients? Maybe, but check that food list (Table 1) back in Chapter 5. You have all the makings well within your weight limit.

2 hfl. cooked rice
1 sp. milk powder
$^1/_2$ c. water
2+ sp. sugar
pinch of salt
cinnamon to taste
1 egg
dash lemon / lime juice
$^1/_2$ sp. margarine
1 hfl. chopped dried fruit
dash of brandy (your basic vanilla substitute)
1 hfl. crushed ginger snaps / crackers

Oil or grease a medium pot. Line it with crushed ginger snaps or crackers. Mix the rice, milk powder, water, sugar, salt, cinnamon, egg, lemon juice, margarine, fruit, and brandy thoroughly and add to the lined pot. Cover with more crushed ginger snaps. Cover and bake in coals or in camping oven until pudding is set, about 20 minutes. Eat hot or cold.

If you're out of some ingredients, improvise. No spare egg? You can still make the pudding. It may not be as rich, but no one's measuring on a taste meter. Substitute a spoonful of flour or cornmeal and a little more water. No margarine? Use oil. Ditto for the seasonings—not everyone carries lemon juice or even cinnamon (although no backpacker carrying cinnamon has ever been known to starve in the wilderness). Maybe throw in some Swiss Miss powdered chocolate drink instead of sugar and cinnamon. Fine. And of course the cookie crumbs can be left out. Experiment. Enjoy.

## Noodles

If pasta palls, go East. Chinese wheat or rice noodles, Japanese buckwheat noodles (*soba*) are great boiled, fried or baked. They can substitute for almost all the rice recipes: Trout Tandoori; Fried Rice Chinese Style; Trout, Rice and Bean Salad; or Fried Rice with Vegetables and Chicken.

## Cooking Noodles ❖

Noodles don't double in bulk when cooked, but the more water you use, the less they stick together and to the pot. Use the large pot, half to three-quarters full of water, add salt, boil and throw in the noodles. Two very generous handfuls will get two of you through a meal. The water should boil rapidly as they cook. They taste done in about 10 to 12 minutes (at moderate to high altitudes). If you plan to use them in another dish, you need time to put it together, just drain the noodles, add fresh cold water to cover and let them stand. This prevents them from sticking together. When everything is ready, drain them again and away you go. If you make a sauce, use the noodle water as the liquid base. It's already hot and flavorful.

## Cold Noodle Salad ❖

*¹/₂ packet Japanese buckwheat noodles (soba), cooked and drained*
*sesame oil / regular cooking oil*
*rice vinegar / regular vinegar*
*1 hfl. dried mixed vegetables, rehydrated*
*sprinkling of mung bean sprouts (optional)*
*salt, pepper to taste*

Mix all ingredients in a pot. Adjust seasonings. Serve.

## Beans ❖

Beans are so good, nutritious and easily prepared that it's a pity they weigh so much. Nevertheless, they are definitely worth taking along, in limited amounts. And it doesn't matter what kinds you bring. Red, kidney, white, or black beans can all be used with equal ease. Put a couple handfuls in a pot, cover with cold water, cover the pot and soak overnight or for four to five hours during the day. Empty the old water, cover again with fresh water, and cook until the beans are tender, 25 to 40 minutes, depending on the amount and kind of beans and the heat of the fire. That's all there is to it. Use the cooking liquid for making sauces.

Lentils and split peas may be substituted for beans in most of these recipes. *Note*: Watch your fuel supply if cooking beans on a camp stove. It may cost you other meals down the line.

## Fried Rice and Beans ❖

As any Mexican cook will tell you, the combination of rice and beans is a nutritional powerhouse. It's also plain good eating. Spice it up with chili powder, cayenne or hot sauce and you've got a ready-made fiesta. To the recipe Fried Rice with Vegetables and

Chicken add cooked beans and fry till done. If spicy, make sure you've got a full water bottle within reach.

## Four-Wheel Drive Vegetarian Chili ❖

You need a Land Rover to get all the ingredients of this great chili into your car campsite, but the 25 skeptics who recently ate it under the baton of Marc Girouard would now gladly lease a limo if necessary. And if you're a backpacker, just dry the finished product on your home dehydrator and rehydrate over the camp stove. Same results, same bliss.

*1 c. dried red kidney (or black or pinto) beans, soaked overnight, rinsed, and*
    *simmered in water until done, about one hour*
*3 onions, chopped*
*4 Tbs. oil*
*2 green peppers, chopped*
*2-3 jalepeño peppers, minced and with seeds removed*
*3 cloves garlic, crushed or minced*
*2 bay leaves*
*1/2 Tbs. ground cumin*
*2 Tbs. chili powder*
*1 12-oz. bottle of beer (preferably ale or porter)*
*salt (optional) and pepper to taste*
*1 c. corn (fresh or frozen)*
*fresh cilantro*
*cheddar cheese, grated*
*sour cream*

While beans are cooking, sauté in a big pot the onions in the oil, then add and sauté the green peppers, jalepeños, garlic, bay leaves, cumin and chili powder till soft. Pour the beer into the pot, add the cooked beans and 1 1/2 qts. canned tomatoes drained of juices, plus seasonings and corn. Bring to boil. Simmer one hour or longer. (You've brought coals or a hotshot camping stove along so there's no eco-disaster built into the cooking time.) Serve topped with chopped fresh cilantro, cheese, and sour cream. (Omit sour cream if backpacking. It won't keep.)

## Baked Rice and Beans in Cheese Sauce ✹
*1 hfl. boiled rice*
*1 hfl. cooked beans*

*2 c. white sauce*
*3 sp. sliced cheese*
*cayenne, chili powder, hot sauce*

To the white sauce, add the cheese and stir till melted. Add the rice and beans, mix. Bake in coals 10 to 15 minutes till set. Serve with mariachi music and plenty of water.

## Refried Beans ❖

*2 hfl. cooked beans and the cooking liquid*
*cooking oil*
*hot sauce, pepper*
*sliced cheese*

Drain the beans but reserve the liquid. Heat oil in the frying pan. Mash the beans with a fork or spatula as they're frying. If the beans get too dry, add some of the reserved liquid. Fry slowly, season with pepper and hot sauce. Slice cheese to taste over them. Eat with biscuits and you get a great Tex-Mex meal.

## Ranch Omelet ❖

For two adults, scramble three eggs with refried beans and some dried tomatoes. Serve with plenty of hot sauce.

## Bean and Rice Salad ❖

*2 hfl. beans, cooked, drained, cooled*
*2 hfl. cooked rice*
*1 poached trout (optional)*
*1 hfl. bean sprouts*
*salt, pepper, lemon juice, sesame oil, mustard powder*

Mix all ingredients together. Season to taste. This is a wonderful meal, even without the trout.

## Bean and Sprouts Salad ❖

Same as above, though without the rice. Use half beans and half mung-bean sprouts. Season as above.

## Bean Sprouts

We always bring some dry mung beans to sprout on the trail. They're a great snack, excellent in soups, fried rice, sauces, soufflés and salads. The first night, soak a handful in a plastic bag. In the morning, drain the water, close the bag and keep in a dark place. While hiking, we carry them in the smallest nested pot; at camp, they're stored in the backpack. Rinse once or twice a day to keep moist, but not wet. They'll sprout in about three days. They don't need to be cooked, but do get moldy fast, so when they're ready, use them. Then begin a new batch.

# Drinking Your Dinner: Soups and Stews

The dry soup mixes that you buy in the local market taste all right, but they're not very filling. If they're going to be your supper, you need to jack them up, give them some body and thus a bit of soul. A handful of uncooked rice or noodles, as much cooked rice and beans as you want, a clove of garlic, a slice of onion, vegetables from your home dehydrator, broken crackers, poached fish, cheese—whatever seems to fit your soup mix will thicken the pot. Starting from scratch is easy, too. Here are a couple examples:

### Fish Stew or Chowder ❖

Clean two or three fish, but save the heads. Toss fish and heads into the big pot, cover with water and poach. Save the liquid in another pot, remove and bury the bones, heads and skin, then combine the fish and liquid. If necessary, add water. Toss in two handfuls of rice (less if you have more fish), and as much chopped onion and garlic as you can spare. Season with salt, pepper, herbs and even a dash of hot sauce. Boil slowly until the rice is done. The thicker the better, so a packet of dry soup mix, especially leek, helps immeasurably. Ignore the packet's directions, and keep tinkering with the seasonings until it tastes just right.

VARIATIONS:
- For Chinese-style hot-and-sour soup, add a good dash of vinegar and considerable black pepper.
- For New England-style chowder, add a spoonful of milk powder just before it comes off the fire.

### Black Bean Soup ❖

Soak overnight and cook two handfuls of black beans in the big pot. If you've got a packet of chicken or beef soup stock, add that, as much dried chopped onion as you can spare, some chips of jerky, lots of garlic, salt, pepper and cayenne. Bring to a boil and let simmer for an hour if you've got the time and the coals are working right. Long cooking gives it more flavor, but even 20 minutes is fine since all the ingredients have already been cooked. Just before serving, add a dash of lemon juice or vinegar and a good hit of brandy. That's it. You'll want seconds, guaranteed. And if you don't have black beans, use what you have and just call it by a different name.

### Lentil or Pea Soups ❖

If you prefer lentils or dried peas to beans and noodles, take them to use as you would for bean soup. Like beans, lentils and peas need two- to three-hours' soaking time before cooking.

## Pancakes and Crêpes

There's something about the cold morning air, a warm fire, a hot griddle and real maple syrup that makes pancakes almost a ritual necessity on a backpacking trip. Here's how to make them.

Ready-made pancake mixes are available in supermarkets. Natural ones are available in some health food and whole food stores. They're adequate. The only problem is you can't unmix them. All you can do with them is make pancakes. If you try using it as a flour supplement or substitute in breads and cakes, you'll end up with something that tastes and looks like a pancake with elephantiasis. The same goes for sauces. You get a warm pancake batter (with cheese), edible only in life-threatening situations. As long as you're taking flour, eggs and milk powder anyway, why not start from scratch?

Pancake batter is made of flour, eggs and milk, to which some shortening and a leavening agent such as baking powder are added. Change the proportions and you get different kinds of pancakes—like crêpes, for example. There are only a few general rules:

- Always add the liquid ingredients to the dry. This is a conservation principle: if you start with too much liquid, you'll waste a lot of flour thickening the batter. But starting with flour, you can add the liquid gradually until the batter is just right. Water is usually expendable.

- You don't need to grease your pan if the batter is made right. The oil or shortening goes in the batter, not in the pan. A thin film of oil won't hurt, but with a decent pan—it doesn't even have to be teflon-coated—it won't be necessary. Crêpes need a little oil in the pan, but not much.

- Heat the pan before you pour the batter in. Test by splashing a few drops of water into the pan. If they dance, sizzle and evaporate, you're ready to go.

- The first pancake is a test run. If it sticks to the pan or isn't golden brown, the pan isn't "tempered" yet. Scrape it off. The second won't stick. If the first one tastes like a sodden brick, you need more liquid. A runny mess means you need more flour. Refine the batter—the rest of the pancakes will be good.

## Basic Pancakes ❖

At home, the usual proportion for pancakes is roughly 2:2:2—two cups flour, two cups milk and two eggs. In the wilderness, the proportions are the same, though the quantity is reduced. A Sierra cup holds around six heaping spoonfuls of flour, which makes way too many pancakes for two adults. Our recipes make from 10 to 12 inflated "silver dollar" pancakes, more than enough for two. The cakes are thick, light and filling. You could write home about them, except there isn't a post office within three-days' walk.

*4 heaping sp. flour*
*1 sp. milk powder*
*dash of salt*
*¹/₂ sp. sugar (optional)*
*1 egg, beaten*
*2 sp. oil/melted margarine*
*¹/₂ c. water*

In a small pot, mix the flour, milk powder, salt, and, if you like, the sugar and leavening agent. Don't worry if you don't have baking powder or soda; they're not necessary, and frankly, we rarely use them for pancakes at any altitude, home or away. Add the beaten egg and oil to the dry ingredients and stir quickly. To hell with any lumps! Now add the water gradually, stirring. The batter will be thick. So you may need to add a bit more water, just enough to keep it thick but still smooth enough to flow off a spoon, like a thick velvet ribbon. Don't worry about getting a perfectly smooth batter. Lumps will disappear in the cooking.

To cook, drop a large spoonful of batter in the middle of the heated pan. If it looks pitifully small, add a dollop more. The cake is ready to flip (only once) when bubbles begin to form on the surface. Flip and let it cook another few minutes. The second side never takes as long as the first. That's it. Eat! Or, if the first one is good, make three or four pancakes at one time so that one of you can have a decent breakfast. Then trade places.

VARIATIONS:

- Use the same proportions, but separate the egg and use only the yolk. After the batter is ready, beat the white until it's stiff but not dry, exactly as you would for a soufflé. Fold the beaten white into the batter gently, to preserve as much of the air as possible. Cook as above. The result will be so light that you'll seriously rethink the theory of gravity.

- Chop apricots, apples, banana chips into tiny pieces and add to the batter.

- Add a half-spoonful of sourdough starter to the dry ingredients and omit the baking powder (See Starting the Sourdough, page 290). Whole wheat or buckwheat flour, a mixture of flour and cornmeal work well and make great pancakes. So do flour with ground up RyKrisp, ginger snaps or vanilla wafers. Just remember that each kind of flour has a different moisture content, so adjust the liquid accordingly.

## Crêpes ❖

Crêpes are French pancakes. They should be paper-thin, to wrap other foods in. To achieve the thinness, change the proportions of flour to liquid to eggs. At home, it would be roughly 2:2:4 (two cups flour, two cups milk and four eggs). At 9,000 feet, you're unlikely to have that many eggs to spare. So stick with one egg and follow the basic pancake recipe with the following changes:

Omit the baking powder or soda. Instead of a spoonful of milk powder, use a half-spoonful and increase the water to make a thin batter—thin enough to look drinkable, like a homemade smoothie.

No self-respecting crêpe recipe includes oil in the batter. If tradition counts with you, leave it out and spread a thin film of oil on the pan for each crêpe. We, however, are not so self-respecting, and after making sure the Academie Française is not meeting in the nearest bog, we throw in a spoonful anyway.

If you have time to fish before breakfast, set the crêpe batter aside, covered, in a cool spot. Crêpe batter is happier if it sits a while. When you get back, poach your fish, crank up a sauce and savor trout crêpes.

COOKING THE CRÊPES:

Pour two or three spoons of batter into a sizzling pan. Tilt the pan away from you, then to the side, then toward you so the batter spreads out roughly in a circle as thin as you can get it. The more you practice, the easier it gets and the rounder and thinner the crêpes will be. They'll only take a minute or so to cook and are ready to turn when the center looks almost, but not quite, dry. Either work a spatula underneath to turn it, or pick it up in your hand and flip it over. The second side takes less time than the first. The result should be cooked but also pliable, so it can be wrapped around food.

CRÊPE FILLINGS:
- For trout crêpes, see page 271
- For cheese crêpes, see page 273 under Sauces/White Sauce

# Fruit Crêpes

Simmer a handful or so of mixed dried fruits in water to cover. Add a spoonful or two of sugar. Stir and simmer till a thick stewed fruit is formed. Stuff crêpes with the fruit, sprinkle sugar and cinnamon on top and serve. These can also be flambéed after dark, as homage to the inventor of Crêpes Suzette.

# Breads

Anybody who can make pancakes can make pan-fried bread. And anybody who can make the dough for pan-fried breads can add some yeast and bake the bread in a pot in the coals. And anybody who can do that can just as easily make a cake. No excuses.

For pancakes, the liquid ingredients outnumber the dry ones and you end up with batter. In bread, the opposite is true and you end up with dough. The dough can be picked up without running down your sleeve and dripping all over your shoe. It can be folded or spindled without harm. A cake is somewhere in between: in other words it is a stiff sweet batter and the promise of dessert.

There's considerable lore about campfire breads and cakes, such as bannock, the basic pan bread. It is so basic that it consists of little more than flour and water with a little baking powder and salt tossed in for luck. Or sourdough, the old-time, homemade substitute for yeast once carried around in pots hung from the saddle in California's gold country. But lore's a bore when you're hungry. Here are some of our favorite mountain breads.

## Pan-Fried Breads ❖

This recipe is so uncompromisingly basic that it has little to recommend it except to give you an idea of how simple bread-making is. Try it once for experience, then move on to the tastier variations.

In the medium-sized pot, mix together four heaping spoonfuls of flour, $1/4$ spoonful of baking powder, and a pinch of salt. Add enough water to make a stiff but smooth dough that you can pick up and handle without half of it sticking to your fingers. Have the flour sack handy so you can keep both hands floured, and if necessary, add small increments of flour to the dough to get the right consistency. Put a layer of oil in the frypan to preheat, and form six to eight small patties of dough, about the size of a muffin and $1/2$" to $3/4$" thick. (If you like flipping them in the air, cook one at a time.) Let them brown slowly over a moderate bed of coals. If the fire is too hot, the crust will cook too fast, leaving the insides half raw. Flip or use a spatula to turn them, as often as you like. They're done when they sound hollow to the tap of a finger, roughly 15 minutes, and they are more than enough for two ravenous adults.

## Cornmeal Muffins ❖

In the medium pot, mix together two heaping spoonfuls of flour and two of cornmeal. Add a pinch of salt, a spoonful of sugar and one of oil, a half spoonful of milk powder, and a quarter spoonful of baking powder. Mix thoroughly, then add enough water to make a smooth dough, easy to handle but not sticky. Keeping your hands lightly floured, form the dough into whatever shape suits you. Cook as above. The result is indecently good, a cross between English muffins and old-fashioned corn fritters, or something like famous Southern hush puppies. Eat them plain, with a sprinkling of sugar, or split open and covered with maple syrup. They're also great with grilled or foil-baked fish.

VARIATIONS:

- For part of the cornmeal or flour, substitute a packet of dry instant oatmeal.

- Dust the muffins with cornmeal before you fry them.

- Season with pepper, nutmeg, cinnamon, sesame seeds or a small amount of crushed nuts.

## Griddle Breads ❖

Does anyone still own a griddle or even know what one is? Those old, flat cast-iron disks or slabs that used to cover openings in wood-burning stoves were griddles (or, as the Scots would say, girdles). By extension, so were (and still are) cast-iron frying pans. Put a cover over them, and you've got the hardware for griddle-baked breads. True, unless you've got a Winnebago, a pack horse, or the world's second biggest llama, it's unlikely you'll have iron to cook on in your campsite. Not to worry. That lightweight Teflon pan and a metal plate (or aluminum foil) will do just as well, as will a camping oven.

The main difference between the pan-fried breads above and griddle breads is that with a covered griddle, you don't always need to use oil in the pan. Just a sprinkling of flour. Watch.

## Scottish Griddle-Baked Scones ❖

*1 c. flour (remember, 1 c. here means a Sierra cupful)*
*³/₄ sp. baking powder or baking soda*
*large pinch of salt*
*2 sp. sourdough starter*
*water*

Mix the dry ingredients together. Add the sourdough starter and just enough water to make a soft dough. Flour your hands, mix. Pat into a round shape about ¹/₄" to ¹/₂" thick. (If much thicker, they'll burn on the outside before the inside is done.) Cut into six wedge-shaped pieces. Place on a lightly floured frying pan.

(Optionally, you may lightly oil the pan and then coat with flour.) Cover with the pan with a metal plate, pot lid, or aluminum foil. Place over "slow" coals. When browned on bottom, turn to brown the other side. When the middle is just dry, they're done. Put on your Scottish kilt, grab a caber to defend against ravenous lowlanders, slather with honey or jam, and eat while reciting the lesser poems of Robert Burns.

SCONE VARIATIONS:
- If traveling with a cooler, substitute buttermilk or sour cream or yogurt for the sourdough starter.
- Add an egg.
- Add a handful of milk powder.
- Add a spoonful of sugar.

## Griddle Corn Bread ❖

This is a skillet-baked variation of Cornmeal Muffins, page 286, and our other corn breads, page 299, though we've altered the proportions here.

*1 c. flour*
*$^1/_2$ c. cornmeal*
*1 sp. baking powder*
*1 sp. sugar*
*1 sp. milk powder*
*large pinch of salt*
*1 egg*
*large squirt of oil or 1 spoonful of melted margarine*
*water*

Mix the dry ingredients together. Add the slightly beaten egg, the oil and just enough water to make a moist, pliable dough that you can gently knead. Shape into a round, about $^1/_4$" thick, cut into wedge-shaped slices, bake in a lightly floured, covered skillet over "slow" coals. Turn once when lightly browned. Bake about 10 to 15 minutes.

## Irish Soda Bread ❖

The chief difference between the Scottish griddle-baked scones above and this recipe is in the cudgel you use to fend off the churls who want to pry the bread from hearth and hand. Down the caber, up the shillelagh!

*1 c. flour*
*¹/₂ sp. baking soda (or in a pinch, baking powder)*
*large pinch of salt*
*sugar to taste*
*1 sp. milk powder*
*1+ sp. margarine*
*water*

Mix the dry ingredients. Add the margarine, and with your fingers, mix it in until it is the consistency of a coarse cornmeal. Add enough water to make a moist dough. Shape into a round about ¹/₂" thick, then slice into wedges (farls to the Irish), and bake on a covered, oiled skillet over "slow" coals. When browned on the bottom, turn 'em over and continue for another, say, 5-10 minutes, depending on the heat of the flame. Eat to the accompaniment of wild Gaelic verse and a hearty stew. Question: Whaddaya do if you only have baking powder? Right. Rename it Irish Baking Powder Bread and drink a toast to Anna Livia Plurabelle.

VARIATIONS:

- Add raisins, currants, even trail mix.

- Omit oil in the pan. Just flour lightly.

## Baked Breads

Baked breads involve one more step than pan-fried, and a lot more time. The extra step is mixing a leavening agent into the dough to lighten it—to puff it up with a myriad of tiny bubbles, making it rise before it's baked. The mixing must be thorough, so you have to punch and push—or "knead"—the dough fully. There are a number of leavening agents. Yeast is the most famous, sourdough starter is another. We carry several packets of store-bought dry yeast with us, and take along a small plastic bottle with sourdough starter. Baking powder and soda work only under extreme heat (in the act of baking itself) and can't be used for pre-bake rising.

STARTING THE YEAST:

All leavening agents work by slowly releasing gas, which gets trapped in the dough and which, in trying to get out, forces it to expand. Yeast needs warmth to produce the gas. In the wilderness, the sun is your warmth. It's also possible to use the warmth of dying coals, but the sun is always your best bet. Don't plan to let your bread rise at night.

Yeast is also activated by warm water and sugar; it's inert until this is done. Sometimes it gets too inert or stale. Check the date on your yeast packets. It should read at least a couple of months ahead. To activate, sprinkle the amount of yeast you need, usually a packet or less, over a half cup of water that's only warm enough to keep your finger in. Add a couple generous pinches of sugar, mix thoroughly, cover and set aside in a warm place until you're ready to add it to the dough. When the yeast is frothy and expanding, it's ready to use.

STARTING THE SOURDOUGH:

Sourdough is exactly that: a dough made of flour and water that has begun fermenting, thus growing microscopic organisms that give off carbon-dioxide gas and a characteristically sour smell as they feed. In its working form, this is called a "starter" because, like yeast, it initiates the leavening process. Having carried it into the mountains and hung it in a tree to get warm and smelly, you're ready to use it freely in breads, pancakes, etc.

In theory, sourdough starter is a complete substitute for yeast. In frontier days, it was impossible to keep yeast fresh, but sourdough could be replenished every time it was used, thus keeping it alive and ready indefinitely. The best starter comes from the sourdough pot of a friend whose family has kept it, along with great-grandad's Klondike nugget, for a hundred years. Or you can buy dried starter in a health food outlet. But if great-grandad took his starter (and nugget) to the grave, and the store is out, here is a basic starter recipe to make at home before beginning your trip.

Heat a cup of milk, add a cup of water and cool to lukewarm. Thoroughly mix one tablespoon of sugar, a teaspoon of salt and two cups of flour in a large bowl—it's going to expand. Cover the bowl with a towel and leave in a warm place for four or five days or until it looks and smells frothy. Now add a package of yeast. Re-cover the bowl, and let it sit at room temperature for another week. Stir it down each day and don't worry how it smells or looks: the badder the better. Store in a jar in the fridge until you're ready to use it.

Sourdough starter alone was fine for Yukon prospectors, but frankly it takes so long for dough to rise that it often dries out, leaving you with a loaf that looks and feels like a gold brick. We always add yeast to the sourdough starter, hedging our bets. Things move along at a fine pace and the bread tastes better, too.

## Basic Mountain Loaf *

A loaf of bread will be as big or small as you have flour to spare. Everything else is secondary. If you have nothing but flour, water and yeast, you can make bread. It might not win prizes at the Happy Valley bake-a-thon, but it will beat dried-out Triscuits. And with any additional ingredients like salt, milk powder, sugar, oil, sourdough, raisins, nuts, cornmeal, oatmeal, a spare egg, onion, garlic, cinnamon, nutmeg, sesame, poppy or sunflower seeds, to name a few, your breads will become a hedonist camper's dream come true.

The following recipe makes about the smallest loaf that is practical and still plentiful for two people. To double it, use twice as much flour but the same amount of yeast, salt and milk. Smaller pots bake better, though a bigger bread will require a larger pot.

Your basic utensils are: two pots, a plate, a Sierra cup, a spoon and eventually, a bed of hot coals or an Outback Oven.

To one-half Sierra cup of warm water, add a packet of yeast and a couple pinches of sugar. Cover and set in a warm place. In the medium pot, mix together a Sierra cup of flour, a dash of salt, one spoonful each of milk powder and oil or melted margarine. Mix the bubbly yeast into the pot thoroughly. The result will be lumpish, perhaps soggy. Never mind. If a lot of the flour is still dry, add a bit more water, not much. You want a fairly stiff dough, not a batter.

Now turn this out onto a floured plate or flat, clean floured rock. Flour your hands and keep the bag nearby. The aim is to turn this sodden stuff into smooth, springy, velvety dough. You do this by kneading—that is, by folding the dough over and over onto itself. Use the heel of your palm to push the dough away from you, fold it back on itself, give it a quarter turn, repeat, turn, repeat, and so on. If the flour on your hands and the plate doesn't suffice, add flour in very small amounts, and knead thoroughly before adding any more. As you knead, the dough will take shape, becoming firm and springy. Conversely, if it gets too hard to knead (or is hard at the outset), you have too much flour and need a little more liquid, either water or oil, the latter being easier to work in at this stage. Soon, the consistency will be just right. The dough is easy and pleasurable to work. You may find yourself spacing out and kneading just because it feels good. It can't hurt, so enjoy it. No harm if you want to go on for a half hour, though 5 or 10 minutes should suffice. The finished dough will spring slowly back when you poke a finger into it. Don't be dismayed if the dough takes on the hue of your pot-blackened hands or picks up small pieces of dirt. You won't taste or see it, nor contract some dreaded mountain disease.

When the dough is kneaded to perfection, it's ready to rise. Grease or oil the small pot, bottom and sides, and drop in the dough ball. Roll it around so its surface gets fully coated with oil. Now remove the dough, re-oil the pot and dust it with a little flour, a process that helps prevent the baked bread from sticking. Set the dough back in, cover, put it in a warm place and go off to fish, read, sleep, whatever, for an hour or so while the dough rises to double its original bulk.

What's a warm place? Any sun-exposed spot is ideal, unless the sun is searing; then warmth in the shade will be fine. A tent in the sun works. Sometimes we stow the pot in a sleeping bag if the day isn't too warm. Avoid setting the pot near the fire. It may get too hot and bake the bread.

What if it clouds over and gets cold? Not to worry, the rising just takes longer—all day is all right. If it's not ready before bed-time, wait till morning, knead the dough some more to bring the spring back and let it rise again. It's ready to bake when it's doubled in bulk. Incidentally, if you have time, breads are lighter and tastier if you let them rise twice, punching down the dough after the first rising and allowing it to double again. Literally, make a fist and jab the dough in mid-section. It will deflate. Then cover it and let the rising continue.

It's perfectly kosher to peek at the working dough. But it isn't an elevator; you won't be able to see it rise. If things go right, it will rise even if it takes time. If everything goes wrong and it won't rise, just turn the mess into a cake (see Getting a Rise Out of a Dud, page 298). What if it doesn't rise and you don't want a cake? Pretend it's fully risen and bake it anyway. The fire's heat gives a last lift to the dough, so the finished loaf will be fine, somewhat heavy but just as tasty.

Let's assume, however, that the dough did double, it didn't rain, the coals are still hot and you're ready to bake. If you wish, gently spread a light film of oil or melted shortening over the top of the dough with your fingers or the underside of a spoon. The oil will give a beautiful brown color to the top crust.

Oven-baked bread is usually started at a high temperature (400 degrees or higher), then after about 10 minutes the heat is reduced to 350 or 375 degrees to finish the baking, normally about 50 minutes. To reproduce those conditions in a bed of coals isn't easy, though as anyone who has ever made "coffee can bread" at summer camp knows, it's possible. The basic notion is to nestle the pot in a clearing in the warm ash or dirt, pile hot coals around it, then let them cool as the bread bakes. As more coals are needed to maintain the heat, rake them around the pot. On windy days, when the fire burns hot to windward and cool to leeward, rotate the pot 180 degrees every 15 minutes to assure an even distribution of heat.

Baking time differs according to the heat of the fire (which burns slower with wet wood, faster with dry wood, and hotter with soft wood), the size of the loaf and its ingredients. The basic mountain loaf should take between 20 and 30 minutes (or less on an Outback Oven, which, if wind-protected, disperses the heat evenly and bakes the bread faster). Baking time varies; keep checking. If the loaf sounds hollow when you tap it sharply, it's done. Remove the pot from the coals and set it to cool for 10 to 15 minutes. Under the best circumstances, when nothing has stuck to the sides, the loaf will come out when you turn the pot over and give it a couple of sharp raps on the bottom and top edges. Normally, though, you have to run a knife blade around the edges. In the worst of cases, so much will stick to the sides and bottom that you may have to saw the loaf in half and dig it out in sections. Usually, however, patience, cooling, deft use of the knife and a sharp knock of the pot against a rock brings forth a gorgeous golden loaf. Let it cool, then be prepared to defend your share against invaders from outer space—or your partner—intent on scarfing it down in one mega-bite!

No doubt about it, the Basic Mountain Loaf is a taste of camping heaven. Using the rough ratio of a generous cup of flour to an ungenerous half-cup of liquid, a packet of yeast and kneading until you get a smooth, unsticky, springy dough, you can overcome all but the most exotic forms of munchies. But the variations are better, and within each variation are other endless permutations.

### Sourdough Bread ●

Use the same proportions and ingredients as above, but add a spoonful of sourdough starter when you add the yeast. Depending on the starter's thickness, you may have to add a little more water or flour to the dough.

### Raisin-Nut Loaf ●

Also known as cinnamon-nut loaf, apricot-nut loaf, banana-nut loaf, mango-nut loaf, prune-nut loaf, nut-nut loaf. This one's sweet. Double the sugar, and add some cinnamon along with a good dash of baking powder or soda, which help enormously when fruit is involved. At the kneading stage, add half a handful of mixed raisins or finely chopped dried fruits and nuts. Proceed as above. Before baking, sprinkle the top with cinnamon, sugar and more chopped nuts.

### Jelly-Roll Bread ●

While the bread is rising, boil some dried fruit, sugar and water into a thick jelly. Punch down the dough and pat it out on a floured plate. Spread the jelly mixture on top of the flattened dough, roll it up and plop it back into the greased pot for a second rising. You can do the same sort of thing with a sugar-cinnamon-nut paste, using enough margarine to hold it together, and come up with the camping equivalent of a morning danish.

### Oatmeal Bread ●

Prepare a packet of instant oatmeal as though you're making breakfast, let it cool while you put together the dry ingredients (omitting the sugar) and start the yeast. Add the oatmeal along with the yeast and mix thoroughly. Continue as before.

### Herb Bread ●

To the Basic Loaf ingredients, add the following: a large pinch or two of sugar, a handful of uncooked instant oatmeal, a handful of whole wheat flour (or more, to your taste), a mix of dried herbs—dill, thyme, sage—and some caraway seeds if you've thought to bring 'em along instead of the Walkman. Toss in a beaten egg and a spoonful of melted margaine if you can spare them. This is a super bread and goes great with that vegetarian chili (page 279) you've just made.

## Onion and Garlic Bread ✻

Fry a large spoonful of chopped onion and garlic until they're translucent. Mix them into the dry ingredients of the Basic Mountain Loaf.

## Egg Breads ✻

An egg in any of the above recipes enriches the bread and adds more taste. If you use one, you may need more flour.

## Mountain Challah ✻

When you add the yeast, throw in an egg or two. Mix thoroughly. You may need more flour than usual to absorb the extra liquid. If possible, let this loaf rise twice. If you have eggs to spare, use a third, separated, as follows: Throw the white into the dough at the outset along with the other ingredients, but save the yolk. Then, just before baking, beat one-half spoonful of water into the yolk, and brush the top of the loaf with the egg and water mixture. It will produce a burnished golden finish that will drive neighboring backpackers into a near frenzy.

## Bagels ✻

"They're boiled, not baked!" One hears the cry of the purists, the keening sounds of the 2nd Avenue Deli. And they're right. This is so easy and so much fun that it's a wonder nobody thought it possible in a campsite before Rick was handed the recipe on stone tablets one day on a mountain which shall go unnamed.

Okay, you've got the Basic Loaf rising nicely in the sun. Build a fire, get a big pot of water boiling, beat an egg in a Sierra cup and reserve. When the dough's risen, flour your hands, pull a small clump off the dough, roll in your hands, then form a small doughnut round your finger. Do this for as many bagels as you want, but note that you're only going to be able to bake two or three at a time. Ready? Ease about two bagels at a time into the boiling water. Let 'em rise to the surface, about 30 seconds (45 seconds at high altitude), then turn them over with a spoon and let 'em boil another 30 or 45 seconds. Enough. Take 'em out, pat dry with a piece of toilet paper or your sweaty bandanna, coat lightly with the beaten egg, and set in the greased and floured medium-sized pot. Bake as you would the Basic Loaf, about 15 minutes or until golden. Nosh.

VARIATIONS (After boiling but before coating with egg):

• Sprinkle with toasted sesame seeds.

• Sprinkle with poppy seeds.

• Sprinkle with chopped, dried onion.

• Sprinkle with cinnamon and sugar (though Hal considers this heresy).

• Use a mix of whole wheat and white flour.

Note: If a couple of bagels each will do, form the remainder of the dough into a loaf, place in the small, prepared pot, spoon the rest of the beaten egg over the loaf and bake. Presto digito! A little challah to warm the heart.

## Chinese Steamed Buns (baozi) ❋

Continuing on our multi-cultural journey with the dough for the Basic Loaf, we arrive in China Camp in time for breakfast—or was it lunch, or dinner? Do you care? Steamed dumplings will stop your clock anyway, so who's looking?

The dough has risen and you've concocted a steamer (see instructions that follow). Tear off a small clump of dough, flatten it to about three or four inches in circumference on your hand or on a floured plate. Now place a small spoon of filling (see the following suggestions) in the center, and with your fingers work the dough up and around the filling till there's just a small opening at the top. Pinch that closed. When you've got the water boiling, place the buns on the steamer, cover, and steam about 20 minutes. Eat them plain or dipped in a mixture of soy sauce, vinegar, and hot sauce. Note: If you've got leftovers, re-steam them later. They'll be just as good.

FILLINGS:

• Poached trout marinated in soy sauce and ginger

• Chopped pieces of salami, jerky

• Rehydrated veggies seasoned with soy, garlic, ginger

• Left-over stir-fried veggies

• Dried fruit rehydrated with a spoon of sugar (Don't dip this in soy sauce or anything else!)

VARIATIONS:

- Omit stuffing (1). Just tear off a piece of risen dough, fashion into a roll and steam. This is your basic Chinese steamed bread *(mantou)*. Eat plain or, better, as a dunking tool with soups, stews, stir-fried veggies or fish.

- Omit stuffing (2). Tear off a large piece of risen dough, dust a plate with flour, flatten dough to about the size of the plate, sprinkle lightly with salt and a thin coat of oil. Roll up the dough like you would a rug. Now cut the rug into small (2- to 3-inch) segments, press each segment slightly in the middle with the back of a knife or a chopstick. Steam as above.

- Omit stuffing (3). Use a mixture of whole wheat and white flours. Add a small spoon of sugar to the dough when mixing (before kneading).

MAKING THE STEAMER:

Face it, you're not going to carry a Chinese bamboo steamer into the outback, though canoeists have been known to do inscrutable things in their day. So, make a steamer. Here are several options:

- Fill your largest pot with a few inches of water. Place the *baozi* or *mantou* on the next-sized pot lid and place in the big pot. Cover and steam!

- Carry with you one of those folding aluminum steamers small enough to fit in your largest pot.

- Interlace a number of green branches to fashion a steamer big enough to sit on top of a small fry pan. Lay a clean bandanna or handkerchief over it and place the *baozi* or *mantou* directly on the cloth. Cover with a large pot lid or a loosely fashioned dome made of aluminum foil. (You'll be able to use the aluminum foil later for baking.)

## *Scones* ✳

Skillet-baked scones (pages 287-288) are one thing. Oven-baked scones another. We know a couple of blokes who'd be willing to fight the Battle of Culloden over again for the right of first tasting. The chief assumption here is that you've got plenty of honey or jam to apply to these pearls of Inverness.

*1 c. flour*
*1/2 sp. baking powder*

1 heaping sp. sugar
large pinch of salt
1 sp. raisins (optional)
1 sp. milk powder
2 sp. margarine
1 or 2 eggs
water

Mix dry ingredients together. Add margarine, mixing with fingers till the consistency of coarse cornmeal. Beat the eggs and add. Then add just enough water to make a soft dough. Knead it on a floured plate just long enough to form a nice round circle, about $1/4$" to $1/2$" thick. If you've got an extra egg, beat it and brush it on the dough. Sprinkle some sugar on top. Then cut the dough into six or eight wedges. If baking over a campfire, place wedges in a lightly floured Teflon frying pan, cover with foil or a metal plate, set on cleared ground and surround with coals. When golden brown, about 10 to 15 minutes, they're done. If using a camping oven, use a Teflon pan with lid or a small baking sheet which can be covered. Same time. Same station.

VARIATIONS:

- Substitute buttermilk, sourdough starter, or even heavy cream (if the American Heart Association isn't on your case, and you've got a cooler for safekeeping), for the milk powder.

- Add thinly sliced cheddar cheese to taste.

- Add other dried fruits, slightly rehydrated. Strawberries and blueberries are great.

- Substitute instant oatmeal for half the flour.

- Flavor with anise, dill or cinnamon.

- If you happen to have a mashed potato in your back pocket, use it for half the flour.

## Getting a Rise Out of a Dud

What happens if the dough doesn't rise? You did everything right. The yeast bubbled and frothed, the dough kneaded nicely, the sun has been shining for hours. But by mid-afternoon, you have an inert gray mass of dough that looks like it's near death. This happened to us on a recent trip. Our options were to toss it or change it. Rick started to reason, like Marie Antoinette, that if you couldn't give them bread, let them eat cake. What wouldn't rise with yeast might rise with baking powder and whipped egg white. So we added enough water and milk powder to turn the dough into a batter, threw in some baking powder, and came up with a great nut-and-raisin cake.

Some research gave us clues as to why that particular dough didn't rise. Experts have countless reasons to explain failure. Humidity and air temperature affect yeast. Too much sweetener slows down or stops the process. Too much salt also inhibits rising. And too little white or whole wheat flour makes matters worse. That's because wheat flour contains a magic substance, gluten, which gives dough the necessary elasticity it needs to trap the yeast-produced bubbles of gas, allowing the dough to rise. Corn-meal, rye and rice flour, etc. have less or no gluten. The dough is made more porous as these are added, and the gas escapes, leaving you with a mound of play dough.

In our case, the dough had too much maple syrup and cornmeal, relative to the amount of white flour. It's hard to give exact proportions, especially as you may run out of important ingredients on the trail. But as a rough rule of thumb, try these:

First, half a spoonful of sugar or a full spoonful of honey or syrup is plenty for starting the yeast. If you want a sweeter bread, add the rest of the sugar to the dough, but remember that the sweeter the dough, the longer the rising time.

Second, use at least half white or whole wheat flour relative to all the other dry ingredients. If you're running too low on flour for that ratio, consider making cake instead of yeast bread.

## Corn Breads

### Yeast Corn Bread *

If you like corn breads which rise, substitute cornmeal for half the flour in the Basic Mountain Loaf recipe (page 291). Add a healthy hit of baking powder or soda and proceed as above.

### Baking Powder Corn Bread *

If you're low on yeast, use a ratio of four spoonfuls of corn-meal to two of flour and forget the yeast. Add a spoonful of baking powder, a shot of salt, a heaping spoonful of milk powder, two or three spoonfuls of sugar, a beaten egg or two and enough water to make a thick batter, similar in consistency to a thick pancake batter. Turn this into a well-greased pot. Bake at once for about a half-hour. Since corn bread won't sound hollow to the tap, you'll know it's done when the top splits open a bit, and when a knife blade inserted in the middle comes out clean.

# Pizza

Ranger Ron said it couldn't be done west of Chicago. It's all very well, he argued, to bake bread in a pot, but pizza has to be flat, and the oven has to be hotter than you can get in the wilderness. We showed him something. Pizza is just an open-baked hot bread with lots of good things piled on top. If you have a frying pan with a removable handle, or a pie plate and a piece of aluminum foil, you can bake a gorgeous pizza in the wilderness.

### *Hal & Rick's South Side Pizza* ✻
*1 packet yeast*
*¹/₂ c. warm water*
*couple pinches of sugar*
*¹/₂ c. flour*
*dash of salt*
*1 sp. oil*
*¹/₂ c. tomato sauce (see recipes, pages 245-246)*
*mixed dried vegetables, slightly rehydrated: mushrooms, zucchini, onion,*
*    peppers*
*2 cloves garlic, sliced*
*sliced salami or jerky (optional)*
*4-5 sp. sliced cheese*
*pepper to taste*
*hearty sprinkling of dried oregano*
*cooking oil*
*aluminum foil*

In a Sierra cup, mix the warm water, yeast and sugar. Set aside covered in a warm place. When "proofed" (that is, bubbly), add it to the flour, salt and oil in a pot. Mix thoroughly with a spoon, adding more oil and water as necessary to make a workable dough. Knead on a plate till smooth. If it's slightly sticky, that's okay. Set in a warm place to rise in a covered, oiled pot. While the dough is rising, make the tomato sauce and rehydrate the veggies slightly by soaking them in hot water barely to cover till they're partially soft. Drain and set aside.

When the dough has risen, turn it out on a plate and begin to work it into a round, flat shape with your fingers, pushing out from the center in all directions. You can even pick it up and toss it into the air with a spiral motion, like they do at Mama Mia's. It's helpful to catch it. You may need a little flour on your hands for this. When the dough has become a nice, even circle, fit it into a well-oiled frying pan. It should extend part or all the way up the sides. Then spread the tomato sauce over the dough and pile on the vegetables (and salami or jerky). Sprinkle on the cheese, garlic, pepper and oregano. Then drip a very thin layer of oil over the finished product, and cover the pan with foil. Alternatively, place a large tin plate over the pizza and seal it to the frying pan with the foil.

Ranger Ron was right in one respect. The idea is to bake the dough fast, before you burn everything on top. Pizza ovens are extremely hot (about 500 degrees Fahrenheit). But if you put your frying pan on a bed of red hot coals, you'll end up with something you might have to call "cheese-n-charcoal." Instead, set the pan on cleared ground, surround it with hot coals, and slide coals on top of the foil too. Let it bake about 15 minutes. Then work some moderately warm coals under the pan and push others around it and on top. In another 10 minutes or so, the pizza is done. The dough will be crusty, the cheese melted, and mouths watering. Overlook his chagrin and give Ranger Ron a piece. Tell him it's crow!

FRYING PAN OR POT LID

PLATE

COALS

ALUMINUM FOIL

**How to bake a pizza (cutaway view)**

PIZZA

COALS

### *Hal & Rick's Carroll Street Calzone* ✺

Okay, you've got the makings of a pizza dough, but you left the Outback Oven at home and you're in a No Campfire zone. What to do? Simple. Make a calzone. Follow the recipe above for the pizza dough. While it's rising, rehydrate whatever you'd like to be in the filling: risotto; veggies; turkey jerky; beans. To cook, heat an oiled fry pan, place the flattened, rounded dough in the pan, spoon in the filling, and fold half the dough over it, and form a pouch by pinching or pressing the top layer of dough to the bottom layer. Fry till golden brown, then turn with a spatula, brown on the other side and remove to a plate. Call in the carabinieri while eating. There's no telling who'd kneecap you for your portion.

## Cakes

Making cake on a camping trip is sort of like sex on Wednesday afternoon: gratuitous but a lot of fun. It has nothing to do with survival, nor your ability to read a compass, has not one ounce of redeeming moral, social or nutritional value. But as long as you have semi-sweet baking chocolate with you anyway (also great for eating plain because it's unlikely to melt in your pack), some margarine, sugar, eggs, flour, baking powder and powdered milk, and as long as it's Wednesday afternoon and the sun is high, you might as well hunker down, bake a cake, make an icing, slap the two together, lay back and pig out. It's a piece of cake.

### *Basic Ground-Level Two-Step Cake* ✺

Pancakes are the result of frying batter. Cakes are the result of baking batter—batter which contains more sugar and eggs. Here's everything you ever needed to know about the unadorned, ultra-simple, starter cake loved by 93 percent of humankind.

*1 c. flour*
*1 sp. milk powder*
*¹/₂ sp. baking powder*
*dash of salt*
*1 sp. margarine*
*3 sp. sugar*
*1 egg*

*dash of brandy*
*water*
*oil for greasing pot*

In a medium pot, mix together the dry ingredients. In the pot lid, cream together the margarine and sugar, using the underside of a spoon to mix. (If you're out of margarine, oil will work.) Break the egg into the sugar mixture and beat till the glop is smooth. Add the brandy as a substitute for vanilla. Combine both mixtures with enough extra water to make a smooth, thick batter that will pour like a ribbon into a well-greased and floured small baking pot.

Bake the cake in coals cooler than for bread. With an Outback Oven, you bake everything with a low flame anyway, so no need to fiddle with settings. At home, you'd use a moderate oven (350 to 375 degrees). Out here, start with coals just beginning to turn black and try to keep any you add roughly the same color. If you can't, don't worry. Betty Crocker won't be around, peeking over your shoulder. Baking time will vary, as usual, but should run about 25 to 30 minutes. Test for doneness by inserting a knife blade into the center of the cake. If it comes out clean, the cake is done. When cool remove from pot. Eat or ice.

VARIATIONS:

## Basic Man-Eatin' Cake ✻

Follow the preceeding recipe, only separate the egg, reserve the white, and add the yolk to the sugar and butter mixture. When the batter is ready to pour into the baking pot, gently fold in the egg whites, beaten stiff but not dry. This makes the cake even lighter, a cruel blow to weight watchers and lifters alike.

## Advanced Man-Eatin' Cake ✻

For a moister, richer cake, use two eggs, separate both and proceed as above. Add other things to the batter: cinnamon, Kahlua in addition to or instead of the brandy, several squares of chocolate shaved with a knife, or assorted dried fruits and nuts.

## Chocolate Cake ✻

Set up as for Man-Eatin' Cake (Basic or Advanced). In a pot lid, place two squares of semi-sweet baking chocolate or two rows of German Sweet chocolate. Add about a quarter cup water. Stir and melt over the fire, being careful not to burn the chocolate. When melted, add to the egg and sugar mixture along with a little brandy. Proceed as in Man-Eatin' Cake, folding in egg whites last. *Note*: It is not necessary in any of these recipes to separate the eggs, so if you left the wire whisk at home, proceed as for Basic Two-Step Cake. No one will notice the difference.

## Surprise-Delight Cake *

Suppose you don't have all the ingredients and still want to make a chocolate cake. Use what you have. Substitute carob for chocolate; scrape the carob off a Tiger Milk Bar to melt in water. Or melt the whole bar and add it to the egg and sugar mixture. Or use powdered Swiss Miss. If you don't have anything to beat the egg whites with, leave them whole. No baking powder? Use beaten egg whites as a rising agent. No brandy? Forget it. No sugar? Double the amount of chocolate, or use both chocolate and instant cocoa, which has plenty of sugar in it. Stretch your mind. Just keep the proportions of wet and dry about the same so the batter stays the proper consistency.

## Chocolate Icing ❖

*2-3 squares semi-sweet baking chocolate, or 3-4 rows German Sweet chocolate*
*1 sp. margarine*
*$1/4$ c. water*
*dash of brandy*

In a pot lid, melt the chocolate (you can use a combination of the two kinds) in the water. *Note*: the more chocolate you use, the more water you need, but add it moderately. The idea is to have a fairly thick, smooth melt. Add margarine, stir till melted and thoroughly mixed with the chocolate. Remove from heat. Add brandy. Cool till icing begins to thicken. This will take some time, especially on a hot day. To hasten, set icing container in a larger container of cold water. Don't fret, it will harden. In fact, if left too long, it will suddenly harden so much that you may have to warm it slightly to turn it back into spreading consistency. When thickened to that consistency, ice the cake with a spoon or knife. The result is so good you'll have difficulty waiting for your partners to return from a day hike, or wherever they're spending Wednesday afternoon.

To store the iced cake, place the large pot over the cake till time to eat. If there's any left over at night, remove it from the plate and double bag in Ziplocs.

*Note*: Icing can be made without a cake. Hardened, it is the perfect nosh, the equivalent of that box of Bartons you were supposed to bring your Great Aunt Emily on her birthday, but ate them first. Softened and thickened with a spoonful each of milk powder and flour, and a cup or two of water, it transmutes into chocolate pudding!

## Fruit Cake ✻

This is a mixture of fruits and nuts held together with a mixture of eggs, sugar and flour. It's a snap to make and a great way to use up nuts and fruit before packing out. In a medium or large pot lid, put as much cut-up fruit and nuts as you wish. For the smallest fruit cake, about three large handfuls will do. To this, add a beaten egg, three spoonfuls of sugar and a hit of brandy. Mix thoroughly. Now add a dash of salt, a spoonful of baking powder and enough flour (about three spoonfuls) to hold the mixture together. Pour into a well-greased small pot, cover and bake very slowly in moderately hot coals. At home, you'd bake at only 300 degrees, so these coals will be the coolest you've used. Allow an hour or so to cook, and don't expect it to rise much. You'll know when it's done by looking at the top—which should be brown—and testing with a knife for firmness. Run the knife around the edge, turn the pot over and bang it sharply on a rock to get the cake out. If it won't come out whole, cut it in pieces or eat it right from the pot. When the cake is cool, pour some brandy over it and let it sit for as long as you like. It'll keep for days. Incidentally, if it comes out of the pot whole, the cake will be very beautiful.

# Cookies

The hardest part of mountain cookie baking is deciding on the ingredients. Chocolate chip, cinnamon-nut, oatmeal and lemon only begin the possibilities. The ratio of ingredients should be 4:2:1, that's four flour (including oatmeal) to two sugar to one margarine. Begin by "creaming" half a Sierra cup of sugar and two spoonfuls of margarine into a paste. Add an egg and a splash of brandy. To a Sierra cup of flour (or flour/oatmeal), add half a spoonful of baking powder, a pinch of salt, and a spoonful of powdered milk. Combine this with the butter and egg mixture. Then add your special ingredients—shredded chocolate bars, raisins, coconut, chopped nuts, dried fruit, cinnamon, nutmeg, ginger, etc. Add flour or water as necessary to get the right consistency, halfway between pancake batter and bread dough. The finished mixture should be thick and chunky. Taste it for sweetness. If it doesn't taste really sweet, your cookies will be more like biscuits.

Cookies are baked in a greased pan exactly like pizza (page 300). If you have a plate or lid that fits over your frying pan, you can use it instead of foil to hold the top coals. A few coals below will keep the bottom of the pan warm. You can only bake three or four at a time, so filling the cookie jar is an all-day project. In a pinch, you can make them like pan-fried bread. They may burn a bit on the top or bottom, but if you dip them in coffee or hot chocolate, you'll hardly notice.

## Quiche

One of the best things about the kind of improvisational cooking we've been discussing is that you're never quite sure what's going to happen next. For more than five years, we'd been baking breads, inventing variations of chocolate cake, igniting brandy and generally congratulating ourselves on the smooth workings of our unbridled imaginations. But we'd never made a pie. Too much trouble, we argued. Too hard. Anyway, what would we fill it with? The answer came from Polly, a doctor who'd lived in the Andes, floated down the Amazon, and survived 20 years in the jungles of Chicago. Five days into the high Sierras in the midst of a hail storm and high winds, she announced she'd make supper that night for six: quiche.

We wished her luck and set her up in the tent to get out of the wind (it's not easy to work with flour in a gale). Every so often, we'd hear a muffled cry for spices, powdered milk or water and we finally put the entire food pack into the tent so she could work in peace. By sundown, the storm had blown itself out and we were all sitting around the campfire complimenting the chef on her work of art.

## Quiche Improvisation ❉

The first thing to do is to make a pie crust of pastry dough, which is different from bread dough. It consists of a mixture of flour and shortening, with just enough water to hold the two together. Here's what you'll need to make a crust in an 8" fry pan:

*large pot*
*spoon*
*water*
*5 heaping spoonfuls of flour*
*dash of salt*
*4 sp. margarine or shortening*

Mix the flour and salt together. Add the margarine, and knead until the dough has the texture of cornmeal. Don't worry if there are some pea-sized globules. Now add two or three spoonfuls of cold water to the mixture, one at a time, blending it in with the spoon or two forks. Only add enough water to hold the dough loosely together. One way to tell if it's right is to form the dough into a lightly packed ball. If it falls apart, you need more water. If it holds together, set the ball on an ungreased frying pan or pie plate, and press the dough down with the heel of your hand, working it to cover the bottom and sides of the pan. It should be very thin, not more than an eighth of an inch thick. But don't worry if it's thicker. It will bake well and taste great.

If you're camping in France, go ahead and follow the national custom. Partially bake the pie crust next. If you're not in France, skip it. Just go ahead and fill the uncooked crust with goodies:

*3 sp. milk powder + water to make 1 cup*
*2 eggs, well beaten*
*cheese*
*jerky*
*diced dried vegetables: mushrooms, peppers, zucchini, etc. (rehydrated if
    possible)*
*onion (dried and crumbled or chopped)*
*salt and pepper to taste*
*dash of nutmeg*
*1 sp. flour*

In a pot, mix together the cup of milk, beaten eggs, salt, pepper and nutmeg. Add the rehydrated vegetables and onion.

(*Note*: If you can't rehydrate the veggies, don't worry. They'll soften in the baking.) To thicken the pot, add the flour and mix well. Pour the mixture into the pie shell. Sprinkle on as much finely shredded cheese as you can spare. Any cheese will do. The quiche is ready to bake.

If you have another pie pan or tin plate of the right size, invert it to cover the quiche. If not, cover it with aluminum foil like a pizza, and bake exactly as in the pizza recipe (pages 300-301). Set hot coals around and on top. After about 20 minutes, when it's half-done, work some moderately hot coals underneath. The quiche is finished when the filling is firm and slightly browned. The reason it takes up to 40 minutes to bake is that the pan is shallow, making the transfer of heat a slower process. You'll be ravenous by the time it's ready, so you'll eat it hot. But it's possible to eat quiche cold, too.

## Apple Pie ✳

Camping's as American as…? Right, apple pie. So if you're canoeing or car camping and have a load of fresh apples, be patriotic, eat pie. If you're backpacking and were smart enough to bring along a Ziploc bag full of dried apples, ditto. Mom doesn't need to be there in her gingham apron.

*pastry for 2 pie crusts (See Quiche Improvisation recipe, page 307)*
*3-4 fresh apples, pared, cored, sliced (or the equivalent rehydrated)*
*sugar and cinnamon to taste*
*margarine (optional)*

Layer the frying pan with one of the crusts. Fill with the apple, sugar and cinnamon mixture. Dot with margarine (optional). Cover with the second crust, which you've "rolled" out on a plate. Pinch the edges of the two crusts together. Poke top crust with a fork in several places. This lets the steam out while the pie is baking. Cover with aluminum foil or a large metal plate, and bake according to directions for pizza and quiche.

VARIATIONS:
- Convert to an Apple Dumpling by using only one crust. Spread it on pan, fill half the crust, then fold over the other half, pinch and bake as above. This is easier and just as tasty.

- Brush the crust with a mixture of milk, cinnamon and sugar.

## *Fruit Tarts* ✳

If you have a cooler full of fresh peaches, plums, nectarines or pears, and ready access to a fire or a camping oven, make an open tart. You can mix and match the fruit or use one kind only.

*3 fresh peaches*
*4 fresh plums*
*pastry dough for one pie crust*
*sugar to taste*
*1 sp. flour*
*1 egg*

Make the pastry dough as above, and line fry pan or Teflon coated pan. Slice the fruit into a pot, sprinkle on sugar and mix to coat well. Arrange fruit slices in concentric circles on the pie dough. Mix the egg and flour together, then dribble this mixture over the fruit. Seal pan with a top or aluminum foil and bake as above. You may need dueling knives to settle disputes when slicing to serve.

- This will work with dried (and rehydrated) fruit too, though the volume required will be about double the fresh fruit above. Solution: Make a smaller tart! Use a large pot lid lined on the *outside* with aluminum foil to prevent burning, and cover with a plate or another pot lid.

## *Berry Pies and Tarts* ✳

If you're in the right place at the right time, you may find wild berries ripe and ready for the oven. The only difference between berry pies and the fruit pies above is that berries need to be thickened. If you have some cornstarch, or better yet, instant (uncooked) tapioca, you're in biz. (Flour will do in a pinch.) Just add a big spoonful of either to the fresh berries or to rehydrated fruit rolls (rhubarb and strawberries, for example, or blackberries and raspberries). Add sugar to taste and a dash of lemon or lime juice, pour into a pastry-lined pan, cover with a top pastry and pinch the two pastry linings together. Cut a little "X" in the pastry dough to allow hot air to escape, cover with aluminum foil or a metal plate, and bake as above.

# Campground Chutney

## Summer Fruit Chutney

If you haven't eaten all the dried fruit by now, and you've just turned out a fabulous Indian meal (Trout Tandoori, Trout in Curried Sauce, or Fried Rice with Vegetables and Chicken), garnish it with chutney. Stew a handful of fruit in water to cover, stirring till softened and thickened. Add an immodest squirt of vinegar or lemon juice (or both!), a spoon of sugar, and continue to stir till thick. Voilà! Chutney.

# Snow Cones

## The Instant High-Mountain Popsicle

Whenever you're above 7,000 feet, you're likely to come upon a snowfield or remaining patches of last winter's snow hidden from the mid-summer sun. If you're hiking, pull over and make snow cones—they're so refreshing it's like finding a soda fountain along the trail. Fill your Sierra cup halfway with snow and add any or all of the following: instant chocolate, cinnamon and sugar, lemon or lime juice and sugar, Kahlua, brandy, nutmeg, ginger, etc. Eat with a spoon. They're the *real* treasure of the Sierra, madre!

# Cooking in the Rain

Several years ago, we were settled into a campsite when it began to rain. Forty-eight hours later it was still raining. Then it began to snow. Though our sleeping bags got soggy, our spirits didn't even dampen. We kept warm and full. When it's raining or cold outside, we like to keep our insides full of hot foods.

You can't make elaborate meals in the rain. Baking is out—you can't keep wet coals hot. Frying is possible, but unless your fire is protected from the rain or you fry fast, the food gets wet on top while it cooks on the bottom. Also, if the pan fills with water, you'll be poaching, which *is* a practical method. Another good technique in the rain is grilling (a rack will not fill with water). A third choice is cooking in a covered pot, which is our usual choice. Soups and stews are great: hot, easy, filling and needing little tending, so you can stay dry under a tree or tarp as they cook. You're likely to catch fish in the rain, and it's simple to grill them quickly or poach them and add to your pot.

Keep the stored food and matches in waterproof containers inside covered packs. When the sun comes out again, dry any damp food or packets to prevent spoilage. And don't go without at least one hot meal a day in the rain. Even a steaming cup of cocoa and some biscuits, or a bowl of oatmeal will keep the spirits up.

## Stove Cooking Hints

- Conserve fuel, cook fast.

- When frying remember that the circumference of heat over a camp stove is smaller than at home or over an open fire. Thus that large pan of frying fish will stay cooler on the edges than in the middle.

- Ignore suggestions for long, slow simmering in all recipes. Boiling time for half a small pot of water is 5 to 10 minutes. A few more minutes and soup's on.

- Stove safety: Use in a sheltered spot, out of the wind and rain. Unless an emergency requires it, don't cook in the tent, even in the rain. Fuel can spill, fumes can make you sick and tents can burn. Use your ingenuity to cook outside instead.

## Eating on the Trail

When we're camped, deeply immersed in cooking, two meals a day are adequate. When hiking, our eating patterns change. A light, fast, early breakfast gives us a fresh start and enough energy to make that long haul to the pass without cardiac arrest from undigested pancakes in the gut. Eating on the trail is part of a pattern of rest and recovery, necessary to put strength back in the muscles and energy back in the system.

Some backpackers eat continually while hiking. They carry a pouch of gorp, and munch away throughout the day on their mixed dried fruits, nuts, candy, coconut, or whatever. Others prefer to snack at rest stops and have a more substantial lunch at a point where tired muscles, sore feet and spectacular scenery call for a longer break. It's amazing how a good meal makes the body willing to go on, and able to do so.

Keep trail food easily accessible. Why empty your pack every time you want a raisin cookie or a lemon drop? And it should be nourishing. Make sure you have on hand dried fruit, chocolate, cookies, crackers, etc. for energy, as well as salami, nuts, jerky, etc. for strength (protein for muscle restoration) to keep you fit. You also need to replace liquid frequently. Be sure you have enough water to drink often, though not necessarily in great quantity. If you're certain of water sources along the trail, you needn't carry much. Water is heavy. But if you're doubtful, keep your canteen full.

Our style includes frequent stops. Often we're more thirsty than hungry, but we also make sure to get some quick energy by sharing something sweet. We lunch at the top of a pass if the weather is as good as the view. We make cheese and salami sandwiches on crackers, eat nuts, dried fruits, a few bean sprouts and drink plenty of water. If there's a snowfield nearby, we make snow cones for dessert. Otherwise, it's raisin cookies or the last part of yesterday's cake. We take our time; this is a rest stop. Then we set off toward our destination, often cross-country. We try to arrive by mid-afternoon, but not at the expense of as many rest and snack stops as necessary to keep our spirits up and our legs moving. If we need to make camp before our destination, we give ourselves a simple but hot supper. Dehydrated dinners and a backpacking stove are handy at such times.

Some backpackers have a saying about emergency situations, "When in doubt, sit it out." We have no objections to that, but we've added a few words of our own. When we come to a crossroads, a roaring creek or a mountain pass, our saying is, "When in doubt, the food comes out." Friends say that ours are the only camping trips they've ever heard of on which the backpackers invariably *gain* weight. Right. What better vacation could you have, staying full of great food and drink, and coming home rock hard from all the hiking, climbing and packing? Those visions of sugar plums and all the delicacies will embellish every tale you tell, all winter long. Give it a try. You'll love it.

# CHAPTER 11

# Hanging Out

## The Fine Art of Spending Time, Filling Space

Doing nothing is an art—and an oxymoron. *Doing* nothing? Maybe Zen masters and 143-year-old yogis can manage it. And yuppie CEOs who work 100-hour weeks and then just sit still, breathe and wonder how big the universe is for days at a time in the backcountry. Or crane operators whose idea of heaven is to hand tie the most intricate fishing flies. Small children can spend hours squatting wisely in a tidepool watching, just watching. Adults can wake full of energetic intentions and crash into sullen boredom five minutes after the pancakes and brew. But we've also known fanatical hikers who think nothing of 15-mile day trips, or solo backpackers who need to contrive detailed daily schedules while in camp to keep the lonely-blues away.

Hanging out is thus a subjective thing. It depends on what you like to do. Rick breathes quicker if there's a handy peak to climb. Karen fishes for approximately 27 hours a day and is reluctant to permit the sun to set. She is sublimely happy to hear an 800-page novel read aloud while she casts. Sarah, who affects High Photographic Sensibility, takes pictures of wildflowers. Not trees, not wildlife. Certainly not the human relics she travels with. Just flowers. The smaller, the better. We've known birders to abandon small children and all responsibilities in quest of the western tanager; we've known mountain bikers to return at dusk bruised and besotted with pleasure after a day on the trail; we've known canoeists who spend long hours on minor and gratuitous repairs, lovingly touching up the lacquer, masking the dent—

erecting campsite body shops just for the hell of it. We began this book hanging out one day, years ago. Turn back to the tale of the fabled Hidden Lake Soufflé, and you'll see the first words we put down on paper. Active or passive, introvert or extrovert, gregarious or a loner, the possibilities for finding pleasure in hanging out are endless. You've come a long way. Now's the time to enjoy.

## Secrets of the Hammock and Other Lounging Devices

Lots of people get to a campsite and don't want to move. Now or forever. "Wake me when it's time to go home," is the cry from the heart. Up goes the hammock between two sturdy birches; up goes the *Do Not Disturb* sign. Then the trouble begins.

The next time you pull into a car campground, check out the hammocks and their occupants. Looks like the entire melon section of the supermarket encased in individual string bags, doesn't it? People stretched out end-to-end, sinking pathetically in the middle until they look like human nutcrackers. Head and feet high, tush low—a painful, humiliating, miserably uncomfortable position. You can't get a lot of rest that way, and if your back doesn't go out, your dreams of bucolic ease will. You'll enlist on the next day hike and never return.

It's true—an awful lot of people don't know how to lie in a hammock! There's a physics to it, and you should be the first to know. Lie *diagonally*. That creates just enough countervailing forces to maintain you in a horizontal position. It minimizes sag and rests your back. You can lie there for hours, whiling away the time watching clouds and daydreaming. You won't miss the activists. You won't join the potato sack race. Keep a mosquito net hat in the hammock, a stuff sack filled with a few clothes as a pillow, a book and the snack of your choice, and you won't have to touch down till the cows come home.

Other lounging machines are Ensolite pads dragged out of the tent, propped against a rock in the sunlight or shade, air mattresses afloat on the lake or cast on a summer meadow, or the canoe floating at anchor lined with sleeping pads. (Don't use a sleeping bag unless you're awfully good at boarding and alighting dry. Pads dry fast; bags don't.) Lawn chairs, inflated inner tubes, re-sited dome tents, even a smooth, sun-drenched granite rock overlooking the lake—all are outdoor sofa substitutes. Deep-six the alarm clock. We'll wake you for dinner. •

## *Stop Your Ramblin', Stop Your Gamblin'...*

Tom Stienstra, a great wilderness camper and author (see Book List on page 382), tells a fine story about a cutthroat, penny-candy-anté poker game high in the backcountry, where money doesn't count but a steely-eyed bluff is still a bluff. He pulled an inside straight on the last deal in a seven-card stud game, 11,000 feet above the nearest gaming table, and backed down at the prospect of losing his last five M&Ms. A man who knows his priorities.

A camping trip in the county park or in the high Canadian Rockies calls for portable amusements, and if you can't spring Granny's soapstone mah-jongg set loose, a pack of cards will do. We have watched two seasoned couples at a drive-in campsite playing pinochle through a hurricane warning, oblivious to the rising wind, collapsing tents, overturned food hampers and the first heavy drops of rain. You can't tell us they weren't having a glorious camping trip.

The farther you go on foot, the lighter your games will need to be. Miniature plastic chess, checkers or backgammon sets, *si*; Monopoly or croquet, *non*. A cribbage board, dice or Trivial Pursuit cards travel well in a backpack. Hang gliders and bowling balls don't. What fits and what's light is what counts.

## *...Stop Stayin' Out Late at Night*

You say you wanna keep shuffling cards till the wee hours, that one more deal is gonna win the pot. You say your end game against your partner's Indian defense takes time to develop: you're not playing chess against a clock out here. True, but you *are* playing against a huge drain on the flashlight batteries. Unless you're carrying one of those six- or twelve-volt floodlight batteries or a powerful fuel-fed camping lantern, you'll have to close down the house and continue in the morning. Either that or agree to watch the stars the following nights and brush your teeth in the dark. Even hanging out comes with finite options. And sometimes they're non-negotiable.

## *The Library*

One of our own personal camping pleasures is reading aloud. We find so much time for it—during a rest break on the trail, while preparing one of our elaborate meals, while one of us is fishing, or just while hanging out—that over the years we've gotten through some of the world's longest books. As we read, we burn, so that we don't have to carry the book's weight out. This may seem barbarous, but there's a silver lining (of the authors' pockets), too. When we get home, we go out and buy the book again, a treasure on our shelves and increased royalties in the writer's money market account.

The most satisfactory kinds of books for this kind of reading are those long, episodic novels where it doesn't matter if you miss a paragraph or even a whole chapter. Great dialogue counts a lot. So does the ability to tell a good story. Among our favorites have been Mark Twain's *Huckleberry Finn* and *A Connecticut Yankee in King Arthur's Court*, Robertson Davies' *Deptford Trilogy* and his equally wonderful *Salterton Trilogy*, John Barth's *The Sotweed Factor*, Charles Dickens' *Bleak House* (over 900 pages!), Henry Fielding's *Tom Jones* (a lot funnier and longer than the movie), the short stories of P.G. Wodehouse and Ring Lardner, the mystery novels of Dashiell Hammett and a good collection of ghost stories. Jon Carroll, a columnist for the *San Francisco Chronicle* and a fine old gonzo back-packer, once rebuked us for not including the novels of Anthony Trollope on our list. Okay, they're in. And your favorites will be, too, if you let us know before the next edition of this book comes out. In short, bring anything you enjoy reading—magazines, comic books, joke books or box tops—and any other printed material which you won't mind burning or packing out—cross-words, puzzles, games, mantras, amulets, or even recipes: whatever tickles your fancy. And *at least one book per child*, however old or young. More if you can manage it. Read and burn. It's the best of cheap thrills.

## Music

We're a plugged-in generation, so there's no use complaining that the quality of silence in the great outdoors has changed for the worse. In fact, that isn't so. The Walkman has come to the rescue of purists like you and us. It's now possible to bring the baddest neo-punk jam into the wilderness without causing damage to more than two eardrums, a net gain no matter how you figure it. There's no further need for a boom box in a campground. There should be no further need for a radio without earplugs.

There's nothing wrong with amplified sound except when it's unleashed. Kept inside the brain case, it's an acceptable part of the modern camper's gear.

If you're in a crowded campground, similar consideration for the neighbors in the next tent requires the guitar, mouth organ and group sing-a-long to be muted and closed down before the third watch. Make it soft, low and early.

You can no doubt fit a drum set into a canoe, or carry a Fender bass on a pack mule, but backpackers and long-distance hikers who play music have to weigh things in the balance. The manufacturers have. They've come out with a backpacking guitar, a lightweight instrument that looks like a stretch ukelele. It's long, thin, light, reasonably durable, and produces a sound good enough to keep even a member of the Seattle string band "Who's Driving?" happy in the wild woods.

Our friend Jules plays a mandolin while hiking and fashions percussion instruments out of hollow logs. Peter the Headwaiter plays the spoons. Penny whistles. Kazoos, comb-and-paper, and harmonicas are light, easy, fun and cheap: a child's delight. There's no need to deprive anyone of music if it soothes the soul. Just make sure that it soothes others' souls, too. Otherwise take a hike and soothe solo.

## Using Ranger Ron

Campers at county, state and national parks should check out the free entertainment offered by the park services. Local naturalists know their turf and have an affection for it. A guided nature hike or a nighttime illustrated talk by Ranger Ron probably won't be like those awful didactic affairs you remember so well from summer camp and other forced-march jamborees. Take advantage of their sense of place and of the patient pleasures of spotting a real Big Bird, identifying a meadow of ephemeral wildflowers, or geologically reading the terrain. If you can't stand the scholarship, you can always go hang glide off Half Dome, but a snail's pace is often just right: lovely and unimportant, surprising and revealing. What's the hurry?

## Day Trips

Hikers, fishers, climbers and bikers itch to get going. To them, hanging out is filled with motion. An unexplored off-trail

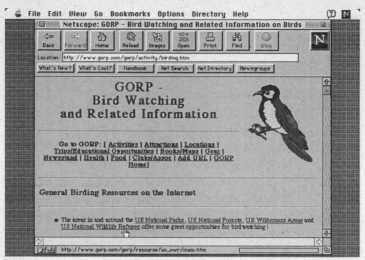

*You'll find lots of birding information on the Internet.*

route, a first-time trail, a nearby stream to fish, a peak to bag: these trigger the imagination, get the blood churning. Anticipation quickens the pulse. A daypack stuffed with food, flashlight, water bottle, maps and compass, warm clothes and rain gear, a minimum first-aid kit, sunscreen and lip balm, and, if on bike, a repair kit, is featherweight compared with the big frame pack that got you to camp. You can make good time, cover a fair amount of ground, and get back to home base before dark. Good planning and common sense make the day safe and filled with satisfactions.

Easiest is a hike along a trail to a ridge, pass, peak or lake that you would otherwise miss if you held to the original itinerary. Fishing a remote, shaded stream may bring you thrills and a late dinner. Lake fishing is less likely to be successful, because you invariably end up fishing in the glare of the sun, when the fish are lying low. It's nearly noon when you get there, and you have to leave around 2 or 3 o'clock to return to camp by sundown. As long as you don't mind a slow few hours of fishing, it can be a scenic and relaxing day. If you're fishing from a canoe, then all bets are on. You can get an early start, stay along the shaded shoreline, check out the inlets, fish from land and have a ball.

And before you set off, secure your campsite. Prepare for hot sun, heavy rain or a ripping wind; any or all could happen while you're gone. Keep food in the shade, leave a rainfly over the tent, and batten down the hatches just in case.

## *Bagging Peaks*

We're not mountain climbers—as in K2, El Capitan or the Jungfrau. But when we're out in the high country and spot a peak in the middle distance, we often take a day trip to climb it. No ropes and crampons, no technical climbing, but careful scrambling and steady going. Planned right, it's safe. Executed right, it's exhilarating, exciting and exhausting. Gazing out over the crest of a 12,000-footer is worth every hard step and passing terror. The heart in your mouth is your own. It's the best place for it as you look down and around from the top of the world, astounded by your audacity and courage. It can become an addiction.

At the top of major peaks, you'll find a register to sign and log your comments. On less important peaks, the equivalent is often a small tin can buried under a cairn of rocks, in which you'll find a small note pad with room for your signature and a remark or two about the state of the union, the view, the weather or the climb.

Preparation and planning are the keys to successful peak bagging. Plan your route early, the day before the climb if possible. Use the topo map. The easiest way to the top is across the widest spaces between the altitude lines on the map. That's where you should trace your route. If your camp is close to the peak, trace the route up the peak with your eyes, looking for rock slides or impenetrable brush which might not show up on the map.

Start the climb early in the morning. We usually eat a quick cold breakfast, pack our daypack and leave close to dawn. Mountain weather is always unpredictable, more so in the afternoon, and the only thing worse than getting caught at the top of a peak in an afternoon hail storm is getting caught there in a lightning-and-hail storm. An electrical storm on the trail in the forest is impressive enough. On an exposed peak, it's positively terrifying. To avoid this nasty business try to bag the peak early in the day.

Your supplies for a peak-bagging expedition will be the same as those above for any day trip. If you don't have a light daypack, rig a stuffsack to one of the straps off your backpack, and sling it over your shoulder.

Dark glasses are *required*, not optional. If you plan to hike over snow fields, you'll also need "blinders" on the sides of your glasses to protect your eyes from reflected glare. Don't have them? Make some the night before with cardboard cutouts from the cookie or biscuit box, and adhesive tape, or rig up a "foreign legion" side shade from a T-shirt or bandanna, which will also protect the back of your neck from sunburn.

Elementary climbing rules should be followed scrupulously:

- Beginners never go alone. Partnered climbing is always preferred whatever the level of experience. Some prefer a minimum of three.

- Don't climb directly below the person above you. Stay off to one side. It's easy to dislodge a large rock or boulder and start a rock slide. Wherever possible, climbers should spread out horizontally or diagonally across the mountain. If you must be in the line of fire of the person above you, wait till she/he has stopped climbing before you head up.

- If you get into an area with rocks jutting above your head, be sure to turn your visor around (like a baseball catcher) before you crack your head on an unseen crag.

- Don't exceed your physical limits and climbing skills. If in doubt, or if you become scared, go back. You get no medals for false valor. Macho Man doesn't live long on the mountain.

- If the going gets too hard, too dangerous, *everyone* turns back together. This is a group effort all the way.

- Topo maps are helpful, but look closely and make decisions as you climb. Rock can be solid or loose. Snow is hard in the mornings and soft in the afternoons. Brush can be full of narrow deer paths or completely impenetrable. Alter your route accordingly, and mark it with trail ducks if you expect to retrace your steps.

- The higher you climb, the more often you need to rest. Altitude thins the air and deprives the lungs and muscles of oxygen. Short breath and sore muscles result and require immediate attention. R&R is mandatory.

- Don't trust the topo map completely. A 30-foot cliff may not show up within 40-foot contour intervals (see *How to Read a Topo Map*, page 183). The "peak" you saw from your camp may not be the true top of the mountain, which may require another half-hour (or half-day) of climbing.

- Don't expect to find an easier way back down the far side of the mountain. You may come upon a sheer drop from the top and find it too dangerous to descend *and* too far to ascend again. It's

safer to mark your trail on the way up and follow that same
trail back.

As you get more interested in climbing, you'll want to refer to
a "mountaineer's guide" (see the Book List on pages 381-386 for
these Sierra Club guides) for a specific mountain range. This set of
small *Tote Books* lists specific climbing routes and "difficulty"
ratings for each route and peak in a given area. There's a guide to
the high Sierra in California, a guide to the Cascade Range in
Oregon and Washington, another for the Wind River Range in
Wyoming, one for the Great Basin Desert, etc. Match your ability
to the difficulty of various climbs, from Class 1 ("hiking") and
Class 2 ("hands are occasionally used for balance") to Class 3
("handholds and footholds are used...some climbers may wish to
be belayed") and even higher classes. Beginners should stick to
Classes 1 and 2; advanced climbers can choose more difficult
peaks and routes. These *Tote Books* also include cross-country
"knapsack routes," which can help you plan off-trail hiking
through areas which might otherwise seem inaccessible with a full
pack. Once you get hooked on bagging peaks, guidebooks like
these are indispensable.

## Mountain Biking

Bikers go faster and farther. A day trip to them may cover
two or three times the distance of a day hike. Trail biking in the
high country challenges stamina and skill and offers solitude and
scenery. With a light pack on the back, tools included, the biker is
unfettered. If, however, the trail is obstructed by fallen trees or is
filled with granite scree, if it climbs or descends too steeply, if it
disappears into dense brush, the mountain biker will have to
dismount, schlep and haul, or turn around and go home. Expecting the unexpected is a cardinal rule for the trail biker. So is
expecting the expected—hikers and backpackers on foot; minor
spills and falls; mechanical failures; fatigue. Be, you should pardon
the expression, prepared.

Some mountain bikers carry a strap so they can shoulder
their bikes up impossible grades. Others grab the handlebars, flip
the front wheel up, and roll the bike ahead on the rear wheel. All
have to dismount to get over tree trunks and logs. This is hard
work, and at a high altitude it's sometimes exhausting, too. Rest.
Swig some water, nosh on a piece of chocolate. Get out the com-

pass and topo map and triangulate your position, even if you know where you are! Anything that takes time and forces you to rest and relax. Take a siesta even though it's only 10 a.m.

When injured, rest some more. Walter Mitty made it across the English Channel at the helm with an unset broken arm, but you won't and shouldn't. He's a fiction. You're a fact. And the fact is that cycling, especially rough trail riding, draws injuries like flies to a feast. Knees and elbows, even encased in long pants and sleeves, are vulnerable, and when scraped and strained require attention and a rest break. Elevate the injury (above the heart). Treat it with the ever-present first-aid kit—a cold pack, disinfectant and an ace bandage—and don't get back on the bike till the swelling's down. No sense sending yourself to the trauma ward when all you want to do is hang out.

## Hanging Out with Children

Everything can be a wonderment—or a bore—to small children, and it's up to you to help make it the first, not the second. If you decide to hang around camp for the day, follow their lead. It could take you (and them) no further than the nearest inchworm. Call it nature study. It may take hours. After all, the worm takes hours doing what it does. Young children may need direction around, rather than through, the still-warm fire, or caution before diving into space, or preferably your arms, from the high scarp overlooking the kitchen. But exploring children are usually happy children, which makes your job that of a benign overseer. As long as they don't get lost or hurt (remember the whistle around their necks?), they can keep busy longer than you may care to imagine. If you're baking bread, give them some dough to knead or feed to the ants. If you're fishing, let them cast, even if the bubble or lure never quite make it into the water. (Keep baby brother out of the range of the hook.) If you're off on a day hike, make sure the five- and six-year-olds have lots to do on the trail—hiding, eating, staring breathlessly at a deer, hearing a story told or telling one.

Water play is as theraputic for children as adults. They don't need a wading pool or San Simeon to be happy. A puddle or stream, a lake or a tide pool will enhance their day and yours. If old enough, they can float in the current of the stream near the canoe or raft. If too young, they can paddle around at the shore-line. For reasons known only to physiologists and low-temperature physicists, toddlers and five-year- olds never seem to get cold. Lips turn blue, gooseflesh appears, yet on they go, insisting on one more splash, one more dunk, one more handful of mud before surrendering to a warm blanket in the sunshine. Yes, we know about the dangers of chill, and so do you, but let them dawdle in the water while the sun is high and they're discovering the joys of the aquatic life. Tide pools are the top of the line in water fun, and entire families can spend whole afternoons wading about touch-ing, watching, feeling and collecting. Shells and stones weigh down packs the next day, but sometimes you have to pay the price.

Rick is one of the world's great grasshopper catchers. He uses them as fishing bait. Now he uses them for Sheri bait. His five-year-old daughter took to the chase as if born to it. Probably some genetic explanation there. Anyway, with the single-mindedness of the true believer, she chased and caught them for the better part of an August day on her third backpacking trip. We're talking hours here, endless pleasure-filled hours, over rocks, along the lake front, through the tall grass. Hal and Rick took turns monitoring the hunt, holding the Ziploc bag. They got tired long before she did. And at the end of the day, she let them loose (hoppers and adults). It seems to have been as much fun watching them depart as it was getting them to arrive.

If you know your edible wild plants, let the kids taste-test them. They seem to love it. Older children often like to use the tree finder—one of those little guides that send you to page 4 if the needles come in threes, then to page 17 if the bark smells like a pineapple. All children appear to like to draw, and we know parents who always take along blank books for the inevitable art projects.

There's a message here and it's simple. If you bring the kids along, allow them the fun they seek, and help them get it. You may have to sacrifice the hammock or the mountain bike, but you'll be repaid in kind down the road when they offer to take *you* back-packing or camping in their favorite wilderness. In the meantime, they can get scrubbed and clean next week at home, and you can burn the clothes in the incinerator.

## Chapter Eleven

# The Stars at Night

Supper is warm and filling, dusk is settling over the camp, and the first star is in the evening sky. The last great arena of the hang-out artist is straight above you, and it's worth a look. Chapter 13 will show you how.

# CHAPTER 12

# Fishing

---

The sky is cloudless, a deep indigo. The sun has already set. It's surprising how fast the warmth vanishes when the sun goes down. A cool breeze blows from the west. Time for parka and knit cap.

We've been fishing from the shore of the lake for about an hour without a bite. Almost in a trance, Rick casts a lure into the depths of the lake and reels it back slowly: twitching it, stopping it, speeding it up; casting left, then right; trying to run it deep, then shallow. Hal goes on reading *Catch 22* aloud. Milo Minderbinder has cornered the world market on guns and is moving in on butter.

A slight tug on Rick's line brings his thoughts back to the lake. Is it a fish nibbling at the lure or just a snag on some undergrowth? To find out, he slows down the lure, twitches it a little, and keeps it moving very slowly. Another tug, and Rick says, "Hey, I think I've got one!"

Half a ton of live, angry fish breaks the surface to our left. The body completely leaves the water, a full six inches above the ripples, then splashes back under the surface. That's when Rick notices his line peeling off the reel. The monster fish is the one on his line.

Rick tightens up on the drag. Not too much, though; that fellow could easily snap his light line. His heart pounds; his hands tremble. This is one big fish.

Reel it in; let it run out on the drag. Reel it in; let it go out again. The fish is getting tired. Rick's getting tired, too. The line gets shorter as man coaxes fish toward the shore. Now we can see it: weary, slightly over on its side. It's in about three feet of water below the rock we stand on. But it's too heavy to yank out, and we have no net.

As if he's walking a dog, Rick slowly leads the fish along the rocky bank to a muddy inlet about 15 feet away. Every three or four feet, the fish twitches. But it's exhausted and hurt. Rick drags it closer to the muddy incline. Now it is in only four inches of water. Then, with a steady pull, he lands the fish. It flops a few times on the beach, but the line holds. Rick reaches down, unhooks it and puts it in our pot: a 16-inch golden trout.

Rick starts to speak, but nothing comes out. His heart is still pounding; he feels a little dizzy. Ten minutes of play has felt like an hour's work. He sits down. Leaning against a rock, eyes closed, it takes 10 minutes more to get back to normal. And then in only an hour, Rick and Hal sit down to the finest, freshest trout amandine dinner they've ever eaten.

Someone once described an airline pilot's job as hours and hours of utter boredom punctuated by a few moments of sheer terror. We could describe mountain fishing as hours and hours of pure relaxation punctuated by a few moments of wild excitement. The most enjoyable part of high mountain fishing is the relaxation: the scenery, the weather, the routine of casting, retrieving and playing the lure or fly.

The picture hanging above Rick's desk at work is not of a string of 14-inch trout. Rather, it's a shot of him casting into a mountain lake at sunset. The peaks above are nearly orange; you can see their reflection in the lake. Standing on a spit of land, his figure is a silhouette against the pale sky. More than anything else, we recommend high-country fishing for the beauty and quiet pleasure it brings. The tasty trout are an additional bonus.

# Mountain Trout: A Fish's Eye View

## *Winter*

If you've never fished for trout before, a good place to begin learning is to experience the lake as the fish does—in the mind's eye of a high-mountain lake trout. During the winter, the lake surface is covered with snow and ice. The water below is close to freezing, and only a little nourishment flows through. The trout, being cold-blooded, respond appropriately: as the temperature descends, so does their metabolism. Though they continue feeding all winter, they need very little food. If you could get into high country in the dead of winter, you'd work very hard for your fish, first to get through the ice, then to get it to bite.

In early spring, which in the mountains means late May and early June, the fishing is also often lean. Occasionally, we've camped at a high lake just as spring is breaking. Parts of the lake are still frozen. And just five or ten feet from shore, huge trout swim slowly along, evidently there for the taking. But nothing seems to work. Flies, lures and moving bait are universally ignored. Sometimes the fish will feed on a small worm or grub buried in the mud. But basically they're just out sunning, warming themselves in the water's upper layers. There's not much to eat yet and the fish aren't hungry. Neither the spawning cycle (which produces lots of yummy eggs) nor the insect hatching cycle (which produces a living feast) have yet begun. As Br'er Rabbit would observe, "They're layin' low."

## Spring: June and Early July

The longer, warmer days of June and early July melt the snow rapidly. Suddenly there is water everywhere. Lakes are overflowing. Meadows turn emerald with lush growth and are dappled with wildflowers. The insect hatch begins. From tiny eggs, insect larvae appear—little white worms called grubs or nymphs which live in the shallows of lakes or streams.

As the lake begins warming, and the body temperature of fish rises, the trout start moving faster. They quickly get hungry. And as the snow melts in the mountain meadows, it washes small grubs down through the lake, so the fish don't have to look far for food. They congregate at the places in the lake where they can find shelter, comfort and nourishment.

Where are these spots? Shelter could mean deep water. However, trout aren't too comfortable in the deepest part of the lake: there's little food, less oxygen and the cold temperatures make them sluggish. In the spring, as the ice melts, the upper 40 feet of the lake will have a good supply of oxygen and water of the right temperature. Shelter in this region might be available under a bank or beneath a rock overhang.

For trout, like for the rest of us, the food question is simple: how to get the most food for the least energy? In the springtime, they do this by finding a quiet place next to a food-bearing flow of water. This allows them to watch the current passively, then dart into it only when a tasty morsel appears. In mountain lakes, these quiet spots are usually found where the shallows drop off rapidly into deep water near where a feeder stream enters the lake. They are often called "holding" areas by fisherfolk.

Another important factor in finding food has to do with the trouts' ability to see. Too little (or too much) light makes it difficult for them to distinguish a moving grub from a twig or pine needle. So fish will usually lurk at the depth of water that offers the right amount of light. They'll feed in shallow water in the early morning, then move deeper during the day, and feed again in the shallows at dusk.

What kind of food do trout look for in the spring? Mainly, grubs. Some grubs float free; some squirm in the mud; many are encased in little "houses" of bark and sand. Open the stomach of a trout and you'll usually find a few partially digested grubs along with lots of dirt, twigs and mud.

Occasionally the fish in these holding areas get a special treat, a batch of trout eggs or roe. Springtime marks spawning season for trout. Many trout swim up into the feeder streams, the females to deposit eggs in warm, shallow water, and the males to fertilize them. Sometimes a batch of eggs is washed from its sandy bed and floats down to the lake. Lake trout are always watching for eggs in the springtime.

How should you fish mountain lakes in the spring? We usually cast fairly deep, near the inlet of a feeder stream, baiting with salmon eggs. Try to find the "drop-off" point and get your eggs just over the ledge. Late in the day, when the water is still warm and the light is losing its glare, those hungry fish will move toward your bait. Chances of a nibble are good.

If you're stream fishing, you can sometimes catch spawners in the shallow creek beds by drawing a lure in front of them—slowly, as if it were an intruder to their nesting area. The fish won't be hungry, but they may grow angry and snap at it in order to protect their turf.

## Summer: July and August

In early and mid-summer, the days turn long and hot in the mountains. The snow is gone. The creeks have slowed. The biggest change from springtime is the proliferation of insect life. Larvae emerge from their twig and sand houses, crawl into the sun on top of a rock, and metamorphose into small flies and bugs. Grasshoppers emerge from eggs and begin hopping through the grassy meadows.

The rushing, running water of the spring is gone. Insect life centers on and around the mountain lakes. Their surfaces become breeding grounds for insects too tiny to see. These in turn become food for larger flying insects which dance along the surface of the water whenever it is calm, eating the smaller ones. From the fish's eye view, the livin' is easy.

Trout continue to spawn during the early summer, with females swimming up feeder streams to lay their eggs. Many of the eggs laid earlier in spring now hatch. Shallow waters are filled with tiny trout, or minnows, which provide excellent nourishment for larger fish. The minnows soon learn the importance of remaining near shelter at all times.

In summer, the lake divides into three layers of water: an upper warm layer, a lower cold layer and a combined middle layer. In the morning, the trout come into the shallows to feed on nymphs and minnows. The water here is cooler then and the low sun makes it easier to see the nymphs (larval flies which swim several inches below the surface of the water) and minnows, which hang out in nooks and crannies for protection.

During midday, the trout move lower, to cooler water. The brighter it gets, the deeper they go. They spend most of these hours nosing around the lake bottom for grubs, larval flies which live in the mud. Occasionally, the fish come across some tasty fish eggs or a small worm. Then in the afternoon, they go back to the shallower areas to feed, primarily in the shade, where it is easier for them to see the surface.

During late afternoon, when the cold-blooded insects are most active on the water and sunlight strikes the lake at an angle, the trout will rise to work the surface. This is when you'll see them jumping. They wait below the still surface for a fly to land and feed. Then they come up—so fast that they just keep going, often completely out of the water. It's always a thrill to see and it's also a prime time to catch dinner.

Yet trout fishing any hour of the summertime day can be a real pleasure. In the morning, we often fish with lures. Lures spin bright and silvery in the water, imitating minnows darting through the upper layers of the lake. During the middle of the day, the fish often seem to "stop biting." They've gone to the cooler depths to forage for grubs. Sometimes they can be caught with salmon eggs, but catching a tan is a better bet, or a nap in the shade after a swim while the old fishing rod, secured by a few sturdy rocks, takes care of itself. If the salmon eggs get soggy, so what?

Afternoons are the most productive times to fish. Everything seems to work. We fish flies when the trout are jumping. We fish lures along the steep drop-offs, often following the shadow line along the shore, as the fish do underwater. We also fish with grasshoppers near the shore in shady places under overhanging bushes. These are the likely spots where grasshoppers may accidentally fall into the lake, spots where the fish will be waiting for them. This time of day usually gives us our best fish memories and stories, and if things work out, a pan full of the freshest supper you could ever want.

## Fall: September and Early October

In the fall, the water level is at the year's lowest. The days get shorter, nights get colder and food gets scarcer. The creeks and streams feeding the lakes have all but dried up. There isn't much insect life flowing through the lake. The temperature layers of the lake water begin to equalize. As the surface water cools, it's easier for the trout to spend time in it.

At this time of year, there are fewer but larger fish in the lakes. They are the survivors, and they want to fatten up for the winter cold spell. They feed on grubs and nymphs, now more plentiful in the shallower stretches, and on insects, which still land on the lake's surface in the late afternoon. Grasshoppers are fewer but fatter and are still choice bait. Everything seems more tempting to the hungry fish.

Fishing in the fall is thus similar to fishing in the summer— with one big exception: with the fish bigger and hungrier, and the action near or on the surface most of the day, it's even easier! There are a couple of other bonuses as well. The weather is better and the wilderness less crowded. Now if you could only arrange vacation time then…

## Lake Structure

There are times, especially late on a summer afternoon, when fish seem to spread out all over a lake. You can catch a fish almost anywhere, as they pop to the surface for fresh bugs or hunt in the shallows for silvery minnows. But most of the day—and most of the year—fish do not lead solitary lives. Like their cousins in the ocean, they form schools in places where the food is easy to come by. Each lake has its unique spots, and finding the ones that hold fish can be baffling.

Once Rick was fishing next to a couple of old-timers on a rocky point. Rick was casting his salmon eggs and lures out toward the middle of the lake, where he figured the big trout would be waiting. Nothing. The old-timers were casting their salmon eggs in the other direction, into a small cove, closer to shore. About every five minutes they reeled in a fish. As they were leaving, they turned to Rick and said, "Hey, young fella, you're fishing in the wrong place. There's an underground feeder stream in this little cove here, and most of the trout in the lake are probably down there waiting for eggs this afternoon. Try it." Twenty minutes later, Rick was heading back to camp with dinner and the next morning's breakfast.

Fish invariably congregate at a junction in the habitat. They sit just below a sharp drop-off, or in the shadow of a submerged boulder, or next to a rocky point, or just below a stream inlet. They follow morning and afternoon shade lines across a lake. It is said that 10 percent of the water holds 90 percent of the trout. No wonder fisherfolk try to keep their special spots secret!

# Rivers and Streams

Stream fishing, like lake fishing, has its unique pleasures and problems. It promises more solitude—a chance to get off by yourself even near the trail. And while it's hard work, it's often productive, and usually satisfying whether you bag a fish or not.

Stream fishing means a lot of hiking for a little angling. It often requires hopping on rocks, or holding onto overhanging branches for dear life or taking off your pants and putting on your boots, or getting your line tangled in thickets of brush, or all of the above. Yet the angler who is willing to fish a mountain stream often will return to camp with a string of trout, having discovered the right tackle and baits and the best places to fish only a spit and a holler from the well-worn path.

Many hiking trails parallel streams, dipping down occasionally to cross them at fordable points. At those points, there are often well-used (and sometimes populated) campsites. But just a few hundred yards in either direction up- or downstream you'll find no sign of human life and often many signs of underwater life. A little scrambling gets you a lot of fishing. And if the fish aren't biting, you can retrace your steps, hike along the trail, leave it again where it approaches the stream, and continue for a whole day, covering long stretches of running water. Along the way, you'll often discover several natural, picture-perfect campsites, too remote for the casual hiker. There you can set up shop for a couple of days of fine early-morning and late-afternoon fishing.

Stream trout eat the same things as lake trout, but they tend to secure their food in a different way. By knowing what, how and where they eat, you can usually find and often catch them. Larvae, grubs, insects, eggs and minnows thrive in streams as well as lakes and fill up the "market basket" of hungry river fish. Your job is to figure out just what the fish are feeding on—you may have to try several riggings and baits before you get the right one—and then go after them. Here's how.

Lake trout, you remember, move around looking for food. River trout, conversely, stay in one place. That's the major difference between the two and makes for a different kind of fishing. As the river water flows, it carries insects, eggs and larvae with it. A fish needn't move to get the food when food is moving to it. This is ecological efficiency at work, and by tapping into its logic, you can imitate nature with your bait and catch a fish.

The fish knows where the food is coming from and where to be to get it. Obviously, it'll come from upstream. The place to be, if you're a stream trout, is in a quiet, well- protected pool, just off the main stream which carries the goodies along. Such pools may be under an overhanging boulder, bank or branch, beneath a rotted log, or at the bend of the river where the flow eddies wide, leaving a quiet spot near one bank. They may be at the far end of a rapids or beneath a miniature waterfall or cascade, all of which act as natural conveyor belts for the food that fish fancy.

Stream trout "hold" in these pools (hence the angling term "holding pools"), and watch the rapidly flowing main current without having to swim against it. When a morsel flows by, they dart out and grab it. Then it's back to the safety of the shadowed pool to watch and wait for more of the same. Like the fish, you can also trace the path of the food. Toss a leaf into the flowing stream or over the cascade. See how it's taken by the current into a calmer spot: that's the pool. Now try to cast your baited hook in such a way that it does the same thing as the leaf. Throw your bait into the current. The eggs, if that's what you're using, will sink slightly, then be carried into the pool below. If you've done your homework and fish are waiting, you'll get a quick bite. River fish are not likely to mouth the bait and spit it out several times as lake fish often do. River fish must get their food on the first bite or watch it disappear downstream.

Sneak up on stream trout from behind. They're facing upstream; you should be hiking and casting upstream also. Cast your bait or lure just above where you suspect they're holding. Let the bait float

**Stream eddies and holding pools**

naturally through the area, as if it just hatched or fell into the water. As the bait floats back to you, reel in just enough line to take up the slack and keep it from snagging—easier said than done!

Several such casts, allowing the bait to flow into the pool, are all you need. Look around for other likely holding pools upstream. Perhaps there's a log blocking the current, or a large rock in the middle of the stream. A fish might lurk behind it, observing the water flow by. Let your bait or lure drift past. Still no bites? Then it's time to move on.

Moving on takes some care. You need to be quiet and cautious at the same time—quiet in order to sneak up on fish which are often just inches below the surface, and cautious to keep from slipping, tripping and falling along overgrown banks and slippery rocks. River trout are easily spooked. Be careful of your shadow dancing on the water. Plan your moves so your shadow falls on the bank instead. That might mean hunching over, even crawling in spots. Keep your casting motion short and low; the sudden movement of your arm and rod can startle fish. Once they sense your motion or are alerted by rocks and gravel you dislodge as you scramble down a bank, they're likely to duck into a safe hiding place for hours.

If you manage to get to the holding pools without sending all the fish to the local fright-recovery unit, and if you have the right bait, your chances of landing a trout are greatly enhanced if you fish early or late in the day. When there's little light on the water, the fish see the surface better and, like their lake cousins, go for living foods on or just below it. At midday, they go as deep as they can, still watching the flowing water for an easy lunch in the deep shade. You might try it yourself.

One last thing. To quiet and caution, add patience. Stream fishing can be frustrating. Your line can get snagged on an overhanging branch, the hook or lure can get hung up on a submerged rock or log, or the trout on your line can free itself by taking your line under a rock and snapping it. But the rewards of solitude, beauty, challenge and good eating more than make up for the hard parts. Take it slow, easy and enjoy.

# Fishing in the Rain

When rain clouds roll in on summer afternoons, many campers head into their tents. *We* put on ponchos and parkas, then head out to fish. Some of our most memorable fishing has been on rainy afternoons.

One theory has it that fish can't possibly conceive of any other creature, especially an over-coddled human, who might prefer to be as wet as they are. Thus, when they see a shiny lure dancing through the rain-splashed water, they figure it's the real thing. Our own theory doesn't attribute quite so much intelligence to the trout. We've found that as the storm moves in, the fish stop biting. They sense the air pressure decreasing—what weather forecasters mean by the barometer falling. Fish—and most other living things—seek shelter.

Once the storm is in full splendor, the barometer steadies, then begins to rise. As the air pressure increases, the rain may still be falling, but the fish sense that the worst is over, and out they go to see what fresh food has entered the lake. The rain washes the surface of the lake clean. New bugs appearing on the surface are likely to be alive. Minnows darting below the surface are likely to be real. And anglers' shadows, broken by the rain-mottled surface, are likely to go unnoticed. While all this is conjecture, the fact is that if you don't mind the wet, fishing in the rain can be highly successful and a lot more fun than huddling in the tent.

# Gear

Mountain trout are usually small. Most range from 8 to 12 inches in length and weigh a little under a pound. A two-to-three pounder in the high country is a monster. And even these require very little in the way of gear to bait, hook and reel into your frying pan.

First, you need a rod and reel. We leave fancy flyfishing, with its graphite rods, hand-tied flies and special line, to the purists. Instead, we use a simple telescoping spinning rod. It telescopes down to a two-foot length, short enough to stick in the backpack, though it's also long and stiff enough to give a good cast. Inexpensive models can even be found in some drugstores. But treat them gently and pack them carefully—expensive or cheap, they're fragile.

Reels come in all shapes and sizes. A look at *Consumer Reports* might be in order before you put your money down. The more expensive reels have better machinery inside—bearings, gears and levers—that last longer and take more abuse. The cheaper "back-packing" reels are lighter, less substantial and more likely to jam up after you drop them onto the ground or into the sand a couple of times. We usually compromise on the best combination of inexpensive and lightweight reel that our discount sports store has in stock when we're buying.

If you're left-handed, you might want a left-handed reel which permits you to wind in with your right hand while holding the rod and reel in your left. On the other hand (!), you might want to learn to fish with a righty's reel. It isn't hard and saves bringing extra gear if you don't mind sharing.

It's a good idea to practice taking the cover off the reel and lubricating the inside mechanism. It won't take many trips before your reel falls into the water or sand for one reason or another. If you don't lubricate it soon afterwards, certainly before your next outing, it will get sticky and much harder to cast properly. For this purpose, you can either buy a special reel lubricant or use any light gear-and-bearing grease.

You'll need fishing line on the reel. We usually deposit our reels at a local bait and tackle shop a few days before each outing and have them wound with four-pound monofilament line. The shop has a special winding machine which lays the line on evenly and regularly.

If you prefer, you can wind the line onto the spool yourself. Set up the rod and reel as if you were going fishing. Thread the line through the rod's eyelets and tie it to the spool of the reel with the bail open. Drop the spool of fresh line into a clean wastebasket. Grasp the line and rod with your right hand about a foot up from the reel. Snap the bail shut and reel the new line in with your left hand. Keep a slight drag on the line with your right hand, and watch the reel as you wind. If you see stray loops or uneven winding, vary the drag until you get it right. Don't allow any lumps, clumps, twirls or snags to grow on the spool. Be sure the line lays down in even symmetrical rows.

Why do you need fresh line each outing? The monofilament tends to shape itself to the spool on which it's wound. Line which has been on your reel for several months tends to lie in the water

**Winding a reel**

in hundreds of little curlicues. As you reel in these curls, they quickly form hundreds of small knots. Then you spend your fishing time untangling knots instead of casting—a disheartening and dull task.

The rest of your backpacking fishing tackle, except for a net, should fit easily into a large Ziploc bag. In that bag, supplies should be divided into smaller bags or plastic boxes. It's important both to save weight when backpacking and to save space in the pack. Don't fill your fishing bag with empty space. Pack lightly but efficiently.

Basically, you'll need the following items:

*Bubbles*: About a dozen clear and torpedo-shaped, if available. These are used mainly for casting weight. A large bubble will get your fly farther into the middle of the lake than a small one.

*Flies*: A dozen small flies will fit into a tiny bag, box or foam-lined case. Buy various colors and shapes, with hook sizes between 8 and 14. Most of our flies are on #10 or #12 hooks. They cost between 50 cents and a dollar each, though hand-tied flies will set you back a lot more.

*Hooks*: One package each of hooks already tied to a small piece of leader, sizes 8, 10, 12 and 14. The leaders have a loop at the other end and can be clipped easily onto a snap or swivel in your rigging.

*Spare Line*: We usually bring 100 yards of four-pound test monofilament on a spool. This can be wound directly onto your reel if you run completely out (as a result, for example, of having consecutively cut away tangled sections). Spare line can also be

### *Fishing tackle*

used as "leader"—line tied directly to a fly or bait. Some people bring 25 yards of two-pound test monofilament to use as leader.

*Snaps*: About 30 of the smallest you can find. These are used at the end of the line to attach bubbles, lures and other riggings.

*Swivels*: About 10, all small. These attach weights or hooks in the middle of a rigging. They can be two- or three-way swivels. They are helpful in dreaming up new ways to rig your bait.

*Weights*: One package (20 weights) of eighth-ounce "egg sinkers." These are sliding weights with a hole down the middle. One package of sixteenth-ounce "split shot," small weights which clamp to a single spot on the line. If you plan long, deep water casts, add a package of quarter-ounce egg sinkers.

*Lures*: About a dozen lures with treble (triple) hooks, sizes 8, 10 and 12. This will allow you to lose a few and still have a reserve. Lures have a habit of snagging; you'll donate quite a number to the lake or stream bottom. The larger, heavier lures can be cast farther. Smaller, lighter lures work better in mountain streams. They don't sink as fast so they're less likely to snag on sunken trees and branches. Check with your favorite expert about his or her special lure before you shop—lures are expensive. We've had the most success with $1\frac{1}{2}$" Super Dupers and half-ounce #6 Panther Martins.

*Salmon Eggs*: Two small bottles of Pautchke's "Balls of Fire," green label. This brand is slightly more expensive but comes highly recommended. Keep the eggs in their glass bottles despite the excess weight. Also keep them cool and in the shade or they'll start to spoil.

*Net:* Get the smallest, lightest net available from a tackle shop. Pack it with the pots, pans and plates and it'll add very little weight and take up hardly any space. It helps a lot in landing fish, especially from a steep, rocky shore.

*License:* You might never meet a ranger or game warden in the backcountry who wants to see your license, but you need one anyway. The fee is steep but worth it, and your money goes to a good cause. It's used by your state's Fish and Game people to restock lakes, maintain hatcheries and keep streams and rivers clear. Don't travel without one. And make sure when you get one to pick up a free copy of your state's fishing regulations. It explains what kind of fishing is legal in which areas at what times of year. Read it carefully.

## Fishing for the Tenderhearted

A lot of people like the idea of fishing but not the reality of executing and eating the results. Solution? Use barbless hooks. It puts sport back into angling and gives the fish a chance. Bait a barbed hook, catch a fish, and you've practically got to eat it because the fish swallows the hook and it's too far down to dislodge without needle-nosed pliers. Use barbed lures and the several hooks often make it impossible to release the fish quickly enough to ensure survival. Barbless means a good fight, a fighting chance for the fish to dislodge the hook, and a quick release if you win.

Where to find barbless hooks? Short of going to Japan and China where everybody fishes with them, try the local fly-fishing shops. Better yet, just take a pliers or a file to your regular stash and press the barbs in or file 'em away. Catch-and-release to your heart's content.

# Bait and Rigging

The best way to find out "if they're biting" and "what to use" is to ask those who are there or who you meet on the trail coming from your lake. If they tell you, "Salmon eggs toward the lake inlet," go to it with salmon eggs. If they tell you, "Lures by the steep north wall," don't use flies by the inlet. Simple enough.

Of course, this presumes the presence of people with information. The farther you go off the beaten track, the fewer ready-made answers you'll find. Alone at a lake, deciding what and where to fish becomes a wonderful challenge. Size up the lake closely for a few moments. Where does the water come in? Where does it leave? Where are the deepest spots? Where are the shady overhangs? Consider the season, the weather and the time of day to figure out where the fish might be.

If you prepare wisely, you're ready in advance for any kind of fishing, deep or shallow, lures or bait. Your lures, fastened to a cork so they won't tangle, can clip easily onto the snap at the end of the line. Your salmon-egg rigging is tied up inside a small plastic bag, available for instant use. If the fish are jumping in the shady section of the lake, you can quickly switch from eggs to a bubble and fly. Or perhaps you feel like putting a grasshopper in the water near the shrubs by the base of a steep cliff, then reading another chapter of your book as you wait for a tug on the line. It's fun and easy to experiment when you've put your riggings together in advance. It's frustrating when that big cahoonga is right there laughing at you, as you try to tie new knots, re-rig a line and catch a grasshopper, all at the same time.

## Fishing Knots, Swivels and Clips

Like Boy Scouts, anglers often wallow lovingly in the intricacy of knotsmanship. "Lark's-head loops" and "Bimini twists" are often cited as prerequisites to catching large fish. Fortunately, this is not the case. Everything in your fishing arsenal can be tied strongly and securely with a simple square knot, and confusion about the fancier systems of connecting line and tackle won't prevent you from catching a single trout. Nevertheless, for the precision angler and other fine-tuners, we include on the next few pages a few simple knots and tying instructions. We often use the clinch knot.

**Improved clinch knot**

**Lark's head knot**

## Bimini twist knot

## Nail knot

## Blood knot

## Double surgeon's knot

## Perfection knot

## Jam knot

Swivels are used to tie one piece of tackle to another so they don't slip or come apart. For example, when you fish with salmon eggs, you may want two groups of eggs suspended above the bottom of the lake. A couple of three-way swivels allow you to connect two short "drop" leaders to the main line with a minimum of fuss.

**Rigging for three-way swivel**

A snap at the end of the line is a must; it'll save you a lot of time when you're making up and changing riggings. You can clip a lure onto the end of your line for fishing deep. Then, if the fish start feeding on surface insects, you can easily detach that lure to clip on a bubble-and-fly rigging. Snaps save you from cutting the line and retying whenever you change tackle. Remember, early morning and evening are the times when it will be most difficult for you to see the line to tie or untangle it, yet those are the times of the most fishing action. If you have a supply of snaps and swivels in your tackle bag, you'll be ready for those quick changes when time counts.

## Salmon Egg Riggings

Trout lay their eggs in shallow rock beds near the headwaters of rivers and streams. These eggs occasionally get jarred loose and float downstream on the streambed, finally settling on the bottoms of lakes. Mountain trout love 'em.

To fish a stream, you need to gauge the amount of weight necessary to keep the egg low in the water. Without any weights at all, salmon egg riggings float near the surface. Too much weight will get your line snagged on the first branch. You should also know the depth and speed of the water to guess the right amount of weight, in the form of split shot(s). Clamp them onto your line about 12" to 16" above the hook. The traditional way to squeeze the split shot tight on the line is to bite down on it with your molars. Your dentist would probably prefer that you use a small pliers or vise-grips for the job. If the split shot is clamped too loosely, it will slide down the line and settle near the hook, making the bait look unnatural. With a couple of salmon eggs on the hook and a couple of split shots tight on the line, you're ready to sneak up and cast it into the nearest holding pool.

On a lake, salmon eggs are usually rigged deep for fishing at times when no fish surface to feed. These riggings are also good for any other bait which isn't supposed to be alive, a bit of salami or scrap of cheese, for example. You want to get these bits of food to where the fish are—along the bottom looking for food that has been washed into the lake. Trout lay eggs in clusters; if they wash away from the shallow stream in which they were laid, they remain clustered as they're carried down into the lake. We usually stick three or four salmon eggs on a #8 hook to simulate nature. One hint on getting them to stay hooked: lay them in the sun about 15 minutes before you use them. This hardens the outside skin and makes them less likely to float off the hook.

When a lake trout spots a cluster of salmon eggs, it will often mouth them, not swallowing them completely at first. It's testing for weirdness, like a hook lurking in its Sunday brunch. Our first suggested rigging is called the "Long Lake Rigging" (after the lake where two old-timers taught it to us). It suspends two clusters of eggs several inches above the lake bottom. When you feel a slight tug on the line, wait just a moment, then "set" the hook in the trout's mouth by pulling up slightly on the rod. The point is to try to snag the fish's lip as it's drawing the bait in for a second mouthing. If you don't wait, you'll pull up empty, for the fish will have let the bait go before taking another taste. With this rigging, you need to hold the line fairly taut at all times so you're sensitive to what's happening at the other end.

**Long Lake rigging**

Our other suggestion is called the "Grizzly Lake Rigging." It rests the bait down on the lake bed and depends on a hungry trout to gobble it up completely. Put a small barrel or doughnut weight on your line *before* you add the swivel, then clip on the leader and the hook. When the fish starts to nibble or mouth the bait, the weight won't give it any resistance. The trout will come back for more in a few moments. If things work right, it won't figure out that the eggs are on a hook until the hook is in its throat or stomach. It's the perfect rigging for reading, sunning, napping and even cooking. You cast, lean the rod against a rock or your leg and wait. The line goes slack. When you feel or see a tug on the slack line, the hook is already set and the fish is ready to be reeled in.

If the lake bottom is full of underwater grasses, you may want to add a little something to your bait to get it to float a few inches above the bottom. That will make it easier for the fish to see as they amble along looking for food. Ask at the bait shop for something that floats: "Power Bait," for example, or "Floating Cheese," or, wonder of wonders, "Garlic Marshmallows." Slather some onto your salmon eggs or just use the floating bait alone on your hook. (If all else fails, you can probably throw the stuff into your spaghetti sauce!)

If you fish with worms, but the fish can't find 'em down in the mud, use a "worm inflator." This is a small plastic bottle with a hollow needle attached. It allows you to squirt some air into the worm to make it, er, more buoyant.

**Grizzly Lake rigging**

With either rigging, the weight should be only as heavy as necessary to get the hook(s) and salmon eggs where you want them. Heavy weights may cast farther, but as soon as a fish bites, that heavier weight gives the trout an advantage. All it has to do is go rapidly in one direction—up, for example—then switch directions with a snap of its head. If the weight is heavy enough, the line will break. Though the fish still has a hook in its mouth, you'll reel in an empty line. We usually start with eighth- or quarter-ounce sinkers and #8 hooks, whatever the rigging.

Any rigging meant to lie on the lake bottom tends to snag as you reel it in. Leave the rigging motionless for several minutes after you cast, so it can settle free of an obstruction that might otherwise snag it immediately. After that, a twitch every few minutes won't hurt and might attract a fish to the moving eggs. When you're ready to cast from a different rock or in another direction, pick up the line quickly from the lake bottom by reeling it in fast. *Keep* reeling fast so the hooks and sinker stay above sharp rocks and dead tree trunks on the bottom of the lake.

There's something else you should know about bait fishing, especially in mountain lakes. Time and again, you'll reel in your hook only to find it empty. You never felt a bite. Did the bait simply get soggy and drift away as you were reeling it in over a rock? Maybe. But more likely a fish got it without your ever knowing what happened. We've sometimes thrown salmon eggs into shallow, clear water (it's practically a ritual as we're getting ready to pack up and head home). Quite often, the fish pop the eggs into their mouths, then spit them out, then eat them for good on the second try. If that egg were attached to a hook, the only way to catch the fish would be to pull back on your line just as the fish mouthed the bait. That's called setting the hook. If you yank back too soon, you'll pull the bait right out of the fish's mouth. If you yank too late, the fish will already have mouthed and spit out the bait, leaving you with an empty hook.

The biggest difference between you and that old-timer on the next rock who's already caught the limit is not age. Nor is it brand of bait. It's that she knows how to feel that first nibble and at just the right time set the hook. The tiniest signal can mean that a trout is mouthing your bait. Some people wait for a slight quiver at the tip of the rod, some look for a movement of the line where it enters the water, some pinch a loop of line lightly between their fingertips. Whatever works. The old-timer's tried them all. You should, too.

## Bubble-and-Fly Rigging

The evening is warm, the air still, the lake calm, and the surface of the water is broken only by the fish jumping for insects. If you're equipped to simulate the insects, you'll almost certainly get a fish. That's where the bubble-and-fly comes in.

This rigging consists of a fly tied onto one end of several feet of leader, either four-pound or two-pound test line, and a teardrop bubble tied on the other. The bubble's weight lets you cast the fly where the fish are feeding. Once the bubble-and-fly lands, the object is to make the fly seem like all those other surface bugs. Watch how the real flies behave, scooting across the water close to shore. Reel in the line with quick short bursts so the fly seems to dart along like its real-life cousins.

**Bubble and fly rigging**

The best thing about bubble-and-fly fishing is that you rarely have to worry about snags. You can spend your time casting and retrieving rather than losing masses of tackle on underwater branches. Once in a while you'll snag a fly on a bush when fishing near shore. Also, be careful of trees and shrubs on your backswing. If you develop good casting habits, you'll while away the hours snagging fish rather than unsnagging line.

Flies come in a wide variety of shapes, sizes and colors. When the fish are jumping in those out-of-the-way backcountry lakes, neither shape nor color seem to matter. Size, however, is important. The fish are small; so are the bugs they eat. Try sizes 10 or 12. We've also noticed that flies produce the best results when they're first cast. They hit the water dry and sit on the surface for the first several casts. Thereafter, they ride slightly below the surface, and the fish are a little less likely to go after them. Sometimes we whip the fly through the air several times between casts in order to dry it off.

Keep moving as you fish bubble-and-fly. After a half-dozen casts in one area or direction, walk on. You can cover a whole lake this way, perfecting your casting technique, seeing the site from startling new perspectives and, if the fish are feeding, bagging dinner into the bargain. We backpack with a number of fanatics who don't care if they ever catch a fish. They just love the feel of casting, and over the years they have become expert at placing the fly a micrometer's distance from an overhanging branch, an inaccessible inlet, or a rocky spit. Now, if we could just get them to move to where the fish are…

## Fishing With Lures

The bigger the trout, the more likely it is to feed on small fish. From the backpacker's point of view, a lure is the closest thing to fishing with small fish; it often gets you the biggest trout. A lure is bright, shiny, silvery, and often spoon-shaped. It dances and flashes through the water, reflecting light much like a minnow. Lure fishing requires a technique simulating the movements of a tiny fish—darting quickly, stopping momentarily, and darting again. The art is in the play of the line, not in the distance of the cast, which can be quite short. As in bubble-and-fly fishing, you have to keep moving—your lure and yourself.

If you're fishing a stream, don't let the lure sink very far or you'll end up with a rock on the end of your line. The art of fishing a lure in a stream is to pick one that's not too heavy, then reel it through the water at a speed which will keep it just off the bottom. If you reel too fast or jerk it too hard, it will pop up to the surface. If you hesitate, it will sink to the bottom and tangle in the first branch or log. You'll definitely want a few spare lures while you're getting the hang of it. Think of the snagged lures as offerings to the spirit of the stream.

The lure simulates the motion of a small fish. If a trout wants to catch a minnow, it has to move fast. The speedy minnow will try to hide instantly, if it senses danger. It can dart into areas too shallow for the big guys, or it can escape under logs or into holes beneath banks. Thus, quickness is essential, for both minnow and trout; as soon as a trout sees the minnow flashing in the water, it strikes. The lure is below the surface. You can't see what's happening. If you feel a nibble, you've usually hooked the fish, because it hits the triple-barbed hook with mouth wide open, intent on swallowing the small fish whole. One minute you're reeling in the lure, the next you've got a big trout, solid on the line.

Suppose the large fish aren't feeding on minnows. They may still be attracted by the lure. They often swim up and seem to check it out, following it toward shore. If they're cautious, their senses will alert them that the lure doesn't sound or smell like a minnow, and they'll move away. It's an angler's nightmare to watch the big one follow a lure up to shore without biting. But frustration goes with the franchise, just as excitement does, and if that fish lives to savor a real minnow today, he'll be there for the taking tomorrow.

Another problem with lures is that they're made to fish deeper than flies. They ride somewhere between 6 and 24 inches below the surface as you reel them in. You can't see what's happening so it's harder to direct their path. Most lures have a three-pronged hook, which is more likely to catch a trout's mouth, but also more likely to snag underwater weeds or branches. Furthermore, if you have a problem with your equipment while the lure is in the water, the moment you stop reeling the treble hook drifts downward to catch on whatever lies there. By the time you fix the reel or untangle the line, the lure is hopelessly hooked on the lake bottom. One thing about lure fishing: it's never dull.

## Fishing with Grasshoppers

An old saying goes, "You can catch any fish if you've got the right bait." Natural bait stimulates all the fish's senses. It's the "r-e-e-l" thing. Grasshoppers are a special treat to lake trout, and depending on the time of day and year, fish will be attuned to the possibility of a large hopper falling onto the lake's surface. Not only will a trout go after one without hesitation, it will often encounter fierce competition from kindred fish for the tasty tidbit.

The challenge of capturing the grasshoppers themselves, however, more than makes up for the ease of landing the fish that bites the hopper that feeds it. There are books on the subject; well, chapters anyway. One suggests chasing hoppers onto a blanket: if they get stuck in the blanket hairs, they're easy pickin'. That's plausible, but not many backpackers carry wool blankets into the high country anymore. Another expert calls for an insect net, also a great idea if you're not backpacking. We have our own methods, summed up by the rueful phrase, "going to great lengths." The bare-handed stab is the classiest technique, though it helps if you're The Flash. Those bugs move fast! The pot-lid slam is inelegant, often resulting in a dented pot lid and a handful of meadow, while the hopper easily eludes this oafish lunge. Our favorite exercise in futility, however, is the "long-distance pole press," invented one morning by Rick as he wandered forlornly through an Eden of grasshoppers with a fishing rod in hand. The long, narrow pole, he noticed, casts only a thin shadow which hoppers don't seem to notice. Once the pole is directly over its victim, you bring it down suddenly, pinning the hopper on the ground. Sometimes instead of pinning the hopper, this artful action stuns it, so you can pick it up while it's still dazed from the blow. Sometimes, instead of stunning the bug, you kill it, which is great if you're fighting a plague of locusts but not so good if you're trying to look like an expert. And sometimes—often, in Hal's case—you miss the grasshopper altogether. That pole is limber, and requires a modicum of hand-eye coordination. No matter how you try, it ain't easy.

Spring meadows are often literally covered with baby grass-hoppers, and the catching's easier. As the year moves on, the hopper population decreases and the adults have more savvy. Like all insects, grasshoppers are cold-blooded. Dependent on the sun's warmth for their energy, they are least active in the morning, and thus theoretically there for the picking, right off leaves and grasses with your fingers. The only trouble in practice is that you can't see them till they flee, always just out of reach, and then you're back to square one: devising cunning strategies.

Some hoppers have wings and fly each time they take off, while others just hop. The key to catching them is to sneak up from behind, thus avoiding their field of vision, which extends roughly from the middle of their right side to the middle of their left. They'll jump just as your hand comes even with their heads, but not before. Try to move your hand slowly into position, per-haps one inch behind the hopper. Be careful not to cast a shadow on it as you move. Then suddenly slap down your open palm. Come down hard, quick and flat! Splat! Usually, you won't kill the hopper, but even if you do the fish won't care. Twelve-year-olds have an uncanny ability to catch grasshoppers this way.

Once you catch enough hoppers, you can keep them alive for as long as two days in a sealed plastic bag. Store them in the shade and be careful not to crush them at the bottom of your pack.

Hopper fishing is done with a rigging similar to a bubble-and-fly. The only difference is that the hook is empty. When you're ready to cast, poke the sharp point of the hook into the underside of the hopper's neck and out again at the belly button. The hopper will stay alive for a short while because its head hasn't been dam-aged. It may even flutter its wings in the water, attracting the fish.

The best place to fish hoppers is under the overhanging limb of a bush or tree where a hopper would be likely to fall in, or where the fish are already jumping. Sometimes when all else fails—the flies and lures and eggs—a hopper will save the day and provide your evening's dining pleasure. They're worth the scramble.

### Hooking a grasshopper

*To set a hook in a grasshopper, first insert the point into the head or upper body under the head. Next, push the hook through the body and turn it so that the point of the hook emerges from the bottom of the grasshopper. Try to leave as little of the hook exposed as possible.*

## Fishing with Other Natural Bait

Rick's grandfather Harry wasn't exactly a fitness fanatic. Fifty pounds overweight, his favorite meal was a can of corned beef hash washed down with a shot of Jack Daniels. Harry's idea of a vacation was shooting craps at a Nevada casino till the wee hours. But one or two mornings afterwards, he'd get up at 7 a.m., grab his old bamboo fishing pole and head out to the local trout stream. Harry would fish from a cement bank, not more than a few feet from his car. Invariably, he'd return with a string of six or eight fish, while others in the same area would leave empty-handed.

Harry's secret? He fished with natural bait. He told Rick that his favorite bait was a "prairie wrinkle." (A "periwinkle" is actually a small sea snail which lives on rocks or pilings along the ocean shore. Don't tell Grandpa.) Oblivious to the malapropism, he'd go on to describe a large fly larva usually called a hellgrammite. Just before dinner, Harry would go down to a shallow stream behind the hotel. He'd stir up the bottom and use an old window screen to catch these one- to two-inch long, worm-like creatures. Whether they were hellgrammites, dragonfly larvae or mayfly pupa didn't matter. As long as they were fat, wet and slimy, the fish loved them.

Most mountain insects develop from larvae which grow in shallow pockets in the mud and under stream rocks. There they build a small nest or shell around themselves made up of whatever materials are on hand—bits of gravel, bark or leaves. When they finally mature, they crawl out of their "cocoon" into the warm sun on top of a nearby rock, and within hours they fly away.

On a camping trip, the best time to become a grub hunter is in the middle of the day, with the sun hanging high and the fish lying low. You can comb the shore of a lake, stir up the bed of a trickling stream or probe the underside of the bark on a rotting log. Anything that's soft, fat and wiggly (your partner excepted) will work as trout bait. Try rigging your mosquito netting with a wire loop and hold it in a stream just below a large rock. Pick up the rock and see what you catch. Teach the kids. They'll love it.

You can fish with these larvae either in their cocoons or out of them, depending on the size of the larvae and your hooks. Insect larvae are usually fished on the bottom, like salmon eggs, but you can also fish them from a bubble as you would a hopper.

## Casting and Reeling

Nothing is more satisfying than catching trout in the wilderness. Nothing is more peaceful and relaxing than the routine of casting and retrieving a lure or fly, working the lake surface in the late afternoon while the fish feed. And nothing is more frustrating than snagging a lure or tangling your line because of improper reeling. The sun is setting, the fish are jumping, and there you are on your hands and knees trying to untangle a seemingly endless number of knots while your lure drifts slowly toward the lake floor to snag on a hidden log or brush. It makes you want to cry.

Prevent this by developing good casting habits. Practice in the local park at home or at the campsite using only a bubble on the line. Grip the rod as shown in the illustration. Point it in the direction you intend to cast. Catch the line on the ball of your forefinger. Then open the bail. With one smooth motion, bring the tip of the rod up, just past vertical, then back down. As the rod passes the "10 o'clock" position in front of you, straighten your forefinger. The line will spin off the reel as it follows the bubble across the lake. Once the bubble or lure is in the water, give the handle on the reel a quick turn to snap the bail back into position. As you continue turning the handle, the line reels regularly and neatly onto the spool, ready to peel off with little resistance on the next cast.

Reeling in the line seems simple, but requires some vigilance at the beginning. Most backpacking reels are small and light; the line is wound in very small loops around a narrow spool. When the line shoots out over the water, it pulls straighter at the bubble end than it does near the reel. The line on the water near you will be twirled and curled, and when you begin to reel in, it might tangle itself into a knot. Even a small knot on the line will foul up smooth casting.

To prevent these tangles, you need to watch the line as you reel in the first 10 or 15 feet. This is distracting: your attention is usually focused where the fish are. Force yourself. Watch for knots and tangles until the line is straight in the water.

Another way to defend against tangles is to grasp the rod and line with your rod hand about a foot in front of the reel as you begin to haul in. As the line slips through your hand, you'll feel any knots and can untangle them on the spot.

What if you reel in a tangle or knot without noticing it? The first indication will be a sudden halt to your lure or bubble as you cast. Knots and tangles catch in the eyelets through which the line passes along the rod. This will stop your cast dead. Then you'll have to decide whether to untangle the mess or just cut it off and continue with the fresh line still on your spool. Most spools contain about three times the amount of line you actually use when casting. If you cut off a length of tangled mess, you'll still have enough

**Casting:** *Hold the line with your forefinger, raise the rod just past vertical, then cast. As the tip passes "10 o'clock," let go of the line.*

for an afternoon's fishing. If you have to cut again, however, you'll be approaching the end of what line is on the reel. Once you hit the bottom of the spool, you'll need to wind on new line, either from the extra four-pound monofilament in your fishing bag, or from another reel (see previous instructions on winding line onto an empty spool).

What happens if you're in a wooded area where branches are too close to permit an overhead cast? Use a side-arm cast. Practice casting *from* either side *to* either side. That way, you'll be prepared to fight your way through brush and cast from a muddy bank overgrown with dense bushes. You can still put the lure or bubble wherever you want it.

## Underwater Snags

Try as you might, the line will occasionally snag on a rock or branch under water. First make sure you haven't actually caught a large fish! The big ones sometimes move so slowly that you might mistake them for a rock. Watch the line carefully in the water as you hold it tight. If it moves at all, it's a fish! Otherwise, you've got a snag. Don't just snap a snagged line. Try loosening its tension and pulling again from all directions. Walk back and forth along the bank, hop around the rocks. You may get lucky and dislodge it. If the weather is warm and the water is not too cold, you can swim out to free it. Sometimes we cut the line and tie it somewhere on shore, and in the heat of the following day we'll screw up our nerve, jump in and retrieve the lure.

If you decide to sacrifice the lure or rigging, be careful not to break your rod in the process of snapping the line. Point the rod in the direction of the snagged lure. Wrap the line two or three times around your hand between the reel and the first eyelet on the rod. (If your skin cuts easily, wrap the line around your shirtsleeve near your wrist. The line, when taut, is knife-like.) Then start walking backward. The line will normally break near the lure, though sometimes the extra pressure will free the lure from the snag. Either way, when the line suddenly goes limp, reel it in. Never snap a line by raising the tip of the pole. That's a guaranteed way to break the pole instead.

# Playing and Landing a Trout: What's a Drag?

When a fish takes your hook, it reacts like any animal with something sharp and painful in its mouth—it runs away. It swims as rapidly and strongly as it can away from the danger it has encountered, toward a secure hiding place. At this point, it's up to the angler to "play" the fish, to let it run against a constant resistance, to tire it out.

If your line is taut, the fish can snap it with a few quick maneuvers. How can a fish which weighs only one pound snap a "four-pound test" line? Easy. The "four-pound" figure indicates only the amount of dead, motionless weight the line can lift vertically off the ground. Even a one-pound fish moving rapidly can exert more than four pounds of force on a taut line. If it does, the line will snap.

Spinning reels are equipped with a "drag" to prevent this. This drag adjustment allows the line to unwind when it is pulled hard by a fish; that is, it unwinds rather than snaps. You should check and adjust the drag each time you fish. Don't wait till the fish hits your lure or bait. You may not have time.

The drag is adjusted with the same screw mechanism that holds the spool in position on the reel. Most light, inexpensive backpacking reels are equipped with cheap drag fittings. The vibration of the reel winding and unwinding, the snapping of the bail, even the bouncing of your pack as you hike along the trail can disturb the drag mechanism, and you'll need to fiddle with it from time to time.

**Adjust the drag**
*with the same screw
that holds the spool on
the reel.*

First check the adjustment. Grab the line below the closed reel and pull. The line should go taut, and then the spool should begin to revolve, allowing the line to peel off. If you can pull hard enough to snap the line without it unwinding, the drag is too tight. If you feel no resistance, it's too loose. When it's adjusted right, a solid tug will unwind the line slowly against a constant resistance. Remember that a very small movement in the adjustment nut— one-eighth or one-quarter of a turn—will make all the difference in the drag. Make sure to check it each time you begin to fish.

If, when you set out to test the drag, the handle and bail revolve, permitting the line to come easily off the spool, the reel's one-way-only ratcheting mechanism is not engaged. It's controlled by a little lever or switch on the reel. It should always be engaged when you fish, so that the reel makes a soft clicking sound as you wind the line in.

## Landing Fish

If a fish gets away while you're trying to land it, it's usually because your heart is going faster than your head. Finally, after all that waiting and all that work, you've got a live, very angry animal on the end of a pathetically thin line, and there are too many things to do all at the same time. The rod is bobbing and weaving, your friends are cheering, whooping and being useless with a million suggestions, none of which you can hear for all the pounding inside your ears. It feels like you're waltzing with a tiger and he knows all the steps.

Okay. You're supposed to remain cool and collected. That's part of the challenge. Anyway, you want to land that thunderbolt. Adjust the drag as you begin to play the fish. Bring it closer to you. Make it work, pulling against the drag, taking the line slowly out again. Then increase the drag just a touch and reel it in again. The fish is now close enough to see. It's a big one! Dinner for four! Better repeat the process. Let it go out again; reel it in again. Is it still fighting mad? Do it again! Don't try to land a biggie until it's tired. Otherwise you're going to end up talking about dinner rather than eating it.

The big ones are the heart stoppers, but the small ones are fun and exhilarating, too. And most of the fish you'll catch in the mountains are going to be small—in the 8-inch to 10-inch bracket: great eating and easy to store. Bring the small fry close to shore, then lift it out of the water and away from the lake all in one fluid motion. If you decide to release the fish—it may be too small or you may only be fishing for sport—get the hook out of the fish's mouth as quickly and gently as possible. Then hold it lightly in your hand and place it under the surface of the water. If it has enough strength to survive, it will dart quickly out of your hand with a sudden, swift motion. If it's nearly dead, it will float motionless in your hand. Don't leave the fish floating there if it doesn't have the strength to swim away. It's as good as dead, and there's no sense polluting the lake with it. Keep it and eat it.

Be careful also about regulations on fish size. In some lakes and streams, there's a legal minimum limit on the size of fish you can keep; smaller fish must be returned to the water. Check in your regulation manual for this information.

The most efficient way to land a larger fish is with a net. This is absolutely imperative if, like us, you enjoy wading out into the lake up to your hips as you fish. Trying to grab a trout with bare hands is more difficult than catching the proverbial greased pig. Net your catch head first so that it will move into the net while trying to escape. Once it's in, lift the net clean out of the water. Then, with your other hand, grab the fish and webbing from the outside with a firm grip around the middle of the fish. Now remove the hook (while holding your rod out of the water, if necessary; it can be done) and release the fish or store it for later eating.

What if you don't have a net? You'll have to beach the fish. Keep in mind when you do this that fish fight harder as the water gets shallower. Play the fish till it's tired, then lead it up to a sandy stretch of shore. With a single, continuous motion, guide the fish onto the beach. Don't jerk the line or it may break. Just pull steadily and the trout will follow the line. The fish might try to twitch and jump when it feels the sand, but if it's tired and your motion is swift and smooth, it won't realize what is happening until it's too late.

What if you have no net and no shore? When fishing from a rocky bank, you'll have to use the "clean-and-jerk" method. If the fish is very tired and the water is shallow, you can use the same motion that you'd use to beach a fish to pull it up out of the water toward land. Once it's airborne and moving in your direction, it may arch its body rapidly, wriggle frantically, or in some other way unhook itself or snap the line. Hopefully it will have enough inertia at this point to continue on its shoreward flight and land on the rocky bank—flipping, flopping and unhooked, but far enough away from the water to prevent a last-minute leap from the frying pan to the watery deep.

You've landed your fish and, like Rick with his 16-inch golden trout, you need time to "come down." Savor the moment and the future bragging rights. Then put the gear in order (the line may be a mess), pack up the plastic bags, and head for the campsite with your catch and a gleam in your eye that spells baked trout and a loaf of bread hot out of the "oven" for supper.

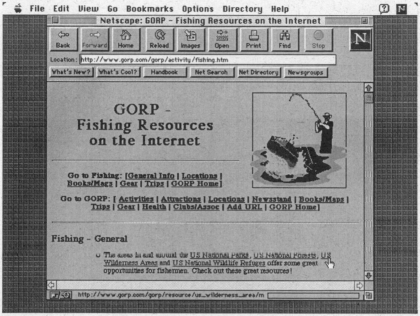

*Angling resources are plentiful on the Net.*

# Star Gazing

## Basic Sky

Being in the backcountry changes your nightlife dramatically. You're a million light years from Main Street, far beyond the reach of the entertainment section, even if you could read it in the failing light. Dinner has been cleaned up and the evening fishing is over; the wind dies down and the clouds disappear. A chill slides into the air. Time for parkas and wool hats, a fire, maybe a ghost story or the lament of a harmonica. You can try to read until the flashlight begins to flicker. You can follow Ben Franklin's "early-to-bed" advice. Or you can stroll down by the lake and watch the moon rise. It's never too late for another cup of hot chocolate and brandy. But in the end, eyes invariably drift upwards toward the Great White Way—the stars in the nighttime sky.

You start to look for the Big Dipper, maybe Scorpio or the Pleiades. Though this is where most non-stargazers' knowledge of the sky ends, we've found that almost everyone has a natural curiosity about the stars and their groupings. If you've packed in a star chart, you'll almost certainly reach for it and try to distinguish Cygnus, the giant swan, from Draco, the great dragon. If you don't have a chart, or have never studied the stars, this chapter will introduce you to one of the greatest pleasures of long summer nights, that of stargazing.

It's an exciting, challenging process to identify planets and constellations. It takes concentration and some patience. Like anything else, the more often you try, the easier and more familiar it gets. At first, however, you're lying on your back, staring into a giant half-dome but the star map is flat, distorting the sky in order to get it down on paper. Also, the sky moves as the earth rotates, so what you see at 7 p.m. will not be the same as what you see at 2 or 3 a.m. The stars also change with the seasons; June's sky is not the same as September's. Trees, clouds and mountains can block your view. A bright moon obscures many stars in its part of the sky. Nonetheless, with a little time and effort, you can slowly find planets, sort out constellations, even identify individual stars. And while you're at it, you're bound to see flashes of shooting stars, blinking satellites, high-flying aircraft and, depending how far north you are, maybe even a glimpse of the aurora borealis—the northern lights.

Star charts throw half the sky at you at once, far too many stars to see or sort out. In this chapter, we show you one small section of the sky at a time. We describe each with pictures, instructions and stories. But before you begin, it's good to know a little basic astronomy.

# Astronomy 101

Everything—the moon, Earth and planets, sun and stars—is moving in space. Astronomical distances are so great, however, that aside from shooting stars, nothing seems to move very fast or very much. Most of the "motion" you observe during the night (or day) is the result of Earth turning. If you picture a spinning ball inside a stationary, star-speckled globe, you'll begin to get the picture. But, from an observational viewpoint, it appears as if all the heavenly bodies do move across the sky. So for expedience's sake, we'll refer to the sun, moon and constellations as the moving entities.

Only the star that happens to sit above the North Pole appears not to move as Earth turns; all the rest do appear to move. During the daytime, the sun moves across the midsection of the sky from east to west. During the night, the moon follows a similar path. Trace the same arc that the sun and moon describe across the sky and look for very bright stars: the brightest ones are probably planets. The sun, moon and planets are close to being on the same plane, which paints a wide stripe inside our star-studded globe. They spin in circles, but they travel across the sky within that stripe.

Divide that stripe into 12 pieces and you have the 12 "houses" of the zodiac. Each house refers to a specific group of stars, or a constellation. Ancient astronomers used these 12 houses to keep track of the seasonal and relative positions of the sun, moon and planets, which appear to be stationed "in front" of any given house at any time of month or year. The naked eye may trick you into thinking that the sun, moon and planets are traveling in a high arc "overhead" while the zodiac is on the horizon, but they are all in that wide stripe running round the equator, just about in the same plane.

It takes the stars in a constellation many millions of years to move in relation to one another. To us, it appears as if they never change position (even though the constellation itself appears to move during the night, due to the spinning of Earth). The sun, moon and planets do move very slowly against the backdrop of the

**Typical star chart**

zodiac constellations. It takes the sun a year to travel slowly through the 12 houses of the zodiac, remaining in each zodiacal house for a month. The moon travels the same path in only a month, and is in each house for three or four days, though even this short passage of time across the constellations is too slow for our eyes to see. On any night, the moon seems locked into its zodiacal house. However fast it seems to rise and set, it never seems to leave "home." What's happening is that the whole night-time sky, with the moon in front of a zodiac constellation, is moving overhead during the night. Saying that the moon is in Virgo means the moon is in that section of the sky occupied by the constellation Virgo. If the sun is in Scorpio, then Scorpio is behind the sun during the day. During an eclipse of the sun, the stars of Scorpio would be visible in that section of the sky.

Of course, you don't *need* to know any of this to enjoy the night sky. If you couldn't care less that the Mars Bar overhead is really the Milky Way, then make up your own constellations.

**North Pole**

Rewrite the sky! (See pages 377-378 for proof that it can be done.) If, on the other hand, you'd like to get a handle on the "classic" sky, the rest of this chapter shows you how. We'll tell you where the constellations are, what they look like, and how to find them.

Go slow at first. The constellations won't go away. If you find one star group a night, you'll be doing well, and the odds are strong that you'll never forget where it is. Tomorrow night it may be in a slightly different place, but not by much. With a little practice, you'll spot it in September as easily as in July, at 11 o'clock as well as at 9 o'clock.

We start you off with the major constellations—the easy, circumpolar ones, which revolve in a tight ring around the North Star. Then we proceed to describe the smaller, more distant, and more difficult or obscure ones.

We use several arbitrary devices to clarify directions and relationships between and among the constellations. First, compass directions (east, southwest, etc.) refer to the earthly horizon. Thus if you're lying on your back looking at the North Star and we send you southwest toward a constellation, trace the direction as you would on a compass: toward southwest on the ground. This may sound obvious, but it isn't when you realize that *all* stars are located literally south of the North Star. Secondly, we assume in our directions that you're facing the sky, holding your star map above you—looking *up* at it—and that it's oriented correctly toward the earthly horizon. Thirdly, we show you the sky at a theoretical 9 p.m. To figure out where things are earlier, turn your

**Zodiac**

star map clockwise; later, turn it counterclockwise. A good star map or chart will allow you to adjust for the month. Our theoretical June should not upset your own calculations, whatever the time of year.

## Ursa Major (Big Dipper), Ursa Minor (Little Dipper), Draco (Dragon)

Almost everyone can locate the Big Dipper: seven bright stars, visible even in the city, a clear constellation in winter as well as in summer. Draw a line through the two stars on the end of the Big Dipper's bowl, then follow that line three times its length to reach Polaris, the North Star. During the night, all the other stars in the sky will seem to move, while the North Star will remain in place. You can check that you have the right star with your compass, as long as you realize that magnetic north, toward which your compass needle points, is not quite the same as true north, where Polaris sits.

The Big Dipper is actually the hind quarters and tail of Ursa Major, the Big Bear. If you look closely, you can find the bear's paws and outline, but it's not easy. Housatonic Indians saw the four bowl stars as a bear and the three handle stars as a hunter with two dogs in pursuit. The middle handle star is really a double star; the hunter carried a pot in which to cook the bear. The hunter chased the bear from spring until autumn, and when the animal was wounded in the fall, its blood was visible in the leaves of the forest.

For centuries, the Big Dipper has guided people to the North Star which, seemingly "fixed" in the sky, has in turn guided mariners and land navigators in their travels. The North Star acts as the tip of the handle of the seven-star Little Dipper, also known as Ursa Minor. The Persians saw the Little Dipper as a date palm. It was a jackal in Egypt.

Ancient Norsemen called it the "Hill of Heaven," abode of the guardian of the rainbow bridge connecting heaven and earth. It really doesn't look much like a small bear.

Beginning between the North Star and the two "pointer" stars of the Big Dipper is a long winding string of stars that goes southeast around the Little Dipper, then back northwest, encircling the Little Dipper on three sides. Then it goes southwest again, ending in a rectangle of four stars. This is the constellation Draco, the Dragon. The Hindus saw it as an alligator and the Egyptians a crocodile. To the Greeks, it was the monster serpent killed by Hercules. Its teeth were sown on the earth to become a crop of armed men.

## Cassiopeia, Cepheus

From the double star in the Big Dipper's handle, draw a line through Polaris. There, bend the line slightly to the right and keep going the same distance as from the pointers. You'll be in the middle of a five-star W-shaped constellation, Cassiopeia. Cassiopeia was the Queen of Ethiopia until she offended the sea nymphs, who bound her to this seat in the sky. The same five stars looked to the early Arabs like a giant hand, each one marking a fingertip.

Between Cassiopeia and Draco's head (the four-star rectangle), you'll find the five-star constellation Cepheus. It's not as bright as Cassiopeia or the Big Dipper. The Greeks saw it as the "sky father," King of Ethiopia and husband of Cassiopeia. It looks somewhat like a large, A-frame tent, pointing toward Polaris.

## Lyra (Lyre), Cygnus (Swan) Hercules

A line from Polaris through the brightest star in the head of Draco points to Vega. Vega is one of the brightest stars in the sky, only 26 light years away, and part of the five-star constellation Lyra, the lyre or harp. It's said that this harp was invented by Hermes and given to his half-brother Apollo. The Arabs thought of the same constellation as a swooping Stone Eagle of the Desert, with half-closed wings tucked at its sides as it dove for a kill.

A line from Polaris through the brightest star of Cepheus (skirting the back of Cepheus' throne) goes to the star Deneb, the head of the giant swan Cygnus. Cygnus is a large cross in the sky, four bright stars long and three wide. It was known in Arabia as a giant bird called a "Roc" made famous by its conflicts with Sinbad the Sailor. Find the Milky Way stretching across the sky and you'll find Cygnus in full flight along it.

Finally, a line from Polaris skirting west of Draco's head takes you to Hercules. A four-star rectangle forms his body, with different numbers of stars for his arms, legs and weapons. The rectangle is the key to finding Hercules, but none of its stars are exceptionally bright. It's sometimes hard to find. It's usually nearly straight overhead on summer evenings. Moving from east to west, Cygnus, Lyra and Hercules are all about the same distance from the North Star.

## Bootes (Herdsman), Corona Borealis (Northern Crown)

Follow the curve of the Big Dipper's handle away from the bowl. It leads to another very bright star, Arcturus. Stretching toward the North Star from Arcturus, in the shape of a kite or ice cream cone, is the constellation Bootes, the Herdsman. The kite shape is the body; the two legs meet at Arcturus. The Arabs called him the "Shepherd," with the idea that the stars around the North Pole resembled a flock of sheep, and he was always going in circles to herd them. He has also been seen as a hunter in pursuit of Ursa Major, the Great Bear.

Between Bootes and Hercules, about the same distance from Polaris, is a seven-star half-circle. This is Corona Borealis, or Northern Crown. (A similar constellation lies in the southern sky near the South Pole.) To the Shawnee Indians, these seven stars were the "Celestial Sisters," the fairest (brightest) of them the wife of the hunter White Hawk, Arcturus.

## Aquila (Eagle), Delphinus (Dolphin), Ophiuchus (Serpent Holder), Serpens (Serpent)

A line from Polaris through the tail of Cygnus the Swan takes you to Altair, the bright head of the eagle Aquila. Altair is only 16

light years away, bright enough to be seen even through city smog.
Aquila the Eagle, cruciform in shape, is about the same size as
Cygnus, and it's easy to imagine Aquila chasing Cygnus along the
Milky Way, always a little behind and to the east of its prey.

The Koreans saw Altair and its two bright neighbors not as
the head and shoulders of an eagle, but as a prince and his ser-
vants, banished across the Milky Way by an irate father-in-law.
The Prince's bride is our Lyra. Only once a year, on the seventh
day of the seventh moon, could the two lovers meet by crossing a
bridge of magpies over the Milky Way.

Just northeast of the eagle is Delphinus, the five-star dolphin.
It's a small constellation on the edge of the Milky Way, on a direct
line from Polaris through Deneb, the head of Cygnus.

A large area of the sky south of Hercules is taken up by a
vague constellation, Ophiuchus and his two serpents, Serpens
Caput and Serpens Cauda. The head of Serpens Caput is a bright
triangle just south of the Corona Borealis (Northern Crown). The
rest of the serpent stretches south, then east towards the Milky
Way. The key to this constellation is figuring out what it is not.
Once you find Hercules and Corona Borealis to the north and
Scorpio to the south, you can find Ophiuchus with his two serpents in between.

In classical legend, Ophiuchus was the ship's surgeon for
Jason and the Argonauts. He became so skilled that he could
restore the dead to life. This caused Pluto to fear for his kingdom
of the dead, and Ophiuchus was struck with a thunderbolt by Jove
and placed among the constellations.

## *Virgo (Virgin), Leo (Lion)*

Remember the pointer stars of the Big Dipper? If you point
in the opposite direction from Polaris, past the bottom of the
dipper, you come to the bright star Regulus, at the head of Leo.
The lion's mane looks like a backward question mark running east
and then north from Regulus, and a triangle of stars to the southeast represents the lion's back legs and tail. The Greeks called it
the "Nemean Lion," placed in the heavens at the same time as
Hercules, the lion's slayer.

Virgo is a dim constellation, difficult to find. Start with the
Big Dipper's handle and follow it through Arcturus at the base of

Bootes. The next bright star on that arc is Spica in the constellation Virgo. The constellation itself is shaped like a distorted Y, with Spica representing an ear of wheat in the maiden's left hand.

### Pegasus (Horse), Andromeda

A line from Polaris passing just east of Cassiopeia goes to a large bright square of stars. The star in the northwest corner of the square is part of a small bright triangle. This is Pegasus, the horse. The square represents the horse's body; the triangle is the horse's rear legs. Pegasus is always near the horizon, "upside down" with its head away from Polaris. In classical mythology, Pegasus sprang from the blood of Medusa after she was slain by Perseus. Later, Bellerophon attempted to ride Pegasus to heaven, but Jupiter, incensed by such boldness, caused an insect to sting the horse. Pegasus threw his rider and then rose alone to his permanent place among the stars.

The bright triangle of stars at one corner of Pegasus is also the end of the constellation Andromeda, the Woman Chained. Alpheratz, the brightest star in the "Great Square" of Pegasus, is the last star in Andromeda. It's the meeting point for two lines of stars (four stars in each line) that represent Andromeda, the daughter of Cepheus and

Cassiopeia, chained in exposure to the sea monsters as punishment for Cassiopeia's boasts of her own beauty.

## Sagittarius (Archer), Scorpio (Scorpion), Libra (Scales)

These three zodiac constellations are usually close to the southern horizon. Sometimes you can't see them at all; sometimes you see only their northernmost stars. Remember that if Polaris is the head, the zodiac ring of constellations is a giant belt around the waist of the sky. As Earth tilts during seasonal changes and Polaris moves closer to the northern horizon, this ring moves up from the southern horizon. During the winter months, with Polaris higher in the sky, these constellations move below the horizon and cannot be seen.

Scorpio is the most spectacular. A line from Polaris through the Corona Borealis and on through the serpent's head on Ophiuchus passes through three very bright stars near the southern horizon. These are the head and the two claws of the scorpion. The rest of the scorpion's body winds south, through Antares, a bright star, and continues to a curlicue tail. Legend has it that this scorpion killed the hunter Orion. They were placed in the sky so that Orion, still fearful, sinks below the northern horizon as Scorpio rises in the south. Antares, the heart of the scorpion, was known to the Chinese as the "Fire Star."

Sagittarius follows Scorpio across the sky. Four stars represent a bow and arrow; another five are the archer's body. The arrow points towards Scorpio. Ancient Arabs saw this constellation as two sets of ostriches, passing to and from the celestial river of the Milky Way.

The four stars of Libra lie between Scorpio and Virgo, in a roughly rectangular shape. The Greeks considered these stars the claws of Scorpio. Later they became known as a separate constellation.

## Perseus (Winged Warrior), Auriga (Charioteer)

Follow the Milky Way from Cygnus through Cassiopeia. The next constellation is Perseus, a warrior wearing winged sandals. He is holding the head of Medusa in his hand, which he later used to rescue Andromeda from the sea monsters. Perses, the son of Perseus and Andromeda, gave Persia its name. Algol, a bright star in Perseus, was called the "Demon's Head" by the Arabians.

Continuing along the Milky Way, from Cassiopeia through Perseus, you'll come to Auriga. It contains seven stars in a rough circle, including Capella, called the "Goat Star" in ancient Greece and the "Shepherd's Star" in Peru.

## Taurus (Bull), Gemini (Twins), Cancer (Crab)

Follow the last three stars in Perseus away from Polaris and you see seven twinkling stars in a very small cluster. These are the Seven Sisters, the Pleiades (pronounced "Plee-a-dees"). They are also the shoulder of the bull, Taurus. The head of the bull is a bright star, Aldebaran, in the midst of another cluster, and the bull's horns extend into the Milky Way, nearly to Auriga.

Pleiades were seen by Australian aborigines as young girls playing music for dancing young men (Orion's belt). The Finns called this cluster a "little sieve." The second cluster next to Aldebaran, the bull's head, is called Hyades (pronounced "Hie-a-dees"). These were seen by the Greeks as half-sisters to the Pleiades. The whole of Taurus was seen as a bull with huge horns by ancient South American tribes, and as the jaw of an ox by natives in the Amazon region.

Gemini is a big rectangle. Two stars are inside the Milky Way, just beyond Auriga. The other end of the constellation consists of two bright stars, Castor and Pollux, the twins' heads. To the Phoenicians, the constellation represented two gazelles, to the Arabians, two peacocks. In India, it was seen as two horsemen.

Cancer is the most inconspicuous of the zodiac constellations. Its stars are so dim that it is impossible to see them close to a bright horizon. Cancer lies between Gemini and Leo and is roughly in the shape of an upside-down Y with its tail pointing toward the North Star. Greek myths say it is the crab that was crushed by Hercules in his contest with the Hydra, then raised to the sky by Juno. The Egyptians saw it as a scarab, the Chinese as a quail's head.

## *Triangulum, Aries (Ram), Pisces (Fish), Cetus (Whale)*

A line from Polaris through the easternmost star in Cassiopeia takes you through the end of Andromeda's chain, then through a small three-star constellation, Triangulum, to one of the two bright stars in Aries, the ram. This ram was sacrificed after helping Phrixus escape the wrath of his stepmother, Ino. Its fleece was placed in the Grove of Ares (Mars), where it turned to gold and became the object of the Argonauts' quest.

Pisces, the fishes, is a huge V-shaped constellation stretching from one leg near Andromeda to a point south of Aries, then back along another long leg toward Aquarius. Most of the stars in Pisces are dim. Star finders are vague about its shape since it is usually "falling off" the edge of the map and badly distorted. It rarely comes above the horizon and what parts of it that do are usually obscured by mountains or trees since it is always so low in the sky. If you can see a fairly straight line of stars south of Pegasus, you've found half of Pisces.

Cetus, as large as Pisces and lower in the sky, is also rarely seen in the northern hemisphere. This is another huge, rambling constellation. The four stars in Cetus' head are just south of Aries. It represents a whale or sea monster, fabled to be the monster sent to devour chained Andromeda, but turned to stone at the sight of Medusa's head held in the hand of Perseus.

## Aquarius (Waterbearer), Equuleus (Colt), Capricorn (Goat)

Follow the triangle of Pegasus (his head) to the south, and you come to Aquarius. The sun tends to be in Aquarius during the rainy season, hence the relationship with water. In Babylon, the constellation was an overflowing water jar, in ancient Arabia a well-bucket, and in Rome a peacock.

Capricorn, between Aquarius and Sagittarius, is generally depicted with the head and body of a goat ending in a fish's tail. It is another one that is tough to make out in the sky. The ancient Hindus saw it as an antelope. The Chinese considered it a bull.

Equuleus, the colt, is between Delphinus (Dolphin) and Pegasus on the north and Aquarius on the south. It is a small constellation (five stars), representing the brother of Pegasus.

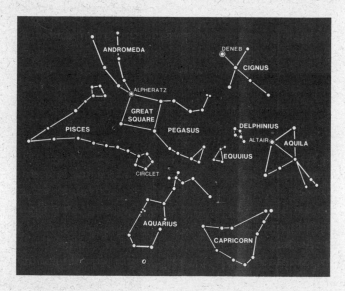

## Orion (Hunter), Canis Major (Greater Dog)

South of Taurus lies Orion, the hunter. It has three bright stars for a belt, and two more representing a sword. The tip of the sword is the star Rigel; Orion's head is the star Betelgeuse. Both are very bright. Orion can be seen from most of Earth, north and south, at one time of the year or other. Mythology holds that he was inflicted with a scorpion sting because of his boastfulness. Then he was placed in the sky in such a way that he could escape whenever his slayer, Scorpio, rose in the east.

Canis Major is a southern-sky constellation, just southeast of Orion. Sirius, its brightest star, lies just on the edge of the Milky Way. From the earliest times, it has been the dog of Orion, shown sitting up and watching his master. The Hindus knew it as the "Deer Slayer," who shot an arrow, which is our belt of Orion. The rest of Orion represented to them a prince, stopped by the arrow from pursuing his daughter, Aldebaran (the bright star in the head of Taurus).

## The Great Horned Wyoming Jackalope and Other Do-It-Yourselfers

If you stand on your head, squeeze your eyes real tight, count to ten and don't pass out or fall asleep, you'll awaken to see the Great Horned Wyoming Jackalope. It's seen especially clearly when reflected in high Rocky Mountain lakes. If you happen to be in Northern California, you might see the Giant Hot Tub, with its pointer stars directing you to a local Zen master. And of course, twinkling through the smog of Southern California comes the Spiraling Red Camaro, complete with sooty black exhaust.

We've picked out everything from grapefruits to beer bottles in the sky, depending on our moods. Rather than getting all strung out making exact identifications, or getting frustrated by not seeing the shapes that the constellations are supposed to be, the important thing is to have fun with the process of discovering the stars. When asked what he liked most about backpacking, a five-year-old friend of ours replied, "I get to eat a lot of cookies and I can stay up as late as I want." On those nights that *you* stay up late, the stars can be enjoyable and agreeable companions, along with a slow-burning fire and some brandy and hot chocolate.

If you really do get turned on by all of this and want more information, see the suggested readings in the Book List on page 386. Or check out the Internet (see below).

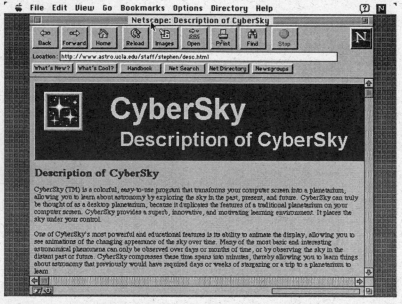

*You can find help with your stargazing on the Net.*

# Epilogue

---

## Looking Ahead

Wilderness camping, like anything else that is complicated and beautiful, is never quite finished. There is always more to learn, about yourself and the wilderness, about technique and enjoyment. There is rarely one way to do things, which means that both common sense and uncommon sensibilities need to be brought to bear on problems and projects. If you accept that as a reasonable proposition, you'll remain open to the ideas, suggestions and experiences of others. And you'll tinker, fiddle and improvise until you've got a camping trip down to where you want it, rather than the way friends, salesmen, old-timers or experts say it should be done. It's at such a point that our book will have served its purpose.

The wilderness is growing smaller. If you want to get a feel for the majesty of the backcountry, you'll have to act fast and with knowledge. The better prepared you are to deal with impassive nature—its demands and your perception of them—the faster you'll be able to get farther into the wilderness. And if your aim in part is to leave the masses behind, if only for a day or two, being able to negotiate the backcountry is a useful skill to have.

Solitude is perhaps our most rapidly dwindling personal resource. Its natural habitat is in the mountains and on the lakes and rivers. In a real sense, then, *we* are the endangered species. If our capacity to be awed by nature is blunted, if we lose the ability to be modest—to be participants in the wilderness rather than masters of it—we diminish ourselves. Wilderness campers are no more high-minded than anyone else, but the very nature of their work—or rather, their play—requires that they stay attuned to the possibilities inherent in the relationship between an individual and the world beyond roads.

If you are high up on a sun-soaked peak one day, enjoying the view and reflecting that the hard, off-trail hike ended at the second most beautiful campsite in the world, that the bubble-and-fly bagged a panful of trout, that the bread rose, the soufflé scored a hit, and the chocolate cake was the best you ever tasted, write a note about it and stick it in the message cairn. Whoever comes along and reads it will treasure your mood and want to make it their own. And who knows? Maybe even we'll come across it sometime down the line. And then we'll know for sure that our book has accomplished its goal.

# Book List

This list is selective and is meant to be used in conjunction with the resources listed in Chapter 2. Dates represent the latest imprints available.

## Camping and Backpacking Books

*A select selection of "how-to" books:*

Dunn, John J., *Winterwise, A Backpacker's Guide*. ADK Mountain Club, 1989. A good all-around book on winter backpacking.

Fletcher, Colin, *The Complete Walker III*. Alfred Knopf, 1994.

Hart, John, *Walking Softly in the Wilderness*. Sierra Club, 1993.

Hampton, Bruce, and David Cole, *Soft Paths: How to Enjoy the Wilderness Without Harming It*. National Outdoor Leadership School, 1988.

Hodgson, Michael, *Wilderness with Children*. Stackpole Books, 1992.

Jeffrey, Nan, *Adventuring with Children*. Foghorn Press, 1992.

Manning, Harvey, *Backpacking One Step at a Time*. Vintage, 1986.

Prater, Gene, *Snowshoeing*, 3rd edition. The Mountaineers, 1988. The bible on the subject.

Silverman, Goldie, *Backpacking with Babies and Small Children*. Wilderness Press, 1991.

Winnett, Thomas, and Melanie Findling, *Backpacking Basics*. Wilderness Press, 1994.

## Guides to Trails, Mountains and Campgrounds

*"Where-to-Go" and "How-to-Get-There" guides:*

*High Sierra Hiking Guides* by Wilderness Press, 2440 Bancroft Way, Berkeley, California 94704.
A series of nine expert little guides, each based on one of the quadrangles established by the U.S. Geological Survey. Small and

light enough to carry with you. The same press publishes guides to other wilderness areas, high-mountain trails, and desert hiking in the western United States. Camping stores will have similar guides to other regions.

*Camping Guides* by Foghorn Press, 555 DeHaro Street, Suite 220, San Francisco, CA 94107.

A series of big books: *California Camping, Rocky Mountain Camping* and *Pacific Northwest Camping,* all written by outdoorsman Tom Stienstra. Also *Southwest Camping* and *Baja Camping.* Camping stores will have similar guides to other states and regions.

*Sierra Club Guides to Natural Areas*
A set of trustworthy regional guides, one each for California; Colorado and Utah; Idaho, Montana, Wyoming; New Mexico, Arizona, Nevada; Oregon and Washington; Florida; New England.

*Falcon Hikers' Guides* by Falcon Press, Helena, Montana. 32 separate guides to particular areas in the U.S.

*Sierra Club Mountaineers' Guides,* Sierra Club Books, distributed by Random House.
A series of 21 *Tote Books,* pocket-size climbing guides to virtually all the major mountain ranges in the United States.

*Trails Illustrated.* Makers of full-color, large-scale topographical maps. Check their catalog for what's available: P.O. Box 3610, Evergreen, Colorado 80439-3425.

## Nature Guides

*The following series provide all you'll ever need to know about bugs, berries, birds and everything else living in the outdoors:*

*Audobon Field Guides.* (Alfred Knopf) Separately published guides to trees, wildflowers, birds, butterflies, fishes, whales and dolphins, insects, reptiles, the night sky, weather, etc.

*Audubon Nature Guides.* (Alfred Knopf) Individual guides to deserts, wetlands, grasslands, Eastern forests, Western forests, etc.

*Nature Study Guild.* Box 972, Berkeley, CA 94701. Regionally configured "finder" guides: ferns, berries, flowers, trees, intertidal life, etc. Nine guides for Eastern North America; nine for the Pacific Coast states; four for the Rocky Mountains and desert states.

*Peterson's Field Guides.* (Houghton Mifflin) 44 titles covering almost everything of interest to the naturalist, by one of the world's preeminent naturalists, Roger Tory Peterson.

*Sierra Club Naturalists' Guides.* (The Sierra Club) Regional guides to the Pacific Northwest, deserts of the Southwest, Southern Rockies, North Atlantic Coast, Middle Atlantic Coast, North Woods of Michigan, Minnesota, South Ontario, the Piedmont of Eastern North America, New England, the Sierra Nevada, and others.

## Reading Maps and Compasses

Kals, W. S., *Land Navigation Handbook: The Sierra Club Guide to Map and Compass.* Sierra Club Books, 1983.

Kjellstrom, Bjorn, *Be Expert with Map & Compass.* Collier Books, 1994. Kjellstrom is the godfather of orienteering.

Randall, Glenn, *The Outward Bound Map and Compass Handbook.* Lyons & Burford, 1989.

## Campsite Cooking

*Pale imitations of what you have just read, but honorable:*

Elias, Thomas S. & Peter A. Dykeman, *Edible Wild Plants, a North American Field Guide.* Sterling Publishing Co., 1990. This is a reprint of a classic.

Fleming, June, *The Well-Fed Backpacker.* Vintage Books, 1986.

Latimer, Carole, *Wilderness Cuisine.* Wilderness Press, 1992.

McHugh, Gretchen, *Hungry Hikers Book of Good Cooking.* Alfred Knopf, 1992.

MacManiman, Gen, *Dry It, You'll Like It.* MacManiman, Inc., 1992.

Miller, Dorcas S., *Good Food for Camp & Trail.* Pruett Publishing, 1993. This is an "all-natural recipes" book.

Yaffe, Linda, *High Trail Cookery.* Chicago Review Press, 1989.

## Outdoor Medicine

*Words of wisdom from the body shop:*

Auerbach, Paul S., M.D., *Medicine for the Outdoors, a Guide to Emergency Medical Procedures and First Aid.* 2nd ed., Little Brown, 1991. A comprehensive (412-page) guide from the author of the definitive medical textbook on the subject.

Bezruchka, Stephen, M.D., *The Pocket Doctor.* 2nd ed., The Mountaineers, 1992. A brief (95-page), handy guide.

Forgey, William, M.D., *Wilderness Medicine.* ICS Books, 1994.

Schimelpfenig, Tod and Linda Lindsey, *NOLS* (National Outdoor Leadership School) *Wilderness First Aid.* NOLS and Stackpole Books, 1992.

Weiss, Eric A., M.D., *A Comprehensive Guide to Wilderness and Travel Medicine.* Adventure Medical Kits, 1992. A trustworthy little guide (106 pages) by the maker of customized medical kits for outdoor activities.

Wilkerson, James, M.D., *Medicine for Mountaineering and Other Wilderness Activities.* 4th ed., The Mountaineers, 1992.

## Canoeing

*Essentials of the craft:*

American National Red Cross, *Canoeing.* Doubleday & Co., 1977.

Davidson, James West, and John Rugge, *The Complete Wilderness Paddler.* Vantage Books, 1983. Comprehensive information on everything from reading water to paddling strokes for all conditions, planning and outfitting a trip, map reading, portages, etc.

Harrison, David and Judy, *Canoe Tripping with Children.* ICS Books, 1990.

Jacobson, Cliff, *Basic Essentials of Canoeing.* ICS Books, 1988.

Landry, Paul, and Matty McNair, *The Outward Bound Canoeing Book.* Lyons and Burford, 1992.

Shears, Nick, *Paddle America, a Guide to Trips and Outfitters in All 50 States.* Starfish Press, 1992. For canoes, rafts and other craft.

## Bicycling

*Touring and cycle repair information:*

Ballantine, Richard, and Richard Gant, *Richard's Ultimate Bicycle Book.* Dorling Kindersley, 1992. This is a big, hardback book, lavishly illustrated.

*Bicycling Magazine's Complete Guide to Bicycle Maintenance and Repair.* Revised and Updated. Rodale Press, 1992.

Coello, Dennis, *Touring on Two Wheels: The Bicycle Traveler's Handbook.* Lyons and Burford, 1988.

Cuthbertson, Tom, *Anybody's Bike Book.* Ten Speed Press, Berkeley, CA, 1992.

Forester, John, *Effective Cycling.* MIT Press, 1993.

Leccese, Michael and Arlene Plevin, *The Bicyclist's Sourcebook, The Ultimate Directory of Cycling Information.* Woodbine House, Inc., 1991.

LeMond, Greg, *Greg LeMond's Complete Book of Bicycling.* Berkeley Publishers, 1990.

Nealy, William, *Mountain Bike: A Manual of Beginning to Advanced Technique.* Menasha Ridge Press, 1992.

Sloane, Eugene A., *Eugene A. Sloan's Book of All-Terrain Bicycles.* Simon & Schuster, 1985.

Van der Plas, R., *The Bicycle Touring Manual.* 3rd expanded edition. Bicycle Books, 1993.

Weaver, Susan, *A Woman's Guide to Cycling.* Ten Speed Press, 1991.

The following are all written by the editors of *Bicycling Magazine* and published by Rodale Press, 33 East Minor Street, Emmaus, PA 18098. They are all short, small books (128 pages seem to be the standard), and sometimes hard to find. Try their distributor, St. Martin's Press, 175 Fifth Avenue, New York, NY 10010 for help. All the titles begin, *Bicycling Magazine's...*

*Basic Maintenance and Repair*
*Bike Touring in the '90s*
*Long Distance Cycling*
*Mountain Biking Skills*
*New Bike Owner's Guide*
*Nutrition for Cyclists*
*600 Tips for Better Bicycling*
*Training for Fitness and Endurance*
*The Complete Guide to Upgrading Your Bike*
*Cycling for Women*

## Fishing

*A guide and a catalog to charm you:*

Anderson, Sheridan, *The Curtis Creek Manifesto.* Frank Amato Publications, Portland, OR, 1988. A boffo and endearing illustrated introduction to the art and joy of fly fishing.

Frank Amato Publications' annual book catalog is one of the most comprehensive lists of books on trout fishing in the world. A book for every kind of trout and every kind of angler. The bias is toward fly fishing, but there are books as well on spinners, spoons and reels, and guides to practically everywhere there's a trout in the Western world. For beginners, pretenders, experts. Address: P. O. Box 82112, Portland, Oregon 97282.

## Children's Car Activities

*Nonelectronic travel games, word games, puzzles:*

*Are We There Yet?* Rand McNally Travel Games, Puzzles and Quizzes, 1991.

Howe, James, *Bunnicula Fun Book.* Morrow Junior Books, 1993. Lots of puzzles, riddles, mazes, mysteries, and for reasons we don't understand, rabbits.

Price, Roger and Leonard Stern, *Mad Libs.* Price Stern Sloan, L.A. This is a series of packaged word games. The individual titles are *The Original #1 Monster, Off-the-Wall,* and *Dinosaur.*

## Stars

*Reliable introductions to astronomy:*

Baker, David, *The Henry Holt Guide to Astronomy.* Henry Holt Co., 1990.

Dickinson, Terrence, *Exploring the Night Sky.* 1991. Winner of the Children's Science Book Award.

Moore, Patrick, *The Pocket Guide to Astronomy.* Simon & Schuster, 1983.

*Peterson First Guide to Astronomy.* Houghton Mifflin, 1988.

*The Miller Planisphere.* Datalizer Slide Charts, Inc., 501 West Gate Street, Addison, Illinois 60101-4524. Ph. 800-837-9675. Indispensable rotating disc showing principal stars visible for every hour in the year at 42 degrees N. Latitude. A compact star map. Comes in two sizes, the smaller of which fits easily into a backpack pouch.

*The Night Sky.* David Chandler, P. O. Box 309, La Verne, CA 91750. 1992. A similar two-sided planisphere, 30-40 degrees N. Latitude. Comes in two sizes, the smaller of which also fits easily into a backpack pouch.

# Index

## S

# About the Authors

*Hal and Bandit*

*Rick and Bandit*

Hal Kahn and Rick Greenspan admit between them to over half a century's experience backpacking and camping. City boys, they took early to the country and its illimitable charms, and for many years have walked, wheeled, paddled, and feasted in the wilderness and campgrounds of the western United States. When they're not out "there," Rick cycles to the College of Alameda where he teaches auto mechanics, and Hal is at Stanford University where he teaches Chinese history. Rick doesn't know a dynasty from a doughnut, but that's all right because Hal couldn't tell a carburetor from a condominium. The only thing they have in common is their love for the outdoors.

Their first book, *Backpacking, A Hedonist's Guide*, was inspired by the fun they've had putting the pleasure principle to work in the wilderness. Their next book, the first edition of *The Camper's Companion*, took off from there, renewing and expanding on that pleasure. And now this new edition, festooned with baubles and bells, pushes the concept to the edge. If you have ideas and suggestions for them, or if you just want to communicate about camping and its delights, write to them at their publisher: Foghorn Press, 555 DeHaro Street, Suite 220, San Francisco, CA 94107. Or phone: (415) 241-9550/1-800-FOGHORN. Fax: (415) 241-9648.

You can also E-mail them at the following addresses:
Rick Greenspan at 71534.3340@compuserve.com
Hal Kahn at wuwei@leland.stanford.edu

# TABLE OF CONTENTS
# Clip-Out Lists and Recipes

As promised, *The Camper's Companion* clip-out and take-it-with-you section. The best wilderness books have pages missing. Somebody has spotted a hint too good to pass up, lifted the information and stowed it in the pack along with the maps and cookies. That's how to treat this book. You'll find each of the packing lists duplicated here, the makings of your very own master list. We've also rerun most of the recipes, which can be used and then incorporated into your campfire. Tear away. If you want to dismantle the fishing or stargazing sections as well, feel free, it's *your* book.

## List of Lists:

❏ The Before-Leaving-Home-Did-I-Turn-Off-the-Gas Check List

❏ Bicycle Touring/Mountain Bike List

❏ Canoeing List

❏ Group Accessories, Individual Needs, Optionals

❏ Backpacking List: Equipment

❏ Backpacking List: Clothing, Boots

❏ First Aid and Medicines

❏ Repair Kit

❏ Maps and Permits

❏ Traveling with a Dog

❏ Kiddy List: For Babies and the Very Young

❏ Fun and Games

❏ Fishing List

❏ Food Planning for Two Six-Day Trips

❏ Food Shopping List

❏ Your Master List

*Select from the lists only those appropriate for your trip.*
*Eliminate duplications.*
*Add individualized items.*
*Combine into handy packet. You may want to seal your lists in plastic or some other protective covering so they last longer.*

# The Before-Leaving-Home-Did-I-Turn-Off-the-Gas Checklist

❑ Leave a schedule/map/ itinerary with someone to call out the Mounties if you don't return on time. Include name and phone number of nearest ranger station.

❑ Get neighbor to watch the house and take in newspapers, take out garbage, feed the pets.

❑ Leave written instructions on plant care.

❑ Leave adequate pet food, and name and phone number of the vet. Alternatively, take pets to the boarding kennel.

❑

❑

❑ Camping equipment:
  ❑ Lubricate all zippers—on tents, sleeping bags, packs— with silicone lube or a light oil (WD-40).
  ❑ Waterproof boots. Use only recommended agent for your particular footwear.
  ❑ Repair/replace damaged or missing parts. *(A leaking inflatable raft can ruin a fishing trip. So can a missing tent pole.)*
  ❑
  ❑

❑ Check car:
  ❑ Tires, belts, hoses and battery cables
  ❑ Wiper blades. Fill windshield washer reservoir with a mixture of Windex & water.

❑ Vital fluids: gas, oil, automatic transmission fluid, brake fluid, coolant

❑ Tire-changing equipment: jack, lug wrench, spare tire

❑ Roof rack: All parts present?

❑

❑

❑ In car:
  ❑ License and car registration
  ❑ Credit cards and cash on board
  ❑ Fire/wilderness permits, fishing licenses
  ❑ Road maps and directions to trailhead or campground
  ❑ Ranger station address and telephone number
  ❑ Sunglasses
  ❑ Accessible rain gear
  ❑ Cooler/ice chest with perishable foods
  ❑ Car meals and snacks
  ❑ Drinking water
  ❑ Dog food and water bowl
  ❑ Litter bag
  ❑ Games, toys, stuffed animals, books, distractions
  ❑ Personal needs: music/story tapes, Walkman, pencil, paper
  ❑ Clean clothes for return drive home
  ❑

❑ Did I leave the gas on, the toilet running?

# Bicycle Touring/Mountain Bike List

- ❑ Bicycle in top running order
- ❑ Cycling shorts
- ❑ Helmet *(with built-in visor for intense sun)*
- ❑ Cycling shoes
- ❑ Shoe covers
- ❑ Cycling gloves
- ❑ Rain gear
- ❑ Sunglasses *(shield type)*
- ❑ Safety glasses *(for mountain biking)*
- ❑ Shoulder strap *(for carrying a mountain bike up or over rough terrain)*
- ❑ Rear-view mirror
- ❑ Horn/bell
- ❑ Panniers
- ❑ Pannier rain covers *(or plastic garbage bags in which all gear is stowed)*
- ❑ Lock
- ❑ Headlamp plus extra batteries
- ❑ Fold-up reflective triangle
- ❑ Water bottle(s)
- ❑ Litter bag
- ❑ Talcum powder *(for saddle sores and flat tires)*
- ❑ Optional: *(for high-tech cycling)*
  - ❑ Small radio *(for weather reports)*
  - ❑ Cyclometer *(indicates speed, distance traveled, etc.)*
  - ❑ Two-way radio that fits in helmet *(lets you chat with a partner while biking)*
- ❑
- ❑
- ❑

- ❑ Tool and Repair Kit
  - ❑ 6" crescent wrench
  - ❑ Folding Allen wrench set *(metric/standard)*
  - ❑ 2 four-way cone wrenches *(metric/standard)*
  - ❑ Small vise-grips with wire-cutter built in
  - ❑ Swiss Army knife *(Tinker model includes Phillips and standard screwdrivers)*
  - ❑ Paper towels and hand cleaner
  - ❑ Pump *(does it fit your tire valve?)*
  - ❑ Spare tube *(right size?)*
  - ❑ Talcum powder *(to dust spare tube before wrapping in a plastic bag)*
  - ❑ Plastic bag
  - ❑ Patch kit: fresh, unopened tube of glue plus several patches in a plastic bag
  - ❑ 2-3 tire irons *(plastic, aluminum or steel)*
  - ❑ Duct tape
  - ❑ Pocket vise
  - ❑ Spoke wrench *(does it fit your spokes?)*
  - ❑ 3-4 extra spokes taped to frame
  - ❑ Chain tool
  - ❑ 4 spare chain links
  - ❑ Chain lube
  - ❑ Extra rear brake cable *(cut off one end)*
  - ❑ Extra derailleur cable *(cut off one end)*
  - ❑ Extra nuts and bolts *(for all-purpose emergencies)*
  - ❑ Safety wire
  - ❑ 2-3 $CO_2$ cartridges *(will save lots of tire-pumping)*
  - ❑
  - ❑

# Canoeing List

- ❏ Canoe *(a very hard item to forget, but we know people who've had to go back for it)*

- ❏ Roof rack and tie-down line

- ❏ Paddles and one spare

- ❏ Personal Flotation Device: one per person

- ❏ Dry sacks *(or duffels lined with plastic garbage bags)*

- ❏ Waterproof map case *(or a large Ziploc bag)*

- ❏ Portage harnesses, tumpline *(to convert duffels, sacks into carrying packs)*

- ❏ Knee pads plus cushions for children

- ❏ 50-foot length of 3/8" line: one per multi-canoe party *(for rescue, etc.) Note:* Plastic lines float.

- ❏ Two 15-foot end lines *(bow and stern)*, 3/8" diameter

- ❏ Foul-weather gear

- ❏ Sneakers with drainage holes cut in them

- ❏ Watertight food containers

- ❏
- ❏
- ❏

- ❏ Large sponge *(your handy "bilge pump")*

- ❏ Bailer

- ❏ Portaging yoke *(if required)*

- ❏ Optional
  - ❏ Extra flotation *(styrofoam inserts)*
  - ❏ Booster seat *(for children)*
  - ❏ Legless, folding backpacking chair
  - ❏ Rowing seat
  - ❏ Golf umbrella *(or tarp for paddling in rain)*
  - ❏ Thigh straps
  - ❏ Extra tie-down straps
  - ❏ Spray skirt

- ❏ Repair kit
  - ❏ Duct tape
  - ❏ Patch material *(appropriate to canoe-type, e.g., epoxy plus glass cloth scraps)*
  - ❏ Swiss Army knife *(with scissors, sharp blades)*
  - ❏ Small putty knife
  - ❏ Sandpaper
  - ❏ Paper towels
  - ❏ Lacquer thinner
  - ❏ Small paint brush

- ❏
- ❏
- ❏
- ❏

# Group Accessories, Individual Needs, Optionals

## Group Accessories

- ❑ Maps and permits
- ❑ Compass
- ❑ GPS *(global positioning system)* device
- ❑ Star chart
- ❑ Tree guide/bird book/wild-flower guide
- ❑ 2 boxes kitchen matches with sulphur heads *(strike anywhere)*. Everyone carries some in a Ziploc bag.
- ❑ First-aid kit
- ❑ Drugs and medicines
- ❑ Repair kit *(see itemized list)*
- ❑ Toothpaste, dental floss
- ❑ Small towel
- ❑ Liquid *(biodegradable)* dish soap and pot scrubber
- ❑ Lantern *(car/canoe/horse camping only)*
- ❑ Mosquito repellent *(two bottles)*
- ❑ Plastic spade *(to bury human waste)*
- ❑ Paper and pencil
- ❑ Camera, film, extra battery
- ❑ Extra pack straps
- ❑ Garbage bags *(one for each member of the party)*
- ❑ Extra Ziploc bags (10-12)
- ❑ Extra tent pegs
- ❑ Extra ground cloths/ponchos *(one for each tent)*
- ❑ Backpacking (Sven) saw
- ❑ Book for reading aloud
- ❑ 2-person inflatable backpacking raft plus paddles *(when other weight considerations permit)*
- ❑ Toilet paper *(enough for everybody)*

## Individual Needs

- ❑ Pocket knife
- ❑ Sunglasses *(in hard case)*
- ❑ Matches *(from Group Accessories list)*
- ❑ Flashlight *(such as a Mallory AA compact flashlight or another weighing about three ounces with batteries, and which can be held in the mouth when both hands are needed)* *Caution:* Remove batteries before storing for winter. This will avoid a corroded, ruined flashlight six months later.
- ❑
- ❑

## Optionals

- ❑ Ring clip to carry the car keys
- ❑ Fishing license
- ❑ Camera and tripod
- ❑ Binoculars
- ❑ Paperback book
- ❑ Toothbrush, toothpaste, comb, barrettes, ponytail bands
- ❑ Towel and bar of *(biodegradable)* soap
- ❑ Sanitary napkins, tampons, etc.
- ❑ Birth control devices
- ❑ Glasses case and extra glasses
- ❑ Contact lens solution
- ❑ Personal medications or prescriptions
- ❑ Nail clippers
- ❑ Playing cards, chess set, etc.
- ❑ Security blanket, stuffed animal, etc.
- ❑ Walking stick
- ❑

# Backpacking List: Equipment

## Tent and Sleeping Gear:

- ❏ Sleeping bags
- ❏ Ensolite, Ridge Rest, or Therm-A-Rest pads
- ❏ Tent, rainfly, stakes, poles *(Note: a two-person tent will not sleep three. Add another tent, rainfly, etc.)*
- ❏ Spare tent stakes
- ❏ Ground tarps/ponchos: one per tent
- ❏
- ❏

## Packs and Protection:

- ❏ Backpacks
- ❏ 4 straps per pack
- ❏ 4 extra pack straps
- ❏ Bear-proof storage canister *(for bear-infested parks)*
- ❏ Large green garbage bags *(or pack covers)*
- ❏ Ponchos/tarps *(as rain gear in addition to ground tarp for tent)*
- ❏ Stuff sacks for clothes and personals
- ❏ Day-pack *(or a strap-rigged stuff-sack to double as day-pack)*
- ❏ Flashlights plus new batteries and bulbs
- ❏ Dog packs, as necessary
- ❏ Child carrier, as necessary
- ❏
- ❏
- ❏

## Cooking, Fire, Water Gear:

- ❏ 3 nested pots and lids
- ❏ Sierra cups
- ❏ Tin plates
- ❏ Spatula
- ❏ Forks and spoons *(or chopsticks)*
- ❏ Frypan
- ❏ Backpack grill
- ❏ Camp stove plus fuel and funnel
- ❏ Matches *(2-plus boxes; strike-anywhere type)*
- ❏ Lighter fluid/fire starter paste in tube or cubes
- ❏ Candle
- ❏ Scouring pad/sponge
- ❏ Aluminum foil *(2 folded sheets for baking)*
- ❏ Light mesh bag *(as dish drainer, suspended from tree)*
- ❏ Pair of garden gloves *(for cooking, wood gathering)*
- ❏ Sven saw *(for gathering dead wood)*
- ❏ Canteens/water bottles
- ❏ Collapsible water container
- ❏ Water-purifier system
- ❏ Food storage:
  - ❏ plastic egg carton *(half-dozen or one dozen sizes)*
  - ❏ plastic pill box *(as "spice rack")*
  - ❏ plastic bottles, jars *(as condiment, syrup, oil, margarine containers)*
  - ❏ spare Ziploc bags *(10 each, small & large)*
- ❏
- ❏

# Backpacking List: Clothing, Boots
*For high-altitude temperatures: 20s-90s Fahrenheit*

- ☐ 1 pair pants *(jeans or cotton/canvas)*
- ☐ 1 pair shorts *(lightweight; doubles as swimsuit)*
- ☐ 3 pair socks *(inner and outer)*
- ☐ 3 underwear
- ☐ 2 cotton shirts *(one long-sleeved, one short)*
- ☐ Long johns *(cotton/polypropylene/wool)*
- ☐ 1 sweater or sweatshirt
- ☐ Down parka *(or Gore-Tex shell and layered sweaters)*
- ☐ Baseball cap or sun visor
- ☐ Wool (ski) hat
- ☐ Sunglasses *(with UV protection)*
- ☐ Boots
- ☐ Moccasins/tennies/reef slippers *(for stream crossings, fishing, in camp)*
- ☐
- ☐
- ☐
- ☐

- ☐ Mosquito-netting "hat" *(slips over visor; indispensable for "that" time of year)*
- ☐ Pocket knife
- ☐ Personal toiletries: *(mandatory)*
  - ☐ toothbrush
  - ☐ toothpaste, dental floss *(Group Accessory)*
  - ☐ toilet paper *(Group Accessory)*
- ☐ Personal toiletries: *(optional)*
  - ☐ comb/brush
  - ☐ barrettes/ponytail bands
  - ☐ razor
  - ☐ glasses case
  - ☐ small towel *(share)*
  - ☐ birth control devices
  - ☐ contact lens solution
  - ☐ nail clippers *(Group Accessory)*
- ☐
- ☐
- ☐
- ☐

# First Aid and Medicines
*Quantities for Four-Person Trip*

## First Aid:

❑ Moleskin *(1 or 2 packets)*
❑ Adhesive tape *(1 small half-inch roll)*
❑ Band-Aids *(12 assorted sizes)*
❑ Gauze pads *(6 assorted sizes)*
❑ Ace bandage *(1)*
❑ Butterfly bandages *(4)* *(Attention: mountain bikers)*
❑ Hydrogen peroxide *(Attention: mountain bikers)*
❑ Instant cold pack *(Attention: mountain bikers)*
❑ Tweezers/surgical locking hemostat *(1)*
❑ Small mirror *(for shaving, inspecting eyes, signaling)*
❑ Baby-wipes or similar "dry washes" *(4, unless there's a baby aboard, in which case thousands!)*
❑
❑

## Drugs and Medicines:

❑ Aspirin or its equivalent
❑ Mosquito repellent *(2 bottles for four people; look for "reduced DEET" on the label)*
❑ Sunscreen
❑ Lip balm
❑ Hand lotion
❑ Optional:
  ❑ Vitamins
  ❑ Neosporin/Bacitracin *(first-aid ointment)*
  ❑ Caladryl itching lotion
  ❑ Antacid pills
  ❑ Snakebite kit
  ❑ Aspirin with codeine
  ❑ Lomotil diarrhea medicine
  ❑ Electrolyte replacement tablets
  ❑ Athlete's-foot treatment
  ❑ Desitin/Zinc ointment
  ❑ Talcum powder *(Attention: cyclists)*

# Repair Kit

❑ Swiss Army knife
❑ 50-foot length of nylon rope
❑ Small vise-grips
❑ Heavy duty *("carpet")* thread plus two large needles
❑ Light nylon thread plus two small needles
❑ Nylon patch material *(called "ripstop" tape)*
❑

❑ Patch kit for rubber raft
❑ Extra flashlight bulb(s) plus batteries *(two per flashlight)*
❑ Safety pins
❑ Spare clevis pins and key wires for backpacks
❑ Roll of half-inch adhesive tape *(see First Aid and Medicine List)*
❑
❑

# Maps and Permits

- ❑ Spare change for phone call
- ❑ Campsite reservation
- ❑ Fire permit
- ❑ Wilderness permit
- ❑ Fishing license
- ❑ Driver's license
- ❑ Automobile registration
- ❑ Road map

- ❑ Trail map
- ❑ Topo map
- ❑ Sea chart *(Attention: canoeists)*
- ❑ Waterproof map pouch or Ziploc bag
- ❑ Compass
- ❑ Star chart
- ❑

# Traveling with a Dog

- ❑ Check that dogs are permitted at your hiking venue
- ❑ Dog pack
- ❑ Dog food *(minimum two packets moist food per day)*
- ❑ Leash
- ❑ Flea collar

- ❑ Name tag with address, phone number
- ❑ Water bowl for car
- ❑ Extra food for car
- ❑ Tweezers/hemostat *(to extract porcupine quills, etc.)*
- ❑

# Kiddy List: For Babies and the Very Young

- ❑ Whistle *(hang a loud one around child's neck)*
- ❑ Extra clothes: *(depending on ages and affinity for dirt)* 4 pairs of pants, 3 shirts, 4 pairs of socks for one-week trip
- ❑ Diapers: *(mix of cloth and disposable)* one dozen each for one-week trip, cloth for sunny weather and disposables for inclement weather
- ❑ Diaper-washing gear: 2 plastic buckets, biodegradable soap, clothes line
- ❑ Baby wipes
- ❑ Tie-on hat
- ❑ Rain suit *(for use at meals as well)*

- ❑ Plastic bags as "outer" socks *(quart/gallon size depending on size of foot)*
- ❑ Life jacket *(for swimming, boating, canoeing)*
- ❑ Syrup of ipecac *(induces vomiting)*
- ❑ Fever-scan forehead-type thermometer
- ❑ Baby Tylenol and chewable amoxicillan
- ❑ Zinc oxide/Desitin
- ❑ Games
- ❑ Books
- ❑ Favorite toys
- ❑ Comforters: stuffed animal, favorite blanket, etc.
- ❑ Edible hiking incentives!

# Fun and Games

- ❑ Paper and pencil
- ❑ Playing cards
- ❑ Star chart
- ❑ Tree guide
- ❑ Wildflower guide
- ❑ Bird book
- ❑ Binoculars
- ❑
- ❑
- ❑ Books
- ❑ Camera, including extra battery and film
- ❑ Musical instruments
- ❑ Pocket chess/checkers
- ❑ Lightweight games
- ❑ Frisbee
- ❑
- ❑

# Fishing List

*Quantities for 2 Anglers, 5-Day Trip: Spinning Tackle Only*

- ❑ Fishing license
- ❑ Telescoping rod
- ❑ Rod case *(to prevent snapping in backpack)*
- ❑ Spinning reel, lubricated and in good working order
- ❑ Fresh 4-pound test monofilament line on reel
- ❑ Spare 4-pound test line *(one small spool)*
- ❑ Spare 2-pound test line *(one small spool)*
- ❑ 6 bubbles
- ❑ 8 flies
- ❑ 10 lures *(vary by weight, size, color)*
- ❑
- ❑
- ❑ 2 bottle corks *(to carry lures, five per cork)*
- ❑ 8 snap swivels
- ❑ 2 packets No. 12 hooks (six per packet), for 8"-15" fish
- ❑ 1 packet No. 14 hooks (six per packet), for 8"-12" fish
- ❑ 8 weights: split shot, egg sinkers *(vary in size, weight)*
- ❑ Bait *(bottled salmon eggs; power bait; cheese; worms)*
- ❑ Worm threader *(optional)*
- ❑ Net
- ❑ Large Ziploc bags (the "tackle box")
- ❑ Swiss Army knife
- ❑

# Food Planning for Two Six-Day Trips

| | Trip One Min. Cooking (weight=lbs.) | Trip Two Max. Cooking (weight=lbs.) | Weight Difference (2nd trip) |
|---|---|---|---|
| **Ready to Eat Foods:** | | | |
| Dried fruit, Raisins | 3.0 | 3.0 | |
| Chicken/Beef Jerkey | 1.8 | 1.8 | |
| Dried Vegetables | 1.5 | 1.0 | 0.5 less |
| Cheese | 3.5 | 2.5 | 1.0 less |
| Nuts | 0.8 | 0.5 | 0.3 less |
| Cookies | 1.5 | 1.5 | |
| Crackers | 1.5 | 1.5 | |
| Chocolate | 2.0 | 2.0 | |
| Granola and Coconut | 0.8 | 0.5 | 0.3 less |
| Sprouts | 0.1 | 0.1 | |
| **Rice, Pasta, Soups:** | | | |
| Minute Rice | 1.0 | 0.7 | 0.3 less |
| Dried Minestrone | 0.8 | 0.8 | |
| Dried Pea Soup | 0.8 | 0.0 | 0.8 less |
| Spaghetti Sauce | 0.8 | 0.8 | |
| Spaghetti and Ramen | 1.2 | 1.0 | 0.2 less |
| **Flour, Sugar, Cereals:** | | | |
| Instant Oatmeal | 0.4 | 0.0 | 0.4 less |
| Flour | 1.5 | 3.0 | 1.5 more |
| Yeast, Baking Powder | 0.0 | 0.3 | 0.3 more |
| Cornmeal | 0.3 | 0.3 | |
| Sugar | 0.5 | 1.0 | 0.5 more |
| **Dairy, Oils, Spices:** | | | |
| Powdered Milk | 0.5 | 0.8 | 0.3 more |
| Eggs | 1.0 | 1.7 | 0.7 more |
| Hot Chocolate | 1.5 | 1.5 | |
| Tea/Coffee | 0.2 | 0.2 | |
| Cooking Oil | 0.0 | 0.5 | 0.5 more |
| Margarine | 0.5 | 0.5 | |
| Spices, Condiments, Syrup | 2.5 | 2.5 | |
| Total Weight | 30.0 | 30.0 | |

# Food Shopping List

*No quantities given here. If drying food at home, purchase fresh fruit and vegetables up to a month in advance of trip; purchase meat and poultry no more than a week before trip.*

- ❏ Flour
- ❏ Cornmeal
- ❏ Sugar
- ❏ Yeast
- ❏ Baking powder
- ❏ Baking soda
- ❏ Powdered milk
- ❏ Semi-sweet baking chocolate
- ❏ German sweet baking chocolate
- ❏ Instant hot chocolate
- ❏ Tea
- ❏ Coffee
- ❏ Rice
- ❏ Beans
- ❏ Mung beans
- ❏ Pasta: spaghetti
- ❏ *Soba*
- ❏ Instant ramen
- ❏ Chinese noodles
- ❏ Nori (Japanese seaweed)
- ❏ Raisin cookies
- ❏ Ginger snaps
- ❏ Ak-Mak crackers
- ❏ Saltines
- ❏ Instant soups
- ❏ Instant oatmeal
- ❏ Cooking oil
- ❏ Sesame oil
- ❏ Rice vinegar
- ❏ Soy sauce
- ❏ Maple syrup
- ❏ Brandy
- ❏ Hot sauce
- ❏ Lemon/lime juice
- ❏ Salami
- ❏ Cheese
- ❏ Margarine
- ❏ Dried fruit/fresh fruit for drying
- ❏ Vegetables for drying
- ❏ Dried meat (jerky) or turkey/chicken for drying
- ❏ Nuts: almonds, cashews, filberts
- ❏ Eggs/powdered eggs
- ❏ Raisins
- ❏ Powdered ginger
- ❏ Garlic
- ❏ Cinnamon
- ❏ Cayenne
- ❏ Paprika
- ❏ Tarragon
- ❏ Basil
- ❏ Thyme
- ❏ Curry powder/*garam masala* (pepper, cumin, cinnamon, cardamom, coriander, cloves, mace, nutmeg)
- ❏ Salt
- ❏ Pepper
- ❏ Car food
- ❏ Chicken
- ❏ Salad stuff
- ❏ French bread
- ❏ Cheese
- ❏ Juices
- ❏ Fresh fruit
- ❏ Dog food
- ❏ Baby food
- ❏

# Food Preparation Fundamentals

## *Definitions*

*Boiling:* Cooking in a liquid at its boiling point. Remember that the higher the altitude, the lower the temperature at which this occurs. That's the good news, because it takes less time to get the water bubbling. The bad news is that the lower boiling temperature means you have to cook the food longer than at sea level. The following chart indicates the differences:

| Altitude | Boiling Point of Water | |
|---|---|---|
| | Fahr | Cent |
| Sea Level | 212 | 100 |
| 2,000 ft. | 208 | 98 |
| 5,000 ft. | 203 | 95 |
| 7,500 ft. | 198 | 92 |
| 10,000 ft. | 194 | 90 |
| 15,000 ft. | 185 | 85 |

*Baking:* Cooking in enclosed heat. At home, this means using an oven. In the wilderness, it means nesting a covered pot in coals. For best results, the pot is *not* set directly on top of the coals, but on a cleared spot in the middle of the ashes of a fire. It is then *surrounded* by the hot coals. Foil-wrapped food placed on or under coals (or both) is also "baked."

*Frying:* Cooking in fat over direct heat. The fat may be any cooking oil— vegetable, corn, peanut, canola, safflower or sesame—or vegetable shortenings like Crisco, Spry, etc. Margarine works too, if you keep it cool and in a tightly lidded container. Butter and olive oil spoil too rapidly to be practical. Bacon drippings are fine for frying, but bacon doesn't last much longer than butter. We travel with a plastic bottle of vegetable oil and several sticks of margarine in a small plastic container.

*Grilling:* Cooking over direct heat on a rack, a grill or a stick, a.k.a. broiling or barbecuing. Backpacking grills are lightweight and small. Sticks, if used, should be pointed at one end, green so they don't burn, and long, so your hand doesn't cook along with the food. If the stick is big enough, it's called a spit, and if the food on it is rotated while cooking, this is known as roasting, a technique best left to Tudor kings with very large fireplaces.

*Poaching:* Cooking by simmering gently in just enough water to cover. Simmering describes what water does just below the boiling point: rather than bubble actively, it moves only slightly. This point is hard to maintain on an open fire, but happily it doesn't matter. Boiling works fine instead of poaching.

## *Practical Measurements*

KEYS AND SYMBOLS USED IN RECIPES:
- ❖  =  Can be prepared on camp stove or campfire
- ✺  =  Can be prepared with campfire or camping oven

❋ = Can be prepared only with campfire
c. = Sierra cupful
hfl. = Handful(s)
sp. = Camping kit spoonful

• *Measurements*: Our motto is "more or less." You won't have measuring spoons or cups and you don't need them. Approximations, guesses and tasting will suffice. In the following recipes, all of which make enough for two hungry adults, we try to keep quantities approximate. Where we use measures, they mean the following:

• *Spoonful*: A standard camping-kit spoon, about soup-spoon size.

• *Cup*: A Sierra-type cup, actually about a cup and a quarter by normal measurements. Sierra cups are lightweight, stack easily, and are less likely to burn your lips when drinking hot liquids than ordinary metal cups, because the rim is made of a heat-resistant alloy. They are available at all camping supply stores.

• *Handful*: Just that, an average adult handful.

• *Pots*: Our small one holds 4 cups, our medium 8 cups, and our large 12 cups.

## Cooking in the Rain

You can't make elaborate meals in the rain. Baking is out—you can't keep wet coals hot. Frying is possible, but unless your fire is protected from the rain or you fry fast, the food gets wet on top while it cooks on the bottom. Also, if the pan fills with water, you'll be poaching, which *is* a practical method. Another good technique in the rain is grilling (a rack will not fill with water). A third choice is cooking in a covered pot, which is our usual choice. Soups and stews are great: hot, easy, filling and needing little tending, so you can stay dry under a tree or tarp as they cook. You're likely to catch fish in the rain, and it's simple to grill them quickly or poach them and add to your pot.

Keep the stored food and matches in waterproof containers inside covered packs. When the sun comes out again, dry any damp food or packets to prevent spoilage. And don't go without at least one hot meal a day in the rain. Even a steaming cup of cocoa and some biscuits, or a bowl of oatmeal will keep the spirits up.

## Stove Cooking Hints

• Conserve fuel, cook fast.

• When frying remember that the circumference of heat over a camp stove is smaller than at home or over an open fire. Thus that large pan of frying fish will stay cooler on the edges than in the middle.

• Ignore suggestions for long, slow simmering in all recipes. Boiling time for half a small pot of water is 5 to 10 minutes. A few more minutes and soup's on.

- Stove safety: Use in a sheltered spot, out of the wind and rain. Unless an emergency requires it, don't cook in the tent, even in the rain. Fuel can spill, fumes can make you sick and tents can burn. Use your ingenuity to cook outside instead.

## Other Helpful Hints

*Meal size*: Camp cooking is cooking in miniature; i.e., a little goes a long way. Be prepared to scale down your normal at-home expectations as to how much you need. You don't want leftovers. Most are hard to store without attracting strange visitors. Plan meals with this in mind. If necessary, feed the last spoonful to the fire or the dogs.

*Utensils*: Pots and pans should be reasonably clean. Make sure the handles don't burn. If you have to stir something on the fire, lengthen your stirring spoon by tying on a stick. Garden gloves also work well to keep your hands protected.

*Water*: Have enough on hand for both cooking and cleaning up as you go. A dirty mixing pot often is needed for baking a few minutes later. Lids keep dirt and ashes out. Whenever you remove a pot top, set it on a clean rock or plate. Before replacing, check to be sure you won't be adding any unwanted twigs or leaves.

*Fire*: You want coals more than flame. A blaze burns rather than cooks. It also consumes a lot of fuel.

*Fire Area*: A fire requires a flat, cleared area, free of brush and clear of any overhanging branches. Don't put it too near your tent, or a slight wind may fill it with smoke. If the fire area is near some natural "chairs" (a big log will do) or "tables" (like a large flat rock), life is easier.

*Ingredients*: Keep them at hand. You don't want to run all over the campsite for garlic or soy sauce.

*White or Wheat Flour?* We use unbleached white flour in all the recipes, but whole wheat works just as well.

*Shade*: Keep all food in the shade while you're in camp. You may need to move the food stash several times a day, but it's so little trouble, especially if you keep the perishables together, and so sensible it should become part of your daily routine. If you leave for the day, place the perishables somewhere out of the arc of the sun.

*Tent*: A veritable kitchen cabinet—use it. If there are several stages to your food preparation and you need to put something aside, store it in the tent beyond the reach of flies, bees and mosquitos. Make sure, however, that you don't burn a hole in the tent floor with a hot pot. Feel the bottom of the pot, place it on a stone or a plate if necessary, and keep it away from sleeping bags and Ensolite pads. Don't forget to zip the mosquito flap all the way. Also, be careful of smelly spills. A tent reeking of raw fish or dried white sauce is likely to attract unwanted guests, such as ants or bears. If you have a spare poncho, spread it in the tent before storing food inside. If you do spill anything on the tent floor, wash it thoroughly before dark.

*Covering Food*: Foods you cook uncovered at home may need to be covered over an open fire to keep out ash and dirt. In such cases, set the lid on loosely and watch that the contents don't burn.

*Washing Up*: Make a wash-up area at the very edge of your campsite so as not to attract insects and animals. Carry water to the wash-up site rather than carrying dirty utensils to a lake or stream. Be sure any detergent, even "biodegradable" varieties, goes into the ground. Those bubbles that you see more and more of these days, even in the remotest wilderness areas, won't be going away. We usually wash pots with no soap at all: a little hot water and a good scrubber do fine. If you want to use soap, do so sparingly. A few drops are enough.

*When to Eat What?* One hot meal a day usually suffices. Two are sometimes essential. The hot-breakfast fanatic has to be fed; there's no getting around it. The hot-dinner fanatic also has to be fed. Now, if they're the same person…Don't try to convert anyone to anything while out on the trail. If you're a minimalist, cut back your own rations, but don't force your partner the carbo-loader to abstain on your account. Just remember that there is no fixed order to meals in the mountains, hot or cold. If you want nothing but desserts for breakfast, enjoy. One day we made and ate a chocolate cake with chocolate icing, a cherry pie and a loaf of sweet sourdough nut bread. The next day roots and grubs looked great. There's no accounting for the suddenness or strangeness of an attack of the munchies, so you might as well not fight it.

*Invidious Comparisons*: Whatever you cook in the wilderness won't be the same as what you make at home. The aim is not to duplicate what you can do seated at the controls of a 21st-century kitchen, but to make do with what you've got. The soufflé you bake at 9,000 feet might fall flat. It might not even warrant the name you give it. But it will be full of eggs, cheese and trout and will taste at least as good as an omelet. So if you're a hot shot chef in the lowlands, don't despair when things turn out differently from what you think is "right." Hopefully, you'll enjoy the cooking as much as the eating.

## Cleaning and Storing Fish

Unless you're a pelican or a down-at-the-heels samurai, you'll want to clean your fish before eating it—an easy task. Ideally, you should do it as soon after your catch as possible, but that's often impossible. You may be on a day hike or out in the raft or too busy catching more to get far enough away from the lake to clean the one you've just caught. In those cases, stow the fish is a Ziploc bag or a pot, or thread it on a stick. Try to keep the fish out of the sun.

Fish are easy to clean, but it's also easy to foul the environment while doing it. While floating on a pristine backcountry lake, nothing is more depressing than to look down and see fish entrails floating in the water. Always clean fish far from all freshwater sources—and from your campsite. And don't even begin to clean them until you've found a spot with soft soil or sand and have dug a hole or trench at least four or five inches deep with your heel or a cup. That will be your Dispose-All.

To clean a fish, you need a sharp knife and some rinse water. Hold the fish in your hand, belly up. Slit the belly from the vent (the small hole just in front of the back fin) to just behind the head. If you plan to cut off the head (lots of folks leave it on), do it now. Cut on a diagonal line from just behind the front fins through to the spinal column. The fish is going to be slippery; so hold on tight. But that backbone is tough, so be careful you don't take your hand off along with the head as the sharp knife severs the bone.

The fish is now opened. Most of the entrails will spill out on their own (into the hole you've dug). Remove the remainder with your hand, scraping away the tissue along the backbone with a thumbnail or knife. That's all there is to it! Rinse out the cavity, put the fish in a bag or pot, clean your knife and hands, pour out the dirty rinse water, cover up the hole and head for supper.

Fish are best cooked and eaten immediately after catching and cleaning. But this too is not always possible. To store the cleaned fish overnight, keep them in a plastic bag inside a pot. You don't need to use any water. Cover the pot and set a heavy rock on it to discourage late four-legged diners. The cold night air will preserve the fish and breakfast will be great.

## Cooking Fish Without a Pan

You've bagged a couple rainbows and your partner has taken the required snapshot. The fish are fresh and cleaned; a feast is in order. There are many ways to cook fish: frying or poaching in a pan, stewing or baking in a pot, or grilling or broiling over an open flame. For starters, let's say you've left your frying pan in the car—at the time it seemed too heavy. The pot lids are too small and light to use as substitutes. The fish are biting on everything from hand-tied flies to matzoh balls, and the idea of one more fish stew palls. What to do? Go primitive. Use a stick, a rock, the flame or coals as your pan or oven.

## Trout on the Coals ❉

*2 rainbow trout*
*1 campfire, flames low, coals just cooling*
*pepper / hot sauce to taste*
*lemon / lime juice*

Toss the fish in the coals! Honest. It works. If you were squeamish about ashes in your food, you wouldn't be here anyway. The worst that'll happen is the fish will be charred beyond recognition. So who needs recognition? Extricate the blackened trout after three to five minutes (depending on the heat of the coals). Use a spare plate to scrape away the charred skin. The flesh will be fine and flaky. Add pepper/hot sauce and a squirt of lemon juice from the miniature plastic bottle. Make Neanderthal noises while eating.

## Trout on a Stick ❉

*2 rainbow trout*
*1 campfire, moderate flames, coals red hot*
*1 green, sharpened hardwood stick*
*cooking oil*
*pepper, salt to taste*
*lemon / lime juice*

Strictly speaking, this is a way to grill, not roast, fish. But the chances of dropping the fish into the fire are good, so you get the best of both techniques. Rub oil on the sharpened stick, lay the oiled part in the cleaned, open belly of the fish, poke the point of the stick into the head to secure it. Truss the fish by poking twigs through one side of the belly, over the stick, and through the other side of the belly. Season it to taste and grill over red-hot coals. The smaller the fish, the less time it takes: an 8-inch trout should be ready in about 6-7 minutes. Check flesh with a fork or knife (or your fingers, if you've lost the cutlery, too). If it flakes easily, it's ready to eat.

## Trout on a Rock ❖

2 rainbow trout
1 campfire, very hot
1 big, flat rock
Cooking oil

Heat the rock in the fire. Work it to the edge of the fire ring, oil the fish, set it on the flat face of the rock, turning once during the cooking. No utensils? Gather round the rock and eat with your hands. Incoherent Cro-Magnon grunting is appropriate here.

## Grilled Trout ❖

2 freshly caught small trout
cooking oil
soy sauce / tamari
rice vinegar / lemon juice
1 campfire, red-hot coals
1 lightweight, wire-mesh grill or 3-pronged backpacking grill

Oil the grill to prevent the fish from sticking. Set it about 5" above the coals. Let the grill get very hot before it receives the trout. Sprinkle cavity with soy sauce and rice vinegar, also a light coat of same on the trout's skin. Toss on grill. (If using a three-pronged grill, set the fish on it gently. Otherwise it'll end up in the fire.) After about five minutes, turn the fish. A small spatula is useful for this, though chopsticks or a knife and fork will do as well. Use the flake test for doneness: that is, with a fork pry up a piece; if is flakes off easily, the fish is finished, and you've just begun to eat. It will remind you of that great Japanese restaurant you went to last year.

## Baked Trout

One of the best and easiest ways to cook fish without a pan is to wrap it in aluminum foil, set it on a bed of hot coals, and cover it with another bed of coals, or use a camping oven for similar effects. As the recipes below show, there are endless variations to this way of cooking. We carry enough foil for at least one meal made this way. About two-and-a-half feet can be folded small and tucked inconspicuously in a pack pouch. It's usable only once. And remember, foil doesn't burn, so pack out the remains.

You can either wrap the fish individually or fashion a flat "oven pan." First, crimp the edges up on all sides so the juices won't spill out. Second, keep the "lid" opening toward you and not the fire; that way you can open the foil with a minimum of movement when the baking is done, without losing the juices.

## Foil-Baked Trout ✺

2 10" trout
rosemary / tarragon
salt, pepper to taste
1 clove garlic, sliced thin
small dab of margarine
hot coals
1-2 ¹/₂ ft. heavy aluminum foil

Rub the cavity with the margarine, then season it with the herbs and garlic. Foil-wrap the fish tightly and place on a bed of coals. Cover with hot coals. Note: coals have a habit of cooling, so expect the fish to take about 15 minutes to bake. You may need to add fresh coals if the originals lose a lot of their heat along the way. If you get good at it, you can test for doneness by poking a fork through the foil, while the fish are cooking. If the fork slides in and out easily, meeting little resistance, dinner is done. Or take the whole shmeer out of the fire, open, check, eat, or return for a little more cooking.

VARIATIONS ON FOIL-BAKED TROUT:

- Bake in soy sauce, garlic, ginger and sesame oil.

- Stuff the fish with finely chopped nuts and prunes soaked for an hour or so in brandy and warm water. Add a dash of sesame oil.

- Lay the fish on a bed of cooked rice; add a mixture of chopped nuts and cut-up dried fruits (apricots, raisins, apples, prunes), salt, curry powder and lemon juice.

- If you find any roe (fish eggs) when cleaning the fish save them. Put the roe back in the cavity with whatever else strikes your fancy and bake.

- Cajun Red. This calls for bread crumbs, but a mixture of flour and cracker crumbs will do. To the mixture add paprika, oregano, salt (optional), red pepper flakes (or cayenne). Beat an egg with a little milk powder and water. Dip trout first into egg mixture, then into "crumb" mixture. Bake in foil as directed.

## Pan-Fried Fish ❖

If you carry a cast-iron frying pan into the mountains, you'll develop very strong calf muscles but you won't get too far. If, however, you bring a light-weight, teflon-coated pan, the slight increment in weight will be repaid many times over in versatility and pleasure. You can't cook a pancake on a stick, and it's hell to fry a fish without a pan.

Pan-fried trout are so easy and satisfying that you may not get beyond them in a week in the mountains. Small lake or stream trout are tender, cook fast and need almost nothing to enhance their flavor. A pan, lightly greased and set on a grill or nestled between rocks about four to five inches above a bed of coals, and a string of cleaned, lightly seasoned trout are all you need for a first-rate meal. The oil should be hot before you add the fish. Turn them over after about four or five minutes (sooner if they're small or if the fire is very hot) and cook for another four or five minutes. Sprinkle generously with lemon juice. That's all, folks.

As soon as the flesh flakes with a fork, it's done. Be careful at this stage; an overcooked fish loses a lot of flavor. When in doubt, take the fish off the fire sooner rather than later. You can always put it back, but you can't reverse a burn-out. All our suggestions for minutes per side are approximate. We don't wear watches in the wilderness. It's better to feel for doneness, following the clock in your head, than to put a stopwatch on the food in your pan.

One other precaution: make sure the oil doesn't burn. It starts to smoke and turns black if it gets too hot. At the smoking stage, add more oil to the pan to reduce the temperature. By experimenting with the heat of the fire and the height of the pan above it, you'll soon get the right combination and the fish will cook to perfection.

## Pan-Fried Trout ❖

*4 eight-inch trout, cleaned, with heads left on*
*cooking oil / margarine*
*salt, pepper to taste*
*lemon juice*

Heat a mixture of oil and margarine if you can spare them; otherwise one or the other. Brown the trout on one side, about 4 minutes; turn and finish cooking. Salt and pepper to taste. Test for doneness by flaking. Turn out on plate, pour the cooking oils over fish, add a dash of lemon juice.

## Trout Amandine #1 (Trout with almonds) ❖

Prepare as Pan-Fried Trout. Add a handful of chopped almonds to the pan after you have removed the cooked fish. Brown the almonds quickly in the cooking oils. Do not burn. Spread almonds over the trout and the juices over all. This is simple and elegant, maybe the best of all ways to prepare a freshly caught small trout. Don't worry if you only have peanuts or cashews. It'll taste just as good, and Escoffier is not likely to pop out from behind a tree to point an accusing finger.

## Trout Amandine #2 ❖

Dust the fish with a handful of seasoned flour. To season flour add any combination of spices to it and mix: pepper, rosemary, tarragon, basil, ginger. Prepare as per Trout Amandine #1.

## Trout Meunière (Flour-dipped, Pan-Fried Trout) ❖

"Meunière" means a miller, someone who grinds grain to make flour. This is one of the classic ways of preparing fresh whole trout. Note that "sp." here means "spoon," as in "mess-kit" spoon. Quantities are not important.

*4 fresh, cleaned trout, with heads left on*
*2-4 sp. margarine/cooking oil*
*2 sp. flour*
*salt, pepper to taste*
*lemon/lime juice*

Dip the trout in flour to coat. Heat oils—a mix of the two is great—and add fish. Season to taste. Brown on one side, about 4 minutes. Turn and complete cooking. Add a dash of lemon juice. Serve. Why leave the head on in these recipes? For both taste and style. The cheek meat on a fish is the tenderest of all. Why give it to the scavengers? And a whole cooked trout is beautiful. That's reason enough.

TROUT MEUNIÈRE VARIATIONS:

- Prepare as per recipe, but use a mixture of flour and cornmeal. Some old-timers put the flour-cornmeal mixture in a bag, drop in the fish, shake and fry.

- Make a small cup of milk with instant powdered milk and water, dip the fish into the milk, then the flour or flour- cornmeal mixture. Cook as in recipe.

- Substitute an egg for the milk. Crack it into a pot lid and beat lightly with a fork. To make it go farther, add a spoonful of water or milk to the egg. Dip the fish into the egg and then into the seasoned flour.

- Suppose you run out of flour and cornmeal and still want to coat the fish? Crush a couple of RyKrisps (or whatever other crackers you have) between a plate and your Sierra cup. Using this coarse meal, proceed with or without egg or milk.

- A piece of stale bread or biscuit can also replace flour or cornmeal. Just make a fine layer of crumbs by rubbing the bread between your hands. Ground-up nuts, seeds, left-over rice—almost anything'll do. Use your imagination.

## Cajun Blackened Trout ❖

Mardi Gras at the campground. Ideally this calls for an iron skillet, but you don't have one. Teflon will do in Little N'orleans. This one will set your socks on fire.

*2 fresh, cleaned trout (optional: filet the trout)*
*3 sp. cooking oil*
*paprika to taste*
*onion, garlic powder to taste (or dried onion flakes and minced fresh garlic)*
*pepper, cayenne, chili powder to taste*

Get that pan as hot as you dare without wrecking the Teflon coating. Season the trout inside and out (or, if fileted, top and bottom). Fry till blackened—right, *blackened*—on both sides. Eat by the light of your flaming socks.

## Trout Flambé ❖

Plan to serve this spectacular dish after dark for best effect. Prepare as in any of the pan-fried recipes. Just before eating, pour a little brandy in a Sierra cup, hold it over the fire until it's warm to the touch and light it with a match. As the brandy catches fire, pour it over the trout. A soft blue flame will dance over and around the trout for up to half a minute and will add another delicate flavor to the dish.

## Poached Trout ❖

A poached fish is a finished product. Seasoned well and not over-cooked, it's as tender as you'll get a trout. But a poached fish is also part of a process that involves other methods of cooking. The six recipes following this one will show you how to combine several methods of preparing fish in order to end up with something definitely more than the sum of its parts.

*2 fresh, cleaned trout*
*seasonings to taste: pepper, Italian herbs*
*lemon juice*
*frying pan filled with boiling water*

Put enough water in your frying pan to barely cover the fish. Season it with salt and herbs to taste. Place the pan over the fire and let the water come to a slight boil. The fish will curl up. That's all right. There's also no need to turn the fish over. It's done when the skin peels off easily, and the flesh has lost its "transparent" look and comes off the bone at a nod and beckon. This takes about 10 minutes from the time the water begins to boil.

Remove the pan from the heat, the fish from the pan, and then with fork, knife or fingers peel off the skin and flake the flesh from the bones. Ideally, the backbone will come off in one piece, taking most of the skeleton and leaving you with a simple mop-up operation close to the fins. It's simple, but work fast or you'll end up wearing a halo of flies and other airborne participants. When finished, place the fish in the tent until ready to use and go bury the skin and bones. If you won't be using the poaching water (see Trout in Curried Sauce, Fried Rice Chinese Style or Hidden Lake Soufflé for possibilities), throw it out far from both your living area and the lake or stream.

## Trout Tandoori ❖

This is a curry dish, filling and fiery. Eat it, and you'll find the rainbow at the end of the pot. (Note: hfl. = handfuls)

*3 small rainbow trout, cleaned and poached*
*2 hfl. rice, boiled*
*assorted chopped nuts, dried fruits, about a small dishful*

*chopped dried onion, as much as you like*
*cooking oil*
*2-3 large pinches garam masala to taste*
*cayenne pepper (optional)*
*lemon/lime juice (optional)*

Heat up just enough oil to cover the bottom of your frying pan. Toss in the poached fish, rice, nuts and fruit. Season with garam masala and cayenne to taste. Add a dash of lime juice. Stir frequently. Done when hot. Serve with a Campground Chutney. Guaranteed to warm whatever in you is not.

## Trout in Curried Sauce ❖

The ingredients are the same as for Trout Tandoori. Add the poached trout to a cup of white sauce made with the poaching liquid, and flavored with *garam masala* and cayenne. Serve over boiled rice with nuts and fruits on the side, and a big helping of chutney.

## Fried Rice Chinese Style ❖

*3 small trout, cleaned and poached*
*2 hfl. rice, boiled*
*2+ cloves garlic, chopped*
*sesame oil/peanut oil/cooking oil*
*powdered ginger*
*dry mustard*
*black pepper*
*soy sauce*

Heat oils (a mixture is desirable but not necessary) in frying pan. Add poached trout, rice and spices. Fry, stirring, till hot. Then add soy sauce to taste and stir thoroughly. *Note:* the soy sauce provides all the salt you'll need. The Chinese have a saying: Chinese food doesn't taste good unless you use chopsticks. You have now been warned.

## Hidden Lake Soufflé ✱

A soufflé is a concoction made by putting cooked food—in this case, poached trout—into a sauce, pumping it up with air provided by beaten egg whites and baking. This definition may not satisfy the cognoscenti, and our methods will probably plunge them into a deep culinary depression, but they work. The results are unspeakably good.

A soufflé is a three-stage affair: poaching the fish, making a white sauce with the poaching liquid, and folding in beaten egg whites before baking. (Note: "c." = Sierra cup) Here are the instructions:

*2-4 small (8") trout, cleaned and poached*
*$^1/_2$ c. thick white sauce*
*1-2 eggs, separated*
*salt, pepper to taste*

Never separated egg whites from yolks? Crack the egg in half gently against the side of a pot, or strike a knife against the shell. Hold half the shell in each hand. Most of the white will drool into the container by itself. Help the rest by moving the yolk back and forth between the shell halves. Don't kill yourself to get all the white. It's okay if a little yolk stays along.

After separating the eggs, mix a spoonful of the cooked sauce into the yolks so they won't hard-boil, then add them to the sauce to make it thicker and richer. Now toss in the poached fish and seasonings. Stir and remove sauce from heat. Reserve (in tent if there are flies).

Beat egg whites with the spring-loaded swizzle stick or a wire whisk. (If you can spare two eggs, all the better, but one will do, too.) The idea is to get them stiff but not dry. Out here in the wilderness, this isn't always possible or necessary. Basically you're trying to whip air into them. The bigger the pot and the more you agitate the egg whites, the better your chances of ending up with the right product. We've tried to use forks as beaters with little luck. Our trusty swizzle stick was just the ticket until it finally broke down this past year. It seems irreplaceable. (Try some old bar or kitchen-supply stores.) A miniature wire whisk works okay.

Fold the beaten egg whites into the sauce, gently as she goes. Just turn the sauce over on the whites with a spoon till they're pretty thoroughly incorporated. Lose their air and the soufflé will end up with a specific gravity close to that of lead.

Now grease and lightly flour the middle-sized pot (even if you have to do some dish washing and pot juggling to get it free and clean), and pour in the soufflé mixture. It should come about one-third of the way up the pot, depending on how much fish you have. Cover and bake.

You've already got a fire going (to poach and thicken the sauce) so by now the coals are glowing red. Scoop out a pot-sized depression in the ashes near the front of the fire and set the pot down—not on the coals, but on the cleared ground or warm ashes. With a heavy stick, pile coals around the pot until it's nestled up to its lid in heat. If the coals are too hot, the soufflé will burn. If they're too cool, it'll take ages to cook and you'll do a slow burn with it. Ideally, the coals should have lost their most intense heat; the fiery red glare should be going out of them. Baking time will be about 20 to 30 minutes, or a chapter from a good book. You may need to add coals to the pile to keep its warmth constant.

It's permissible to peek but be careful not to knock everything awry or get ashes in the pot. Don't worry if the outside of the soufflé is slightly burned; the inside will be as tasty as promised. The soufflé *will* actually rise, to almost double its bulk, and will look spectacular. Savor it quickly, however, for it deflates rapidly after taken off the heat. But by then, appetite will take over from aesthetics. Tuck in, eat up.

## *Trout Crêpes* ❖

Once you can poach a fish and prepare a sauce, you also have the makings of the filling for crêpes.

*2-3 fresh trout, cleaned and poached*
*1 ¹/₂ c. thick white sauce, made with poaching liquid*
*seasonings to taste*
*2 c. crêpe batter*

Crêpes are made with eggs, so you don't need any in the sauce. Keep the sauce warm, near the fire, and covered while you make the crêpes. It's neither easy nor necessary to make all the crêpes at once, so eat them in turns as they come off the fire. Put a crêpe on a plate, spoon sauce into it, wrap and eat. Then let your partner(s) follow suit.

## Trout, Rice and Bean Salad ❖

Here's another use of poached trout, especially if you've had an abundance of luck on the lake. Take the leftover poached, flaked trout and add it to our famous Bean and Rice Salad.

## Sashimi (Japanese-style Raw Fish)

Here are some important facts about preparing *sashimi* in the wilderness:

## Raw Trout

- The fish must be absolutely fresh. They can't sit around for a couple hours in a pot, even cleaned. You need to eat them soon after catching or keep them alive until you have enough (say, four or five 8" trout) for a meal. Incidentally, if you're fishing near a snowfield, you can pack your catch in snow immediately, and have them as iced as your local fishmonger's.

- There's not much flesh on a small trout. Some is also lost in skinning and boning. Don't expect a filling meal, but *sashimi* is a perfect lunch snack.

- There are two ways to prepare it. For both, clean the fish thoroughly. For the first method, skin it and peel the flesh from the bones. To skin a fish, begin by cutting under the fins and yanking them toward the head. Then slice along the backbone from head to tail. With your knife, loosen the skin around the gills. Now work your fingers, the knife or both, under the skin at the head and strip it back toward the tail. Once the fish is skinned, cut away the flesh, beginning at the backbone and working down. Toward the end, fingers work better than a knife. Place the raw fish in a Sierra cup.

- For the second method, bone the fish first, then remove the skin. Spread open the cleaned and beheaded fish, gutted side facing you. With your knife, cut gently along one side of the backbone from top to tail. Do the same on the other side. This severs the spine from the skeletal bones or ribs, and it can be pulled out, working from neck to tail. Last, get the skeletal bones out. Starting from the tail, work your blade under the bones gently toward the neck, turn the knife around, and then come back toward the tail. Starting from the neck, lift the bones away. This leaves a whole, flat, boned fish with the skin still on the "under" side. You can now remove the flesh from the skin by working your blade under the flesh and scraping it away. Start at the tail, which you can grasp for leverage, and move up. You'll have the fish in one piece this way. Again put it into a Sierra cup.

- One word of caution. All this boning and skinning tends to draw flies. Unless you're fast, you may want to do it in your tent. If so, spread a poncho on the floor so the tent will stay clean even if you're messy.

- You need a spicy condiment with your *sashimi*, as well as some soy sauce. The Japanese use a fiery green horseradish called *wasabi*. This comes in powdered form. You add enough water to make a paste, which is then added to the soy sauce. The fish is dipped into it and eaten straight away. You needn't carry a packet of dried *wasabi*. Dry mustard, particularly the good hot kind, will do just as well and is, frankly, more functional, since you can use it in many other dishes. Either way, *sashimi* is great!

## Sauces

You've been in the mountains eight days and are low on supplies. You have some RyKrisps left, a lump of degenerating cheese, a few spoonfuls of flour, some oil that looks like it came from a crank case and a handful of milk powder. The prospects of catching a trout are dim. You want a hot meal. Not to worry! If you know how to make a sauce, you're in business. A combination of oil, flour, milk powder and water will give you a base for the cheese and whatever spices you have left. When it's all melted, thick and steaming hot, you've got yourself a kind of rarebit which can be eaten on the crackers for a filling, hearty meal.

This kind of sauce, practically a meal in itself, can also stretch other foods far and in many directions. It has almost as many names as uses: cream sauce, white sauce, bechamel. It's basically equal parts shortening (usually butter) and flour, which are heated for a few minutes before you slowly add liquid (usually milk or the stock with which you've been cooking). That's it. Some seasonings, cheese, perhaps an egg yolk give you sauce thick enough to eat alone or use in a soufflé, crêpes, curry or cream soup.

At home, you'd use real butter and whole milk. Over an open fire and with neither on hand, the technique changes a bit, but the principle is the same.

### *White Sauce* ❖

*3 sp. margarine / shortening / oil*
*3 sp. flour*
*1-2 c. poaching liquid, or 1-2+ c. water*
*1 sp. milk powder*
*salt, pepper, curry powder, nutmeg, paprika to taste*

In a small pot, melt the margarine (or, in descending order of preference, shortening or oil: they all work). Add an equal amount of flour (heaping spoonfuls if a very thick sauce is desired). Stir this mixture over the heat for a minute or two to kill the taste of the raw flour. In your kitchen you'd use a low flame. At a campfire, that isn't so easy; alternate the pan on and off the heat to prevent the sauce from burning. If you are using the poaching liquid from the fish, add this a little at a time, stirring. If you are using the milk powder and water, add the milk powder to the mixture, then add the water a little at a time, stirring. The mixture will thicken almost instantly. Continue to add liquid slowly. By the time you've added a cupful or more, the sauce will have thinned out, much to the relief of anyone who thought they were being conned into making kindergarten paste. Keep stirring till smooth. Add seasonings to taste. The sauce is done when reasonably thick and smooth. Don't lose heart if the flour and milk powder aren't completely absorbed by the liquid. It'll still be hot, filling and delicious. When done, add whatever else you want: poached fish, crushed biscuits, cheese, cooked rice, noodles.

## United Nations Rarebit ❖

It would be an insult to the Welsh to call this by its conventional name, so we'll let the National Security Council decide its provenance. Anyway, it'll stick to more than ribs and keep you fat and happy.

*3 c. white sauce*
*3-4+ sp. sliced cheese*
*1 egg (optional)*
*hot sauce*
*brandy*

Add as much sliced cheese as you can spare to the completed white sauce. If you have an extra egg, beat it well and add. Continue to stir till cheese is melted. Season with hot sauce to taste and a dash of brandy from the medicine kit. Serve on crackers, boiled rice or fresh baked bread.

If the sauce is too thick or pasty, keep adding liquid till you get the right consistency. If it's too thin, either let the sauce boil down while stirring, or in a pot lid, make 5 or 6 marble-sized balls of dough from flour and shortening or oil. Drop these into the sauce and stir. They'll thicken the sauce without leaving it filled with lumps of unabsorbed flour, which you'd get if you added flour alone to the sauce.

## Tomato Sauce ❖

Here is the stripped-down fighting version of the homemade sauce you weren't able to dehydrate this year. As long as you have some dried tomatoes and onions, perhaps some dried mushrooms and jerky, you're in business. You'll use this sauce for pasta and for the pizza you can't live without.

*1 lg hfl. dehydrated tomatoes*
*1 hfl. dehydrated onions*
*1 clove garlic, sliced*

*1 hfl. dehydrated mushrooms*
*2 sp. sliced or diced jerky (optional)*
*mixed Italian spices*
*salt, pepper to taste*
*water*

Cover the tomatoes with twice their volume of water. Bring to boil and stir frequently while the tomatoes are rehydrating. Add water as necessary. The tomatoes will not completely transform into a sauce, but enough so to give a first-rate illusion of same, in about 20 minutes. About half way through the cooking, add the onions, mushrooms, garlic, jerky and spices. Continue to cook till the ingredients absorb most of the water and become saucy. Adjust seasonings. Ta da!

*Note*: If this is going to be the base of your pizza, omit the onions, mushrooms and jerky, as they'll go on separately.

# Rice, Noodles and Beans

## Rice

Put two generous handfuls of white rice in the medium pot with a pinch of salt. Add enough water to come up to just below the middle knuckle of your forefinger. This is enough rice for two adults. We can't explain the knuckle measure. It was taught to us years ago, and for reasons that are still mysterious, it's invariably correct. Neither the size of the finger nor the size of the hand nor the size pot seem to matter. Remember: the water will boil faster in the mountains than at sea level. Thus the knuckle measure will give you more water to start off with than you'd use for a good fluffy rice at home.

White rice cooks in about 10 to 15 minutes, depending on the heat of the fire. Brown rice requires more water, to about the middle of the knuckle, and more time to cook. Allow about 25 minutes. To make the pot easier to clean, pour water in it immediately after you've spooned out the rice, and keep it warm near the fire. By wash-up time, the pot almost cleans itself!

## Fried Rice With Vegetables & Chicken ❖

*2 hfl. boiled rice*
*1 c. mixed dried vegetables, rehydrated in water to cover*
*1 hfl. chopped nuts*
*sliced/diced chicken jerky (optional)*
*1 clove garlic, sliced*
*cooking oil*
*hot sauce, spices to taste*

Heat the oil in the frying pan, add garlic and nuts till just turning brown, then veggies and spices. Stir and saute till done; add cooked rice, stir till thoroughly mixed. Adjust seasonings.

## Rice Pudding ⁕

This can be a meal in itself—dessert and main course combined.

*2 hfl. cooked rice*
*1 sp. milk powder*
*¹/₂ c. water*
*2+ sp. sugar*
*pinch of salt*
*cinnamon to taste*
*1 egg*
*dash lemon/lime juice*
*¹/₂ sp. margarine*
*1 hfl. chopped dried fruit*
*dash of brandy (your basic vanilla substitute)*
*1 hfl. crushed ginger snaps/crackers*

Oil or grease a medium pot. Line it with crushed ginger snaps or crackers. Mix the rice, milk powder, water, sugar, salt, cinnamon, egg, lemon juice, margarine, fruit, and brandy thoroughly and add to the lined pot. Cover with more crushed ginger snaps. Cover and bake in coals or in a camping oven until the pudding is set, about 20 minutes. Eat hot or cold.

If you're out of some ingredients, improvise. No spare egg? You can still make the pudding. It may not be as rich, but no one's measuring on a taste meter. Substitute a spoonful of flour or cornmeal and a little more water. No margarine? Use oil. Ditto for the seasonings—not everyone carries lemon juice or even cinnamon (although no backpacker carrying cinnamon has ever been known to starve in the wilderness). Maybe throw in some Swiss Miss powdered chocolate drink instead of sugar and cinnamon. Fine. And of course the cookie crumbs can be left out. Experiment. Enjoy.

## Noodles

If pasta palls, go East. Chinese wheat or rice noodles, Japanese buckwheat noodles (*soba*) are great boiled, fried or baked. They can substitute for almost all the rice recipes: Trout Tandoori; Fried Rice Chinese Style; Trout, Rice and Bean Salad; or Fried Rice with Vegetables and Chicken.

## Cooking Noodles ❖

Noodles don't double in bulk when cooked, but the more water you use, the less they stick together and to the pot. Use the large pot, half to three-quarters full of water, add salt, boil and throw in the noodles. Two very generous handfuls will get two of you through a meal. The water should boil rapidly as they cook. They taste done in about 10-12 minutes (at moderate to high altitudes). If you plan to use them in another dish, you need time to put it together, just drain the noodles, add fresh cold water to cover and let them stand. This prevents them from sticking together. When everything is ready, drain them again and away you go. If you make a sauce, use the noodle water as the liquid base. It's already hot and flavorful.

## Cold Noodle Salad ❖

*¹/₂ packet Japanese buckwheat noodles (soba), cooked and drained*
*sesame oil / regular cooking oil*
*rice vinegar / regular vinegar*
*1 hfl. dried mixed vegetables, rehydrated*
*sprinkling of mung bean sprouts (optional)*
*salt, pepper to taste*

Mix all ingredients in a pot. Adjust seasonings. Serve.

## Beans ❖

Beans are so good, nutritious and easily prepared that it's a pity they weigh so much. Nevertheless, they are definitely worth taking along, in limited amounts. And it doesn't matter what kinds you bring. Red, kidney, white, or black beans can all be used with equal ease. Put a couple handfuls in a pot, cover with cold water, cover the pot and soak overnight or for four to five hours during the day. Empty the old water, cover again with fresh water, and cook until the beans are tender, 25-40 minutes, depending on the amount and kind of beans and the heat of the fire. That's all there is to it. Use the cooking liquid for making sauces.

Lentils and split peas may be substituted for beans in most of these recipes. *Note*: Watch your fuel supply if cooking beans on a camp stove. It may cost you other meals down the line.

## Fried Rice and Beans ❖

As any Mexican cook will tell you, the combination of rice and beans is a nutritional powerhouse. It's also plain good eating. Spice it up with chili powder, cayenne or hot sauce and you've got a ready-made fiesta. To the recipe Fried Rice with Vegetables and Chicken add cooked beans and fry till done. If spicy, make sure you've got a full water bottle within reach.

## Four-Wheel Drive Vegetarian Chili ❖

You need a Land Rover to get all the ingredients of this great chili into your car campsite, but the 25 skeptics who recently ate it under the baton of Marc Girouard would now gladly lease a limo if necessary. And if you're a backpacker, just dry the finished product on your home dehydrator and rehydrate over the camp stove. Same results, same bliss.

*1 c. dried red kidney (or black or pinto) beans, soaked overnight, rinsed, and simmered in*
*    water until done, about one hour*
*3 onions, chopped*
*4 Tbs. oil*
*2 green peppers, chopped*
*2-3 jalepeño peppers, minced and with seeds removed*
*3 cloves garlic, crushed or minced*
*2 bay leaves*
*¹/₂ Tbs. ground cumin*

2 Tbs. chili powder
1 12 oz. bottle of beer (preferably ale or porter)
salt (optional) and pepper to taste
1 c. corn (fresh or frozen)
fresh cilantro
cheddar cheese, grated
sour cream

    While beans are cooking, sauté in a big pot the onions in the oil, then add and sauté the green peppers, jalepeños, garlic, bay leaves, cumin and chili powder till soft. Pour the beer into the pot, add the cooked beans and $1^1/_2$ qts. canned tomatoes drained of juices, plus seasonings and corn. Bring to boil. Simmer one hour or longer. (You've brought coals or a hotshot camping stove along so there's no eco-disaster built into the cooking time.) Serve topped with chopped fresh cilantro, cheese, and sour cream. (Omit sour cream if backpacking. It won't keep.)

## Baked Rice and Beans in Cheese Sauce ✸

1 hfl. boiled rice
1 hfl. cooked beans
2 c. white sauce
3 sp. sliced cheese
cayenne, chili powder, hot sauce

    To the white sauce, add the cheese and stir till melted. Add the rice and beans, mix. Bake in coals 10 to 15 minutes till set. Serve with mariachi music and plenty of water.

## Refried Beans ❖

2 hfl. cooked beans and the cooking liquid
cooking oil
hot sauce, pepper
sliced cheese

    Drain the beans but reserve the liquid. Heat oil in the frying pan. Mash the beans with a fork or spatula as they're frying. If the beans get too dry, add some of the reserved liquid. Fry slowly, season with pepper and hot sauce. Slice cheese to taste over them. Eat with biscuits and you get a great Tex-Mex meal.

## Ranch Omelet ❖

    For two adults, scramble three eggs with refried beans and some dried tomatoes. Serve with plenty of hot sauce.

## Bean and Rice Salad ❖

2 hfl. beans, cooked, drained, cooled
2 hfl. cooked rice

1 poached trout (optional)
1 hfl. bean sprouts
salt, pepper, lemon juice, sesame oil, mustard powder

Mix all ingredients together. Season to taste. This is a wonderful meal, even without the trout.

### Bean and Sprouts Salad ❖

Same as above, though without the rice. Use half beans and half mung-bean sprouts. Season as above.

### Bean Sprouts

We always bring some dry mung beans to sprout on the trail. They're a great snack, excellent in soups, fried rice, sauces, soufflés and salads. The first night, soak a handful in a plastic bag. In the morning, drain the water, close the bag and keep in a dark place. While hiking, we carry them in the smallest nested pot; at camp, they're stored in the backpack. Rinse once or twice a day to keep moist, but not wet. They'll sprout in about three days. They don't need to be cooked, but do get moldy fast, so when they're ready, use them. Then begin a new batch.

# Drinking Your Dinner: Soups and Stews

The dry soup mixes that you buy in the local market taste all right, but they're not very filling. If they're going to be your supper, you need to jack them up, give them some body and thus a bit of soul. A handful of uncooked rice or noodles, as much cooked rice and beans as you want, a clove of garlic, a slice of onion, vegetables from your home dehydrator, broken crackers, poached fish, cheese—whatever seems to fit your soup mix will thicken the pot. Starting from scratch is easy, too. Here are a couple examples:

### Fish Stew or Chowder ❖

Clean two or three fish, but save the heads. Toss fish and heads into the big pot, cover with water and poach. Save the liquid in another pot, remove and bury the bones, heads and skin, then combine the fish and liquid. If necessary, add water. Toss in two handfuls of rice (less if you have more fish), and as much chopped onion and garlic as you can spare. Season with salt, pepper, herbs and even a dash of hot sauce. Boil slowly until the rice is done. The thicker the better, so a packet of dry soup mix, especially leek, helps immeasurably. Ignore the packet's directions, and keep tinkering with the seasonings until it tastes just right.

VARIATIONS:
- For Chinese-style hot-and-sour soup, add a good dash of vinegar and considerable black pepper.

- For New England-style chowder, add a spoonful of milk powder just before it comes off the fire.

## Black Bean Soup ❖

Soak overnight and cook two handfuls of black beans in the big pot. If you've got a packet of chicken or beef soup stock, add that, as much dried chopped onion as you can spare, some chips of jerky, lots of garlic, salt, pepper and cayenne. Bring to a boil and let simmer for an hour if you've got the time and the coals are working right. Long cooking gives it more flavor, but even 20 minutes is fine since all the ingredients have already been cooked. Just before serving, add a dash of lemon juice or vinegar and a good hit of brandy. That's it. You'll want seconds, guaranteed. And if you don't have black beans, use what you have and just call it by a different name.

## Lentil or Pea Soups ❖

If you prefer lentils or dried peas to beans and noodles, take them to use as you would for bean soup. Like beans, lentils and peas need two- to three-hours' soaking time before cooking.

# Pancakes and Crêpes

There's something about the cold morning air, a warm fire, a hot griddle and real maple syrup that makes pancakes almost a ritual necessity on a backpacking trip. Here's how to make them.

Ready-made pancake mixes are available in supermarkets. Natural ones are available in some health food and whole food stores. They're adequate. The only problem is you can't unmix them. All you can do with them is make pancakes. If you try using it as a flour supplement or substitute in breads and cakes, you'll end up with something that tastes and looks like a pancake with elephantiasis. The same goes for sauces. You get a warm pancake batter (with cheese), edible only in life-threatening situations. As long as you're taking flour, eggs and milk powder anyway, why not start from scratch?

Pancake batter is made of flour, eggs and milk, to which some shortening and a leavening agent such as baking powder are added. Change the proportions and you get different kinds of pancakes—like crêpes, for example. There are only a few general rules:

- Always add the liquid ingredients to the dry. This is a conservation principle: if you start with too much liquid, you'll waste a lot of flour thickening the batter. But starting with flour, you can add the liquid gradually until the batter is just right. Water is usually expendable.

- You don't need to grease your pan if the batter is made right. The oil or shortening goes in the batter, not in the pan. A thin film of oil won't hurt, but with a decent pan—it doesn't even have to be teflon-coated—it won't be necessary. Crêpes need a little oil in the pan, but not much.

- Heat the pan before you pour the batter in. Test by splashing a few drops of water into the pan. If they dance, sizzle and evaporate, you're ready to go.

- The first pancake is a test run. If it sticks to the pan or isn't golden brown, the pan isn't "tempered" yet. Scrape it off. The second won't stick. If the first one tastes like a sodden brick, you need more liquid. A runny mess means you need more flour. Refine the batter—the rest of the pancakes will be good.

## Basic Pancakes ❖

At home, the usual proportion for pancakes is roughly 2:2:2—two cups flour, two cups milk and two eggs. In the wilderness, the proportions are the same, though the quantity is reduced. A Sierra cup holds around six heaping spoonfuls of flour, which makes way too many pancakes for two adults. Our recipes make from 10 to 12 inflated "silver dollar" pancakes, more than enough for two. The cakes are thick, light and filling. You could write home about them, except there isn't a post office within three-days' walk.

*4 heaping sp. flour*
*1 sp. milk powder*
*dash of salt*
*$^1/_2$ sp. sugar (optional)*
*1 egg, beaten*
*2 sp. oil/melted margarine*
*$^1/_2$ c. water*

In a small pot, mix the flour, milk powder, salt, and, if you like, the sugar and leavening agent. Don't worry if you don't have baking powder or soda; they're not necessary, and frankly, we rarely use them for pancakes at any altitude, home or away. Add the beaten egg and oil to the dry ingredients and stir quickly. To hell with any lumps! Now add the water gradually, stirring. The batter will be thick. So you may need to add a bit more water, just enough to keep it thick but still smooth enough to flow off a spoon, like a thick velvet ribbon. Don't worry about getting a perfectly smooth batter. Lumps will disappear in the cooking.

To cook, drop a large spoonful of batter in the middle of the heated pan. If it looks pitifully small, add a dollop more. The cake is ready to flip (only once) when bubbles begin to form on the surface. Flip and let it cook another few minutes. The second side never takes as long as the first. That's it. Eat! Or, if the first one is good, make three or four pancakes at one time so that one of you can have a decent breakfast. Then trade places.

VARIATIONS:

- Use the same proportions, but separate the egg and use only the yolk. After the batter is ready, beat the white until it's stiff but not dry, exactly as you would for a soufflé. Fold the beaten white into the batter gently, to preserve as much of the air as possible. Cook as above. The result will be so light that you'll seriously rethink the theory of gravity.

- Chop apricots, apples, banana chips into tiny pieces and add to the batter.

- Add a half-spoonful of sourdough starter to the dry ingredients and omit the baking powder). Whole wheat or buckwheat flour, a mixture of flour and cornmeal work well and make great pancakes. So do flour with ground up RyKrisp, ginger snaps or vanilla wafers. Just remember that each kind of flour has a different moisture content, so adjust the liquid accordingly.

## Crêpes ❖

Crêpes are French pancakes. They should be paper-thin, to wrap other foods in. To achieve the thinness, change the proportions of flour to liquid to eggs. At home, it would be roughly 2:2:4 (two cups flour, two cups milk and four eggs). At 9,000 feet, you're unlikely to have that many eggs to spare. So stick with one egg and follow the basic pancake recipe with the following changes:

Omit the baking powder or soda. Instead of a spoonful of milk powder, use a half-spoonful and increase the water to make a thin batter—thin enough to look drinkable, like a homemade smoothie.

No self-respecting crêpe recipe includes oil in the batter. If tradition counts with you, leave it out and spread a thin film of oil on the pan for each crêpe. We, however, are not so self-respecting, and after making sure the Academie Française is not meeting in the nearest bog, we throw in a spoonful anyway.

If you have time to fish before breakfast, set the crêpe batter aside, covered, in a cool spot. Crêpe batter is happier if it sits a while. When you get back, poach your fish, crank up a sauce and savor trout crêpes.

COOKING THE CRÊPES:

Pour two or three spoons of batter into a sizzling pan. Tilt the pan away from you, then to the side, then toward you so the batter spreads out roughly in a circle as thin as you can get it. The more you practice, the easier it gets and the rounder and thinner the crêpes will be. They'll only take a minute or so to cook and are ready to turn when the center looks almost, but not quite, dry. Either work a spatula underneath to turn it, or pick it up in your hand and flip it over. The second side takes less time than the first. The result should be cooked but also pliable, so it can be wrapped around food.

## Fruit Crêpes

Simmer a handful or so of mixed dried fruits in water to cover. Add a spoonful or two of sugar. Stir and simmer till a thick stewed fruit is formed. Stuff crêpes with the fruit, sprinkle sugar and cinnamon on top and serve. These can also be flambéed after dark, as homage to the inventor of Crêpes Suzette.

# Breads

Anybody who can make pancakes can make pan-fried bread. And anybody who can make the dough for pan-fried breads can add some yeast and bake the bread in a pot in the coals. And anybody who can do that can just as easily make a cake. No excuses.

For pancakes, the liquid ingredients outnumber the dry ones and you end up with batter. In bread, the opposite is true and you end up with dough. The dough can be picked up without running down your sleeve and dripping all over your shoe. It can be folded or spindled without harm. A cake is somewhere in between: in other words it is a stiff sweet batter and the promise of dessert.

There's considerable lore about campfire breads and cakes, such as bannock, the basic pan bread. It is so basic that it consists of little more than flour and water with a little baking powder and salt tossed in for luck. Or sourdough, the old-time, homemade substitute for yeast once carried around in pots hung from the saddle in California's gold country. But lore's a bore when you're hungry. Here are some of our favorite mountain breads.

## Pan-Fried Breads ❖

This recipe is so uncompromisingly basic that it has little to recommend it except to give you an idea of how simple bread-making is. Try it once for experience, then move on to the tastier variations.

In the medium-sized pot, mix together four heaping spoonfuls of flour, a $^1/_4$ spoonful of baking powder, and a pinch of salt. Add enough water to make a stiff but smooth dough that you can pick up and handle without half of it sticking to your fingers. Have the flour sack handy so you can keep both hands floured, and if necessary, add small increments of flour to the dough to get the right consistency. Put a layer of oil in the frypan to preheat, and form six to eight small patties of dough, about the size of a muffin and $^1/_2$ to $^3/_4$ inches thick. (If you like flipping them in the air, cook one at a time.) Let them brown slowly over a moderate bed of coals. If the fire is too hot, the crust will cook too fast, leaving the insides half raw. Flip or use a spatula to turn them, as often as you like. They're done when they sound hollow to the tap of a finger, roughly 15 minutes, and they are more than enough for two ravenous adults.

## Cornmeal Muffins ❖

In the medium pot, mix together two heaping spoonfuls of flour and two of cornmeal. Add a pinch of salt, a spoonful of sugar and one of oil, a half spoonful of milk powder, and a quarter spoonful of baking powder. Mix thoroughly, then add enough water to make a smooth dough, easy to handle but not sticky. Keeping your hands lightly floured, form the dough into whatever shape suits you. Cook as above. The result is indecently good, a cross between English muffins and old-fashioned corn fritters, or something like famous Southern hush puppies. Eat them plain, with a sprinkling of sugar, or split open and covered with maple syrup. They're also great with grilled or foil-baked fish.

VARIATIONS:

- For part of the cornmeal or flour, substitute a packet of dry instant oatmeal.

- Dust the muffins with cornmeal before you fry them.

- Season with pepper, nutmeg, cinnamon, sesame seeds or a small amount of crushed nuts.

## Griddle Breads ❖

Does anyone still own a griddle or even know what one is? Those old, flat cast-iron disks or slabs that used to cover openings in wood-burning stoves were griddles (or, as the Scots would say, girdles). By extension, so were (and still are) cast-iron frying pans. Put a cover over them, and you've got the hardware for griddle-baked breads. True, unless you've got a Winnebago, a pack horse, or the world's second biggest llama, it's unlikely you'll have iron to cook on in your campsite. Not to worry. That lightweight Teflon pan and a metal plate (or aluminum foil) will do just as well, as will a camping oven.

The main difference between the pan-fried breads above and griddle breads is that with a covered griddle, you don't always need to use oil in the pan. Just a sprinkling of flour. Watch.

## Scottish Griddle-Baked Scones ❖

*1 c. flour (remember, 1 c. here means a Sierra cupful)*
*³/₄ sp. baking powder or baking soda*
*large pinch of salt*
*2 sp. sourdough starter*
*water*

Mix the dry ingredients together. Add the sourdough starter and just enough water to make a soft dough. Flour your hands, mix. Pat into a round shape about a ¹/₄"-¹/₂" thick. (If much thicker, they'll burn on the outside before the inside is done.) Cut into 6 wedge-shaped pieces. Place on a lightly floured frying pan. (Optionally, you may lightly oil the pan and then coat with flour.) Cover with the pan with a metal plate, pot lid, or aluminum foil. Place over "slow" coals. When browned on bottom, turn to brown the other side. When the middle is just dry, they're done. Put on your Scottish kilt, grab a caber to defend against ravenous lowlanders, slather with honey or jam, and eat while reciting the lesser poems of Robert Burns.

SCONE VARIATIONS

- If traveling with a cooler, substitute buttermilk or sour cream or yogurt for the sourdough starter.

- Add an egg.

- Add a handful of milk powder.

- Add a spoonful of sugar.

## Griddle Corn Bread ❖

This is a skillet-baked variation of Cornmeal Muffins and our other corn breads though we've altered the proportions here.

*1 c. flour*
*¹/₂ c. cornmeal*
*1 sp. baking powder*
*1 sp. sugar*
*1 sp. milk powder*
*large pinch of salt*
*1 egg*
*large squirt of oil or 1 spoonful of melted margarine*
*water*

Mix the dry ingredients together. Add the slightly beaten egg, the oil and just enough water to make a moist, pliable dough that you can gently knead. Shape into a round, about ¹/₄" thick, cut into wedge-shaped slices, bake in a lightly floured, covered skillet over "slow" coals. Turn once when lightly browned. Bake about 10-15 minutes.

## Irish Soda Bread ❖

The chief difference between the Scottish griddle-baked scones above and this recipe is in the cudgel you use to fend off the churls who want to pry the bread from hearth and hand. Down the caber, up the shillelagh!

*1 c. flour*
*¹/₂ sp. baking soda (or in a pinch, baking powder)*
*large pinch of salt*
*sugar to taste*
*1 sp. milk powder*
*1+ sp. margarine*
*water*

Mix the dry ingredients. Add the margarine, and with your fingers, mix it in until it is the consistency of a coarse cornmeal. Add enough water to make a moist dough. Shape into a round about ¹/₂" thick, then slice into wedges (farls to the Irish), and bake on a covered, oiled skillet over "slow" coals. When browned on the bottom, turn 'em over and continue for another, say, 5-10 minutes, depending on the heat of the flame. Eat to the accompaniment of wild Gaelic verse and a hearty stew. Question: Whaddaya do if you only have baking powder? Right. Rename it Irish Baking Powder Bread and drink a toast to Anna Livia Plurabelle.

VARIATIONS

• Add raisins, currants, even trail mix.

• Omit oil in the pan. Just flour lightly.

## Baked Breads

Baked breads involve one more step than pan-fried, and a lot more time. The extra step is mixing a leavening agent into the dough to lighten it—to puff it up with a myriad of tiny bubbles, making it rise before it's baked. The mixing must be thorough, so you have to punch and push—or "knead"—the dough fully. There are a number of leavening agents. Yeast is the most famous, sourdough starter is another. We carry several packets of store-bought dry yeast with us, and take along a small plastic bottle with sourdough starter. Baking powder and soda work only under extreme heat (in the act of baking itself) and can't be used for pre-bake rising.

STARTING THE YEAST:

All leavening agents work by slowly releasing gas, which gets trapped in the dough and which, in trying to get out, forces it to expand. Yeast needs warmth to produce the gas. In the wilderness, the sun is your warmth. It's also possible to use the warmth of dying coals, but the sun is always your best bet. Don't plan to let your bread rise at night.

Yeast is also activated by warm water and sugar; it's inert until this is done. Sometimes it gets too inert or stale. Check the date on your yeast packets. It should read at least a couple of months ahead. To activate, sprinkle the amount of yeast you need, usually a packet or less, over a half cup of water that's only warm enough to keep your finger in. Add a couple generous pinches of sugar, mix thoroughly, cover and set aside in a warm place until you're ready to add it to the dough. When the yeast is frothy and expanding, it's ready to use.

STARTING THE SOURDOUGH:

Sourdough is exactly that: a dough made of flour and water that has begun fermenting, thus growing microscopic organisms that give off carbon-dioxide gas and a characteristically sour smell as they feed. In its working form, this is called a "starter" because, like yeast, it initiates the leavening process. Having carried it into the mountains and hung it in a tree to get warm and smelly, you're ready to use it freely in breads, pancakes, etc.

In theory, sourdough starter is a complete substitute for yeast. In frontier days, it was impossible to keep yeast fresh, but sourdough could be replenished every time it was used, thus keeping it alive and ready indefinitely. The best starter comes from the sourdough pot of a friend whose family has kept it, along with great-grandad's Klondike nugget, for a hundred years. Or you can buy dried starter in a health food outlet. But if great-grandad took his starter (and nugget) to the grave, and the store is out, here is a basic starter recipe to make at home before beginning your trip.

Heat a cup of milk, add a cup of water and cool to lukewarm. Thoroughly mix one tablespoon of sugar, a teaspoon of salt and two cups of flour in a large bowl—it's going to expand. Cover the bowl with a towel and leave in a warm place for four or five days or until it looks and smells frothy. Now add a package of yeast. Re-cover the bowl, and let it sit at room temperature for another week. Stir it down each day and don't worry how it smells or looks:

the badder the better. Store in a jar in the fridge until you're ready to use it.

Sourdough starter alone was fine for Yukon prospectors, but frankly it takes so long for dough to rise that it often dries out, leaving you with a loaf that looks and feels like a gold brick. We always add yeast to the sourdough starter, hedging our bets. Things move along at a fine pace and the bread tastes better, too.

## Basic Mountain Loaf ✱

A loaf of bread will be as big or small as you have flour to spare. Everything else is secondary. If you have nothing but flour, water and yeast, you can make bread. It might not win prizes at the Happy Valley bake-a-thon, but it will beat dried-out Triscuits. And with any additional ingredients like salt, milk powder, sugar, oil, sourdough, raisins, nuts, cornmeal, oatmeal, a spare egg, onion, garlic, cinnamon, nutmeg, sesame, poppy or sunflower seeds, to name a few, your breads will become a hedonist camper's dream come true.

The following recipe makes about the smallest loaf that is practical and still plentiful for two people. To double it, use twice as much flour but the same amount of yeast, salt and milk. Smaller pots bake better, though a bigger bread will require a larger pot.

Your basic utensils are: two pots, a plate, a Sierra cup, a spoon and eventually, a bed of hot coals or an Outback Oven.

To $1/2$ a Sierra cup of warm water, add a packet of yeast and a couple pinches of sugar. Cover and set in a warm place. In the medium pot, mix together a Sierra cup of flour, a dash of salt, one spoonful each of milk powder and oil or melted margarine. Mix the bubbly yeast into the pot thoroughly. The result will be lumpish, perhaps soggy. Never mind. If a lot of the flour is still dry, add a bit more water, not much. You want a fairly stiff dough, not a batter.

Now turn this out onto a floured plate or flat, clean floured rock. Flour your hands and keep the bag nearby. The aim is to turn this sodden stuff into smooth, springy, velvety dough. You do this by kneading—that is, by folding the dough over and over onto itself. Use the heel of your palm to push the dough away from you, fold it back on itself, give it a quarter turn, repeat, turn, repeat, and so on. If the flour on your hands and the plate doesn't suffice, add flour in very small amounts, and knead thoroughly before adding any more. As you knead, the dough will take shape, becoming firm and springy. Conversely, if it gets too hard to knead (or is hard at the outset), you have too much flour and need a little more liquid, either water or oil, the latter being easier to work in at this stage. Soon, the consistency will be just right. The dough is easy and pleasurable to work. You may find yourself spacing out and kneading just because it feels good. It can't hurt, so enjoy it. No harm if you want to go on for a half hour, though 5 or 10 minutes should suffice. The finished dough will spring slowly back when you poke a finger into it. Don't be dismayed if the dough takes on the hue of your pot-blackened hands or picks up small pieces of dirt. You won't taste or see it, nor contract some dreaded mountain disease.

When the dough is kneaded to perfection, it's ready to rise. Grease or oil the small pot, bottom and sides, and drop in the dough ball. Roll it around so its surface gets fully coated with oil. Now remove the dough, re-oil the pot and dust it with a little flour, a process that helps prevent the baked bread from sticking. Set the dough back in, cover, put it in a warm place and go off to fish, read, sleep, whatever, for an hour or so while the dough rises to double its original bulk.

What's a warm place? Any sun-exposed spot is ideal, unless the sun is searing; then warmth in the shade will be fine. A tent in the sun works. Sometimes we stow the pot in a sleeping bag if the day isn't too warm. Avoid setting the pot near the fire. It may get too hot and bake the bread.

What if it clouds over and gets cold? Not to worry, the rising just takes longer—all day is all right. If it's not ready before bedtime, wait till morning, knead the dough some more to bring the spring back and let it rise again. It's ready to bake when it's doubled in bulk. Incidentally, if you have time, breads are lighter and tastier if you let them rise twice, punching down the dough after the first rising and allowing it to double again. Literally, make a fist and jab the dough in mid-section. It will deflate. Then cover it and let the rising continue.

It's perfectly kosher to peek at the working dough. But it isn't an elevator; you won't be able to see it rise. If things go right, it will rise even if it takes time. If everything goes wrong and it won't rise, just turn the mess into a cake (see Getting a Rise Out of a Dud). What if it doesn't rise and you don't want a cake? Pretend it's fully risen and bake it anyway. The fire's heat gives a last lift to the dough, so the finished loaf will be fine, somewhat heavy but just as tasty.

Let's assume, however, that the dough did double, it didn't rain, the coals are still hot and you're ready to bake. If you wish, gently spread a light film of oil or melted shortening over the top of the dough with your fingers or the underside of a spoon. The oil will give a beautiful brown color to the top crust.

Oven-baked bread is usually started at a high temperature (400 degrees or higher), then after about 10 minutes the heat is reduced to 350 or 375 degrees to finish the baking, normally about 50 minutes. To reproduce those conditions in a bed of coals isn't easy, though as anyone who has ever made "coffee can bread" at summer camp knows, it's possible. The basic notion is to nestle the pot in a clearing in the warm ash or dirt, pile hot coals around it, then let them cool as the bread bakes. As more coals are needed to maintain the heat, rake them around the pot. On windy days, when the fire burns hot to windward and cool to leeward, rotate the pot 180 degrees every 15 minutes to assure an even distribution of heat.

Baking time differs according to the heat of the fire (which burns slower with wet wood, faster with dry wood, and hotter with soft wood), the size of the loaf and its ingredients. The basic mountain loaf should take between 20 and 30 minutes (or less on an Outback Oven, which, if wind-protected, disperses the heat evenly and bakes the bread faster). Baking time varies; keep checking. If the loaf sounds hollow when you tap it sharply, it's done. Remove the pot from the coals and set it to cool for 10-15 minutes. Under the best circumstances, when nothing has stuck to the sides, the loaf will come out when you turn the pot over and give it a couple of sharp raps on the bottom and top edges. Normally, though, you have to run a knife blade around the edges. In the worst of cases, so much will stick to the sides and bottom that you may have to saw the loaf in half and dig it out in sections. Usually, however, patience, cooling, deft use of the knife and a sharp knock of the pot against a rock brings forth a gorgeous golden loaf. Let it cool, then be prepared to defend your share against invaders from outer space—or your partner—intent on scarfing it down in one mega-bite!

No doubt about it, the Basic Mountain Loaf is a taste of camping heaven. Using the rough ratio of a generous cup of flour to an ungenerous half-cup of liquid, a packet of yeast and kneading until you get a smooth, unsticky, springy dough, you can overcome all but the most exotic forms of munchies. But the variations are better, and within each variation are other endless permutations.

## Sourdough Bread ✦

Use the same proportions and ingredients as above, but add a spoonful of sourdough starter when you add the yeast. Depending on the starter's thickness, you may have to add a little more water or flour to the dough.

## Raisin-Nut Loaf ✦

Also known as cinnamon-nut loaf, apricot-nut loaf, banana-nut loaf, mango-nut loaf, prune-nut loaf, nut-nut loaf. This one's sweet. Double the sugar, and add some cinnamon along with a good dash of baking powder or soda, which help enormously when fruit is involved. At the kneading stage, add half a handful of mixed raisins or finely chopped dried fruits and nuts. Proceed as above. Before baking, sprinkle the top with cinnamon, sugar and more chopped nuts.

## Jelly-Roll Bread ✦

While the bread is rising, boil some dried fruit, sugar and water into a thick jelly. Punch down the dough and pat it out on a floured plate. Spread the jelly mixture on top of the flattened dough, roll it up and plop it back into the greased pot for a second rising. You can do the same sort of thing with a sugar-cinnamon-nut paste, using enough margarine to hold it together, and come up with the camping equivalent of a morning danish.

## Oatmeal Bread ✦

Prepare a packet of instant oatmeal as though you're making breakfast, let it cool while you put together the dry ingredients (omitting the sugar) and start the yeast. Add the oatmeal along with the yeast and mix thoroughly. Continue as before.

## Herb Bread ✦

To the Basic Loaf ingredients, add the following: a large pinch or two of sugar, a handful of uncooked instant oatmeal, a handful of whole wheat flour (or more, to your taste), a mix of dried herbs—dill, thyme, sage—and some caraway seeds if you've thought to bring 'em along instead of the Walkman.

Toss in a beaten egg and a spoonful of melted margaine if you can spare
them. This is a super bread and goes great with that vegetarian chili you've
just made.

## Onion and Garlic Bread ✴

Fry a large spoonful of chopped onion and garlic until they're translucent.
Mix them into the dry ingredients of the Basic Mountain Loaf.

## Egg Breads ✴

An egg in any of the above recipes enriches the bread and adds more taste. If
you use one, you may need more flour.

## Mountain Challah ✴

When you add the yeast, throw in an egg or two. Mix thoroughly. You
may need more flour than usual to absorb the extra liquid. If possible, let this
loaf rise twice. If you have eggs to spare, use a third, separated, as follows:
Throw the white into the dough at the outset along with the other ingredients,
but save the yolk. Then, just before baking, beat $1/_2$ spoonful of water into the
yolk, and brush the top of the loaf with the egg and water mixture. It will
produce a burnished golden finish that will drive neighboring backpackers into
a near frenzy.

## Bagels ✴

Okay, you've got the Basic Loaf rising nicely in the sun. Build a fire, get a
big pot of water boiling, beat an egg in a Sierra cup and reserve. When the
dough's risen, flour your hands, pull a small clump off the dough, roll in your
hands, then form a small doughnut round your finger. Do this for as many
bagels as you want, but note that you're only going to be able to bake two or
three at a time. Ready? Ease about two bagels at a time into the boiling water.
Let 'em rise to the surface, about 30 seconds (45 seconds at high altitude), then
turn them over with a spoon and let 'em boil another 30 or 45 seconds.
Enough. Take 'em out, pat dry with a piece of toilet paper or your sweaty
bandanna, coat lightly with the beaten egg, and set in the greased and floured
medium-sized pot. Bake as you would the Basic Loaf, about 15 minutes or
until golden. Nosh.

VARIATIONS (After boiling but before coating with egg):

- Sprinkle with toasted sesame seeds.

- Sprinkle with poppy seeds.

- Sprinkle with chopped, dried onion.

- Sprinkle with cinnamon and sugar (though Hal considers this
  heresy).

- Use a mix of whole wheat and white flour.

Note: If a couple of bagels each will do, form the remainder of the dough into a loaf, place in the small, prepared pot, spoon the rest of the beaten egg over the loaf and bake. Presto digito! A little challah to warm the heart.

## Chinese Steamed Buns (baozi) ✱

The dough has risen and you've concocted a steamer (see instructions that follow). Tear off a small clump of dough, flatten it to about three or four inches in circumference on your hand or on a floured plate. Now place a small spoon of filling (see the following suggestions) in the center, and with your fingers work the dough up and around the filling till there's just a small opening at the top. Pinch that closed. When you've got the water boiling, place the buns on the steamer, cover, and steam about 20 minutes. Eat them plain or dipped in a mixture of soy sauce, vinegar, and hot sauce. Note: If you've got leftovers, re-steam them later. They'll be just as good.

FILLINGS:

- Poached trout marinated in soy sauce and ginger
- Chopped pieces of salami, jerky
- Rehydrated veggies seasoned with soy, garlic, ginger
- Left-over stir-fried veggies
- Dried fruit rehydrated with a spoon of sugar (Don't dip this in soy sauce or anything else!)

VARIATIONS:

- Omit stuffing (1). Just tear off a piece of risen dough, fashion into a roll and steam. This is your basic Chinese steamed bread *(mantou)*. Eat plain or, better, as a dunking tool with soups, stews, stir-fried veggies or fish.
- Omit stuffing (2). Tear off a large piece of risen dough, dust a plate with flour, flatten dough to about the size of the plate, sprinkle lightly with salt and a thin coat of oil. Roll up the dough like you would a rug. Now cut the rug into small (2- to 3-inch) segments, press each segment slightly in the middle with the back of a knife or a chopstick. Steam as above.
- Omit stuffing (3). Use a mixture of whole wheat and white flours. Add a small spoon of sugar to the dough when mixing (before kneading).

MAKING THE STEAMER:

Face it, you're not going to carry a Chinese bamboo steamer into the outback, though canoeists have been known to do inscrutable things in their day. So, make a steamer. Here are several options:

- Fill your largest pot with a few inches of water. Place the *baozi* or *mantou* on the next-sized pot lid and place in the big pot. Cover and steam!
- Carry with you one of those folding aluminum steamers small enough to fit in your largest pot.

- Interlace a number of green branches to fashion a steamer big enough to sit on top of a small fry pan. Lay a clean bandanna or handkerchief over it and place the *baozi* or *mantou* directly on the cloth. Cover with a large pot lid or a loosely fashioned dome made of aluminum foil. (You'll be able to use the aluminum foil later for baking.)

## Scones ❋

Skillet-baked scones are one thing. Oven-baked scones another. We know a couple of blokes who'd be willing to fight the Battle of Culloden over again for the right of first tasting. The chief assumption here is that you've got plenty of honey or jam to apply to these pearls of Inverness.

*1 c. flour*
*¹/₂ sp. baking powder*
*1 heaping sp. sugar*
*large pinch of salt*
*1 sp. raisins (optional)*
*1 sp. milk powder*
*2 sp. margarine*
*1 or 2 eggs*
*water*

Mix dry ingredients together. Add margarine, mixing with fingers till the consistency of coarse cornmeal. Beat the eggs and add. Then add just enough water to make a soft dough. Knead it on a floured plate just long enough to form a nice round circle, about a ¹/₄" to ¹/₂" thick. If you've got an extra egg, beat it and brush it on the dough. Sprinkle some sugar on top. Then cut the dough into 6 or 8 wedges. If baking over a campfire, place wedges in a lightly floured Teflon frying pan, cover with foil or a metal plate, set on cleared ground and surround with coals. When golden brown, about 10-15 minutes, they're done. If using a camping oven, use a Teflon pan with lid or a small baking sheet which can be covered. Same time. Same station.

### VARIATIONS

- Substitute buttermilk, sourdough starter, or even heavy cream (if the American Heart Association isn't on your case, and you've got a cooler for safekeeping), for the milk powder.

- Add thinly sliced cheddar cheese to taste.

- Add other dried fruits, slightly rehydrated. Strawberries and blueberries are great.

- Substitute instant oatmeal for half the flour.

- Flavor with anise, dill or cinnamon.

- If you happen to have a mashed potato in your back pocket, use it for half the flour.

## Getting a Rise Out of a Dud

What happens if the dough doesn't rise? You did everything right. The yeast bubbled and frothed, the dough kneaded nicely, the sun has been shining for hours. But by mid-afternoon, you have an inert gray mass of dough that looks like it's near death. This happened to us on a recent trip. Our options were to toss it or change it. Rick started to reason, like Marie Antoinette, that if you couldn't give them bread, let them eat cake. What wouldn't rise with yeast might rise with baking powder and whipped egg white. So we added enough water and milk powder to turn the dough into a batter, threw in some baking powder, and came up with a great nut-and-raisin cake.

Some research gave us clues as to why that particular dough didn't rise. Experts have countless reasons to explain failure. Humidity and air temperature affect yeast. Too much sweetener slows down or stops the process. Too much salt also inhibits rising. And too little white or whole wheat flour makes matters worse. That's because wheat flour contains a magic substance, gluten, which gives dough the necessary elasticity it needs to trap the yeast-produced bubbles of gas, allowing the dough to rise. Cornmeal, rye and rice flour, etc. have less or no gluten. The dough is made more porous as these are added, and the gas escapes, leaving you with a mound of play dough.

In our case, the dough had too much maple syrup and cornmeal, relative to the amount of white flour. It's hard to give exact proportions, especially as you may run out of important ingredients on the trail. But as a rough rule of thumb, try these:

First, half a spoonful of sugar or a full spoonful of honey or syrup is plenty for starting the yeast. If you want a sweeter bread, add the rest of the sugar to the dough, but remember that the sweeter the dough, the longer the rising time.

Second, use at least half white or whole wheat flour relative to all the other dry ingredients. If you're running too low on flour for that ratio, consider making cake instead of yeast bread.

## Yeast Corn Bread ✱

If you like corn breads which rise, substitute cornmeal for half the flour in the Basic Mountain Loaf recipe. Add a healthy hit of baking powder or soda and proceed as above.

## Baking Powder Corn Bread ✱

If you're low on yeast, use a ratio of four spoonfuls of cornmeal to two of flour and forget the yeast. Add a spoonful of baking powder, a shot of salt, a heaping spoonful of milk powder, two or three spoonfuls of sugar, a beaten egg or two and enough water to make a thick batter, similar in consistency to a thick pancake batter. Turn this into a well-greased pot. Bake at once for about a half-hour. Since corn bread won't sound hollow to the tap, you'll know it's done when the top splits open a bit, and when a knife blade inserted in the middle comes out clean.

## Hal & Rick's South Side Pizza ✷

1 packet yeast
$^1/_2$ c. warm water
couple pinches of sugar
$^1/_2$ c. flour
dash of salt
1 sp. oil
$^1/_2$ c. tomato sauce
mixed dried vegetables, slightly rehydrated: mushrooms, zucchini, onion, peppers
2 cloves garlic, sliced
sliced salami or jerky (optional)
4-5 sp. sliced cheese
pepper to taste
hearty sprinkling of dried oregano
cooking oil
aluminum foil

In a Sierra cup, mix the warm water, yeast and sugar. Set aside covered in a warm place. When "proofed" (that is, bubbly), add it to the flour, salt and oil in a pot. Mix thoroughly with a spoon, adding more oil and water as necessary to make a workable dough. Knead on a plate till smooth. If it's slightly sticky, that's okay. Set in a warm place to rise in a covered, oiled pot. While the dough is rising, make the tomato sauce and rehydrate the veggies slightly by soaking them in hot water barely to cover till they're partially soft. Drain and set aside.

When the dough has risen, turn it out on a plate and begin to work it into a round, flat shape with your fingers, pushing out from the center in all directions. You can even pick it up and toss it into the air with a spiral motion, like they do at Mama Mia's. It's helpful to catch it. You may need a little flour on your hands for this. When the dough has become a nice, even circle, fit it into a well-oiled frying pan. It should extend part or all the way up the sides. Then spread the tomato sauce over the dough and pile on the vegetables (and salami or jerky). Sprinkle on the cheese, garlic, pepper and oregano. Then drip a very thin layer of oil over the finished product, and cover the pan with foil. Alternatively, place a large tin plate over the pizza and seal it to the frying pan with the foil.

Ranger Ron was right in one respect. The idea is to bake the dough fast, before you burn everything on top. Pizza ovens are extremely hot (about 500 degrees Fahrenheit). But if you put your frying pan on a bed of red hot coals, you'll end up with something you might have to call "cheese-n-charcoal." Instead, set the pan on cleared ground, surround it with hot coals, and slide coals on top of the foil too. Let it bake about 15 minutes. Then work some moderately warm coals under the pan and push others around it and on top. In another 10 minutes or so, the pizza is done. The dough will be crusty, the cheese melted, and mouths watering. Overlook his chagrin and give Ranger Ron a piece. Tell him it's crow!

## *Hal & Rick's Carroll Street Calzone* ✳

Okay, you've got the makings of a pizza dough, but you left the Outback Oven at home and you're in a No Campfire zone. What to do? Simple. Make a calzone. Follow the recipe above for the pizza dough. While it's rising, rehydrate whatever you'd like to be in the filling: risotto; veggies; turkey jerky; beans. To cook, heat an oiled fry pan, place the flattened, rounded dough in the pan, spoon in the filling, and fold half the dough over it, and form a pouch by pinching or pressing the top layer of dough to the bottom layer. Fry till golden brown, then turn with a spatula, brown on the other side and remove to a plate. Call in the carabinieri while eating. There's no telling who'd kneecap you for your portion.

# Cakes

Making cake on a camping trip is sort of like sex on Wednesday afternoon: gratuitous but a lot of fun. It has nothing to do with survival, nor your ability to read a compass, has not one ounce of redeeming moral, social or nutritional value. But as long as you have semi-sweet baking chocolate with you anyway (also great for eating plain because it's unlikely to melt in your pack), some margarine, sugar, eggs, flour, baking powder and powdered milk, and as long as it's Wednesday afternoon and the sun is high, you might as well hunker down, bake a cake, make an icing, slap the two together, lay back and pig out. It's a piece of cake.

## *Basic Ground-Level Two-Step Cake* ✳

Pancakes are the result of frying batter. Cakes are the result of baking batter—batter which contains more sugar and eggs. Here's everything you ever needed to know about the unadorned, ultra-simple, starter cake loved by 93 percent of humankind.

*1 c. flour*
*1 sp. milk powder*
*$^1$/$_2$ sp. baking powder*
*dash of salt*
*1 sp. margarine*
*3 sp. sugar*
*1 egg*
*dash of brandy*
*water*
*oil for greasing pot*

In a medium pot, mix together the dry ingredients. In the pot lid, cream together the margarine and sugar, using the underside of a spoon to mix. (If you're out of margarine, oil will work.) Break the egg into the sugar mixture and beat till the glop is smooth. Add the brandy as a substitute for vanilla. Combine both mixtures with enough extra water to make a smooth, thick batter that will pour like a ribbon into a well-greased and floured small baking pot.

Bake the cake in coals cooler than for bread. With an Outback Oven, you bake everything with a low flame anyway, so no need to fiddle with settings. At home, you'd use a moderate oven (350-375 degrees). Out here, start with coals just beginning to turn black and try to keep any you add roughly the same color. If you can't, don't worry. Betty Crocker won't be around, peeking over your shoulder. Baking time will vary, as usual, but should run about 25 to 30 minutes. Test for doneness by inserting a knife blade into the center of the cake. If it comes out clean, the cake is done. When cool remove from pot.

VARIATIONS:

## *Basic Man-Eatin' Cake* ✶

Follow the preceeding recipe, only separate the egg, reserve the white, and add the yolk to the sugar and butter mixture. When the batter is ready to pour into the baking pot, gently fold in the egg whites, beaten stiff but not dry. This makes the cake even lighter, a cruel blow to weight watchers and lifters alike.

## *Advanced Man-Eatin' Cake* ✶

For a moister, richer cake, use two eggs, separate both and proceed as above. Add other things to the batter: cinnamon, Kahlua in addition to or instead of the brandy, several squares of chocolate shaved with a knife, or assorted dried fruits and nuts.

## *Chocolate Cake* ✶

Set up as for Man-Eatin' Cake (Basic or Advanced). In a pot lid, place two squares of semi-sweet baking chocolate or two rows of German Sweet chocolate. Add about a $1/4$ cup water. Stir and melt over the fire, being careful not to burn the chocolate. When melted, add to the egg and sugar mixture along with a little brandy. Proceed as in Man-Eatin' Cake, folding in egg whites last. *Note*: it is not necessary in any of these recipes to separate the eggs, so if you left the wire whisk at home, proceed as for Basic Two-Step Cake. No one will notice the difference.

## *Surprise-Delight Cake* ✶

Suppose you don't have all the ingredients and still want to make a chocolate cake. Use what you have. Substitute carob for chocolate; scrape the carob off a Tiger Milk Bar to melt in water. Or melt the whole bar and add it to the egg and sugar mixture. Or use powdered Swiss Miss. If you don't have anything to beat the egg whites with, leave them whole. No baking powder? Use beaten egg whites as a rising agent. No brandy? Forget it. No sugar? Double the amount of chocolate, or use both chocolate and instant cocoa, which has plenty of sugar in it. Stretch your mind. Just keep the proportions of wet and dry about the same so the batter stays the proper consistency.

## *Chocolate Icing* ❖

*2-3 squares semi-sweet baking chocolate, or 3-4 rows German Sweet chocolate*

*1 sp. margarine*
*¹/₄ c. water*
*dash of brandy*

In a pot lid, melt the chocolate (you can use a combination of the two kinds) in the water. *Note*: the more chocolate you use, the more water you need, but add it moderately. The idea is to have a fairly thick, smooth melt. Add margarine, stir till melted and thoroughly mixed with the chocolate. Remove from heat. Add brandy. Cool till icing begins to thicken. This will take some time, especially on a hot day. To hasten, set icing container in a larger container of cold water. Don't fret, it will harden. In fact, if left too long, it will suddenly harden so much that you may have to warm it slightly to turn it back into spreading consistency. When thickened to that consistency, ice the cake with a spoon or knife. The result is so good you'll have difficulty waiting for your partners to return from a day hike, or wherever they're spending Wednesday afternoon.

To store the iced cake, place the large pot over the cake till time to eat. If there's any left over at night, remove it from the plate and double bag in Ziplocs.

*Note*: Icing can be made without a cake. Hardened, it is the perfect nosh, the equivalent of that box of Bartons you were supposed to bring your Great Aunt Emily on her birthday, but ate them first. Softened and thickened with a spoonful each of milk powder and flour, and a cup or two of water, it transmutes into chocolate pudding!

## Fruit Cake ✶

This is a mixture of fruits and nuts held together with a mixture of eggs, sugar and flour. It's a snap to make and a great way to use up nuts and fruit before packing out. In a medium or large pot lid, put as much cut-up fruit and nuts as you wish. For the smallest fruit cake, about three large handfuls will do. To this, add a beaten egg, three spoonfuls of sugar and a hit of brandy. Mix thoroughly. Now add a dash of salt, a spoonful of baking powder and enough flour (about three spoonfuls) to hold the mixture together. Pour into a well-greased small pot, cover and bake very slowly in moderately hot coals. At home, you'd bake at only 300 degrees, so these coals will be the coolest you've used. Allow an hour or so to cook, and don't expect it to rise much. You'll know when it's done by looking at the top—which should be brown—and testing with a knife for firmness. Run the knife around the edge, turn the pot over and bang it sharply on a rock to get the cake out. If it won't come out whole, cut it in pieces or eat it right from the pot. When the cake is cool, pour some brandy over it and let it sit for as long as you like. It'll keep for days. Incidentally, if it comes out of the pot whole, the cake will be very beautiful.

# Cookies

The hardest part of mountain cookie baking is deciding on the ingredients. Chocolate chip, cinnamon-nut, oatmeal and lemon only begin the possibilities. The ratio of ingredients should be 4:2:1, that's four flour (including oatmeal) to two sugar to one margarine. Begin by "creaming" half a Sierra cup of sugar and two spoonfuls of margarine into a paste. Add an egg and a splash of brandy. To a Sierra cup of flour (or flour/oatmeal), add half a spoonful of baking powder, a pinch of salt, and a spoonful of powdered milk. Combine this with the butter and egg mixture. Then add your special ingredients—shredded chocolate bars, raisins, coconut, chopped nuts, dried fruit, cinnamon, nutmeg, ginger, etc. Add flour or water as necessary to get the right consistency, halfway between pancake batter and bread dough. The finished mixture should be thick and chunky. Taste it for sweetness. If it doesn't taste really sweet, your cookies will be more like biscuits.

Cookies are baked in a greased pan exactly like pizza. If you have a plate or lid that fits over your frying pan, you can use it instead of foil to hold the top coals. A few coals below will keep the bottom of the pan warm. You can only bake three or four at a time, so filling the cookie jar is an all-day project. In a pinch, you can make them like pan-fried bread. They may burn a bit on the top or bottom, but if you dip them in coffee or hot chocolate, you'll hardly notice.

# Quiche

One of the best things about the kind of improvisational cooking we've been discussing is that you're never quite sure what's going to happen next. For more than five years, we'd been baking breads, inventing variations of chocolate cake, igniting brandy and generally congratulating ourselves on the smooth workings of our unbridled imaginations. But we'd never made a pie. Too much trouble, we argued. Too hard. Anyway, what would we fill it with? The answer came from Polly, a doctor who'd lived in the Andes, floated down the Amazon, and survived 20 years in the jungles of Chicago. Five days into the high Sierras in the midst of a hail storm and high winds, she announced she'd make supper that night for six: quiche.

We wished her luck and set her up in the tent to get out of the wind (it's not easy to work with flour in a gale). Every so often, we'd hear a muffled cry for spices, powdered milk or water and we finally put the entire food pack into the tent so she could work in peace. By sundown, the storm had blown itself out and we were all sitting around the campfire complimenting the chef on her work of art.

## *Quiche Improvisation* ✳

The first thing to do is to make a pie crust of pastry dough, which is different from bread dough. It consists of a mixture of flour and shortening, with just enough water to hold the two together. Here's what you'll need to make a crust in an 8" fry pan:

*large pot*
*spoon*
*water*
*5 heaping spoonfuls of flour*

*dash of salt*
*4 sp. margarine or shortening*

Mix the flour and salt together. Add the margarine, and knead until the dough has the texture of cornmeal. Don't worry if there are some pea-sized globules. Now add two or three spoonfuls of cold water to the mixture, one at a time, blending it in with the spoon or two forks. Only add enough water to hold the dough loosely together. One way to tell if it's right is to form the dough into a lightly packed ball. If it falls apart, you need more water. If it holds together, set the ball on an ungreased frying pan or pie plate, and press the dough down with the heel of your hand, working it to cover the bottom and sides of the pan. It should be very thin, not more than an eighth of an inch thick. But don't worry if it's thicker. It will bake well and taste great.

If you're camping in France, go ahead and follow the national custom. Partially bake the pie crust next. If you're not in France, skip it. Just go ahead and fill the uncooked crust with quiche goodies:

*3 sp. milk powder + water to make 1 cup*
*2 eggs, well beaten*
*cheese*
*jerky*
*diced dried vegetables: mushrooms, peppers, zucchini, etc. (rehydrated if possible)*
*onion (dried and crumbled or chopped)*
*salt and pepper to taste*
*dash of nutmeg*
*1 sp. flour*

In a pot mix together the cup of milk, beaten eggs, salt, pepper and nutmeg. Add the rehydrated vegetables and onion. (*Note:* If you can't rehydrate the veggies, don't worry. They'll soften in the baking.) To thicken the pot, add the flour and mix well. Pour the mixture into the pie shell. Sprinkle on as much finely shredded cheese as you can spare. Any cheese will do. The quiche is ready to bake.

If you have another pie pan or tin plate of the right size, invert it to cover the quiche. If not, cover it with aluminum foil like a pizza, and bake exactly as in the pizza recipe. Set hot coals around and on top. After about 20 minutes, when it's half-done, work some moderately hot coals underneath. The quiche is finished when the filling is firm and slightly browned. The reason it takes up to 40 minutes to bake is that the pan is shallow, making the transfer of heat a slower process. You'll be ravenous by the time it's ready, so you'll eat it hot. But it's possible to eat quiche cold, too.

## Apple Pie ✱

Camping's as American as...? Right, apple pie. So if you're canoeing or car camping and have a load of fresh apples, be patriotic, eat pie. If you're backpacking and were smart enough to bring along a Ziploc bag full of dried apples, ditto. Mom doesn't need to be there in her gingham apron.

*pastry for 2 pie crusts*
*3-4 fresh apples, pared, cored, sliced (or the equivalent rehydrated)*
*sugar and cinnamon to taste*
*margarine (optional)*

Layer the frying pan with one of the crusts. Fill with the apple, sugar and cinnamon mixture. Dot with margarine (optional). Cover with the second crust, which you've "rolled" out on a plate. Pinch the edges of the two crusts together. Poke top crust with a fork in several places. This lets the steam out while the pie is baking. Cover with aluminum foil or a large metal plate, and bake according to directions for pizza and quiche.

VARIATION

- Convert to an Apple Dumpling by using only one crust. Spread it on pan, fill half the crust, then fold over the other half, pinch and bake as above. This is easier and just as tasty.

- Brush the crust with a mixture of milk, cinnamon and sugar.

## Fruit Tarts ✹

If you have a cooler full of fresh peaches, plums, nectarines or pears, and ready access to a fire or a camping oven, make an open tart. You can mix and match the fruit or use one kind only.

*3 fresh peaches*
*4 fresh plums*
*pastry dough for one pie crust*
*sugar to taste*
*1 sp. flour*
*1 egg*

Make the pastry dough as above, line fry pan or Teflon coated pan. Slice the fruit into a pot, sprinkle on sugar and mix to coat well. Arrange fruit slices in concentric circles on the pie dough. Mix the egg and flour together, then dribble this mixture over the fruit. Seal pan with a top or aluminum foil and bake as above. You may need dueling knives to settle disputes when slicing to serve.

- This will work with dried (and rehydrated) fruit too, though the volume required will be about double the fresh fruit above. Solution: Make a smaller tart! Use a large pot lid lined on the *outside* with aluminum foil to prevent burning, and cover with a plate or another pot lid.

## Berry Pies and Tarts ✹

If you're in the right place at the right time, you may find wild berries ripe and ready for the oven. The only difference between berry pies and the fruit pies above is that berries need to be thickened. If you have some cornstarch, or better yet, instant (uncooked) tapioca, you're in biz. (Flour will do in a pinch.)

Just add a big spoonful of either to the fresh berries or to rehydrated fruit rolls (rhubarb and strawberries, for example, or blackberries and raspberries). Add sugar to taste and a dash of lemon or lime juice, pour into a pastry-lined pan, cover with a top pastry and pinch the two pastry linings together. Cut a little "X" in the pastry dough to allow hot air to escape, cover with aluminum foil or a metal plate, and bake as above.

# Campground Chutney

### *Summer Fruit Chutney*

If you haven't eaten all the dried fruit by now, and you've just turned out a fabulous Indian meal (*Trout Tandoori, Trout in Curried Sauce*, or *Fried Rice with Vegetables and Chicken*), garnish it with chutney. Stew a handful of fruit in water to cover, stirring till softened and thickened. Add an immodest squirt of vinegar or lemon juice (or both!), a spoon of sugar, and continue to stir till thick. Voilà! Chutney.

# Snow Cones

### *The Instant High-Mountain Popsicle*

Whenever you're above 7,000 feet, you're likely to come upon a snowfield or remaining patches of last winter's snow hidden from the mid-summer sun. If you're hiking, pull over and make snow cones—they're so refreshing it's like finding a soda fountain along the trail. Fill your Sierra cup halfway with snow and add any or all of the following: instant chocolate, cinnamon and sugar, lemon or lime juice and sugar, Kahlua, brandy, nutmeg, ginger, etc. Eat with a spoon. They're the *real* treasure of the Sierra, madre!

# Leave No Trace

**Leave No Trace, Inc.,** is a program dedicated to maintaining the integrity of outdoor recreation areas through education and public awareness. Foghorn Press is a proud supporter of this program and its ethics.

## Here's how you can Leave No Trace:

### Plan Ahead and Prepare
- Learn about the regulations and special concerns of the area you are visiting.
- Visit the backcountry in small groups.
- Avoid popular areas during peak-use periods.
- Choose equipment and clothing in subdued colors.
- Pack food in reusable containers.

### Travel and Camp with Care
*On the trail:*
- Stay on designated trails. Walk single file in the middle of the path.
- Do not take shortcuts on switchbacks.
- When traveling cross-country where there are no trails, follow animal trails or spread out your group so no new routes are created. Walk along the most durable surfaces available, such as rock, gravel, dry grasses, or snow.
- Use a map and compass to eliminate the need for rock cairns, tree scars, or ribbons.
- If you encounter pack animals, step to the downhill side of the trail and speak softly to avoid startling them.

*At camp:*
- Choose an established, legal site that will not be damaged by your stay.
- Restrict activities to areas where vegetation is compacted or absent.
- Keep pollutants out of the water by camping at least 200 feet (about 70 adult steps) from lakes and streams.
- Control pets at all times, or leave them at home with a sitter. Remove dog feces.

### Pack It In and Pack It Out
- Take everything you bring into the wild back out with you.
- Protect wildlife and your food by storing rations securely. Pick up all spilled foods.
- Use toilet paper or wipes sparingly; pack them out.
- Inspect your campsite for trash and any evidence of your stay. Pack out all trash—even if it's not yours!

### Properly Dispose of What You Can't Pack Out
- If no refuse facility is available, deposit human waste in catholes dug six to eight inches deep at least 200 feet from water, camps, or trails. Cover and disguise the catholes when you're finished.
- To wash yourself or your dishes, carry the water 200 feet from streams or lakes and use small amounts of biodegradable soap. Scatter the strained dishwater.

### Keep the Wilderness Wild
- Treat our natural heritage with respect. Leave plants, rocks, and historical artifacts as you found them.
- Good campsites are found, not made. Do not alter a campsite.
- Let nature's sounds prevail; keep loud voices and noises to a minimum.
- Do not build structures or furniture or dig trenches.

### Minimize Use and Impact of Fires
- Campfires can have a lasting impact on the backcountry. Always carry a light-weight stove for cooking, and use a candle lantern instead of building a fire whenever possible.
- Where fires are permitted, use established fire rings only.
- Do not scar the natural setting by snapping the branches off live, dead, or downed trees.
- Completely extinguish your campfire and make sure it is cold before departing. Remove all unburned trash from the fire ring and scatter the cold ashes over a large area well away from any camp.

**For more information, call 1-800-332-4100.**

# FOGHORN PRESS

Founded in 1985, Foghorn Press has quickly become one of the country's premier publishers of outdoor recreation guidebooks. Through its unique Books Building Community program, Foghorn Press supports community environmental issues, such as park, trail, and water ecosystem preservation. Foghorn Press is also committed to printing its books on recycled paper.

Foghorn Press books are sold throughout the United States. Call 1-800-FOGHORN (8:30-5:30 PST) for the location of a bookstore near you that carries Foghorn Press titles. If you prefer, you may place an order directly with Foghorn Press using your Visa or MasterCard. All of the titles listed below are now available, unless otherwise noted.

## The Complete Guide Series

The Complete Guides are the books that have given Foghorn Press its reputation for excellence. Each book is a comprehensive resource for its subject, from *every* golf course in California to *every* fishing spot in the state of Washington. With extensive cross references and detailed maps, the Complete Guides offer readers a quick and easy way to get the best recreational information available.

### California titles include:

- *California Beaches* (704 pp) $19.95, available 5/96
- *California Boating and Water Sports* (608 pp) $18.95, available 6/96
- *California Camping* (848 pp) $19.95
- *California Fishing* (832 pp) $19.95
- *California Golf* (896 pp) $19.95
- *California Hiking* (856 pp) $18.95
- *California In-Line Skating* (496 pp) $18.95, available 5/96
- *Tahoe* (704 pp) $18.95

### Other regional titles include:

- *Alaska Fishing* (640 pp) $19.95
- *Baja Camping* (294 pp) $12.95
- *Pacific Northwest Camping* (720 pp) $19.95, new edition available 4/96
- *Pacific Northwest Hiking* (808 pp) $18.95
- *Rocky Mountain Camping* (576 pp) $14.95
- *Washington Fishing* (608 pp) $18.95, available 4/96

## The Easy Series

The Easy books are perfect for families, seniors, or anyone looking for easy, fun weekend adventures. No special effort or advance planning is necessary—just head outdoors, relax, and enjoy. Look for Easy guides to Southern California and other favorite destinations in the fall of 1996.

- *Easy Biking in Northern California* (224 pp) $12.95, available 4/96
- *Easy Camping in Northern California* (240 pp) $12.95
- *Easy Hiking in Northern California* (240 pp) $12.95

## The Great Outdoor Getaways Series

For outdoor adventure, nothing beats Foghorn's Great Outdoor Getaways guides. Full of terrific ideas for day trips or weekend journeys, these books point you in the right direction for fun in the Great Outdoors.

• *Great Outdoor Getaways to the Bay Area & Beyond* (632 pp) $16.95
• *Great Outdoor Getaways to the Southwest* (448 pp) $16.95

## The Dog Lover's Companion Series

Foghorn's Dog Lover's series is for travelers who want to bring their canine companions along for the ride. Readers will find regional listings of pet-friendly restaurants, hotels, parks, walks, and hikes that will keep their dogs' tails wagging. Watch for guides to Atlanta, Chicago, Boston, and Florida.

• *The Bay Area Dog Lover's Companion* (352 pp) $13.95
• *The California Dog Lover's Companion* (720 pp) $19.95

## The National Outdoors Series

• *America's Secret Recreation Areas—Your Recreation Guide to the Bureau of Land Management's Wild Lands of the West* (640 pp) $17.95
• *The Camper's Companion—The Pack-Along Guide for Better Outdoor Trips* (464 pp) $15.95
• *Epic Trips of the West—Tom Stienstra's Ten Best* (208 pp) $9.95
• *Our Endangered Parks—What You Can Do to Protect Our National Heritage* (224 pp) $10.95
• *Wild America—The Complete Guide to More Than 600 Wilderness Areas* (704 pp) $19.95, available 7/96

A book's page length and availability are subject to change.

**For more information, call 1-800-FOGHORN or write to:**
**Foghorn Press**
**555 DeHaro Street,**
**The Boiler Room, Suite 220**
**San Francisco, CA 94107**